GATED COMMUNITIES?

Gated Communities?

Regulating Migration in Early Modern Cities

EDITED BY
Bert De Munck
Universiteit Antwerpen, Belgium
and
Anne Winter
Vrije Universiteit Brussel, Belgium.

Routledge
Taylor & Francis Group

LONDON AND NEW YORK

First published 2012 by Ashgate Publishing

Published 2016 by Routledge
2 Park Square, Milton Park, Abingdon, Oxon OX14 4RN
711 Third Avenue, New York, NY 10017, USA

First issued in paperback 2017

Routledge is an imprint of the Taylor & Francis Group, an informa business

British Library Cataloguing in Publication Data
Gated communities? : regulating migration in early modern cities.
  1. Migration, Internal – Europe – History – 16th century. 2. Migration,
  Internal – Europe – History – 17th century. 3. Migration, Internal – Europe – History –
  18th century. 4. Migration, Internal – Law and legislation – Europe – History.
  5. Internal migrants – Europe – History. 6. Indigenous peoples – Urban residence –
  Europe – History. 7. Migrant labor – Europe – History. 8. Municipal government –
  Europe – History. I. Munck, Bert De, 1967- II. Winter, Anne, Ph. D.
  304.8'094'0903–dc22

Library of Congress Cataloging-in-Publication Data
Munck, Bert De, 1967–
  Gated communities? : regulating migration in early modern cities / Bert De
  Munck and Anne Winter.
    p. cm. Includes bibliographical references and index.
  ISBN 978-1-4094-3129-9 (hardcover : alk. paper)
  1. Gated communities—Europe—History. 2. Emigration and immigration—
  Government policy—History. I. Winter, Anne, Ph. D. II. Title.
  HT169.59.E9M86 2011
  307.77094—dc23

                                                                    2011022336

ISBN 13: 978-1-138-11717-4 (pbk)
ISBN 13: 978-1-4094-3129-9 (hbk)

Contents

List of Tables and Figures

Tables

Figures

Notes on Contributors

Eleonora Canepari is a Marie Curie postdoctoral fellow at the Centre National de la Recherche Scientifique (CNRS) in Paris and a fellow of the Centre for Reformation and Renaissance Studies, University of Toronto. Her research focuses on migrations, working class and the making of networks in the urban space. She has published *Stare in compagnia. Strategie di inurbamento e forme associative nella Roma del Seicento* (Soveria Mannelli, 2008).

Jason Coy is an Associate Professor of History at the College of Charleston, South Carolina. He received his doctorate from the University of California, Los Angeles, in 2001. Professor Coy is the author of *Strangers and Misfits: Banishment, Social Control, and Authority in Early Modern Germany* (Studies in Central European Histories 47, Leiden, 2008). He is the co-editor of a volume of essays on symbolic performance, communication and power relations in the Holy Roman Empire during the early modern period – entitled *The Holy Roman Empire, Reconsidered* – that appeared in 2010 as the inaugural volume in the Spektrum series, sponsored by the German Studies Association and published by Berghahn Press.

Tim Hitchcock is Professor of Eighteenth-Century History at the University of Hertfordshire, and has spent the last 20 years helping to create a 'new history from below' which puts the experiences and agency of the poor and of working people at the heart of our understanding of the history of eighteenth-century Britain. He has authored or edited 10 books on the histories of poverty, gender and sexuality – including *Down and Out in Eighteenth-Century London* (London, 2004) and, with Robert Shoemaker, *Tales from the Hanging Court* (London, 2006). He is a co-director of the Old Bailey Online, 1674 to 1913 (www.oldbaileyonline.org) and London Lives, 1690–1800 (www.londonlives. org).

Yves Junot is *maître de conférences* and member of the Calhiste research team (EA 4343) at the University of Valenciennes (France). His research concentrates on the social and economic history of the early modern period, with particular attention for the Spanish Low Countries. His PhD (University of Lille3, 2002, under the supervision of Philippe Guignet) on the burghers of Valenciennes in the long sixteenth century exposed the social dynamics of an urban society confronted with an intense growth in textile manufacturing and a purging of its elites after the Protestant revolt. He is currently investigating geographical mobility and migration in the Southern Low Countries after the civil war (late sixteenth and early seventeenth centuries) in relation to pacification policies, economic recovery and identity discourses.

Aleksej Kalc is a researcher and lecturer in Modern and Contemporary History at the University of Primorska (Science and Research Centre and the Faculty of Humanities Koper, Slovenia). His main research interests are demography and the history of migrations and related political and social issues in border and ethnically mixed areas. Recent publications include a study on immigration and urban change in eighteenth-century Trieste: *Tržaško prebivalstvo v 18. stoletju: priseljevanje kot gibalo demografske rasti in družbenih sprememb* (Koper, 2008).

Leo Lucassen studied Social and Economic History at the University of Leiden (MA in 1985). In 1990 he was granted a PhD (*cum laude*) from Leiden for his dissertation on the history of Gypsies in the Netherlands 1850–1940. In 1989–1990 he was attached to the Law Faculty of the University of Nijmegen and in 1990–1991 to the Faculty of Social Sciences of the University of Leiden. Between 1991 and 1996 he worked as fellow of the Royal Dutch Academy of Sciences (KNAW) at the History Department in Leiden, and in 1996 received the D.J. Veegensprijs of the *Hollandse Maatschappij van Wetenschappen*. In 1998 he moved to the University of Amsterdam (UvA), where he directed a Netherlands Organization for Scientific Research (NWO) pioneer project on the assimilation of immigrants in the Netherlands. In the year 2002–2003 he was a fellow of the Netherlands Institute for Advanced Study (NIAS) in Wassenaar. In 2005 he returned to Leiden, where he shares the chair of Social History with Professor Wim Willems. Since September 2007 Leo Lucassen has been full-time Professor of Social History at the Leiden History Department, and he is member of the Academia Europaea.

Jan De Meester is a doctoral researcher at the Centre for Urban History at the University of Antwerp. His research is part of the Research Foundation Flanders (FWO) project 'The Integration of Artisan-Immigrants into the Urban Labour Market: The Duchy of Brabant, 1450–1800' and the IAP programme 'City and Society in the Low Countries 1200–1800: Space, Knowledge, Social Capital'. His main fields of interest are craft guild history and migration history. The impact of migration on early modern urban labour markets is the focal point of his research.

Vincent Milliot is Professor of Modern History at the University of Caen. He works on the European police of the Enlightenment. His most recent book is *Un policier des Lumières, suivi de Mémoires de J.C.P. Lenoir, ancien lieutenant general de police de Paris écrits dans les pays étrangers dans les années 1790 et suivantes* (Seyssel, 2011). He has also edited and co-edited *Police et migrants, France 1667–1939* (Rennes, 2001); *Les mémoires policiers, 1750–1850. Écritures et pratiques policières du Siècle des Lumières au Second Empire* (Rennes, 2006). *Métiers de police, Être policier en Europe, XVIIIe–XXe siècle* (Rennes, 2008); and *Réformer la police. Les mémoires policiers en Europe au XVIIIe siècle* (Rennes, 2009).

Leslie Page Moch obtained her PhD at the University of Michigan in 1979. She held positions at the universities of Illinois, Texas and Michigan-Flint; the Ecole des Hautes Etudes en Sciences Sociales in Paris; and Michigan State University, where she has been a professor in the History department since 1996. Books such as *Paths to the City* (Beverly Hills, 1983), *Moving Europeans: Migration in Western Europe since 1650* (Bloomington, 1992; 2nd rev. edn, 2003) and *The Pariahs of Yesterday: Bretons in Paris* (Durham NC, forthcoming) explore comparative migration history and urban migration history in particular. Moch is currently at work on a project with Russian historian Lewis Siegelbaum that will analyse the history of migration in the Russian Empire, Soviet Union and Russian Federation.

Bert De Munck is Senior Lecturer in the Department of History at the University of Antwerp, Belgium, teaching social and economic history of the early modern period, history and social theory and public history. He is director of the Centre for Urban History at the same university and main editor of the journal *Stadsgeschiedenis (Urban History)*. His research revolves around apprenticeship and the circulation of knowledge, craft guilds and civil society, and the 'repertoires of evaluation' regarding skills and products. His publications include *Technologies of Learning: Apprenticeship in Antwerp from the 15th Century to the End of the Ancien Régime* (Turnhout, 2007) and, co-edited with Steven Kaplan and Hugo Soly, *Learning on the Shop Floor: Historical Perspectives on Apprenticeship* (London/New York, 2007).

Ulrich Niggemann studied History at the universities of Göttingen and Bonn. From 2002 to 2003 he was a research assistant at the *Acta Pacis Westphalica*e edition project in Bonn, and since 2003 he has been a research assistant at the Early Modern History Department of the University of Marburg. He received a doctorate there in 2007 with a thesis on immigration politics and

Huguenot settlement in late seventeenth-century Germany and England. Since 2008 he has worked on a postdoctoral research project on memorial culture, historiography and political norms in early modern Europe. His publications include a monograph based on his doctoral thesis, articles on migration history, as well as English and American funeral sermons.

Hanna Sonkajärvi received her PhD in History from the European University Institute in Florence, Italy, in 2006. She holds an MA in Political Science (2001) from the University of Freiburg, Germany. After having worked as a research fellow at the University of Trier, she now works (since October 2007) as a research assistant (Wissenschaftliche Mitarbeiterin) at the University of Duisburg-Essen, Germany. Her fields of expertise include the social, political and military history of early modern western Europe, in particular France and the Southern Low Countries.

Anne Winter studied History at the Vrije Universiteit Brussel (VUB) and the London School of Economics (LSE), and obtained her PhD at the VUB in 2007. First employed as a PhD fellow and subsequently postdoctoral fellow of the Research Foundation Flanders (FWO) at the VUB, she was appointed lecturer in Early Modern and Urban History at the same university in 2010, after carrying out research stays at Somerville College (Oxford) and the Ecole des Hautes Etudes en Sciences Sociales (Paris). Her research concentrates on the social and economic history of the Low Countries in the early modern period and nineteenth century in a comparative perspective, with a particular interest in migration, social policies, urbanization and labour relations in the transitional period 1750–1850.

Acknowledgements

The seeds for this book were planted during the session 'The Integration of Economic Immigrants in Early Modern and Industrializing Cities', which we co-organized at the IXth International Conference on Urban History in Lyon, 27–30 August 2008, together with Sylvia Hahn (Universität Salzburg). The papers presented at that session and the discussions stimulated by discussants Andreas Gestrich (German Historical Institute London) and Leo Lucassen (University of Leiden) unearthed a remarkable blind spot in existing historiography – i.e. the local regulatory mechanisms dealing with immigration and integration in early modern cities. In order to integrate research scattered across different fields and subfields and to examine the multilayered and multidimensional character of such forms of regulation we organized a follow-up conference at the Palace of the Academy in Brussels, 4–5 September 2009, the contributions to which formed the basis for the chapters in this book. The organization of the follow-up conference was made possible by generous support from the Royal Flemish Academy of Belgium for Science and the Arts, the Research Foundation Flanders (FWO) and the FWO Research Network (WOG) 'Labour, Labour Relations and Labour Markets in Western Europe, 1500–2000' (dir. Hugo Soly). We are very grateful to Frank Winter and Jeremy Schreiber for proofreading and correcting several chapters, and we are hugely indebted to all contributors to this book and to the participants at the Lyon session and the Brussels conference for their critical and stimulating insights and comments.

Bert De Munck and Anne Winter

Chapter 1

Regulating Migration in Early Modern Cities: An Introduction

Bert De Munck and Anne Winter

Contrary to earlier views of early modern Europe as an essentially sedentary society, research over the past decades has amply demonstrated that migration was a pervasive characteristic of European society in the early modern period. Many people moved, over various distances, to different destinations, for different reasons and for different periods of time.[1] Only a fraction of all mobility was directed towards towns, but these migrations were of great importance for urban economic and demographic development in the early modern period.[2] Because early modern cities as a rule recorded more deaths than births, most cities relied on a permanent influx of newcomers in order to maintain their population size, let alone grow.[3] In a fast-growing town the majority of the population was likely to have been born outside the city limits, while the proportion of immigrants could easily amount to more than 30 per cent in a relatively stable population.[4] As most migration was temporary, the total volume of urban immigration and emigration was much higher than the number of urban immigrants at any given

---

[1]   Among others, see: Peter Clark and David Souden (eds), *Migration and Society in Early Modern England* (London, 1987); Steve Hochstadt, 'Migration in Preindustrial Germany', *Central European History*, 16/3 (1983): pp. 195–224; Olwen Hufton, *The Poor of Eighteenth-Century France* (Oxford, 1974) pp. 69–106; Jan Lucassen, *Migrant Labour in Europe 1600–1900: The Drift to the North Sea* (London, 1987); Leslie Page Moch, *Moving Europeans: Migration in Western Europe since 1650* (Bloomington, 2003), pp. 22–101; Daniel Roche, *Humeurs vagabondes. De la circulation des hommes et de l'utilité des voyages* (Paris, 2003); Charles Tilly, 'Migration in Modern European History', in William H. McNeill and Ruth S. Adams, *Human Migration: Patterns and Policies* (Bloomington, 1978), pp. 48–74.

[2]   On recent calculations of the volume of urban immigration in early modern Europe: J. Lucassen and L. Lucassen, 'The Mobility Transition Revisited, 1500–1900: What the Case of Europe Can Offer to Global History', *Journal of Global History*, 4/3 (2009): pp. 347–77.

[3]   Paul Bairoch, *De Jericho à Mexico. Villes et économie dans l'histoire* (Paris, 1985), pp. 264–71; Jan de Vries, *European Urbanization, 1500–1800* (London, 1984), pp. 175–98; Moch, *Moving Europeans*, pp. 44–6.

[4]   Hochstadt, 'Migration'; Moch, *Moving Europeans*, p. 44.

moment might suggest, and the total proportion of persons engaged in urban migration patterns at some point of their lives was substantial throughout the early modern period.[5]

While the precise demographic contribution of urban migrants remains subject to debate, even critics of the model of urban natural decrease do not question the magnitude of urban migration in the early modern period, or its importance as 'the linchpin of the urban economy'.[6] The constant flow back and forth of labourers, domestic servants, tradesmen and artisans played a key role in the development of early modern labour and commodity markets and in the diffusion of technology, and was essential to the working of the urban economy.[7] Early modern European cities were therefore characterized by permanent flows of migrants in and out of the city, guided by as varied motivations as finding jobs, schooling, patronage, business opportunities, shelter, alms, health care or marriage partners. The existence of a diverse and often temporary group of migrants – both short-distance and long-distance – was an essential element of everyday city life which left an important mark on the demographic, economic, social, political and cultural characteristics of individual cities.

Yet whereas actual patterns of migration to early modern cities have by now received a good deal of attention, the ways in which urban groups and authorities attempted to *influence* and *control* these movements have only recently started to be treated as a subject of historical research, reflection and discussion. Most studies dealing with urban migration policies have so far tended to concentrate either on distinct migrant groups or on specific institutional mechanisms of inclusion and exclusion. Studies of the first type tend to favour migrant communities with distinct ethnic, religious, occupational or wealth characteristics, such as merchant *nations*, Jews, Moriscos, Huguenots and the *compagnonnages*.[8] While these studies have yielded major insights, urban policies

---

[5]   de Vries, *European Urbanization*, pp. 200–206, also Moch, *Moving Europeans*, pp. 43–7.

[6]   de Vries, *European Urbanization*, pp. 196–7; Allan Sharlin, 'Natural Decrease in Early Modern Cities: A Reconsideration', *Past and Present*, 79/1 (1978): p. 138; Ad van der Woude, 'Population Developments in the Northern Netherlands (1500–1800) and the Validity of the "Urban Graveyard" Effect', *Annales de Démographie Historique* (1982): pp. 55–75.

[7]   de Vries, *European Urbanization*, p. 200ff.; Moch, *Moving Europeans*, p. 43ff.

[8]   F.R.P. Ackhurst and Stephanie C. Van D'Elden (eds), *The Stranger in Medieval Society* (Minneapolis, 1997); Jacques Bottin and Donatella Calabi (eds), *Les étrangers dans la ville. Minorités et espace urbain du bas Moyen Âge à l'époque moderne* (Paris, 1999); Donatella Calabi and Stephen Turk Christensen (eds), *Cultural Exchange in Early Modern Europe: Volume 2: Cities and Cultural Exchange in Europe, 1400–1700* (Cambridge, 2007); Raingard Esser, '"They obey all magistrates and all good lawes ... and we thinke our cittie happie to enjoye them": Migrants and Urban Stability in Early Modern English Towns', *Urban History*, 34/1 (2007): pp. 64–75; Jean-Pierre Jessenne (ed.), *L'image de l'autre dans l'Europe du Nord-Ouest à travers l'histoire* (Lille, 1996);

directed towards the large majority of migrants who did *not* belong to any such recognizable (minority) group have received considerably less attention, yielding the unjust impression that regulation was directed mainly at conspicuously 'different' newcomers. Studies of the second type have been more attentive to the ways in which the presence of newcomers of *all* types was related to a wide range of local mechanisms of inclusion and exclusion – which were connected, in turn, to a wide range of urban institutions. Collective institutions such as urban citizenship,[9] guilds,[10] associational life[11] and public and private poor relief systems[12] were all characterized by certain legal, social, cultural and/or financial barriers to prospective members, while differential treatment by institutions of control and repression – from policing to tribunals – reinforced distinctions between 'insiders' and 'outsiders'.[13] Yet while many case studies have enhanced our insight into the functioning of these various institutions, they often only

Lien Bich Luu, *Immigrants and the Industries of London, 1500–1700* (Aldershot, 2005); Denis Menjot and Jean-Luc Pinol (eds), *Les immigrants et la ville. Insertion, intégration, discrimination (XIIe–XXe siècles)* (Paris, 1996); Hugo Soly and Alfons K.L. Thijs (eds), *Minderheden in Westeuropese steden (16de–20ste eeuw)* (Brussels, 1995); Francesca Trivellato, *The Familiarity of Strangers: The Sephardic Diaspora, Livorno, and Cross-Cultural Trade in the Early Modern Period* (New Haven, 2009); Cynthia M. Truant, *The Rites of Labour: Brotherhoods of Compagnonnage in Old and New Regime France* (Ithaca/London, 1994). An early example of a more comprehensive focus: Etienne François (ed.), *Immigration et société urbaine en Europe occidentale, XVIe–XXe siècle* (Paris, 1985).

9   Marc Boone and Maarten Prak (eds), *Individual, Corporate and Judicial Status in European Cities (Late Middle Ages and Early Modern Period)* (Leuven/Apeldoorn, 1996); Joost Kloek and Karin Tilmans (eds), *Burger. Geschiedenis van het begrip van de Middeleeuwen tot eenentwintigste eeuw* (Amsterdam, 2002); Rainer C. Schwinges (ed.), *Neubürger im Späten Mittelalter. Migration und Austausch in der Städtelandschaft des alten Reiches (1250–1550)* (Berlin, 2002).

10   Stephan R. Epstein and Maarten Prak (eds) *Guilds, Innovation, and the European Economy, 1400–1800* (Cambridge, 2008); Heinz-Gerhard Haupt (ed.), *Das Ende der Zünfte. Ein europäischer Vergleich* (Göttingen, 2002); Jan Lucassen, Tine de Moor and Jan Luiten van Zanden (eds), *The Return of the Guilds* (Cambridge, 2008); Maarten Prak, Catharina Lis, Jan Lucassen and Hugo Soly (eds), *Craft Guilds in the Early Modern Low Countries: Work, Power and Representation* (Aldershot, 2006).

11   A state of the art in Nicholas Eckstein and Nicholas Terpstra (eds), *Sociability and its Discontents: Civil Society, Social Capital, and their Alternatives in Late-Medieval and Early-Modern Europe* (Turnhout, 2010).

12   Andreas Gestrich, Lutz Raphael and Herbert Uerlings (eds), *Strangers and Poor People: Changing Patterns of Inclusion and Exclusion in Europe and the Mediterranean World from Classical Antiquity to the Present Day* (Frankfurt am Main, 2009); Katherine A. Lynch, *Individuals, Families, and Communities in Europe, 1200–1800: The Urban Foundations of Western Society* (Cambridge, 2003).

13   Marie-Claude Blanc-Chaléard, Caroline Douki, Nicole Dyonet and Vincent Milliot (eds), *Police et migrants. France, 1667–1939* (Rennes, 2001); Jason P. Coy, *Strangers and Misfits:*

obliquely address their relation to the constant coming and going of migrants, and seldom address the *interactions* between these different institutional mechanisms at the urban level.

To be sure, the observation that urban authorities often sought to attract 'wanted' and repel 'unwanted' migrants is a familiar *topos* in late medieval and early modern urban historiography.[14] Yet the contentious, malleable and multilayered nature of the distinction between 'wanted' and 'unwanted' migrants has so far been insufficiently explored. While rich merchants and invalid beggars were obviously on opposite sides of the distinction, the boundaries between wanted and unwanted migrants were never clear-cut and remained subject to many different interpretations. Institutions such as burghership, guild membership or relief systems all mobilized different repertoires of inclusion and exclusion whose intentions and effects could vary widely through space and time. On close inspection, there has in fact been very little systematic research into the actors, interests and power relations that determined the shifting boundaries between those considered wanted or unwanted, and a comprehensive view of the wide range of institutional mechanisms that governed inclusion and exclusion in early modern towns remains underdeveloped.

The aim of this book is to move beyond the 'selective' perspectives of studies focusing on specific immigrant groups or particular institutions, and to venture into the multilayered and multidimensional reality of urban migration regulation from different local perspectives in order to lay bare the complex interactions of interests, conflicts, actors and negotiations involved in the regulation of migration in different urban contexts of early modern Europe. Because local categories formed the prime organizing principle of social, political and economic regulation, *all* immigration from across the city boundaries is considered part of the research focus, both regional and long-distance, temporary and permanent. And while we use the terms 'policies' and 'regulation' throughout the book, this does not imply that urban authorities necessarily pursued anything like a *conscious* or *coherent* policy with regard to migration. Rather, regulations impinging on migration were often a by-product of interventions in the labour market, housing, policing or welfare arrangements, shaped by the pressures of different urban interest groups and producing a

---

Banishment, Social Control, and Authority in Early Modern Germany (Leiden, 2008); Daniel Roche (ed.), *La ville promise. Mobilité et accueil à Paris (fin XVIIe–debut XIXe siècle)* (Paris, 2000).

[14]   See for instance Marc Boone, 'Les villes de l'espace flamand au bas Moyen Age. Immigrations et migrations internes', in Stéphane Curveiller and L. Buchard (eds), *Se déplacer du Moyen Âge à nos jours* (Calais, 2009), pp. 99–112; Maria R. Boes, 'Unwanted Travellers: The Tightening of City Borders in Early Modern Germany', in Thomas Betteridge (ed.), *Borders and Travellers in Early Modern Europe* (Aldershot, 2007), pp. 87–112.

varied and sometimes incongruous range of institutional mechanisms. The main research focus therefore lies with uncovering the interactions between the variety of institutional mechanisms of exclusion and inclusion, and on the interests, conflicts and power relationships that shaped the shifting boundaries between wanted and unwanted migrants.

*   *   *

This book brings together a range of case studies on the regulation of early modern urban migration in different spatial and historical contexts in order to flesh out the institutional arenas, conflicts and actors in which repertoires of inclusion and exclusion were moulded. The collection is the result of an international workshop on the theme organized in Brussels on 4–5 September 2009, which was a follow-up to a session organized at the IXth International Conference on Urban History in Lyon, 27–30 August 2008. The different chapters address a wide range of historical contexts, and take us from sixteenth-century Antwerp, Ulm, Lille and Valenciennes, over seventeenth-century Berlin, Milan and Rome, to eighteenth-century Strasbourg, Trieste, Paris, London and Antwerp, with comparisons up to the present day.

    With each of the chapters addressing the central theme in different ways in distinct urban contexts, together they sketch a varied and lively image of the many ways in which urban authorities and other institutions intervened in the movements of people entering, leaving and inhabiting their city. They bring to the fore how the intricate mix of coercion and conciliation that shaped the local government structure of early modern cities also made room for a certain degree of permanent negotiation and bargaining over the different interests involved. While local elites were themselves not homogeneous groups, they interacted with guilds, relief administrations, central governments, other local authorities, church communities, workers' coalitions, public protesters and other interest groups when devising and bringing into practice local migration policies. At the same time, the studies highlight how policy concerns over migration tended to be concentrated in a number of specific domains which can loosely be grouped under the headings of markets, communal resources and social stability. In their analysis of the 'how' and 'why' of interventions in these domains, the case studies both confirm some existing insights and add up to a number of important new insights which together provide a coherent and stimulating framework for future research.

Markets

It is a familiar observation from existing studies that early modern town authorities often sought to attract wealthy merchants, skilled artisans and other newcomers with resources deemed particularly valuable, and tried to prevent the arrival and settlement of less resourceful migrants whose presence was not considered useful – aspirations which we could translate as attempts to intervene in the markets and circulation of labour, capital and goods in order to ensure adequate supplies of all three *in situ*. Privileged access to burghership or guilds, tax exemptions, grants and other privileges functioned as typical instruments of attraction, while financial requirements or other means of exclusion from corporative structures and social provisions, together with expulsions, were mobilized against the settlement of the unwanted poor.[15]

Most chapters in this book bear out that the regulation of markets represented an important consideration in urban migration policies. Given that migration played a crucial role in the circulation and allocation of labour, goods and capital in early modern cities, attempts by local (and central) authorities to regulate these markets were directly related to opportunities and restrictions for movement and settlement. The chapters by De Meester, Kalc, Niggemann and Winter testify that migration policies were intimately tied up with questions of labour market regulation: while migration restrictions could lead to labour shortages, measures tolerating or even attracting migrant workers were often part of policies designed to augment the local labour supply and/or to import specific skills and technical knowledge. Likewise, Canepari, Niggemann and Kalc remind us how attempts to enlarge or diversify local production and commercial activity to shore up cities' shares in international markets of goods and capital went hand in hand with active recruitment policies towards resourceful merchants, bankers and specialized manufacturers, be it in sixteenth-century Rome, seventeenth-century Potsdam or eighteenth-century Trieste. The latter case is in itself a powerful example of the crucial role of migration policies in attempts to influence early modern markets: policies aimed at attracting merchants, manufacturers and workers, and at facilitating the flows of goods, capital and people, indeed played a key role in the Habsburgs' voluntarist

---

[15] Erika Kuijpers and Maarten Prak, 'Burger, ingezetene, vreemdeling. Burgerschap in Amsterdam in de 17e en 18e eeuw', in Kloek and Tilmans (eds), *Burger*, p. 121; Marc Boone and Peter Stabel, 'New Burghers in the Late Medieval Towns of Flanders and Brabant: Conditions of Entry, Rules and Reality', in Schwinges (ed.), *Neubürger*, p. 320; Ulrich Niggemann, *Immigrationspolitik zwischen Konflikt und Konsens. Die Hugenottenansiedlung in Deutschland und England (1681–1697)* (Cologne/Weimar/Vienna, 2008), pp. 290–301; Alfons K.L. Thijs, 'Minderheden te Antwerpen (16de–20ste eeuw)', in Soly and Thijs (eds), *Minderheden*, pp. 26–31.

scheme to transform Trieste from a small town into a maritime emporium in the eighteenth century.

At the same time, the different case studies warn against treating the distinction between wanted and unwanted migrants in this respect as self-evident, by providing insight into the dynamics of conflict and processes of negotiation that were bound up with the distinction. Given the instability of urban labour markets and the vulnerability of wage-dependent existence, periods of unemployment could often transform 'useful' workers into 'burdensome' poor and vice versa, even in relatively specialized branches of sixteenth-century textile production (Junot). Moreover, newcomers could be considered 'wanted' by some and 'unwanted' by others. A most obvious conflict of interest in this respect was that between workers and employers: as labour shortages were likely to strengthen the bargaining position of local workers – at least in the short run – and increases in labour supplies tended to push down wages, workers often opposed the influx of additional manpower which was welcomed or stimulated by employers, as exemplified in the chapters by De Meester, Niggemann and Kalc. In a similar vein, while mercantilist interests sought the attraction of wealthy merchants or craftsmen-entrepreneurs, the latter were often received with considerably less enthusiasm by established commercial or artisan communities.

Several chapters stress how guilds often played a crucial role in the articulation of conflicts and negotiations over local migration policies, both because of their economic role in the regulation of labour and product markets, and of their political role in local government. While guilds in an older historiography have often been portrayed as essentially homogenous and protectionist institutes which strove to exclude immigrants,[16] recent research has yielded a more complex picture. Masters sometimes appear to have closed ranks when socio-economic pressures jeopardized their status and well-being, as was the case in Nantes and Lyon in the eighteenth century. Conversely, stable guild systems and the absence of modernization could result in greater openness and higher social mobility for new entrants – if only because of greater career prospects for masters' sons outside the guilds.[17] Even declining guilds could be relatively open as a result of masters' sons not following in their fathers' footsteps.[18]

---

[16]   A state of the art on guild historiography in James R. Farr, *Artisans in Europe, 1300–1914* (Cambridge, 2000). See also footnote 10.

[17]   Edward J. Shephard, 'Social and Geographic Mobility of the Eighteenth Century Guild Artisan: An Analysis of Guild Receptions in Dijon, 1700–1790', in Steve L. Kaplan and Cynthia Koepp (eds), *Work in France: Representations, Meaning, Organization, and Practice* (Ithaca, 1986), pp. 97–131.

[18]   Maurice Garden, 'The Urban Trades: Social Analysis and Representation', in Kaplan and Koepp (eds), *Work*, pp. 287–97.

In addition, guild entry policies were also influenced by internal divisions and power relations within the guilds. Merchants coordinating guild-based *Verlag* systems, for instance, were in theory likely to favour the influx of masters (who provided them with finished products), while large artisan-entrepreneurs rather stood to gain from the influx of journeymen. Small masters, from their part, could be opposed to both in an attempt to preserve a certain equality among masters.[19] Depending on their numbers and degree of organization, journeymen could at times enforce a right of preference by which masters were prevented from hiring outsiders ('unfree' journeymen) when 'free' journeymen (who had finished an apprenticeship term and sometimes a journeymen's trial as well) were available.[20]

The case studies developed here confirm that guilds were not *a priori* against or in favour of immigration, but rather constituted arenas of tension between small-scale manufacturers, large-scale entrepreneurs, journeymen, workers and apprentices who had different interests and concerns with regard to the immigration and inclusion or exclusion of new groups. While generalization is difficult because of the limited number of case studies, one tentative suggestion in this respect is that small-scale artisans appear to have been most likely and able to mobilize exclusive measures when local markets were fairly small, internal differences within the guild limited and their influence in guilds large – conditions which were most likely in servicing trades aimed at local markets. In guilds and sectors where the influence of large-scale artisan-entrepreneurs was larger, as in the building industry of sixteenth-century Antwerp, small-scale artisans and journeymen were more likely to call for inclusive measures to prevent 'unfree' workers (non-guild members) from undercutting wages and working conditions (De Meester). Finally, when small-scale artisans and wage workers faced concentration trends and had very little political influence, they were most likely to engage in radical anti-immigrant protests as their main (and last) line of defence, as in the case of the anti-Huguenot protests by London's Weavers' Company in the seventeenth century (Niggemann).

---

[19]   Bert De Munck, *Technologies of Learning: Apprenticeship in Antwerp from the 15th Century to the End of the Ancien Régime* (Turnhout, 2007), chapter 2.3. Also: Catharina Lis and Hugo Soly, 'Export Industries, Craft Guilds and Capitalist Trajectories, 13th to 18th Centuries', in Prak et al. (eds), *Craft Guilds*, pp. 119–26; Catharina Lis and Hugo Soly, 'Subcontracting in Guild-Based Export Trades, 13th–18th Centuries', in Epstein and Prak (eds), *Guilds*, pp. 81–113.

[20]   Bert De Munck, 'One Counter and Your Own Account: Redefining Illicit Labour in Early Modern Antwerp', *Urban History*, 37/1 (2010): pp. 26–44. Also: Catharina Lis and Hugo Soly, '"An Irresistible Phalanx": Journeymen Associations in Western Europe, 1300–1800', in Catharina Lis, Jan Lucassen and Hugo Soly (eds), *Before the Unions: Wage Earners and Collective Action in Europe, 1300–1850* (Amsterdam, 1994), pp. 11–52.

In addition, several chapters highlight how conflicts within guilds were complicated by interventions by local and central authorities. Local authorities did not always take the same sides in conflicts over migration policies in relation to labour and product market regulation. While the Antwerp city government sided with wealthy entrepreneurs during the city's building boom of the early sixteenth century, for instance, it became more sympathetic to the interests of small-scale artisans and workers when the building market came to rest at the end of the century. Moreover, central authorities could and did intervene in local negotiation processes over guild regulations and market access, for instance when they decided to overrule the masons' guild regulations in sixteenth-century Antwerp because of military interests (De Meester); brushed aside demands for protectionist measures in local retail activities in order to stimulate free enterprise (Kalc); lifted local immigration restrictions for particularly 'useful' industries (Winter); or awarded local privileges in order to attract and support the presence of Huguenots in seventeenth-century Germany (Niggemann). In most of these cases, central governments intervened to reinforce market mechanisms and undercut local regulatory activity, mainly out of a mercantilist striving to develop industry and commerce.

Another important observation that emerges from several chapters is that newcomers were themselves not necessarily willing to be integrated in guilds or other corporative structures, which next to certain privileges also implied local obligations and restricted spatial manoeuvrability. The 'unfreedom' of non-citizen journeymen and apprentices in sixteenth-century Antwerp, for instance, gave them a competitive edge in the labour market (De Meester), much like the seasonal Grizon craftsmen in eighteenth-century Trieste (Kalc). Conversely, exemption from guild membership was in some cases mobilized as a privilege to lure skilled manufacturers or merchants, like the Huguenots in seventeenth-century German states (Niggemann), or was actively sought after by wealthy groups wanting to keep their options open, from sixteenth-century Genoa (Canepari) to eighteenth-century Strasbourg (Sonkajärvi). Much appears to have depended on whether newcomers intended to settle down in their new place of residence, in which case they had a stronger interest in being integrated in existing structures of regulation and protection, or whether they intended only a short (be it repeated) stay, in which case the costs of inclusion could outweigh its benefits.

Conflicts over market access, conditions and regulation, then, were rife in early modern urban migration policies. While the underlying interests were relatively similar in many situations, differences in economic and political contexts and power relationships, in the structure of social institutions such as guilds and city governments, and in the degree and nature of interference by central authorities led to actual negotiation processes and bargaining strategies differing from town to town. The influence of these factors extended not only to the design of migration policies, but also to their enforcement. Indeed, several authors remind us that norm and practice in market and guild regulations were not necessarily the same thing: rather, actual in-the-field power relationships, and the willingness or unwillingness of local and central authorities to enforce certain regulations, often mattered more than normative prescriptions. What is more, in order to understand conflicts and bargaining processes adequately, we need to probe deeper into the interests and field of tensions which confronted the actors involved. In particular, interests in both the design and enforcement of migration policies with regard to market regulation had to be weighed against those pertaining to two other important policy concerns: communal resources and social stability.

Communal Resources

An important local policy domain in early modern cities was the management and allocation of communal resources. The term is used here to designate communal local provisions like common rights and poor relief to which access was mediated via non-market criteria such as moral entitlement and belonging, and which were disproportionately concentrated in cities. These communal resources acted as a buffer against market forces for urban workers, and offered vital compensations for discrepancies between wages and survival.[21] Because communal resources were managed on an essentially local basis, migration impacted upon the composition and size of the pool of potential claimants. Existing research has therefore suggested that the endeavour to keep out chargeable newcomers was a major motivation in urban policies against alien beggars and vagrants.[22] Yet while relief entitlements are often cited as a reason for

---

[21]   Marco H.D. van Leeuwen, 'Logic of Charity: Poor Relief in Preindustrial Europe', *Journal of Interdisciplinary History* 24/4 (1994): pp. 600–606; Catharina Lis and Hugo Soly, *Poverty and Capitalism in Pre-Industrial Europe* (Brighton, 1979), chapters 3–5; Catharina Lis and Hugo Soly, 'Policing the Early Modern Proletariat, 1450–1850', in David Levine (ed.), *Proletarianization and Family History* (Orlando, 1984), pp. 163–228.

[22]   Dirk van Damme, 'Onderstandswoonst, sedentarisering en stad-platteland-tegenstellingen. Evolutie en betekenis van de wetgeving op de onderstandwoonst in België (einde achttiende tot einde negentiende eeuw)', *Belgisch Tijdschrift voor Nieuwste Geschiedenis*, 21/3 (1990): pp. 484–9; Abram de Swaan, *In Care of the State: Health Care, Education, and Welfare in Europe and the USA in the Modern Era* (Oxford, 1988), pp. 30–41; Thijs, 'Minderheden', p. 31; Catharina Lis, Dirk Van Damme and Hugo Soly, *Op vrije voeten. Sociale politiek in West-Europa (1450-1914)* (Leuven, 1985).

the exclusion of newcomers, a number of recent studies have highlighted how the development of urban relief schemes, especially by voluntary and private associations, was also linked to a process of community building.[23] Although they excluded certain groups, they therefore also acted as mechanisms for the inclusion of others.

Several chapters in this volume move beyond these paradoxes by demonstrating that also in this domain inclusion and exclusion were the subject of conflicts of interest. As Junot's chapter on the textile towns of Walloon Flanders shows, it was hard to discriminate between economic and religious migrants or between 'useful' newcomers and potential claimants to poor relief. By highlighting the inherent contradictions between attempts to shield local provisions from newcomers and attempts to enlarge the local labour supply, several chapters provide insights into the complex ways in which concerns over migrants' access to communal resources were tied in with a broader process of negotiation over the costs and benefits of migration which pitted the interests of employers against those of relief administrators. To the extent that immigration benefited local employers by depressing the cost of labour, it increased pressure on communal provisions which made up for the discrepancies between wages and survival. Relief providers and administrators therefore often sought to avoid the additional burden which immigration could entail by restricting the immigration of poor and vulnerable groups – which happened for instance in the Jewish community of eighteenth-century Trieste (Kalc), or was the function of the migration restrictions that accompanied the reorganization of Antwerp's poor relief board in 1779 (Winter). Yet several chapters demonstrate that immigration restrictions were difficult to enforce in practice, especially in large cities with limited policing effectives (Kalc, Milliot), while they could also encounter opposition by employers (Junot, Winter). Such measures were therefore almost all seconded and sometimes replaced by more retroactive means to avoid migrants becoming a burden on local relief provisions: making access to relief conditional on a certain length of residence or other criteria of local belonging (Winter) and/or simply expelling migrants if and when they became chargeable (Coy). But when large numbers of poor migrants sought relief, even retroactive forms of exclusion could prove unfeasible – or as the Antwerp authorities emphatically complained in the late eighteenth century: '[T]hey are still humans, and ... we cannot let them perish.'[24]

---

[23]   Lynch, *Individuals*, chapter 3; Katherine A. Lynch, 'Behavioral Regulation in the City: Families, Religious Associations, and the Role of Poor Relief', in Herman Roodenburg and Pieter Spierenburg (eds), *Social Control in Europe, Volume 1, 1500–1800* (Columbus, 2004), pp. 200–19.

[24]   See the chapter by Anne Winter in this volume.

The policy outcome of the trade-off between encouraging immigration and economizing on relief expenses was therefore shaped by power relationships between employers, relief administrators and recipients, but in this constellation local labour market structures also seem to have mattered a great deal. In general, employer interests and labour supply needs appear to have had more chance of prevailing in urban economies that relied most strongly on a permanent influx of newcomers, like international port towns such as Amsterdam, while relief economizing concerns were more likely to gain priority in cities where employers relied mainly on a skilled but low-paid local workforce, like the textile producing Antwerp or silk producing Lyon in the eighteenth century. Both Winter and Lucassen moreover indicate that reciprocity could be an additional consideration pertaining to the exclusion or inclusion of poor migrants, so that urban policies in this respect were also influenced by those of other local authorities as well as by regional or national legislation.

All the same, while local relief provisions, both public and private, were probably the most important type of communal resource, the concept could be extended to include local employment and business opportunities – especially to the extent that they were viewed as scarce communal goods in the 'moral economy' described by Niggemann. In this view, German craftsmen opposed Huguenot immigration primarily because it increased competition for 'Nahrung', the concept adopted by Werner Sombart to characterize a premodern economic ideology which disapproved of market ideology and revolved around the possibility to make an honest living.[25] In that perspective, also resonating in De Meester's discussion of the building trades in sixteenth-century Antwerp, local income opportunities were considered a kind of communal resource which some wanted to protect from infringements by newcomers – for instance by linking it to burghership. The extent to which they actually succeeded in doing so was, however, dependent upon local contexts, interests and power relationships.

Social Stability and Incorporation

Immigration could run counter to another major policy concern of early modern town elites, that of public order and social stability. The majority of migrants who belonged to the poor and vulnerable classes were often perceived as a potential threat to public order, especially given their alleged proneness to engage in begging, vagrancy, prostitution, libertinage, thieving, rioting

---

[25]   For critical observations on this concept, see various contributions in Josef Ehmer and Catharina Lis (eds), *The Idea of Work in Europe from Antiquity to Modern Times* (Farnham, 2009).

and other dangerous or criminal behaviour in the eyes of early modern elites and middling groups. Recent research on the development of early modern policing, particularly in France, has highlighted how the expansion and professionalization of urban police forces were intimately tied up with a growing ambition to control and monitor the whereabouts and activities of newcomers.[26] Next to repressive and control measures, more incorporative instruments such as the granting of burgership could also be mobilized to integrate newcomers within the existing social hierarchy.

The chapters by Coy, Junot and Milliot in particular confirm that controlling, detecting and correcting materially or morally dangerous behaviour by low-status newcomers was often a central concern of urban migration policies. Many of the case studies in this book cite the existence of entry regulations and passport formalities at the city gates, and of requirements for landlords and innkeepers to inform local authorities of the characteristics and antecedents of their lodgers. However, the efficiency of these measures was heavily dependent upon the development of urban policing (Milliot), and often failed to deny entry except to the most destitute or potentially dangerous of newcomers (Kalc). Retroactive policies such as expulsions were therefore also mobilized to exclude not only the burdensome but also the violators of social and moral norms (Coy).

Conversely, several chapters at the same time highlight how attempts to restrict or regulate immigration with an eye to social stability, just like concerns about relief, could conflict with employers' interests in expanding the local labour supply. Coy's study provides an instructive illustration on how efforts to restrict and monitor immigration with an eye to protecting moral standards and social stability had to strike a delicate balance with local needs for migrant labour in sixteenth-century Ulm. Kalc's discussion of how calls for a permit system to regulate the number and conduct of porters in eighteenth-century Trieste were systematically boycotted by merchants who feared labour shortages is in turn a telling example of how concerns about public order could remain subservient to employers' interests in unlimited immigration.

Whether because of inefficient control instruments or predominant employer interests, early modern cities remained confronted with a permanent influx of migrants from all social classes that created challenges in terms of social stability that could not be resolved by selective migration policies alone. After all, migration was not necessarily a destabilizing factor. On the contrary, given the demographic and economic needs of early modern cities, migration was necessary for the reproduction of urban life. Yet to the extent that newcomers were essentially unknown and unconnected individuals in an order based on

---

[26]   Roche, *La ville promise*; Blanc-Chaléard et al. (eds), *Police et migrants*.

belonging and reputation, something which is stressed by Canepari, migration was a phenomenon that required close monitoring and suitable integration mechanisms. An important consideration in this respect, and one made in several chapters, is that not only the immigration of the *classes dangereuses* but also that of more resourceful groups created challenges in terms of social stability, and that the monitoring and integration of *all* types of newcomers were key concerns in urban migration policies.

The main challenge should therefore be described as *incorporation*, i.e. the allocation of newcomers to their appropriate status and corporative groups in the existing urban hierarchy, in order to channel their entitlement to communal resources while ensuring their commitment to the communal normative framework and the political status quo. Burghership and guild membership were important instruments for the incorporation of better-off groups. Burghership was in the first instance a legal status that defined one's membership of the urban *communitas* and conferred upon its bearer a range of political rights, legal prerogatives, fiscal and economic privileges and social benefits.[27] Existing research has highlighted how burghership was the cornerstone of a corporative rhetoric centred on the urban *communitas*, celebrated by pledges of allegiance, processions and other manifestations of corporative identity and sealed with the stipulation that guild masters must be burghers.[28] Yet the great variety in criteria for its acquisition leaves open many questions as to the precise ways in which burghership could function as a means of integration.[29]

---

[27]   Marc Boone, 'Droit de bourgeoisie et particularisme urbain dans la Flandre bourguignonne et habsburgoise (1384–1585)', *Belgisch Tijdschrift voor Filologie en Geschiedenis*, 74 (1996): p. 713; An Kint, 'Becoming Civic Community. Citizenship in Sixteenth-century Antwerp', in Boone and Prak (eds), *Individual*, pp. 157–70; Kuijpers and Prak, 'Burger', pp. 115–19; Anna Maria Pult Quaglia, 'Citizenship in Medieval and Early Modern Italian Cities', in Stephan G. Ellis, Gudmundur Hálfdanarson and Ann Katherine Isaacs (eds), *Citizenship in Historical Perspective* (Pisa, 2006), pp. 107–14; Angelika Schaser, 'Städtische Fremdenpolitik im Deutschland der Frühen Neuzeit', in Alexander Demandt (ed.), *Mit Fremden leben. Eine Kulturgeschichte von der Antike bis zur Gegenwart* (Munich, 1995), p. 144; James S. Amelang, 'Cities and Foreigners', in Calabi and Christensen (eds), *Cultural Exchange*, pp. 42–55.

[28]   Cf. Boone and Prak (eds), *Individual*; Pult Quaglia, 'Citizenship'; Eberhard Isenmann, 'Bürgerrecht und Bürgeraufnahme in der spätmittelalterlichen und frühneuzeitlichen Stadt', in Schwinges (ed.), *Neubürger*, p. 205ff. According to An Kint, 'Becoming Civic Community', p. 160 burghership did *not* function as the cornerstone of the urban community in sixteenth-century Antwerp.

[29]   Via birth, residence, purchase and/or marriage. See for instance Kint, 'Becoming Civic Community', p. 161; Kuijpers and Prak, 'Burger', pp. 119–24; Isenmann, 'Bürgerrecht und Bürgeraufnahme'; Amelang, 'Cities and Foreigners', pp. 45, 47; Christopher R. Friedrichs, *The Early Modern City* (London/New York, 1995), pp. 143–4; Jonathan Barry, 'Civility and Civic

What is clear is that burghership and guild membership can be seen as instrumental in *incorporation* policies as well. While established groups sometimes sought to exclude newcomers from accessing these corporative institutions, De Meester and Niggemann demonstrate how membership of the citizenry and guilds could be actively promoted as a way to integrate newcomers' interests with those of established groups. Conversely, Sonkajärvi's study illuminates how the failure to incorporate privileged newcomers into local repertoires of allegiance – in this case through noblemen's adherence to national rather than local citizenship – undermined the existing political and judicial order of eighteenth-century Strasbourg. Further down the social ladder, intermediate statuses of accepted but non-citizen resident – *Beywoner* in sixteenth-century Ulm (Coy), *simple manant* in sixteenth-century Tournai (Junot), *Temporal-Schirm* in eighteenth-century Strasbourg (Sonkajärvi) or residence permit holders in eighteenth-century Trieste (Kalc) – were devised to monitor processes of conditional incorporation of less resourceful groups.

An important observation here is again that neither upmarket nor downmarket newcomers were necessarily willing to take on these statuses of incorporation, especially if they also entailed local obligations and limited manoeuvrability, as the cases of Italian merchants (Canepari) and Strasbourg noblemen (Sonkajärvi) indicate. Burghership should therefore not necessarily be taken as a measure of successful integration, or as the outcome of a personal negotiation process between an 'outsider' on the one hand and an established community on the other. Rather, the inclusion or exclusion of immigrants from corporative structures was part of a wider collective negotiation process over the positions, rights and privileges of different migrant groups in which many different concerns and interest groups played a role.

Identities and Communities

Possibly partly as a reaction against too strong a focus on these matters in earlier minority studies, the chapters rarely consider culture and religion as relevant policy concerns in themselves. Rather, they play down the role of religious differences as a cause of conflict between immigrant Huguenots and local craftsmen in seventeenth-century German cities (Niggemann), stress the malleability of religious distinctions as compared to other concerns in eighteenth-century Strasbourg (Sonkajärvi); illustrate how local policies of

Culture in Early Modern England: The Meanings of Urban Freedom', in P. Burke et al. (eds), *Civil Histories: Essays Presented to Sir Keith Thomas* (Oxford, 2000), pp. 181–96, pp. 186, 191.

reconciliation enabled a flexible accommodation of dissenting migrants in cities of Walloon Flanders even at the height of religious conflict in the late sixteenth century (Junot); and provide examples of peaceful religious coexistence, as in seventeenth-century Amsterdam (Lucassen) or eighteenth-century Trieste (Kalc). At the same time, these references show that religious identities were nevertheless considered relevant – be it actively construed and malleable – distinctions by different actors in most urban contexts discussed here. To a certain extent religion, like culture, can be considered part of the corporative identity structure that underlay conceptions of urban citizenship and belonging. Hence policy makers' concerns for a certain degree of homogeneity or categorization in this respect could be considered part of a more general concern for public order and social stability.[30]

More generally, several of the case studies indicate that the choices made by the actors involved need to be understood in relation to their ideas about community formation and belonging. The defence and distribution of communal resources inevitably depended on how the community was conceived in moral and political terms. The connection between the status of burgher and the exclusive right to own real estate – as existed in Strasbourg – suggests that the idea of political and social standing and privileges being conditional upon settledness was deep-rooted. According to Canepari, being a 'foreigner' in early modern Italian cities was largely synonymous with lacking a permanent residence. In Strasbourg, abandoning burgher status required swearing an oath which committed the ex-burgher to leaving the city.

Processes of state formation and loss of city autonomy were sources of important tensions in this domain.[31] A former autonomous imperial city (*Reichsstadt*) which came under the sovereignty of the French king at the end of the seventeenth century, the case of Strasbourg illustrates the frictions and conflicts that arose between local and national repertoires of belonging. The conflicts which surfaced after the annexation therefore appear to have been less the result of increased immigration *per se* than of a confrontation between two different modes of classifying inhabitants – related to two different repertoires of political allegiance (Sonkajärvi). As discussions of tax exemptions and the possession of real estate by non-burghers illustrate, the definitions of legal status, social position and privilege were fundamentally related to political claims

---

[30]   Additional concerns like the evasion of conscription (Kalc), or the spread of contagious disease (Milliot), can likewise be considered part of efforts to protect the military and sanitary assets of a local community, and hence to maintain its social stability.

[31]   See for instance Maarten Prak, 'Burghers into Citizens: Urban and National Citizenship in the Netherlands during the Revolutionary Era (c. 1800)', *Theory and Society*, 26 (1997): pp. 403–20.

on the urban territory. Both ownership of real estate by non-burghers and tax exemptions ran counter to traditional ideas on 'communal resources' – or else were at least based on another definition of *communitas*. The interference of the central government in sixteenth-century Antwerp (De Meester) might serve as an early example of the same field of tension.

Shifting political claims on local territories entailed shifting definitions of 'foreignness' and different modes of migration control. Canepari's discussion of foreigners' legislation in the state of Milan shows how it became increasingly difficult to be classified as 'local' in the course of the seventeenth century. Milliot's chapter demonstrates more directly how both increasing mobility and state formation impacted upon the identification and classification of individuals in eighteenth-century France. These processes brought about growing concerns with social disaffiliation and disintegration, and, hence, led to the professionalization and specialization of police and administrative forces. The latter were in turn felt to interfere with corporative and neighbourhood-like models of belonging, participation and governance. What Milliot refers to as 'enlightened opinion' appears to have been at odds with 'old community regulation' in this respect – among other things because from the perspective of local communities it entailed a certain 'de-territorialization'.

The extent to which the growing influence of central authorities appears to have undermined local repertoires of belonging and allegiance is a question that is explored further in Lucassen's chapter. By highlighting similarities in the migration regimes of early modern cities and modern states he provides new and stimulating perspectives for further systematic comparisons of intentions, effects and limitations of migration policies in a long-term perspective. Hitchcock's chapter, finally, is an important counterpoint to many of the insights from the other chapters in laying bare the limits of migration regulation. It argues that even in eighteenth-century England, with its highly formalized relief and settlement system and arguably the most centralized state of the time, migration in practice remained largely unregulated and many poor migrants could travel around unmolested. Furthermore, it demonstrates that unsettledness was a daily experience and accepted reality for many migrants and local authorities respectively, and at times provided an alternative, non-territorial sense of identity. Hence, while urban authorities and other institutions engaged in complex discussions on the positions and entitlements of migrants, the precise effects and implications of these policies on the actual manoeuvrability and agency of even the most destitute migrants remains a focal point for further research.

Conclusions and Suggestions for Further Research

The different case studies addressed in the chapters of this book demonstrate that merchants, entrepreneurs, small-scale artisans, workers, relief payers, relief recipients and local and central administrations could all have different and often opposing interests with regard to the influx and incorporation of urban migrants in early modern Europe. On the whole, these different interests and conflicts crystallized around three main areas of concern: the regulation of (labour) markets, social stability and communal resources. The degree of overlap between the social groups embodying these different concerns, as well as the power relationships between them, interacted with social and economic contexts and institutions to shape urban migration policies in practice. Several chapters bring to light not only dynamics of conflict, but also arenas of negotiation – of which riots and public protests were only the most visible, and exceptional, manifestation. In one way or another, the outcomes tended to be compromises in that they attempted to accommodate different concerns and interests. In practice this meant that migration policies often combined elements of attraction, restriction and exclusion. The very poor, criminal, uprooted and riotous ranked as the most unwanted type of newcomers, while docile and useful workers, together with skilled and wealthy newcomers, were higher on the wanted list. Yet the chapters show that the boundary between wanted and unwanted migrant was not fixed, but fluctuated according to power relationships between different interest groups involved in the trade-off between attempts to augment the local labour supply, economize on relief expenses and maintain social stability.

Policies made use of both proactive and retroactive instruments of selection and restriction, but both ran up against limits of enforcement. As a result, the integration even of groups deemed less useful or welcome was often a *conditio sine qua non* for urban authorities to deal with the permanent flux of migrants. It is important to stress in this respect that the opposition between inclusion and exclusion is a too linear pair of concepts to describe the multilayered reality that newcomers to early modern cities faced. Local policy makers seem to have been more concerned about the status of the immigrants residing in the city – and hence their obligations and the nature of their entitlements to communal resources – than about their presence as such. So the approach centred on inclusion and exclusion should perhaps be substituted by a more malleable one centred on models, mechanisms and levels of *incorporation*. There were in any case various levels and notions of 'integration' in play, on the part of both established urban communities and newcomers alike. Not all newcomers were necessarily willing to follow the incorporative trajectories outlined for them, while expectations and entry conditions vis-à-vis migrants could vary considerably. Inevitably, these issues were linked to fundamental notions of sociability and community and identity formation, which materialized in distinct ways of defining 'foreigners'.

In the end, it is at the level of the different mechanisms of incorporation and status ascription that long-term transformations materialized. As a result of the choice made to present a range of case studies, long-term trends and transformations remain underexposed in this volume. Yet, we feel that the insights yielded by the different chapters provide important starting points for further research in this direction. One main question in this respect centres on the influence of the growing intrusion of market forces on considerations related to labour market regulation and access to communal resources. To the extent that work for wages became increasingly important as a labour allocation mechanism in the course of the early modern period,[32] employers' interests against immigration restrictions are likely to have gained in force. But workers' growing wage dependency at the same time increased the importance of residual welfare provisions as a buffer against the potentially disruptive effects of proletarianization for social and political stability.[33] Growing reliance on relief provisions is in turn likely to have heightened anti-immigration considerations from the perspective of taxpayers and relief recipients who sought to restrict newcomers' potential encroachments on local relief provisions. In other words, the growth of wage dependency is likely to have amplified conflicts of interest over the costs and benefits of immigration between employers and relief providers respectively. If this was indeed the case, this may in turn have been related to the growing role of police control as an alternative way to organize and monitor society: as conceptions of 'Nahrung', charity and neighbourly help came under increasing pressure by market forces, police control may have taken their place as a prime means to maintain social stability *and* to deal with the ongoing rising tensions over immigration. In this context, further research is needed along the lines set out by Lucassen on the role of state formation in shifting definitions of foreignness and remoulding policies of migration. Exploring these questions in a long-term perspective will require taking into consideration the many different manifestations of conflicts and compromises over the costs and benefits of regulating migration through time and space.

---

[32]   On the relative and absolute rise of wage labour in the course of the early modern period: Charles Tilly, 'Demographic Origins of the European Proletariat', in Levine (ed.), *Proletarianization*, pp. 30–36.

[33]   Leeuwen, 'Logic of Charity'; Catharina Lis and Hugo Soly, 'Policing'; Larry Patriquin, *Agrarian Capitalism and Poor Relief in England, 1500–1860: Rethinking the Origins of the Welfare State* (Basingstoke, 2007), pp. 45–78.

One general conclusion of this book is that labour market regulation cannot be separated from the management of local resources and moral and ideological sensitivities regarding local communities – an observation which can help to articulate new questions for further research too. Urban burghership is for instance an institution that could benefit from further research from a comparative long-term perspective with regard to the field of tension between labour market regulation, communal resources and community building. The fact that citizenship could often be purchased, while in some cases it was free of charge and in other situations it was granted on an ad-hoc basis, made it into an instrument by which foreigners could be excluded or taxed.[34] However, burghership was a very diverse and multilayered institution as well. Both power struggles within the city and the need to include or exclude specific social groups according to economic circumstances have led to a wide range of different citizenship types. Burghership was often passed on via 'ius sanguinis' (having one or two citizen-parents), but sometimes conferred on everyone born within the urban territory ('ius soli') or awarded after a certain length of residence (from one to 15 years or more).[35] Moreover, although early modern urban citizenship was often linked to guild membership, and urban 'freedom' in England was even to be acquired through apprenticeship (next to inheritance and marriage), in France or Rome one could become a guild master without being a burgher.[36]

On the whole, burghership was related to the claims of urban elites to local communal resources. As such, the privileged position of the urban 'patriciate' and corporative middling groups was justified by the assumption that their material interests guaranteed loyalty to the 'common good'.[37] But in order to understand differences and long-term transformations comparative research is needed. For this, burghership should be linked to both lower and higher levels of identification and belonging. On the one hand, more research is needed on the alternative patterns of incorporation and identification of non-burghers,

---

[34]   E.g. Boone, 'Droit de bourgeoisie'; Kuijpers and Prak, 'Burger', pp. 119–23.

[35]   Thijs, 'Minderheden', pp. 17–20; Kint, 'Becoming Civic Community', p. 161; Amelang, 'Cities and Foreigners', p. 47.

[36]   Friedrichs, *The Early Modern City*, pp. 143–4; Barry, 'Civility and Civic Culture', p. 191; Amelang, 'Cities and Foreigners', p. 45. Why, moreover, could burghership sometimes be conditional upon membership of a guild, as was the case in London and Zurich, rather than the other way around? Marc Boone et al. 'Introduction. Citizenship between Individual and Community', in Boone and Prak (eds), *Individual*, p. 5. See also the chapter by Canepari in this volume.

[37]   Marc Boone, '"Cette frivole, dampnable et desraisonnable bourgeoisie". De vele gezichten van het laatmiddeleeuwse burgerbegrip in de Zuidelijke Nederlanden', in Kloek and Tilmans (eds), *Burger*, p. 45; Ulrich Meier, 'Gemeinnutz und Vaterlandsliebe. Kontroversen über die normativen Grundlagen des Bürgerbegriffs im späten Mittelalter', in Schwinges (ed.), *Neubürger*, pp. 53–82.

and on the social and cultural significance of intermediate categories such as *ingezetene, manant, Beywoner, Schirmbürger* and so on.[38] On the other hand, interactions between urban citizenship and non-local, especially national, categories of belonging are in need of further research.[39] When Venice and Florence turned into 'territorial states' in the sixteenth century, for instance, citizenship changed from an identificational to a juridical concept. While urban burghership had been intimately tied in with the social and political body of the 'commune', belonging to the state was less and less connected to *participation* in governmental (and perhaps economic) affairs.[40] How can this be tallied with the recent idea that there was at the same time a return to the territorial idea of early 'communes', whereby the *ius sanguinis* of the late medieval cities (which enabled extending urban citizenship to the *contado*) was replaced with citizenship being reserved for actual residents and perhaps to those who owned real estate and paid taxes?[41]

In order to link questions of burghership and belonging to economic factors, additional research on the political economy of guilds may prove helpful. While the old image of guilds as exclusive cartels of masters who jealously guarded their production monopoly and their labour market monopsony have fallen into disrepute, the factors determining the relative openness or closedness of guilds are in need of further qualification. Important differentiations need to be made, for instance, between entry policies towards apprentices, journeymen and masters, while also the nature of the industrial activities, production relations and political power of and within different guilds needs to be taken into account. Hence, it is of major importance to examine guilds' regulations and their

---

[38]   For studies from a legal perspective, see for instance J. Gilissen, 'Le statut des étrangers en Belgique du XIIIe au XXe siècle', in *Recueils de la société Jean Bodin, vol. X* (Paris, 1984), pp. 233–308; Pelus-Kaplan, Marie-Louise, 'Travail, immigration et citoyenneté dans les villes hanséatiques, XVIe–XVIIe siècles, d'après les exemples de Lübeck, Hambourg et Danzig', in Pilar Gonzalez-Bernaldo, Manuela Martini and Marie-Louise Pelus-Kaplan (eds), *Etrangers et societes. Représentations, coexistences, interactions dans la longue durée* (Rennes, 2008), pp. 337–50. Also: Schaser, 'Städtische Fremdenpolitik', 147–9. In Amsterdam, the juridical status of 'ingesetene' in 1668 appears to have been created in order to include a welcome category of artisans as it gave access to the local guilds (while at the same time excluding them from communal office) – but research is still very much in its infancy here: Kuijpers and Prak, 'Burger', p. 122.

[39]   Interesting perspectives: Prak, 'Burghers into Citizens'; Tamara Herzog, *Defining Nations: Immigrants and Citizens in Early Modern Spain and Spanish America* (New Haven, 2003); Renaud Morieux, *Une mer pour deux royaumes. La Manche, frontière franco-anglaise (XVIIe–XVIIIe siècles)* (Rennes, 2008).

[40]   Pult Quaglia, 'Citizenship'.

[41]   Pierre Racine, 'La citoyenneté en Italie au moyen âge', *Le moyen âge*, 115/1 (2009): pp. 87–108.

implications for labour market regulation from a micro-perspective in order to understand when, why and how guilds encouraged or restricted immigration of skilled (and at times unskilled) masters, journeymen and apprentices.

Analogous observations can be made with regard to poor relief arrangements. Although long-term trends in poor relief are typically described as shifts from private and religious forms of charity to public poor relief and businesslike insurance schemes, different perspectives abound. While some have studied the development of public poor relief in the context of proletarianization and state formation,[42] others have focused on private and bottom-up initiatives such as poor boxes.[43] Recently, poor relief has been approached from the perspective of community building, as a result of which incorporative strategies towards the shamefaced poor are stressed.[44] Further research should, in our opinion, not only address different types of mutual aid and charity providers from the perspective of exclusion and incorporation, but should also consider the interconnections and fields of tension between different levels and types of poor relief.[45] In order to understand long-term transformations related to the incorporative and exclusionary mechanisms at the urban level we need to examine poor relief as a whole – including confraternities, guilds and parishes on the one hand, and public and private poor relief schemes on the other.

---

[42]   E.g. Lis and Soly, *Poverty and Capitalism*; Hugo Soly, 'Continuity and Change. Attitudes Towards Poor Relief and Health Care in Early Modern Antwerp', in Ole Peter Grell and Andrew Cunningham (eds), *Health Care and Poor Relief in Protestant Europe, 1500–1700* (London, 1997): pp. 85–107; de Swaan, *In Care of the State*.

[43]   E.g. Sandra Bos, *'Uyt liefde tot malcander'. Onderlinge hulpverlening binnen de Noord-Nederlandse gilden in internationaal perspectief (1570–1820)* (Amsterdam, 1998); Sandra Bos, 'A Tradition of Giving and Receiving: Mutual Aid within the Guild System', in Prak et al. (eds), *Craft Guilds*, pp. 174–93; Sigrid Fröhlich, *Die Soziale Sicherung bei Zünften und* Gesellenverbanden: *Darstellung, Analyse, Vergleich* (Berlin, 1976); Marco van Leeuwen, *The Logic of Charity: Amsterdam, 1800–1850* (London/New York, 2000); Marcel van der Linden (ed.), *Social Security Mutualism: The Comparative History of Mutual Benefit Societies* (Bern, 1996).

[44]   Lynch, *Individuals*; Lynch, 'Behavioral Regulation'.

[45]   Manon van der Heijden, 'New Perspectives on Public Services in Early Modern Europe', *Journal of Urban History*, 36/3 (2010): pp 269-284. A case study in which the differences between guilds and trade-related poor boxes are examined: Bert De Munck, 'Fiscalizing Solidarity (from Below): Poor Relief in Antwerp Guilds between Community Building and Public Service', in Manon van der Heijden, Elise van Nederveen Meerkerk, Griet Vermeesch and Martijn van der Burg (eds), *Serving the Urban Community: The Rise of Public Facilities in the Low Countries* (Amsterdam, 2009), pp. 168–93.

PART I
Repertoires of Inclusion and Exclusion: Guilds and Citizenship

Chapter 2

Migrant Workers and Illicit Labour: Regulating the Immigration of Building Workers in Sixteenth-Century Antwerp

Jan De Meester

The strong linkage between economy and demography was a distinct characteristic of early modern cities. Economic changes resulted in demographical shifts, and in this process migration movements were crucial. Strong urban economies attracted immigrants and discouraged potential emigrants from leaving. An economic downturn led to a surplus of emigrants and a shortage of immigrants.[1] This historical pattern applies to sixteenth-century Antwerp. Until the fall of Antwerp in 1585, when Spain regained control of the city, its economic preponderance within the Netherlands was overwhelming.[2] Its demographic growth was accordingly. In 1480 Antwerp counted approximately 33,000 inhabitants. This figure increased to around 55,000 in 1526 and to 84,000 in 1542. The city's demography, along with its economic situation, peaked in 1568, with 105,000 inhabitants.[3] As historical-

[1]   Clé Lesger, 'Migratiestromen en economische ontwikkeling in vroegmoderne steden. Nieuwe burgers in Antwerpen en Amsterdam, 1541–1655', *Stadsgeschiedenis*, 1/1 (2006): p. 97.

[2]   Herman van der Wee, *The Growth of the Antwerp Market and the European Economy (Fourteenth-Sixteenth Century)* (3 vols, The Hague, 1963); An Kint, *The Community of Commerce: Social Relations in Sixteenth-Century Antwerp* (unpublished PhD dissertation, New York, 1996), pp. 47–109; Oscar Gelderblom, 'The Decline of Fairs and Merchant Guilds in the Low Countries, 1250–1650', *Jaarboek voor Middeleeuwse Geschiedenis*, 7 (2004): pp. 215–20; Wilfrid Brulez, 'Brugge en Antwerpen in de 15de en 16de eeuw. Een tegenstelling?', *Tijdschrift voor geschiedenis*, 83 (1970): pp. 15–37; Wilfrid Brulez, 'De Handel', *Antwerpen in de XVIde eeuw* (Antwerp, 1975), pp. 109–42; Jan Arthur Van Houtte, 'Déclin et survivance d'Anvers (1550–1700)', *Studi in Onore di Amintori Fanfani* (6 vols, Milan, 1962), vol. 2, pp. 705–26; Bruno Blondé and Michael Limberger, 'De gebroken welvaart', in Raymond Van Uytven (ed.), *Geschiedenis van Brabant van het hertogdom tot heden* (Leuven, 2007), pp. 307–11.

[3]   Jan De Vries, *European Urbanization 1500–1800* (London, 1984), p. 272; René Boumans, 'L'évolution démographique d'Anvers (XVe–XVIIe siècle)', *Bulletin statistique*, 34 (1948): pp. 1683–91; René Boumans and Jan Craeybeckx, 'Het bevolkingscijfer van Antwerpen in het

demographical analyses demonstrate, early modern cities like Antwerp struggled with high mortality rates. This so-called 'urban graveyard' effect generally prevented natural demographic growth.[4] Reconstructed birth and mortality rates for Antwerp confirm that natural population increase was impossible in the Scheldt town.[5] One implication is that immigrants were responsible for Antwerp's enormous population growth in the sixteenth century. Migration historians estimate that immigrants easily constituted half of the population of fast-growing early modern cities.[6] For sixteenth-century Antwerp such a figure may even be an underestimation: between 1526 and 1542 more than 2,000 immigrants arrived in the city annually.[7]

Although there were different reasons for moving to Antwerp in the sixteenth century, labour market opportunities were certainly the main pull-factor.[8] Next to being a world centre of industry, commerce and transport, Antwerp also functioned as a major service centre for a large hinterland. The city and its strong economy were thus attractive to merchants, skilled craftsmen and unskilled labourers alike. That the labour market was flooded with many 'fortune seekers' naturally had myriad consequences. This contribution seeks to explore how different actors on the labour market – including entrepreneurs, craft guilds and central and local governments – reacted to the massive influx of labour migrants. Depending on the economic situation, these actors had different interests regarding the regulation of the labour market. Attempts to regulate the labour market in sixteenth-century Antwerp logically resulted in attempts to regulate labour migration. In this chapter I investigate how negotiations between the different parties concerning the regulation of labour migration were carried out and how they evolved. I will argue that such

---

derde kwart der XVIe eeuw', *Tijdschrift voor geschiedenis*, 60 (1974): pp. 394–405; Jan Van Roey, 'De bevolking', in *Antwerpen in de XVIde eeuw* (Antwerp, 1975), pp. 95–108.

[4]   Katherine A. Lynch, *Individuals, Families, and Communities in Europe, 1200–1800: The Urban Foundations of Western Society* (Cambridge, 2003), pp. 39–43.

[5]   Herman van der Wee and Jan Matterné, 'De Antwerpse wereldmarkt tijdens de 16de en 17de eeuw', in Jan van der Stock (ed.), *Antwerpen. Verhaal van een metropool 16de–17de eeuw* (Ghent, 1963), p. 20.

[6]   Leslie Page Moch, *Moving Europeans: Migration in Western Europe since 1650* (Bloomington, 2003), pp. 40–44.

[7]   Kint, *Community of Commerce*, pp. 34–36.

[8]   For a summary of traditional push-pull factors, see Peter Stabel, *De kleine stad in Vlaanderen. Bevolkingsdynamiek en economische functies van de kleine en secundaire stedelijke centra in het Gentse kwartier (14de–16de eeuw)* (Brussels, 1995), pp. 28–9; Erika Kuijpers, *Migrantenstad. Immigratie en sociale verhoudingen in seventiende-eeuws Amsterdam* (Hilversum, 2005), p. 21; Jan De Meester, 'Arbeidsmigratie vanuit westelijk Noord-Brabant naar Antwerpen in de zestiende eeuw', *Jaarboek De Ghulden Roos*, 68 (2009): p. 138.

negotiations resulted in the development of a kind of strategy for controlling the influx of labour immigrants,[9] not least because local as well as central authorities realized that well-organized labour mobility would benefit the expansion of the labour market.[10]

As it is not viable to examine the entire labour market in a single chapter, this contribution will concentrate on the Masons' guild, which was one of the most important craft guilds within the urban economy. My chapter fits into the recent historiographical trend of considering guilds as institutions which had a considerable and wide-ranging impact on the urban economy and society, and as powerful lobbyists that to a great extent steered the intricacies of city politics.[11] In sixteenth-century Antwerp craft guilds had considerable political influence. Although they were not represented in the Antwerp magistrate or town executive, the urban authorities regularly involved them in the city's administration.[12] If a guild strongly pressed its case there was good chance that the authorities would take *ad hoc* decisions in the guild's favour.[13] In this chapter I will examine how the Masons' guild members and authorities reacted to the massive influx of labour immigrants and how they tried to influence the

---

[9]   Leo Lucassen, 'Gelijkheid en onbehagen. De wortels van het integratiedebat in West-Europa', in Leo Lucassen and Wim Willems (eds), *Gelijkheid en onbehagen. Over steden, nieuwkomers en nationaal geheugenverlies* (Amsterdam, 2006), pp. 16–17.

[10]   Alfons Thijs, 'Minderheden te Antwerpen (16de–20ste eeuw)', in Hugo Soly and Alfons Thijs (eds), *Minderheden in West-Europese steden (16de–20ste eeuw)* (Brussels, 1995), pp. 29–40; Anne Winter, *Divided Interests, Divided Migrants: The Rationales of Policies Regarding Labour Mobility in Western Europe, ca. 1550–1914* (Global Economic History Network (GEHN) Working Paper, 15), 2005, pp. 1–10.

[11]   Peter Stabel, 'Guilds in Late Medieval Flanders: Myths and Realities of Guild Life in an Export-Oriented Environment', *Journal of Medieval History*, 30 (2004): pp. 187–90.

[12]   René Boumans, *Het Antwerps stadsbestuur voor en tijdens de Franse overheersing. Bijdrage tot de ontwikkelingsgeschiedenis van de stedelijke bestuursinstellingen in de Zuidelijke Nederlanden* (Bruges, 1965), pp. 21–44; Guido Marnef, *Antwerpen in de tijd van de Reformatie. Ondergronds protestantisme in een handelsmetropool 1550–1577* (Antwerp, 1996), pp. 35–46; Jan van den Nieuwehuizen, 'Bestuursinstellingen van de stad Antwerpen (12de eeuw–1795)', in Raymond van Uytven, Claude Bruneel and Herman Coppens (eds), *De gewestelijke en lokale instellingen in Brabant en Mechelen tot 1795* (Brussels, 2000), pp. 462–510; Jan Vanroelen, 'Het stadsbestuur', in *Antwerpen in de XVIde eeuw* (Antwerp, 1975), pp. 49–51.

[13]   Catharina Lis and Hugo Soly, 'Living Apart Together. overheid en ondernemers in Brabant en Vlaanderen tijdens de tweede helft van de 18de eeuw', in Jan Craeybeckx and Etienne Scholliers, *Arbeid in Veelvoud. Een huldeboek voor Jan Craeybeckx en Etienne Scholliers* (Brussels, 1988), p. 135; Catharina Lis and Hugo Soly, 'Craft Guilds in Comparative Perspective: The Northern and Southern Netherlands, a Survey', in Maarten Prak, Catharina Lis, Jan Lucassen and Hugo Soly (eds), *Craft Guilds in the Early Modern Low Countries: Work, Power and Representation* (Aldershot, 2006), p. 12.

development of a (labour) migration policy. An important consideration in this respect is that the corporative world was not homogeneous. Craft guilds were constructed and transformed in a dynamic interplay of unequal balances of power between different interest groups, each of which had their own objectives, aspirations and strategies.[14] Guilds' attempts to regulate labour migration is therefore assumed to have been a multifaceted process: all regulations resulted from negotiations and struggle in which the positions of the various actors were not predetermined and could easily change depending on the labour market situation.

In most Antwerp craft guilds, entry to the trade required the completion of an apprenticeship, the production of a master piece and the payment of entrance fees. At the same time, in most guilds there existed important social divisions among masters. While wealthy masters enjoyed opportunities for accumulating capital, other masters became proletarianized as *de facto* wage workers for their more affluent colleagues. Moreover, in some guilds, including the Masons' and the Carpenters' guilds, there was a distinction between 'free' and 'unfree' journeymen. The status of free journeyman developed in the course of the fifteenth and sixteenth centuries. Whereas previously only prospective masters needed to meet apprenticeship requirements, now free journeymen also had to complete an apprenticeship.[15] Free journeymen enjoyed a 'right of preference', which prevented masters from hiring outsiders or unfree journeymen who had not finished an apprenticeship term. Masters were allowed to recruit unfree journeymen only when no free journeymen were available. In some guilds free journeymen also had to make a trial piece in order to distinguish them from unfree journeymen.[16]

This chapter takes a closer look at the negotiations between the different actors on the building market with regard to the regulation of labour migration. The chapter is structured around two central questions. Firstly, was the Masons' guild exclusive or inclusive with regard to immigrant master artisans? And

---

[14]   Lis and Soly, 'Craft Guilds', pp. 30–31; Catharina Lis and Hugo Soly, 'Corporatisme, onderaanneming en loonarbeid. Flexibilisering en deregulering van de arbeidsmarkt in Westeuropese steden (veertiende-achttiende eeuw)', *Tijdschrift voor sociale geschiedenis*, 20/4 (1994): 365–8.

[15]   Bert De Munck, Piet Lourens and Jan Lucassen, 'The Establishment and Distribution of Craft Guilds in the Low Countries, 1000–1800', in Prak et al. (eds), *Craft Guilds*, pp. 32–72; Bert De Munck, 'One Counter and Your Own Account: Redefining Illicit Labour in Early Modern Antwerp', *Urban History*, 37/1 (2010): 26–44; Bert De Munck, *Technologies of Learning: Apprenticeship in Antwerp from the 15th Century to the End of the Ancien Régime* (Turnhout, 2007).

[16]   De Munck, 'One Counter'.

secondly, how did it try to regulate labour migration? By analysing a range of normative sources – such as ordinances of the urban and central administrations and statutes and privileges of the Masons' guild – and by looking at sources for resolving conflict – such as petitions and trial records – this chapter will examine negotiations over the relationship between immigrants and the Masons' guild, with particular reference to potential conflicts of interests within the guild. My argument is that the Masons' guild was not averse to immigrants as such, but that much discussion centred on their corporative status. Conceptions about illicit labour and the distinction between free and unfree workers were key to discussions about immigrant labour in the building industry.

The Building Industry and the Masons' Guild

The decision to examine the building industry, and especially the Masons' guild, was an obvious one. During the sixteenth century the construction industry was among the biggest employers in Antwerp. It is estimated that it employed around 20 per cent of the working population during periods of heavy building activity.[17] Because of the demographic boom in sixteenth-century Antwerp, the private building industry flourished and various major public works were carried out. In 1480 Antwerp counted 5,673 houses intra and extra muros. In 1496 the number had grown to 6,798.[18] In 1526 8,720 houses were counted and by 1568 the number had increased to 13,173, which amounts to an increase of 106 new houses per year in the period 1527–1568.[19] Because a large number of houses had been destroyed in the wake of the siege by Maarten Van Rossum in 1542,[20] actual building activity must have been even higher. Furthermore, a city ordinance of 26 November 1546 decreed that all new houses had to be built in

---

[17]   Etienne Scholliers, *De levensstandaard in de XVe en XVIe eeuw te Antwerpen. Loonarbeid en honger* (Antwerp, 1960), p. xv; Jan Van Roey, *De sociale structuur en de godsdienstige gezindheid van de Antwerpse bevolking op de vooravond van de Reconciliatie met Farnèse (17 augustus 1585)* (PhD dissertation, University of Ghent, 1963).

[18]   Joseph Cuvelier, *Les dénombrements de foyers en Brabant (XIVe–XVIe siècle)* (Brussels, 1912), pp. 462–3.

[19]   Hugo Soly, 'Grondspeculatie en kapitalisme te Antwerpen in de 16de eeuw', *Economisch en Sociaal Tijdschrift*, 26 (1973): pp. 294–5; Hugo Soly, *Urbanisme en kapitalisme in Antwerpen in de 16de eeuw. De stedebouwkundige en industriële ondernemingen van Gilbert van Schoonbeke* (Brussels, 1977), pp. 51–4.

[20]   Floris Prims, *Geschiedenis van Antwerpen* (22 vols, Antwerp, 1938–1946), vol. 16, pp. 115–20; Hugo Soly, 'Huurprijzen en reële opbrengst van arbeiderswoningen te Antwerpen in de eerste helft van de 16de eeuw', *Bijdragen tot de geschiedenis*, 53 (1970): p. 89.

brick.[21] Besides considerable private building activity, the period between 1526 and 1568 was also characterized by very intense public building, with peaks during the years 1542–1552 and 1561–1564.[22] Between 1542 and 1552 new fortification walls were built, measuring 4,500 metres in length and featuring nine bastions and five monumental gates. Also, a new city district, the so-called *Nieuwstad*, was added to the city. The *Nieuwstad* covered an area of 25 hectares and included three canals. Eighty-five new streets, totalling 8,800 metres in length, were constructed in the sixteenth century, along with four market places. Seven major public buildings were erected, including a new city hall. Nine churches were built or rebuilt.[23]

Antwerp's building boom in the sixteenth century both restructured the internal relations within the Masons' guild and weakened the guild's grip on urban building activities. Affluent entrepreneurs in the guild gained the upper hand over their less wealthy 'colleagues', especially during periods when public work projects and residential construction were thriving.[24] Public building projects were mostly contracted in large units or *taswerken*, an important characteristic of which was that contractors were paid only after completion of the works. This meant that contractors had to be able to advance the wages and the costs of building materials. Large mason-masters thus typically also become merchants in construction materials, and even possessed brickyards and stone pits.[25] As a result of this process, large-scale entrepreneurs, some of whom worked outside the guild and transformed themselves into real estate agents, took over the building market – the most notable of which was Gilbert Van Schoonbeke, who established the largest construction company in the Low Countries.[26] While the guild's master artisans had to work and act in accordance

21   Stadsarchief Antwerp (SAA), Privilegekamer (PK) 915, fols 70v and 71r.

22   Soly, 'Grondspeculatie', pp. 294–5; Hugo Soly, 'Economische vernieuwing en sociale weerstand. De betekenis en aspiraties der Antwerpse middenklasse in de 16de eeuw', *Tijdschrift voor geschiedenis*, 83 (1970): pp. 521–4.

23   Soly, *Urbanisme*, pp. 371–93.

24   Lis and Soly, 'Craft Guilds', p. 21; Hugo Soly, 'Nijverheid en kapitalisme te Antwerpen in de 16de eeuw', in *Album Charles Verlinden ter gelegenheid van zijn dertig jaar professoraat* (Ghent, 1975), pp. 341–2; Etienne Scholliers, 'Vrije en onvrije arbeiders, voornamelijk te Antwerpen in de 16de eeuw', *Bijdragen voor de geschiedenis der Nederlanden*, 11 (1956): pp. 290–95; De Munck, 'One Counter'.

25   SAA, GA 4001, fol. 45v and SAA, GA 4267, fol. 2.; Jean-Pierre Sosson, 'Les métiers: norme et réalité. L'exemple des anciens Pays-Bas méridionaux aux XIVe et XVe siècles', in Jacqueline Hamesse and Colette Muraille-Samaran (eds), *Le travail au moyen âge. Une approche interdisciplinaire* (Actes du colloque international de Louvain-la-Neuve, 21–23 May 1987) (Louvain-la-Neuve, 1990) ; Hugo Soly, *Urbanisme en kapitalisme*.

26   Hugo Soly, 'Grondspeculatie'.

with guild regulations, these entrepreneurs, often working outside the guild, felt free to employ anybody they wanted. By the beginning of the 1540s it had become impossible for small masters to compete with their affluent colleagues. For example in 1547 a (sub)contractor working on Antwerp's fortification walls had to testify in writing that he would deliver 50 labourers per day.[27]

An indication of the changing labour relations within the building industry is the emergence of the status of *vrije gezel* or free journeyman in guild documents. The masons' foundation privileges of 9 April 1423 and 21 August 1458 mention only masters and apprentices as guild members.[28] Apprentices who had completed their apprenticeship (first two, later four years)[29] and produced a trial piece could become a master, though only after paying an admission fee and offering a meal to the guild's board. The fact that these entry conditions were expensive led to the problematic though not uncommon situation of ex-apprentices who, despite being qualified to do so, were financially unable to set up as independent masters. This formed the backdrop to the creation of the status of free journeyman: well-off young men now entered apprenticeships with a view to becoming masters, whereas poor apprentices registered with the intention of becoming journeymen.[30] It is impossible to state when precisely the journeyman status was first acknowledged in the Masons' guild – it is mentioned for the first time in a trial record of 1537[31] and the ordinances of 1554 and 1558[32] – but it can hardly be coincidental that it entered the stage at a time when many major public works had to be completed.

Labour relations in construction activity were under increasing pressure by growing levels of immigration. Antwerp's building activities created a demand for thousands of construction workers. According to the famous Italian architect Donato Buoni, at least 2,000 workers were needed just to begin work on the fortification walls.[33] It is not known how many workers were employed for construction of the city walls, though historians believe there was full employment among skilled artisans as well as unskilled building labourers in Antwerp during this period. Indeed, the construction of just one canal in the *Nieuwstad* required approximately 500 workers per week.[34] The wages of

27   Scholliers, 'Vrije en onvrije arbeiders', pp. 294–5.
28   Stadsarchief Antwerp (SAA), Gilden en Ambachten (GA) 4001, fols 44v–46; 4267, fols 1–6v.
29   SAA, GA 4001, fol. 45; GA 4267, fol. 3.
30   De Munck, *Technologies of Learning*, pp. 155–6.
31   SAA, GA 4267, fols 254–7.
32   SAA, GA 4267, fols 20–21v and 24–25v.
33   Scholliers, *De levensstandaard*, pp. 131–2.
34   SAA, PK 2214.

building workers in Antwerp increased as compared to other cities and these (high) wages attracted immigrants to the Scheldt town.[35] Workers' wages occasionally even skyrocketed, thereby forcing reaction from the authorities. In 1560–1561, for example, officials from several cities and villages in the southern Netherlands, fearing the emigration of their workers, repeatedly requested the central government to limit the wages paid in Antwerp.[36] Obviously, in this context large-scale entrepreneurs had a major interest in the deregulation of labour relations and immigration, and increasingly sought to recruit migrant workers from outside the guild system.

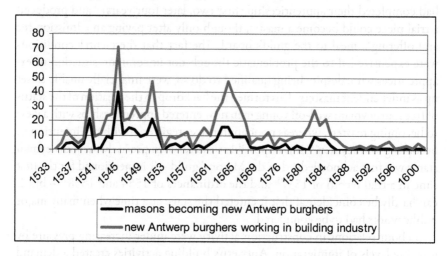

Figure 2.1   Number of new Antwerp burghers in the building industry, 1533–1600

Source: SAA, Vierschaar, 142–53, Burgherbooks 1533–1600.

Unfortunately, a lack of sources precludes mapping the total immigration of building workers to sixteenth-century Antwerp. The only serial source which gives information about migration flows are the burgherbooks.[37] The occupational data show that at least 6 per cent of the new burghers in the sixteenth century worked in construction. Due to the particularity of the source materials these

35   For wages of masons in other cities in the Netherlands, Johan Dambruyne, *Corporatieve middengroepen. Aspiraties, relaties en transformaties in het 16de eeuwse ambachtswezen* (Ghent, 2002), pp. 838–40; Scholliers, *De levensstandaard*, pp. 223–6.

36   *Recueil des ordonnances des Pays-Bas*, série 2 (8 vols, Brussels, 1910–1978), vol. 7, p. 445.

37   For a critical look on the Antwerp burgherbooks, Jan De Meester, 'De gebruiks- en meerwaarde van poortersboeken voor historici. Casus. Antwerpen in de zestiende eeuw (vervolg)', *Vlaamse Stam*, 43/4 (2007): pp. 322–6.

were probably all master artisans. If all labourers, workers, transport workers and the like who figure in the burgherbooks are taken into account, the figure may well increase to more than 10 per cent. Figure 2.1 in any case shows that the registration of new burghers who were working in the building industry peaked during periods in which public works were being carried out.

Hence, while many small masters were 'obliged' to work as wage labourers for the large masters, journeymen and small masters alike were pressured by the massive influx of immigrants. As large contractors increasingly turned to recruiting foreign labourers outside guild structures to help finish the job, tensions crystallized around the relationship between migrant labour and guild membership. In the following two paragraphs, I will first focus on the attitudes towards immigrants who wished to establish themselves as master masons, before turning to the question of 'unfree' workers who operated outside the guild system.

Guild Membership and Burghership

Traditionally, corporative organizations have been regarded as closed and exclusive institutions which resisted admitting not only immigrants but even locals who were not sons of masters in order to limit competition against established master artisans. The guilds were said to have imposed continuous obstacles to this end, including lengthy apprenticeships, difficult master trials, high admission fees and other requirements.[38] However, recent research into the position of apprentices within Antwerp craft guilds has shown that the guilds did not systematically exclude immigrants. In fact, the craft guilds sought to bind journeymen and apprentices to the guilds and can therefore be considered as having been highly inclusive.[39] In the late medieval town of Bruges craft guilds were also relatively open institutions: some counted up to 75 per cent immigrants among their new guild members.[40]

In this chapter I take the concept of burghership as a possible indication of the guild's exclusiveness or inclusiveness towards immigrants. It is common

---

[38]   Henri Pirenne, *Early Democracies in the Low Countries: Urban Society and Political Conflict in the Middle Ages and the Renaissance* (New York, 1963); Hans Van Werveke, 'Ambachten en erfelijkheid' in *Mededeelingen van de Koninklijke Vlaamse Academie voor Wetenschappen, Letteren en Schoone Kunsten van België*, 4/1 (Antwerp, 1942); Floris Prims, *Het herfsttij van het corporatisme* (Antwerpen, 1945); Jan Arthus Van Houtte, *Economische geschiedenis van de Lage Landen, 800–1800* (Haarlem, 1979).

[39]   De Munck, *Technologies of Learning*, chapter 2.3.

[40]   Stabel, 'Guilds', pp. 194–5.

opinion that non-burghers were excluded from becoming masters in Antwerp guilds.[41] A glance at the guilds' statutes confirms this view. Some Antwerp guilds declared burghership a requirement not only for promotion to mastership but also for mere entry into the guild as *gezel* or even apprentice. This was the case with the Masons' guild. The sources do not reveal why the craft guilds and, apparently, the city authorities held strongly to the connection between guild membership and burghership. Nor is it clear why apprentices in the building sector also had to obtain burghership. Floris Prims claims that the city magistrate wished to connect recognition of the craft guilds as independent institutions to the city's burgher policy, and that the impetus for excluding non-burghers from guild membership came from the craft guilds themselves.[42] According to Prims the *kordewagenkruiers* guild, having experienced many problems with immigrant masters before it was officially recognized as a guild, urged city authorities to include in their foundation privilege that only burghers could be allowed into the guild.[43] The condition that only burghers could enter a craft guild also featured in Antwerp's customary law; even for certain commercial activities – the so-called *poortersneringen* – burghership was required. One such *poortersnering* was the trade in building materials: someone who wished to trade in building materials did not necessarily have to be member of the Masons' guild, yet had to be a burgher.[44] Burghership requirements implied a comparative disadvantage for immigrants. After all, anyone born in Antwerp, including children of non-burghers, automatically became a burgher. Yet immigrants who wanted to become a burgher had to purchase citizenship, for a sum which was the equivalent of 16 to (after mid-century) 25 days' work by a master artisan.

The Antwerp law and the guilds' statutes appear unequivocal about the fact that every master artisan had to be a burgher of the city. Yet in studying guild history one often uncovers a different reality.[45] Examination of the fiscal registers that Jan Van Roey used to study the social structure of the Antwerp population at the end of the sixteenth century shows that many immigrants

---

[41]   Frans Blockmans, 'Het vroegste officiële ambachtswezen in Antwerpen', *Bijdragen voor de geschiedenis der Nederlanden*, 8 (1953): pp. 190–91 and Francine De Nave, 'De oudste Antwerpse lijsten van nieuwe poorters (28 januari 1390–28 december 1414)', *Handelingen van de Koninklijke Commissie voor Geschiedenis*, 134 (1973): 115.

[42]   Prims, *Geschiedenis van Antwerpen*, vol. 3, pp. 144–5.

[43]   Prims, *Geschiedenis van Antwerpen*, vol. 3, pp. 142–5.

[44]   Gérard De Longé, *Recueil des anciennes coutumes de Belgique. Coutumes du pays et duché de Brabant. Quartier d'Anvers* (4 vols, Brussels, 1870–1874), vol. 1, p. 544; vol. 2, p. 224 and vol. 4, p. 66.

[45]   Jean-Pierre Sosson, *Les travaux publics de la ville de Bruges XIVe–XVe siècles* (Brussel, 1987), pp. 339–48.

had been master artisans for many years, or even decades, without ever being registered as Antwerp burghers.[46] The occupational census of 1571 reveals that even many deans were not burghers.[47] Likewise, the matriculation lists of apprentice dry-shavers demonstrate that many masters were not burghers even when they enlisted apprentices.[48] The city magistrate was probably aware of such anomalies and occasionally even created them, as in the case of the serge weavers of Hondschoote. After it was sacked in 1582, many inhabitants of Hondschoote fled north and a group of serge weavers requested the Antwerp authorities to be able to bring their famous industry to the city.[49] The boards of the craft guilds formally objected to this proposal, but the city authorities decided to accommodate them: the first 24 masters received free housing and workshops and were allowed to enter a guild without having to become burghers.[50]

The attitude of the urban authorities towards non-burghers was therefore ambiguous. In practice, they allowed non-burghers to become master artisans, yet they proclaimed city ordinances (*stadsgeboden*) which strongly prohibited non-burghers from entering craft guilds. This ambiguity was already in place in the fifteenth century, but became more pronounced in the sixteenth and early seventeenth centuries.[51] The attitude of the city magistrate is evident not only in the *stadsgeboden* but also in the craft guild ordinances, which were ratified by the city authorities. More importantly, however, the attitudes of members of the Masons' guild towards non-burghers entering their guild become clear by looking at the ordinances. In most cases the establishment of guild ordinances resulted from complaints formulated by individual members or by the guild's board. The foundation privilege of 1423 for the Masons' guild was clear on this point: no one could become a master, or even an apprentice, unless he was a burgher.[52] The renewed *principaele brief* of 1458 went even further, stating that no one could enter the guild, become an apprentice or work as a subcontractor without being a burgher.[53]

---

[46]   Roey, *De sociale structuur*.

[47]   SAA, Tresorij, 1702.

[48]   Rijksarchief Antwerp, Fonds Antwerpen, 39 and Jan De Meester, 'Hulp vanuit onverwachte hoek: de inschrijvingslijsten van de Antwerpse droogscheerders-leerlingen als genealogische bron. Deel 1', *Vlaamse Stam*, 44/4 (2008): pp. 236–42.

[49]   SAA, PK 661, fol. 20.

[50]   SAA, GA 4055, no foliation.

[51]   City ordinances handling the matter of burghership in craft guilds appeared on 10 April 1426; 10 February 1427; 4 August 1500; 24 December 1502; 9 September 1578; 14 August 1603; 22 September 1610; 10 January 1614; 27 February 1617 and 18 November 1627.

[52]   SAA, GA 4001, fols 45–45v.

[53]   SAA, GA 4267, fols 2–3v.

All went well until Antwerp became one big construction site. In 1558, during a period of busy building activities, a complaint from the 'deans and the masters of the Masons' guild' reached the city authorities. The undertone of the petition indicates that small masters had taken the initiative in formulating the complaint. They argued that many mason-apprentices, in blatant contradiction of guild ordinances, were not burghers of the city. Furthermore, when these 'illegal' immigrant apprentices suspected that they would be caught, they simply left town. In fact, the small masters' complaints targeted the large master-entrepreneurs who did not seem to bother about guild regulations. According to the small masters these so-called 'apprentices' in reality were employed as cheap workers. The city administration responded by decreeing that – 'and this time for real' – no immigrant could become a mason's apprentice without being a burgher.[54]

Although the small masters obtained what they wanted, the problem did not disappear after the construction boom had come to an end. A petition of 1610 complained that large masters were still hiring immigrant apprentices who were not burghers. But now the city administration reacted more moderately, decreeing that only apprentices who wished to stay and work in the city after finishing their apprenticeship had to become a burgher.[55] These examples show that large masters in the guild did not take guild regulations concerning the employment of non-burghers seriously and that small masters reacted to their 'misconduct'. In other words, the small masters openly negotiated with the authorities about illegal workers, and the magistrate sometimes lent an ear to their grievances. The large master-entrepreneurs for their part occasionally negotiated with the magistrate about illegal competition which affected them. In 1507 some entrepreneurs, together with the deans of the guild, denounced that a non-burgher was selling building materials.[56] The same complaint reappeared in a petition of 1611, after it had become clear that people from other cities were illegally selling building materials in Antwerp.[57]

We can conclude that most master masons held fiercely to the fact that only burghers could work as masons – masters and apprentices – within the guild system. Nowhere in the sources do we find complaints about new guild members being immigrants *an sich*. It still needs to be investigated whether this is evidence of an exclusive or, on the contrary, inclusive guild attitude towards immigrants. Whatever the answer, the ordinances' focus on burghership shows that problems concerning immigrants entering the guild centred on the status

---

54   SAA, GA 4267, fols 20–21v.
55   SAA, GA 4267, fol. 50.
56   SAA, GA 4267, fols 250–51.
57   SAA, GA 4268, no foliation.

of the newcomers in question. Immigrants were accepted in the guild under condition that they became burghers of Antwerp. The reason why apprentices in the Masons' guild had to become burghers still remains unclear. One explanation is that the city authorities and the guild feared that apprentices would otherwise take their skills elsewhere after their training period.[58] According to Kint the regulations on burghership were by no means intended to exclude immigrants from the guilds. The authorities sometimes even feigned ignorance of the fact that immigrant-artisans capitalized on their mastership for some time before investing in the required citizenship status.[59] The city authorities and the Masons' guild were partners in their endeavour to protect the social fabric of the city and the 'fairness' of the labour market. When the building market changed during the sixteenth century, however, small and large masters developed other interests, strategies and ways of thinking about guild 'ideology' – which forces us to focus on the appreciation of skilled and unskilled labour and conceptions about illicit work by the different actors involved in negotiations over immigrant-labourers.

Illicit Labour? Free and Unfree Workers

Some actors within the guild – small masters and free journeymen in particular – sought to control the influx of immigrants into their corporation as much as possible. But was it possible for the Masons' guild to control or to regulate the influx of migrants who tried to work outside the guild system? After all, numerous actors within and outside the guild – especially large entrepreneurs – had opposing interests concerning the organization of the building industry in sixteenth-century Antwerp. Each party was moreover eager to seek partners to defend his interests. At first sight the sources reveal that the Masons' guild and the city authorities tried to close off the building market outside the craft guild from foreign masters. In 1500 city ordinances clearly stated that a master-artisan should live within the city walls.[60] This *stadsgebod* was repeated in 1502,

---

[58]   See also Stephan R. Epstein, 'Craft guilds, Apprenticeship, and Technological Change in Preindustrial Europe', *Journal of Economic History*, 58/5 (1998): 684–713; Bert De Munck, 'Construction and Reproduction: The Training and Skills of Antwerp Cabinetmakers in the Sixteenth and Seventeenth Centuries', in Bert De Munck, Steven L. Kaplan and Hugo Soly (eds), *Learning on the Shop Floor: Historical Perspectives on Apprenticeship* (New York/Oxford, 2007), pp. 84–110.

[59]   An Kint, 'Becoming Civic Community: Citizenship in Sixteenth-Century Antwerp', in Marc Boone and Maarten Prak (eds), *Individual, Corporate and Judicial Status in European Cities (Late Middle Ages and Early Modern Period)* (Leuven/Apeldoorn, 1996), p. 166.

[60]   SAA, PK 914, fol. 20.

1503, 1541, 1546 and 1557.[61] Yet, the foundation privilege of the Masons' guild stated that labourers from outside Antwerp could be recruited if there was a lot of work, albeit not for longer than 14 days and under the condition that they paid an annuity or *kaarsgeld*. If the municipality or religious institutions needed building workers, they could employ these persons for up to 14 days.[62]

Soon after the Masons' guild received its foundation privilege, the abbey of Saint-Michael in Antwerp filed a complaint with the central government. The abbey invoked an old ducal privilege stating that jobs in convents could be done on-site by anyone to argue that craft guild regulations did not apply to them. Master masons and carpenters who lived outside the city and were not members of Antwerp guilds should therefore be allowed to work on the convent's premises. The central government followed their line of reasoning and ordered the foundation privilege to be nullified.[63] Although this 'incident' occurred well before the sixteenth century, it is important to cite because common opinion maintains that the central government did not intervene in urban guild policies. This example shows otherwise and an examination of central ordinances clearly demonstrates that also in the sixteenth century the central authorities repeatedly intervened in guild regulations to regulate the labour market. In 1544, for example, they invoked the weak state of the economy in Bruges to declare that – contrary to guild statutes – anyone could become a master there without being a burgher.[64] In Antwerp the central government became an important actor in negotiations, especially when large public building projects attracted many foreign building labourers to the city and when the interests of the central government were at stake.

The city authorities and the Masons' guild formulated a new compromise with regard to foreign masters in the new *principaele brief* of 1458. Henceforth the latter would be allowed to work for the city or for religious institutions for as long as they were needed. This was a concession to the central government, though the Masons' guild also achieved a minor victory. Whereas the original privilege had stipulated that non-member masters could work for private clients in Antwerp for 14 days, this was now possible only when no Antwerp masters were available.[65] This all seemed to go well until Antwerp became one big building site in the first half of the sixteenth century. It soon became clear that there was insufficient manpower available for carrying out the private and public building contracts at the same time. One solution for the influx of cheap

---

[61]   SAA, PK 914, fol. 24v, fol. 27v and fol. 112; PK 915 fol. 17, fol. 72 and fol. 253.

[62]   SAA, GA 4001, fol. 45v.

[63]   *Recueil des ordonnances des Pays-Bas*, série 2, vol. 2, pp. 97–9.

[64]   *Recueil des ordonnances des Pays-Bas*, série 2, vol. 5, p. 77.

[65]   SAA, GA 4267, fols 4–4v.

labour was the creation of the status of free journeyman. The Masons' guild, and the small masters in particular, could live with this solution because the free journeymen, having to pay annuities and respect the guild regulations, were integrated into the guild system.

Yet it soon became clear that the large public building projects required many more labourers than there were masters and free journeymen available in the city. Large entrepreneurs increasingly recruited unfree journeymen – i.e. non-guild members – from out of town. While the status of unfree journeyman only appeared in an ordinance in 1544, previous legislation allowed them to be hired for short periods of time under the condition that no free journeymen were available. Different actors within the guild considered unfree journeymen intruders on the labour market. It is noteworthy in this respect that the terms 'unfree' and 'foreign' were generally used interchangeably in the source materials. In most cases when conflict-regulating sources mention unfree journeymen they refer to immigrant labourers. Obviously such labourers could take work from the free journeymen. But an apprentice might also have feared for his future and considered his four-year investment a waste of time and money. Even small masters could see free journeymen as competitors, as large masters resorted to hiring unfree journeymen instead of free journeymen and small masters.

Small masters and free journeymen tried their utmost to keep these intruders out. They had various reasons for this, not least in that they feared for their jobs. The most important motive, however, was that the influx of unfree journeyman exerted a downward pressure on wages and offset the potential wage gains from the increasing labour demand.[66] This is why the small masters and free journeymen negotiated with city authorities about the admission of unfree journeymen to the labour market. In 1537 the deans of the Masons' guild sued a number of large master-entrepreneurs for illegally employing unfree journeymen for long periods. The Antwerp aldermen declared that according to guild regulations such hiring could only be done for 14 days and after payment of *kaarsgeld*.[67] But the city authorities found themselves in an awkward position. They realized that in order to have their public works finished within reasonable delay they had to find ways to circumvent the guild regulations. Entrepreneurs and large master-artisans used the authorities to bypass the guild statutes. From the second quarter of the sixteenth century onward the Masons' guild was therefore divided into different camps with conflicting interests: large masters who tried to make as much money as possible by employing unfree journeymen; small masters who feared descending to the status of mere wage labourers; and free journeymen

---

[66]   Scholliers, 'Vrije en onvrije arbeiders', pp. 294–5.
[67]   SAA, GA 4267, fols 254–7.

who tried to guard their 'right of preference' against competition from outside Antwerp.

The small masters and free journeymen suffered a major setback in 1542, when the construction of the new fortification walls began. The siege by Maarten van Rossum had made clear that it was necessary not only to build the walls but to do so quickly. Several months after the works had started the central government levied all Antwerp building labourers to work on the fortifications and therefore called a halt to all private building activities.[68] The Antwerp magistrate issued three consecutive *stadsgeboden* in 1542 ordering every available building labourer to come to the city walls with his tools.[69] Antwerp citizens soon complained that they could not find masons to build or repair their private dwellings unless they paid exorbitant wages. The city responded in 1544 not only by fixing the masons' wages but also by mandating that if masters and free journeymen refused to work for these wages, the deans of the guild could force them. An even further reaching measure stipulated that unfree journeymen could be employed if no free journeymen were available. Their wages were not to exceed those of free journeymen, and they had to leave town upon the completion of their assignment. Should they wish to continue working as unfree labourers they had to pay the same annuity or *kaarsgeld* to the guild as free journeymen.[70] Although this regulation protected the 'right of preference' of free journeymen, it also legitimized the activities of unfree journeymen.

This put the masters and free journeymen at ease, at least until 1548, when construction tycoon Gilbert Van Schoonbeke secured the building contract for the *Nieuwstad*. This contract stipulated that the job was to be completed within four years, which even by modern standards was unrealistic. Van Schoonbeke hired large subcontractors to handle the job. Each subcontractor needed a large contingent of cheap labour and so they went straight to the city authorities and to the central government. On 24 February 1548 the central government issued, upon advice of the city magistrate, a harsh verdict. All craft guild regulations of the Masons' guild were to be 'temporarily' suspended. Out-of-town masons could enter Antwerp to help build the *Nieuwstad*. They had to purchase a 'work permit' for a small fee, of which the proceeds would go to the guilds.[71] The guild members saw masses of unfree workers flowing into town. Accounts show that thousands of building labourers, many of them immigrant, were employed in the building of the *Nieuwstad* for low wages.[72] This led to a reduction in the

---

68   *Recueil des ordonnances des Pays-Bas*, 2 série, vol. 5, p. 400.
69   SAA, PK 915, fol. 28v, fol. 29 and fol. 29v.
70   SAA, GA 4267, fols 24–5.
71   *Recueil des ordonnances de Pays-Bas*, 2 série, vol. 5, pp. 508–9.
72   SAA, PK 2213–16.

wages of both small masters and free journeymen, who decided that talking with the city magistrate was inadequate and that other 'negotiation methods' were to be employed. Many small masters and free journeymen tried to thwart the construction of the fortification walls and the *Nieuwstad* by leaving the works *en masse*. In August and September 1549 the city magistrate issued several *stadsgeboden* declaring that no one could leave the works, under penalty of severe fines. The city even threatened to break the guilds' monopoly should the free journeymen refuse to work.[73] As a safety measure the city magistrate even ordered beggars and vagrants to work on the fortification walls.[74] In July 1552 major strikes were averted but the works were disrupted by riots. Angry building labourers threatened the magistrate and immigrant labourers were attacked in the streets.[75] Two years later, in July 1554, an uproar against Gilbert Van Schoonbeke shook the city.[76] These actions did not work out in favour of the masters and free journeymen, and the city magistrate responded severely.[77]

When the building market finally calmed down in the second half of the sixteenth century, the Masons' guild began to make progress in their struggle against unfree journeymen as the city magistrate again sided with the craft guilds. In 1558 the city decreed that unfree journeymen could not work unless enlisted in matriculation lists. From then on the deans of the Masons' guild enjoyed wide powers in refusing unfree journeymen from coming to Antwerp to work as masons.[78] Although the city authorities had long sided with the wealthy entrepreneurs, they now sought to take measures to protect guild members against competition from out of town. After all, by the end of the sixteenth century there was major unemployment in Antwerp. In their 1591 *stadsgebod* the city authorities sought to appease small masters and free journeymen by refusing unfree journeymen entry to the city.[79] It appears that by that time the large entrepreneurs had lost their influence with the city government, although it must be remembered that most had left Antwerp well before 1591. After the Fall of Antwerp in 1585, its economy again became much more small scale and the city authorities realized that the craft guilds were welcome partners in rebuilding the urban economy.

---

[73]　SAA, PK 914, fol. 85v°.
[74]　SAA PK 915, fol. 142.
[75]　Scholliers, 'Vrije en onvrije arbeiders', p. 133.
[76]　Soly, 'Economische vernieuwing'.
[77]　SAA, PK 915, fol. 157.
[78]　SAA, GA 4267, fols 24–5.
[79]　SAA, PK 918, fol. 27.

Conclusion

In the sixteenth century, up to its Fall in 1585, Antwerp attracted large numbers of immigrants. As a result its population boomed, especially in the period 1526–1568. As many dwellings were needed to house the newcomers, the private building industry grew rapidly. In combination with intensive public building activities this resulted in a growing need for building labourers. Until the sixteenth century economic life in Antwerp was controlled mostly by craft guilds. One such guild was that of the masons. The Masons' guild became an important player in negotiations over the admittance of thousands of building labourers who were attracted to Antwerp by the city's comparatively high wages. Drawing attention to the citizenship status of new guild members was one way to control the entry of immigrant masons to the craft guild, as guild ordinances required new members to be a burgher of the town. In the early sixteenth century the Masons' guild, with the support of the urban magistrate, appears to have controlled the regulation of labour migration quite effectively.

In the course of the sixteenth century, however, the labour market transformed profoundly. The building industry was one of the sectors that were to a great extent taken over by large entrepreneurs. The Masons' guild appears to have lost influence over the industry and large entrepreneurs operating outside the guild system began to play a major role. These entrepreneurs' interests differed significantly from those of the many small master-artisans. The status of free journeyman appears to have been created to favour the small masters in a period when private and (especially) public building markets were booming. The former soon became allies of the small master-masons against their affluent colleagues. Large entrepreneurs seemed annoyed with guild regulations and sought to recruit as many unfree out-of-town workers as possible. The small masters and free journeymen tried to avoid this scenario by requiring all building workers to be members of the guild. But by now there was too much at stake and the small masters lost the support of the urban and central authorities, who were motivated among other things by military concerns over the fortification walls. The city administration, at times prompted by the central government, decreed various laws allowing unfree labourers to work in the building industry. The Masons' guild lost its grip on the regulation of labour migration as it became clear that corporative regulations were unable to keep up with a rapidly growing economy and changing labour market.

The position of the Antwerp authorities towards the craft guilds in the course of this process was relatively ambiguous. In the early sixteenth century the Antwerp magistrate still sought to reconcile the interests of entrepreneurs, small masters and journeymen, but during the mid-century economic boom both urban and central authorities clearly sided with the entrepreneurs. When the Antwerp economy began to decline again in the late sixteenth century, however, the local authorities again sided with the craft guilds. This demonstrates that during the sixteenth century the labour market to a great extent dictated the regulation of migration, which often resulted in *ad hoc* decisions taken under pressure.[80]

---

[80] Lis and Soly 'Living Apart Together': 135.

Chapter 3

Craft Guilds and Immigration: Huguenots in German and English Cities

Ulrich Niggemann

On Saturday, 3 September 1692 German butchers broke into the shop of the French butcher Jacob le Goulon in Frankfurt-on-Oder. They forcibly took away his sheep and his meat and, finally, they threatened to kill him if he carried on his business.[1] In 1694, the brothers Collin complained that they had been assaulted and seriously injured by German carpenters in Berlin.[2] A few years earlier, in 1685, a Huguenot clockmaker and his pregnant wife were attacked by angry English colleagues in London.[3] Especially violent were the conflicts between Huguenot weavers and the journeymen of the London Weavers' Company, which led to intense rioting in 1675.[4] Many Huguenot immigrants to England and several German states had similar experiences, although not always as violent.[5]

---

[1]   Complaint of Jacob le Goulon, Geheimes Staatsarchiv Preußischer Kulturbesitz, Berlin-Dahlem (GStAPK) I. HA Rep. 122 14 no 1 vol. I, fols 193–193'. Cf. Henri Tollin, *Der hugenottische Lehrstand, Wehrstand und Nährstand zu Frankfurt a.d. Oder* (Magdeburg, 1896), p. 54. All dates are given according to the Julian calendar.

[2]   Complaint of the Brothers Collin, 1 June 1694, GStAPK I. HA Rep. 122 7bII no 10.

[3]   Complaint to the Privy Council, 10 April 1685, The National Archives (TNA), PC 2/71, fols 39v, 44. Cf. Malcolm R. Thorp, 'The Anti-Huguenot Undercurrent in Late Seventeenth-Century England', *Proceedings of the Huguenot Society of London*, 22 (1970–1976): pp. 565–80, at p. 571; Daniel Statt, *Foreigners and Englishmen: The Controversy over Immigration and Population, 1660–1760* (Newark DE, 1995), p. 178.

[4]   *Calendar of State Papers, Domestic* (CSP dom.), Charles II, ed. F. H. Blackburn Danielle and Francis Bickley (vol. 17, Nendeln, 1968), p. 253. Cf. Alfred Plummer, *The London Weavers' Company, 1600–1970* (London/Boston MA, 1972), p. 162; Statt, *Foreigners*, pp. 183–4; Robin D. Gwynn, *Huguenot Heritage: The History and Contribution of the Huguenots in Britain* (Brighton, 2001), pp. 148–9; R.M. Dunn, 'The London Weavers' Riot of 1675', *Guildhall Studies in London History*, 1 (1973): pp. 13–23.

[5]   Cf. Ulrich Niggemann, *Immigrationspolitik zwischen Konflikt und Konsens. Die Hugenottenansiedlung in Deutschland und England (1681–1697)* (Cologne/Weimar/ Vienna, 2008), pp. 285–361.

Early modern cities experienced a constant influx of immigrants, arriving as individuals or in small groups. These everyday movements of labourers and other persons played an important role in urban life. However, larger groups such as the Huguenots fleeing persecution in France required extraordinary administrative efforts, and it was more difficult for them to be incorporated into the labour market than for smaller groups or individuals. This chapter investigates the attitudes of English and German craftsmen towards Huguenot immigration and immigrants in the late seventeenth century. How were these immigrants perceived and how were they treated by resident craftsmen? Do the records of conflict, like those mentioned above, give an adequate and realistic image of what the resident members of craft guilds thought about immigration? What were the reasons for acting the way they actually did?

Historians have long been aware that some serious conflicts occurred between Huguenot immigrants and local craftsmen, and they point to quarrels and controversies concerning the settlement of French refugees in both countries.[6] They differ, however, in their assessment of the intensity of the conflicts and their interpretations of the reasons for them. Some historians, especially during the nineteenth century, saw religious differences between the Calvinist immigrants and the Lutheran, or Anglican, locals as the main source of conflict.[7] For others, economic competition was the main factor. Myriam Yardeni, for instance, points out that the Huguenots were perceived by resident craftsmen as superior in skill. Thus, general xenophobia mixed with fears of economic disadvantages motivated actions against the immigrants. The hostility shown by Englishmen and Germans was 'a clear indication of the value attributed to the Huguenots'.[8] Recently, German historians have argued that the development of 'absolutist'

---

[6]   Henri Tollin, *Geschichte der Französischen Colonie zu Magdeburg* (6 vols, Halle on Saale, 1886–1892); Georg Schanz, *Zur Geschichte der Colonisation und Industrie in Franken* (Erlangen, 1884); August Ebrard, *Christian Ernst von Brandenburg-Baireuth. Die Aufnahme reformirter Flüchtlingsgemeinden in ein lutherisches Land 1686–1712* (Gütersloh, 1885); Reginald L. Poole, *A History of the Huguenots of the Dispersion at the Recall of the Edict of Nantes* (London, 1880); Fernand Baron de Schickler, *Les Églises du Refuge en Angleterre* (3 vols, Paris, 1892); Stefi Jersch-Wenzel, *Juden und 'Franzosen' in der Wirtschaft des Raumes Berlin/Brandenburg zur Zeit des Merkantilismus* (Berlin, 1978); Franz-Anton Kadell, *Die Hugenotten in Hessen-Kassel* (Darmstadt/Marburg, 1980); Malcolm R. Thorp, *The English Government and the Huguenot Settlement, 1680–1702* (PhD thesis University of Wisconsin, Madison, 1972).

[7]   Tollin, *Geschichte*, vol. 1, pp. 276–7; ibid. vol. 2, pp. 21–2, 32, 46, 110–11, 227, 253, 264; ibid. vol. 3/1a, pp. 194–5; ibid. vol. 3/1c, pp. 432, 1280–81; Ebrard, *Christian Ernst*, pp. v–vi, 14–15, 20, 25–7; Alfred Heussner, *Die französische Colonie in Cassel* (Magdeburg, 1903), p. 7.

[8]   Myriam Yardeni, *Le Refuge protestant* (Paris, 1985), p. 129. Similarly, Jersch-Wenzel, *Juden*, p. 76; Barbara Dölemeyer, *Die Hugenotten* (Stuttgart, 2006), pp. 163–4; Gwynn, *Heritage*, p. 142.

states was an underlying cause of conflict between craft guilds and governments. In this view, the Huguenots and their privileges were instrumental in abolishing the self-government of city corporations, and the resistance of craft guilds against the settlement of French immigrants was part of a broader resistance against the expansion of the early modern state.[9]

This chapter attempts to show that the reactions of local craftsmen were both more flexible and more complex. I will argue that it was neither religion nor the development of 'absolutism' that led to conflicts. There was indeed a strong corporate self-consciousness combined with a pre-modern sense of honour that sometimes led craft guilds to react with hostility towards immigrants; but the governments did not develop a programme to abolish the ancient privileges of the corporations by introducing privileged immigrant groups – nor did the guilds principally oppose the settlement of Huguenot craftsmen. Competition played a part in the reaction of resident craftsmen, but not in the sense that they feared superior Huguenot skills. Rather, they disapproved of the concept of competition in general. This becomes clear when we focus on the mentalities and the moral dimension of early modern artisans and craftsmen. In addition to economic cycles and conjunctures, this chapter points to another way of explaining attitudes towards immigrants.

I would like to develop my arguments in three steps. First, I will sketch how the immigration of Huguenot refugees was regulated in legal terms by the state governments. The comparison between Germany and England will show that there are some major differences between both countries, particularly concerning the legal foundations of the Huguenot communities. Second, I will take a closer look at the structure of conflicts and the arguments delivered by the members of guilds. Despite the legal differences, there were many similarities between England and Germany in these respects. However, some important differences concerning the internal structures of the guilds and the development of nationality will be discussed in the final section of this chapter.

Legal Aspects of the Reception of Huguenots

The immigration of Huguenots, especially of Huguenot manufacturers and craftsmen, was highly appreciated and supported by state governments. This applies particularly to the German territorial states, many of which had suffered

---

9 Michael Maurer, 'Mit Ausländern Staat machen? Glaubensflüchtlinge im Absolutismus', *Essener Unikate*, 6/7 (1995): pp. 74–85; Andreas Reinke, 'Die Kehrseite der Privilegierung: Proteste und Widerstände gegen die hugenottische Niederlassung in den deutschen Territorialstaaten', *Comparativ*, 7 (1997): pp. 39–52.

dramatic losses of population during the Thirty Years' War (1618–1648).[10] Influenced by ideas of mercantilist or cameralist thinkers, such as Veit Ludwig von Seckendorff, who taught that an increase in population was one of the most important factors for economic development and public prosperity, the princes sought to repopulate their devastated countries. Rising costs of court culture, standing armies and administrative staff demanded an increase in tax revenues. Aiming towards the enhancement of public wealth, therefore, was not only a token of paternalistic care for their subjects, but also a means to raise revenues.[11] Thus, from the end of the Thirty Years' War, territorial governments adopted specific policies to attract immigrants.[12] In the large migration movement of French Protestants before and after the revocation of the Edict of Nantes by Louis XIV in 1685, they saw an opportunity not only to repopulate depopulated towns and villages, but also to gain qualified manufacturers and craftsmen from one of the most developed countries in Europe.

The principal means employed was the publication of edicts, such as the Edict of Potsdam by Elector Frederic William of Brandenburg-Prussia (29 October 1685) or the *Concessions et Privilèges* by Landgrave Charles of Hesse-Kassel (12 December 1685), which offered important privileges to Huguenot settlers.[13] These and other edicts were circulated at gathering places of the immigrants in Frankfurt-on-Main or Rotterdam, and sometimes even smuggled into France.[14] A large part of the privileges were economic in character: the Huguenots could obtain property and houses as gifts from the sovereign or they were given the

---

[10]   Matthias Asche, *Neusiedler im verheerten Land. Kriegsfolgenbewältigung, Migrationssteuerung und Konfessionspolitik im Zeichen des Landeswiederaufbaus. Die Mark Brandenburg nach den Kriegen des 17. Jahrhunderts* (Münster, 2006), pp. 41–71.

[11]   Veit Ludwig von Seckendorff, *Teutscher Fürsten-Stat* (Jena, 1754, first edition Frankfurt am Main, 1656). Cf. Erhard Dittrich, *Die deutschen und österreichischen Kameralisten* (Darmstadt, 1974), p. 71; Kurt Zielenziger, *Die alten deutschen Kameralisten. Ein Beitrag zur Geschichte der Nationalökonomie und zum Problem des Merkantilismus* (Frankfurt am Main, 1966), pp. 345, 361–2; Michael Stolleis, 'Veit Ludwig von Seckendorff', in Michael Stolleis and Notker Hammerstein (eds), *Staatsdenker in der Frühen Neuzeit* (Munich, 1995), pp. 148–71.

[12]   Ulrich Niggemann, '"Peuplierung" als merkantilistisches Instrument. Privilegierung von Immigranten und staatlich gelenkte Ansiedlungen', in Klaus J. Bade and Jochen Oltmer (eds), *Handbuch Staat und Migration in Deutschland seit dem 17. Jahrhundert* (forthcoming).

[13]   Edict of Potsdam: Ernst Mengin (ed.), *Das Recht der französisch-reformierten Kirche in Preußen. Urkundliche Denkschrift* (Berlin, 1929), pp. 186–96; *Concessions et Privilèges*: Dieter Mempel (ed.), *Gewissensfreiheit und Wirtschaftspolitik. Hugenotten- und Waldenserprivilegien 1681–1699* (Trier, 1986), pp. 51–6.

[14]   Meta Kohnke, 'Das Edikt von Potsdam. Zu seiner Entstehung, Verbreitung und Überlieferung', *Jahrbuch für Geschichte des Feudalismus*, 9 (1985): pp. 241–75. Cf. also Niggemann, *Immigrationspolitik*, pp. 147–51.

building materials for new houses. They would be exempted from most taxes and customs for a certain number of years, and allowed to merchandise their products throughout the country.[15] They also achieved administrative and juridical exemptions: for example, in Hesse-Kassel or Hanover they were freed from mandatory guild membership, whereas in other states, such as Brandenburg, they were promised accession to guild membership without paying the usual duties.[16] In Brandenburg, a Huguenot judge was established, and such an exemption from the ordinary jurisdiction can also be observed in other states, for example in Hesse-Kassel or in particular towns such as Erlangen or Hameln.[17] In most German territorial states, Huguenots were also allowed to worship according to the rites of the French Reformed Church.[18]

Although England had also suffered from depopulation during the civil wars of the 1640s, and although mercantilist thought played an important role there as well, the English government did not adopt an immigration policy comparable to any of the German states. The first Huguenot settlers arrived as early as the 1550s, when they founded communities in London, Canterbury and elsewhere.[19] The Crown also experimented with privileged colonies in the Elizabethan period, but the bulk of Huguenot immigrants, arriving in the 1680s, were not attracted to England as part of a purposeful repopulation programme. The proclamation by Charles II in July 1681 allowed 'distressed Protestants abroad' to settle in England and gave them the right to worship according to

---

[15] Niggemann, *Immigrationspolitik*, pp. 290–93.

[16] *Concessions et Privilèges*, article 8, Mempel (ed.), *Gewissensfreiheit*, pp. 51–6. Cf. Kadell, *Hugenotten*, pp. 312, 575; Walter Mogk, 'Voraussetzungen für die Einwanderung von Hugenotten und Waldensern nach Hessen-Kassel', in Jochen Desel and Walter Mogk (eds), *Die Hugenotten und Waldenser in Hessen-Kassel* (Kassel, 1978), pp. 13–41, at p. 24. Edict of Duke Ernest August of Hanover, article 10, Thomas Klingebiel (ed.), *Die Hugenotten in den welfischen Landen. Eine Privilegiensammlung* (Bad Karlshafen, 1994), pp. 53–5. Cf. Thomas Klingebiel, *Weserfranzosen. Studien zur Geschichte der Hugenottengemeinschaft in Hameln* (Göttingen, 1992), p. 59. Edict of Potsdam, Mengin (ed.), *Recht*. Cf. Jersch-Wenzel, *Juden*, pp. 37, 76. Generally, Niggemann, *Immigrationspolitik*, pp. 299–301.

[17] Edict of Potsdam, article 10, Mengin (ed.), *Recht*, pp. 192–3. Cf. Werner Grieshammer, *Studien zur Geschichte der Réfugiés in Brandenburg-Preußen bis 1713* (Berlin, 1935), pp. 62–71; Jürgen Wilke, 'Rechtstellung und Rechtsprechung der Hugenotten in Brandenburg-Preußen (1685–1809)', in Rudolf von Thadden and Michelle Magdalaine (eds), *Die Hugenotten 1685–1985* (Munich, 1985), pp. 100–114, at pp. 104–5.

[18] Ulrich Niggemann, 'Huguenot Attitudes to Church Administration in Brandenburg-Prussia and Hesse-Kassel', *Proceedings of the Huguenot Society of Great Britain and Ireland*, 29 (2008): pp. 93–104.

[19] William Cunningham, *Alien Immigrants to England* (London/New York, 1969), pp. 149–57; Bernard Cottret, *The Huguenots in England: Immigration and Settlement, c. 1550–1700* (Cambridge, 1991), pp. 8–21; Gwynn, *Heritage*, pp. 33–44.

their own customs, but did not offer any special concessions concerning taxes, jurisdiction or gifts of property. The king promised to issue letters of denization to the immigrants, and he also promised to propose a naturalization bill to Parliament; but the proclamation itself could not make denizens – nor could it enact naturalization. A naturalization act was passed by Parliament as late as 1709, and then quickly revoked in 1712.[20] In the reign of James II, only those Huguenots who conformed to the Church of England could obtain any support from the funds collected in churches.[21]

The differences between the German edicts and the English proclamations are more than just matters of detail. Actually, they are the embodiment of a totally different reaction to Huguenot emigration from France: whereas many German Protestant states adopted an active immigration policy, England only passively allowed Huguenots to settle there.[22] Nonetheless, more Huguenots went to England than to any of the German states. Up to 50,000 French Protestants emigrated to England, including Ireland and the American colonies. Between 15,000 and 20,000 migrated to Brandenburg-Prussia, some 3,000 to Hesse-Kassel, only about 1,000 to Hanover and approximately the same number to Brandenburg-Bayreuth.[23]

In all these cases, the state governments were highly involved from the beginning. Moreover, the central government often took the initiative towards the town authorities. In theory, the central governments were in a strong position in most German cities, especially in the capitals.[24] In practice, however, the power of the central government over the city authorities was always the object of negotiations between the groups involved in a particular case. Not

---

[20]   Proclamation by King Charles II, *Letters of Denization and Acts of Naturalization for Aliens in England and Ireland, 1603–1700*, ed. William A. Shaw (London, 1911), pp. 124–5. Cf. Daniel Statt, 'The Birthright of an Englishman: The Practice of Naturalization and Denization of Immigrants under the Later Stuarts and Early Hanoverians', *Proceedings of the Huguenot Society of London*, 25 (1989): pp. 61–74, at pp. 68–70; William O'Reilly, 'The Naturalization Act of 1709 and the Settlement of Germans in Britain, Ireland and the Colonies', in Randolph Vigne and Charles Littleton (eds), *From Strangers to Citizens: The Integration of Immigrant Communities in Britain, Ireland and Colonial America, 1550–1750* (Brighton/Portland OR, 2001), pp. 492–502.

[21]   Robin D. Gwynn, 'James II in the Light of his Treatment of Huguenot Refugees in England, 1685–1686', *English Historical Review*, 92 (1977): pp. 820–33.

[22]   Niggemann, *Immigrationspolitik*, pp. 147–52.

[23]   Barbara Dölemeyer, 'Rechtliche Aspekte konfessioneller Migration im frühneuzeitlichen Europa am Beispiel der Hugenottenaufnahme', in Joachim Bahlcke (ed.), *Glaubensflüchtlinge. Ursachen, Formen und Auswirkungen frühneuzeitlicher Konfessionsmigration in Europa* (Münster, 2008), pp. 1–25, at pp. 3–4, 24–25.

[24]   For Berlin, see Helga Schultz, *Berlin 1650–1800. Sozialgeschichte einer Residenz* (Berlin, 1992), pp. 28–30.

every order or edict could be enforced by the central government if it met with the resistance of town authorities or interest groups.[25]

Local Conflicts: Cities and Guilds

Complaints from the guilds or urban governments against Huguenots are rarely preserved in the archives. More often we find grievances by French craftsmen who were hindered from exercising their trade by local craftsmen.[26] It often remains unclear what kind of hindrance the local craftsmen formed against the French. In some cases, as we have seen, they committed acts of violence against Huguenots or took away their equipment and products.[27] The most violent conflicts were recorded in London, for example between the Feltmakers' Company and the French hatters at Wandsworth. The Huguenots complained about the ill-treatment they received from the Company, while the Company itself criticized the French for their trading practices.[28] In November 1695, soldiers were deployed to protect French dyers from assaults by their English colleagues.[29]

Despite the sparseness of written complaints by the guilds and the city corporations, in which the guild masters often had an important voice, some conclusions can be drawn from the evidence: there are indications that the indigenous craftsmen were afraid of economic disadvantages. The hatters of Berlin, for example, lamented that before the Huguenot immigration there were already 20 master hatters and two manufactories in the city,[30] while the buttonmakers feared their utter ruin ('eüßersten ruin') because of the 30 masters

25   Cf. Markus Meumann and Ralf Pröve, 'Die Faszination des Staates und die historische Praxis. Zur Beschreibung von Herrschaftsbeziehungen jenseits von teleologischen und dualistischen Begriffsbildungen', in Markus Meumann and Ralf Pröve (eds), *Herrschaft in der Frühen Neuzeit. Umrisse eines dynamisch-kommunikativen Prozesses* (Münster, 2004), pp. 11–49.

26   E.g. complaint by the buttonmaker Louis Lausanne, 13 September 1689, GStAPK I. HA Rep. 122 7bII no 6, fol. 145; by the hatter Gabriel Barbanson, 8 July 1692, GStAPK I. HA Rep. 122 7bII no 10; by Pierre Courriol, 23 September 1694, GStAPK I. HA Rep. 122 18c vol. V, fol. 77; and by the widow le Crû, 2 June 1686, Hessisches Staatsarchiv Marburg (HStAM) Best. 5 no 15464, fol. 20.

27   For further examples, see Niggemann, *Immigrationspolitik*, pp. 321–3.

28   Petitions by French hatters, TNA PC 2/71, fol. 206, 155'; TNA PC 2/73, p. 415; TNA PC 2/75, p. 442. Cf. Thorp, *Government*, pp. 32–6; Statt, *Foreigners*, p. 181; Norman G. Brett-James, *The Growth of Stuart London* (London, 1935), p. 491. Complaints from the Company, TNA PC 2/70, p. 296, 298; TNA PC 2/71, fols 11, 91v.

29   Cf. Thorp, 'Undercurrent', p. 571.

30   Hatters of Berlin, 4 July 1692, GStAPK I. HA Rep. 122 7bII no. 10.

in the city.[31] Similar arguments can be drawn from the petitions of English artisans, who also complained about the great number of foreign craftsmen who, in their view, seized the whole trade.[32]

Can the attitude of the artisans be explained by focusing on fear of competition alone? A closer examination of the sources indicates that a significant part in the political language of German craftsmen was expressed in the concept of 'Nahrung'. The hatters of Berlin, for example, made clear that their 'Nahrung' was diminished by the newcomers because there were already too many hatters in the city. In the same way, the grocers of Halle hoped to achieve an order from the Elector which would ban the French grocers from trading in order to preserve the Germans 'bey unserer wenigen nahrung'.[33] The butchers of Kassel also worried that their 'Nahrung' would be weakened by the French butchers in town.[34] The research topos of fear of competition is clearly not mistaken, but it is only a part of a wider motive on the side of the local craftsmen. The German economic historian Werner Sombart has argued that the concept of 'Nahrung' in premodern sources meant much more than just food; it points to a traditional comprehension of economic principles which was directly opposed to profit seeking. To have his 'Nahrung', to an early modern craftsman, meant to meet his own needs, befitting his particular rank in society.[35] Although Sombart has his critics, it can still be stated that a kind of 'pre-commercial' economic idea did indeed form the views of early modern craftsmen. Of course, they did not follow ideas of equality or socialism, and surely they were not disinclined towards profit; but the guilds provided some kind of order to prevent disproportionate differences between poorer and richer masters which could destroy social stability.[36] Within limits the guilds accepted profit, but beyond this they disapproved of market ideology and of free trade; instead, they aimed at a basic supply for all members of a certain guild, whereas

---

[31]   Buttonmakers of Berlin, 1691, ibid. For further examples, see Niggemann, *Immigrationspolitik*, p. 327.

[32]   General complaint to the Privy Council, 20 May 1686, TNA PC 2/71, fol. 143'; and complaint of the hatters, 18 December 1685, ibid. fol. 91'.

[33]   Hatters of Berlin, GStAPK I. HA Rep. 122 7bII no 10; Grocers' guild at Halle, GStAPK I. HA Rep. 122 16 no 1 vol. I, fols 80–80v.

[34]   Butchers of Kassel, 24 November 1688, HStAM Best. 17f no 586.

[35]   Werner Sombart, *Der moderne Kapitalismus* (6 vols, Leipzig/Berlin, 1928–1955), at vol. 1/1, pp. 14, 31–9, 188–212. Cf. Robert Brandt and Thomas Buchner, 'Einleitung', in Robert Brandt and Thomas Buchner (eds), *Nahrung, Markt oder Gemeinnutz. Werner Sombart und das vorindustrielle Handwerk* (Bielefeld, 2004), pp. 13–28; Thomas Buchner, 'Überlegungen zur Rezeption von Nahrung in der handwerksgeschichtlichen Forschung seit dem Nationalsozialismus', in Brandt and Buchner (eds), *Nahrung*, pp. 67–94.

[36]   Arndt Kluge, *Die Zünfte* (Stuttgart, 2007), pp. 278–82.

profit seeking at the expense of other members of the corporation was decried as selfishness.[37] To protect this 'Nahrung' or the sustenance of every member was exactly what the guilds defined as their principal aim. Every master with his journeymen and apprentices should be able to earn his livelihood from his craft.[38] This idea was certainly part of the 'moral economy' of the early modern labouring classes, which could also be detected in rural communities, in Germany as well as in England and other European countries.[39]

It was on this basis that the guilds claimed their warranted right to have a monopoly on certain works. Thus, the glovers of Hanover reminded the government of their property rights to the craft of glovemaking,[40] and the London Feltmakers' Company recalled the statutes and privileges protecting them against outsiders.[41] Within the municipal area, all guilds in Germany as well as in England claimed their monopoly rights against foreign craftsmen. Huguenots who settled within a town to practise a trade claimed by a guild were, therefore, seen as intruders who had no legitimacy to work. Thus, the rejection of Huguenot craftsmen was much more than fear of competitors; rather, it was a reaction to a violation of property and privilege. Accordingly, the defence of their rights was a defence of a traditional economic conception.

---

[37]　Cf. Helga Schultz, *Das ehrbare Handwerk. Zunftleben im alten Berlin zur Zeit des Absolutismus* (Weimar, 1993), p. 38; Hans-Ulrich Wehler, *Deutsche Gesellschaftsgeschichte* (vol. 1, Munich, 1987), pp. 92–3; Michael Stürmer, *Herbst des Alten Handwerks. Meister, Gesellen und Obrigkeit im 18. Jahrhundert* (Munich, 1986), pp. 107–9; Renate Blickle, 'Nahrung und Eigentum als Kategorien der ständischen Gesellschaft', in Winfried Schulze (ed.), *Ständische Gesellschaft und soziale Mobilität* (Munich, 1988), pp. 73–93.

[38]　Rudolf Wissell, *Des alten Handwerks Recht und Gewohnheit* (6 vols, Berlin, 1971–1988), vol. 2, pp. 279–303; Reinald Ennen, *Zünfte und Wettbewerb. Möglichkeiten und Grenzen zünftlerischer Wettbewerbsbeschränkungen im städtischen Handel und Gewerbe des Spätmittelalters* (Cologne/Vienna, 1971), pp. 12–13; Wehler, *Gesellschaftsgeschichte*, pp. 92–3; Schultz, *Handwerk*, p. 38; Wilfried Reininghaus, *Zünfte, Städte und Staat in der Grafschaft Mark. Einleitung und Regesten von Texten des 14. bis 19. Jahrhunderts* (Münster, 1989), p. 60; Christof Jeggle, 'Nahrung und Markt in Ökonomien städtischer Gewerbe in der Frühen Neuzeit. Methodische Überlegungen am Beispiel des Leinengewerbes in Münster/Westfalen', in Brandt and Buchner (eds), *Nahrung*, pp. 95–130, at pp. 126–9. For England, see Ephraim Lipson, *The Economic History of England* (vol. 3, London, 1956), pp. 330–31; Leslie A. Clarkson, *The Pre-Industrial Economy in England 1500–1750* (London, 1971), p. 103.

[39]　Cf. E.P. Thompson, 'The Moral Economy of the English Crowd in the Eighteenth Century', *Past and Present*, 50 (1971): pp. 76–136. See also Blickle, 'Nahrung', for the 'moral economy' in Bavarian rural communities.

[40]　Niedersächsisches Hauptstaatsarchiv, Hanover, Cal. Br. 8 no 638, fols 1–2.

[41]　Complaint of the feltmakers, 13 February 1685, TNA PC 2/71, fol. 11. Cf. Statt, *Foreigners*, p. 181. Similarly for the goldsmiths, see Thorp, *Government*, pp. 29–30.

If the French wanted to practise their trades legally, they had to register with the guild and to enter it after overcoming due barriers. This is exactly what many corporations stipulated.[42] They also demanded that the French conform to the usage of the guilds; for example, the Huguenot bakers should sell their bread only by using certain market stands, as the German bakers did, and the Huguenot brewers should comply with the times of brewing appointed by the guild.[43] Similar observations could be made for England, where the guilds also tried to control the number of master craftsmen within the municipal area, for example, of London. Thus, the Feltmakers' Company demanded that the norms and standards of fabrication as well as the usages of the guild were maintained.[44] Rather than an expression of hostility in principle against the Huguenots, this was part of the care and protection the guild exercised in favour of all its members.

Interestingly, the governments usually complied with the complaints and demands of the guilds. This was clearly the case in England, where the above-mentioned proclamation by Charles II only promised such 'priviledges and immunitys for the liberty and free exercise of their trades and handicrafts *as are consistent with the Laws*.'[45] Accordingly, the government issued licences for Huguenot craftsmen, but with restrictions concerning the number of journeymen and apprentices, and with validity only beyond the 5-mile zone around the City of London defined by the charters of the companies.[46] The government of Brandenburg, too, sought to force Huguenot craftsmen to enter the guilds. As mentioned before, the Edict of Potsdam had already pointed to regular Huguenot incorporation. Even Hesse-Kassel or Hanover – where French Protestants were freed from mandatory guild membership in theory – tried to restrict this exemption to the greater manufacturers, whereas the small craftsmen were bound to enter a corporation.[47] Thereby, all the governments

---

[42] Elector Frederic III on several petitions, 2 August 1690, GStAPK I. HA Rep. 122 7bII no 8, fol. 122; cf. also the petition of the hatters of Berlin, GStAPK I. HA Rep. 122 7bII no 10; or butchers of Kassel, HStAM Best. 17f no 586.

[43] Elector Fredric III on the complaint of Abraham Clausse, 25 February 1698, GStAPK I. HA Rep. 122 27 no 1, vol. I. Citizenry of Magdeburg, 5 January 1689, GStAPK I. HA Rep. 122 18c vol. I, fols 127–30.

[44] TNA PC 2/71, fol. 11; and order of King James II, TNA SP 31/5, fol. 2. Cf. Statt, *Foreigners*, p. 181. For the goldsmiths, see Thorp, *Government*, pp. 29–30.

[45] Proclamation by King Charles II, 28 July 1681, Shaw, *Letters of Denization*, pp. 124–5 (my italics).

[46] Cf. Statt, *Foreigners*, pp. 180–81; Thorp, *Government*, pp. 33–4; Brett-James, *Growth*, p. 491; and Niggemann, *Immigrationspolitik*, pp. 340–42.

[47] Very explicitly, in Hameln, where according to the 'Koloniereglement' of 14 June 1706, all Huguenot craftsmen had to enter a guild, Klingebiel (ed.), *Hugenotten*, pp. 91–4; Klingebiel,

accepted the claims of the guilds for control of the local trades, and precisely did not attempt to abolish guild control.

Although the guilds demanded membership of Huguenot craftsmen, their admission also caused problems. In Brandenburg so many difficulties arose that the Elector deployed two commissioners to supervise the entrance of Huguenots into the guilds.[48] The records preserve many attempts by guilds to refuse admission to French colleagues. The metalworkers, for example, denied two Frenchmen access to their corporation, although the Elector had ordered them to accommodate the French.[49] French cabinetmakers complained that they were not invited to the assemblies of the guild masters,[50] and two braziers were not incorporated, in spite of their offer to produce a masterpiece.[51]

The fact that the Elector demanded that the guilds accommodate French craftsmen free of charge and without producing a masterpiece contributed to the problems. For the guilds, who maintained that every craftsman had to produce a masterpiece and pay the usual duties if he wished to enter the guild, this was most disturbing. Often they demanded masterpieces and duties despite the privileges of the Huguenots. The drapers of Magdeburg, for example, required 20 *Reichstaler* from Louis Paris for his accession to the guild,[52] and the bookbinders of Halle demanded 10 *Reichstaler* from Arnaud Sarat.[53]

If the guild masters required that Huguenot craftsmen should enter the respective guilds, why then did they refuse to admit them in many cases? Why did they make access so difficult? Was it just chicanery and harassment? I argue that it was not, because the guilds aimed at the protection of their members against an overstaffed trade. According to the ideology of 'Nahrung', an overstaffed trade meant competition and, consequently, ruin for some of the less successful masters. Correspondingly, the hatters of Berlin pointed out that, because there were already 20 masters in the city, they all had 'schlechte und geringe nahrung'.[54] Similarly, the buttonmakers perceived the danger of ruin because there were

---

Weserfranzosen, pp. 128–9, 146–7. For Hesse-Kassel see Niggemann, *Immigrationspolitik*, pp. 338–9.

[48] GStAPK I. HA Rep. 122 7bI no. 1, fols 102–102'. Cf. also Tollin, *Geschichte* vol. 1, p. 425.

[49] GStAPK I. HA Rep. 122 7bII no. 8, fol. 128, mentioning an earlier admonition.

[50] GStAPK I. HA Rep. 122 7bII no. 8, fols 163–163'.

[51] Report of the French commissioners, 16 September 1689, GStAPK I. HA Rep. 122 7bII no. 13, fols 108–109. For further examples, Niggemann, *Immigrationspolitik*, p. 347.

[52] GStAPK I. HA Rep. 122 18c vol. II, fols 75–75'.

[53] GStAPK I. HA Rep. 122 16 no. 1 vol. III, fols 51–51'.

[54] GStAPK I. HA Rep. 122 7bII no. 10.

already 30 masters in the city.[55] Restricted access to the corporation by means of fees and charges as well as a masterpiece were ways of preserving control over the number of workshops in the town and excluding those who had not learned the craft according to the statutes.[56]

It was also a principal task of guilds to maintain control over the quality of products. Thus, guilds had always demanded a certain number of years of apprenticeship, adjacent years of travel and a masterpiece as a condition of becoming a master craftsman. Huguenots, because of the circumstances of their flight from France, often could not produce evidence of their training. Consequently, they were sometimes accused of not having learned their craft sufficiently. For instance, the buttonmakers of Cologne on the Spree refused to incorporate Louis Lausanne because, in their judgement, he had not been trained in the craft.[57] The hatters complained that their French colleagues, having barely finished their apprenticeship, established themselves as master craftsmen.[58] For the same reasons, Huguenots often could not prove their honest birth. It was essential for the guilds to ensure that every member was of honest origin and sufficiently qualified. Qualification and skill were surely central elements in legitimizing the social status of masters and the privileges of the guild. Moreover, they were the quintessence of the guild's reputation.[59] A loss of reputation meant isolation from the respective guilds of other towns and cities and, consequently, the loss of an operating network providing for the exchange of journeymen.[60] The buttonmakers of Cologne on the Spree brought forward this argument clearly: they were afraid that the acceptance of Louis Lausanne as a member of the guild would cause such a serious loss of reputation that no journeymen from outside would ever come to work with them.[61]

Obviously, there were many serious conflicts concerning the accession of Huguenots into the guilds, especially in Brandenburg-Prussia, where the government insisted on incorporating Huguenot craftsmen. Apart from the

---

[55]   Ibid.

[56]   Cf. Bert De Munck, 'Skills, Trust, and Changing Consumer Preferences: The Decline of Antwerp's Craft Guilds from the Perspective of the Product Market, c. 1500–c. 1800', *International Review of Social History*, 53 (2008): pp. 197–233, at pp. 212–15.

[57]   GStAPK I. HA Rep. 122 7bII no. 10.

[58]   Ibid.

[59]   De Munck, 'Skills', pp. 201, 215–22, 231.

[60]   Kluge, *Zünfte*, pp. 107–14; Wissell, *Recht*, vol. 1, pp. 145–273; Schultz, *Handwerk*, pp. 44–50; Wolfram Fischer, *Handwerksrecht und Handwerkswirtschaft um 1800. Studien zur Sozial- und Wirtschaftsverfassung vor der industriellen Revolution* (Berlin, 1955), pp. 52–3.

[61]   GStAPK I. HA Rep. 122 7bII no. 10. Similarly, the shoemakers of Halberstadt, 13 September 1703, Landeshauptarchiv von Sachsen-Anhalt, Magdeburg, Rep. A 13 no. 465, fols 237–40.

aforementioned cases, many further examples could be listed. Nonetheless, it would be a mistake to overstate the conflicts. The contemporary documents only record the conflicts and the governmental interventions. That there are hardly any records showing voluntary and undisputed entrances of Huguenots into the guilds does surely not mean that there were none. Compared with the large number of Huguenots settling in Berlin, for instance, the number of proven conflicts there is quite low.[62] This is also an indication that it was not hostility in principle that determined the behaviour of local craftsmen, but rather their specific conceptions of honesty in trade and just and equal distribution of work and 'Nahrung'.

Nor was it the aim of the governments to abolish guild control. On the contrary, they complied with many of the demands from the corporations while simultaneously struggling to accommodate the numerous Huguenot craftsmen. The fact that local guilds partly complied with the orders of the state governments without resistance and that they carried on negotiating with the state commissioners can be seen as an indication of an ongoing cooperation. The guilds did not perceive the early modern state as opposed to their existence as urban corporations and, therefore, did not try to combat the orders of the government, but instead communicated their complaints and accepted the state as an arbiter.[63]

Differences in the Nature of Local Conflicts

In spite of a very different approach to Huguenot immigration on the part of the governments, as shown in the first section of this chapter, the second section has proven that urban conflicts in Germany and England show a number of similarities. Nevertheless, some differences, especially between London and the German cities and towns, should not be ignored. In contrast to the German cases, in England we can observe intense struggles within the guilds, especially within the great London livery companies. Moreover, there was a strong nationalistic element in the resistance against Huguenot craftsmanship that was generally absent in Germany.

Weavers in London accused the Huguenots of working for lower wages than Englishmen, thereby lowering the general level of wages. In a pamphlet from 1681, the journeymen weavers complained: 'And Weavers all may curse

---

[62]   For statistics, cf. Jürgen Wilke, 'Die Französische Kolonie in Berlin', in Schultz, *Berlin*, pp. 353–430, at pp. 361–7; Jürgen Wilke, 'Zur Sozialstruktur und demographischen Analyse der Hugenotten in Brandenburg-Preußen, insbesondere der in Berlin', in Ingrid Mittenzwei (ed.), *Hugenotten in Brandenburg-Preußen* (Berlin [GDR], 1987), pp. 27–99, at pp. 36–7.

[63]   See Niggemann, *Immigrationspolitik*, pp. 320–61, 536–9.

their fates/because the French work under rates.'[64] Other pamphlets, such as 'England's Advocate', confirmed this argument by pointing out that all English weavers would find employment if the French were sent back home.[65] The resentment was strengthened by the fact that in London divisions between the larger master weavers on the one hand and the smaller masters and journeymen on the other hand were increasing. Thus, the system of independent craftsmen bound together by the guild with its internal solidarity was already in a state of disintegration.[66] For the larger weavers, who were acting as putting-out agents, the French represented a pool of cheap workers. Therefore, they were keen to support immigration, and they entered into an agreement with the French churches in London for the employment of French textile workers.[67] For the English journeymen and wageworkers, this meant a widening of the gap between them and the employing master weavers. Similar tendencies have been traced in other centres of textile production and commerce, such as Antwerp or southern German imperial cities such as Augsburg.[68] The German towns that experienced the greatest influx of Huguenots in the late seventeenth century were not centres like Antwerp, London or Augsburg, however. Most of them were quite small and economically backward. Although there may have been differences between smaller and larger masters, too, these differences did not – at least in the archival evidence – affect the attitudes of craftsmen towards French immigrants.

In England, the fears of the small masters and journeymen of being deprived of their sustenance also joined with a language strongly directed against 'foreigners' and 'aliens', thus introducing a sense of nationality into the discourse, distinguishing Englishness from 'otherness'.[69] English craftsmen

---

[64] Quoted by Cottret, *Huguenots*, p. 195.

[65] *England's Advocate, Europe's Monitor: Being An Intreaty for help, In Behalf of the English Silk-Weavers and Silk-Throsters* ... (London, 1699) [Wing/N2], pp. 9–10, 37–8.

[66] Cf. Brett-James, *Growth*, p. 492; Peter Clark and Paul Slack (eds), *English Towns in Transition, 1500–1700* (Oxford, 1976), pp. 69–70; Clarkson, *Economy*, p. 104; and focusing on the weavers, Dunn, 'Weavers' Riot', p. 13; Statt, *Foreigners*, p. 183.

[67] Statt, *Foreigners*, p. 176. Cf. William C. Waller (ed.), *Extracts from the Court Books of the Weavers Company of London, 1610–1730* (London, 1931), p. xii; Cottret, *Huguenots*, p. 196; Plummer, *Weavers' Company*, pp. 56, 147, 155.

[68] For Antwerp, see Bert De Munck, 'One Counter and Your Own Account: Redefining Illicit Labour in Early Modern Antwerp', *Urban History*, 37/1 (2010): pp. 26–44; and the contribution by Jan De Meester in the present volume. For Augsburg, see Anke Sczesny, 'Nahrung, Gemeinwohl und Eigennutz im ostschwäbischen Textilgewerbe der Frühen Neuzeit', in Brandt and Buchner (eds), *Nahrung*, pp. 131–54.

[69] Cf. Tony Claydon and Ian McBride (eds), *Protestantism and National Identity: Britain and Ireland, c. 1650–c. 1850* (Cambridge, 1998); Linda Colley, *Britons: Forging the Nation 1707–1837* (London, 1994).

repeatedly deplored the great number of foreigners exercising their craft. They demanded that the government protect them against alien labour, referring to the statutes of King Richard III and King Henry VIII.[70] These statutes had been enacted by Parliament to prevent immigrants from working within the city of London without becoming freemen of the respective guilds and from employing more than two foreign journeymen. In the late seventeenth century, they were used as an argument against the settlement of immigrant craftsmen in a very tense situation, resulting from the above-mentioned divisions within the Weavers' Company, as well as from general underemployment in the fast growing London suburbs.[71] At least in London,- we can observe the problems of a modernizing labour market, with its dissolving guild structures and an increasing competition for wages. In most trades the specifically premodern conceptions of craftsmanship were still prevailing, but in the fast expanding textile industry, new developments were manifesting themselves.

Conclusions

Seemingly, the relationship between Huguenot immigrants and local craftsmen was defined by intense conflicts, but a closer examination shows that, compared with the large number of immigrants recorded, the conflicts appear less predominant. Elements of corporate identity, honesty and a certain conception of economy played an important role in the attitude of guild members towards immigration and immigrants. From their point of view, just distribution of work and income lay at the core of corporate craftsmanship, while unrestricted immigration and exercise of trade put every member's sustenance at risk. Thus, adherence to the principle of 'Nahrung' was essential to the common welfare. Therefore, local craftsmen did not disapprove of individual French competitors, but of the concept of market competition in general. They did not think in terms of competition, but they adhered to specifically premodern, subsistence-oriented ideas of economy. This was part of a certain system of thought – their 'moral

---

[70]   Report about rumours produced by journeymen weavers, 27 August 1683, TNA SP 29/431, fol. 29; reference to the 'Statute Lawes for the Regulation of that Trade & preventing Forrainers to invade it', TNA PC 2/71, fol. 11. Cf. Lien Bich Luu, *Immigrants and the Industries of London, 1500–1700* (Aldershot, 2005), p. 143; Daniel Statt, 'The City of London and the Controversy over Immigration, 1660–1722', *The Historical Journal*, 33 (1990): pp. 45–61, at p. 46.

[71]   Christopher G. Clay, *Economic Expansion and Social Change: England, 1500–1700* (2 vols, Cambridge, 1984), at vol. 1, pp. 26–8, and vol. 2, pp. 90–91; James A. Sharpe, *Early Modern England: A Social History 1550–1760* (London, 1987), pp. 85–90; Clarkson, *Economy*, pp. 31–2.

economy' – which they perceived as a quite rational conception for a society in which commodities were always scarce and living was always precarious.

Although these observations are quite similar for Germany and England, there are still some important differences: the rapid growth of London suburbs, the divisions within the larger livery companies and the more developed national consciousness led to intensified hostilities in some branches of production, especially in the textile industries. In fact, some of the larger master weavers came to agreements with the French churches concerning the employment of Frenchmen; but the mass of wage workers in the London Weavers' Company vehemently resented the immigration of Huguenots, fearing that they might undercut wages. In this situation, national resentments helped to formulate arguments against immigration, but the motives remained economic in character.

In conclusion, economic fears resulting from the prospect of dissolution of traditional concepts of craftsmanship informed the sometimes hostile attitude of the guilds towards Huguenot immigration. Yet, there are no indications that the state governments seriously attempted to abolish guild control of the urban trades. Resistance, therefore, was not directed against the state; the guilds incorporated many Huguenots without resistance, but adhered to their traditional economic conceptions and upheld the usual restrictions of access. They accepted immigration, but resented mass immigration.

Chapter 4

Heresy, War, Vagrancy and Labour Needs: Dealing with Temporary Migrants in the Textile Towns of Flanders, Artois and Hainaut in the Wake of the Dutch Revolt (1566–1609)

Yves Junot

In the early modern period, towns experienced a permanent influx of migrants, which was essential for their demographic and economic development. Cities were places for professional recruitment and important job markets. The influx of migrants played a part in urban economic development, but also in urban decline.[1] At the same time, towns were not necessarily a terminus for migrants: variations in economic activity, employment and wages fostered a situation of permanent mobility. Hence, an unknown – and probably rather large – number of urban migrants did not settle down: they were in effect temporary residents and workers.[2] Their presence in turn had a great impact on the supply of accommodation, jobs and poor relief, and could complicate the maintenance of public order. How, then, did urban authorities attempt to regulate the activities of their 'floating population'?

The Southern Low Countries in the late sixteenth century are of great interest for studying urban authorities' responses to temporary migrations. To understand why, we must take into account their geographic position in the urban network, the characteristics of textile manufacturing which dominated the area since the Middle Ages, the religious and military conflicts of the period and the towns' political and social organization. In Flanders, small towns

---

[1]   D. Roche, *La ville promise. Mobilité et accueil à Paris (fin XVIIe–début XIXe siècle)* (Paris, 2000), p. 10; J.L. Pinol (ed.), *Histoire de l'Europe urbaine. De l'Antiquité au XVIIIe siècle* (Paris, 2003), vol. 1, pp. 627, 753–5.

[2]   M.P. Hohenberg and L.H. Lees, *La formation de l'Europe urbaine 1000–1950* (Paris, 1992), pp. 134–5.

functioned as intermediate stages in migrations between the countryside and large cities. They offered a first training in textile manufacturing for unqualified rural workers who afterwards migrated to larger towns to pursue better employment opportunities.[3] The woollen industry dominating the regions of Lille, Douai, Orchies, Tournai, Artois and Hainaut was characterized by a multiplicity of urban centres without one town truly dominating over the others. In the sixteenth century, competition between towns like Lille, Valenciennes and Tournai increased as they developed into major rival centres of *sayetterie*, a branch of the booming new draperies.[4] In addition, the Cambrai area, which was renowned for its linen manufacturing, experienced competition from the growth of fine linen production in Valenciennes. This economic competition exerted a downward pressure on wages and stimulated migration. The search for a better life fostered the geographical mobility of workers, who did not necessarily have any interest in settling down and integrating into an urban society on a permanent basis.

These patterns of mobility were at once stimulated and complicated by the religious and military conflicts of the period. The Dutch Revolt (1566–1609) and the Spanish reconquest intensified religious tensions and entailed severe economic disruptions which fostered large-scale emigrations to England and the northern provinces. These in turn stimulated the expansion of long-distance patterns of circular migration, joining textile centres in Walloon Flanders, the Dutch Republic and England. However, as the Walloon provinces sided with the Spanish crown (Union of Arras, 1579) and fronts remained active against France (until 1598), England (until 1604) and the Dutch Republic (until 1609), these cross-border migrants were treated with heightened official suspicion in the late sixteenth century. As a result, the labour needs of the urban manufacturing sectors at times conflicted with political imperatives that strove to limit movements to and from 'enemy territory'.

These different forms of mobility also posed challenges to the social and political organization of towns, which resembled that of 'urban republics'. It was based on a participative system of citizens with burghership right: privileged inhabitants who enjoyed a set of political, judicial, military, fiscal

---

[3]   P. Stabel, *Dwarfs among Giants: The Flemish Urban Network in the Late Middle Ages* (Leuven/Apeldoorn, 1997), pp. 116, 128–35.

[4]   R.S. Duplessis, 'One Theory, Two Draperies, Three Provinces, and a Multitude of Fabrics: The New Drapery of French Flanders, Hainaut and Tournaisis, c. 1500–1800', in N.B. Harte (ed.), *The New Draperies in the Low Countries and England, 1300–1800* (Oxford/New York, 1997), pp. 130–42.

and economic rights and duties.[5] The municipal authorities were responsible for the maintenance of social cohesion. The town councils, which also supervised guilds and manufacturing, aimed to relieve poverty and maintain social order by developing a new centralized system of poor relief from 1520 onwards.[6] This participative system was in spirit open to newcomers and did not put up any financial barriers to the acquisition of burghership, contrary to the situation in other areas of Europe.[7] Up to the 1560s a large number of immigrant artisans acquired urban citizenship during the prosperous period of the woollen industry: during the first two-thirds of the century more than 40 per cent of the new burghers of Valenciennes were active in textile manufacturing, among whom were many modest saymakers and weavers. By the end of the sixteenth century, however, manual workers tended to disappear from the lists of new burghers, which suggests that channels of integration linked to burghership became more selective and restrictive. This process started in the 1580s, at the time of the revival or the conversion of urban textile activity, when recruitment of labour was again intensifying due to higher production levels.[8]

The main focus of this chapter is to investigate how urban society accommodated temporary residents without weakening social cohesion in a time of socio-economic and political transformation. These 'silent groups' of history are mentioned only rarely in official documents, but their existence can be investigated via judicial archives concerning repressive measures against vagrancy and the heightened supervision of people and movement in the context of the ongoing religious and military conflicts of the late sixteenth century. In the following pages I will first identify the main segments of the floating population as they came into contact with urban authorities and show that they did not have homogeneous profiles: their migratory experiences varied according to economic contexts, survival strategies and religious beliefs. A second section

---

5   P. Guignet, *Le pouvoir dans la ville au XVIIIe siècle. Pratiques politiques, notabilité et éthique sociale de part et d'autre de la frontière franco-belge* (Paris, 1990); Y. Junot, *Les bourgeois de Valenciennes. Anatomie d'une élite dans la ville (1500–1630)* (Villeneuve d'Ascq, 2009), pp. 33–42.

6   P. Bonenfant, 'Les origines et le caractère de la réforme de la bienfaisance aux Pays-Bas sous le règne de Charles Quint', *Revue belge de philologie et d'histoire*, 5 (1926): pp. 887–904 and 6 (1927): pp. 207–30; R. Jütte, *Poverty and Deviance in Early Modern Europe* (Cambridge, 1994), pp. 100–119.

7   On the social exclusion of workers and poor women from the Hanse towns, see M.L. Pelus-Kaplan, 'Travail, immigration et citoyenneté dans les villes hanséatiques, aux XVIe–XVIIe siècles, d'après les exemples de Lübeck, Hambourg et Danzig', in P. Gonzàlez-Bernaldo, M. Martini and M.L. Pelus-Kaplan (eds), *Etrangers et sociétés. Représentations, coexistences, interactions dans la longue durée* (Rennes, 2008), pp. 343–8.

8   Junot, *Les bourgeois de Valenciennes*, pp. 27–8, 48–53, 270–71.

will focus in greater detail on the case of textile workers, who participated in specific migration networks that were tied in with the particular organization of work in the woollen industry (around Lille, Tournai and Valenciennes) and the linen industry (around Cambrai and Valenciennes). A last section will examine the regulative efforts of municipal authorities towards temporary migrants by confronting norms and discourse with actual practice.

The Floating Population: Different Migratory Experiences

In judicial archives, migrants can be traced from one place to another as they were arrested for begging, theft, unauthorized travelling, heresy or other suspicious or illegal activities. Judicial interrogations[9] and petitions for reconciliation[10] shed light on the geographical stages of their journeys, their reasons for taking to the road and their conditions of survival. A wide range of terms was used to describe these migrants as they presented themselves to the urban authorities. These were not free from prejudice, but are illustrative of the latter's ways of thinking. These sources enable us to understand the mobile projects of a 'floating population' that was not wandering about aimlessly, but formed part of migration systems that were structured by migrants' practices and networks.[11] Three main circuits can be distinguished in this respect: war migrations, individual break-ups and mobile textile workers.

War Migrations: Soldiers and Refugees

Given the intensity of warfare in the Low Countries at the end of the sixteenth century, it is no surprise to find many active and demobilized soldiers and deserters among migrants interrogated by the aldermen.[12] With the proximity of

---

[9]   Sample: 40 cases in two criminal registers of Valenciennes from 1590–1593 and 1600–1601 in the Archives municipales de Valenciennes (AMV), FF1 10 and 11, completed with 17 impositions of a fine for housing foreigners in Tournai in the periods 1581–1585 and 1593–1595 in the Belgian Archives générales du royaume (AGR), Chambre des Comptes (CdC), 39999–40001, 40010–40011.

[10]   Sample: seven requests sent to the Conseil Privé in Brussels between 1583 and 1606 by craftsmen who had emigrated mainly from Lille and Tournai (AGR, Conseil Privé espagnol (CPE), 1420 and 1421).

[11]   V. Denis, 'Surveiller et décrire. L'enquête des préfets sur les migrations périodiques, 1807–1812', *Revue d'histoire moderne et contemporaine*, 47/4 (2000): pp. 706–30.

[12]   G. Parker, 'Recrutement' and 'Désobéissance', in P. Janssens (ed.), *La Belgique espagnole 1585–1715, vol 1. La politique* (Brussels, 2006), pp. 55–60, 65–6 (high desertion rate, around 15 per cent).

military operations, many were soldiers who had left camp without permission. Others had retired from the army after many years and resorted to begging, theft and robbery as they experienced difficulties fitting back into civilian life.[13] Military camps were also important temporary job markets for navvies, servants, salesmen and other civilians, who followed the troops in the prospect of work.[14]

The military operations also produced numerous refugees. With many civilians uprooted by warfare and religious persecution, the reconciliation policy launched by Alexander Farnese allowed refugees in enemy territory to return to the pacified provinces. Few craftsmen filed an official request for reconciliation, unlike merchants who worried about their trade and town notables who worried about their positions. Among the inhabitants of Cambrai who took refuge in France and filed a request to return to the Low Countries in 1581–1583, there was only one tailor. In his reasons for applying, he stressed his Spanish and Tridentine loyalty. In contrast, the woollen weavers who wanted to return to Tournai from Antwerp by means of the reconciliation treaty concluded between Tournai and Farnese in 1581 systematically avoided mentioning political or religious considerations.[15] They explained their departure from Tournai by the 'decline of manufacturing during the wars' and the impossibility of earning their living.[16] They presented themselves to the authorities as migrant workers rather than political or religious refugees.

Individual Break-Ups: Relegated Craftsmen

Investigations carried out by aldermen shed light on the processes of social degradation that took place when craftsmen crossed the social borders which separated them from vagrants. It is not always easy to establish who was poor by birth and who was relegated to poverty by individual accidents of life.[17] An inhabitant of Lille, Gillebert Regnart – *sayetteur* and maker of *changeants*, born around 1553 – was the son of a herring wholesaler who had been ruined by

---

13   See the example of Anthoine de Gorat in AMV, FF1 10, fols 13v, 45, 48.

14   See the example of Douais-born shoemaker Loys Sorret in AMV, FF1 11, fols 71–3, 75, 79, 80r.

15   Alfons K.L. Thijs, 'Structural Changes in the Antwerp Industry from the Fifteenth to the Eighteenth Century', in H. Van der Wee (ed.), *The Rise and Decline of Urban Industries in Italy and in the Low Countries (Late Middle Ages–Early Modern Times)* (Leuven, 1988), p. 208: the intense activity of the Antwerp industry until the beginning of the 1580s was made possible through a massive immigration of Flemish and Hainaut workers.

16   AGR, CPE, 1420.

17   Nor is it in the case of contemporary problems of poverty: S. Paugam, 'La pauvreté en Europe, entre statut transitoire et destin social', *L'état des inégalités en France* (Paris, 2006), p. 155.

misfortune. He belonged to an eminent family – his cousins were aldermen – and began to work for several masters in Lille when he was 16. He was however condemned for rape around 1576, after which he appears to have embarked on a vagrant life. He begged for bread in Bruges around 1578, was subsequently condemned to the galleys for six years in Spain and stayed in Granada and Lisbon until 1585. Back in the Low Countries, he wandered from fair to fair to earn his living, passing through Lille and Aix-la-Chapelle. Under arrest in Valenciennes in 1591, he declared that he was begging because of 'the death of his craft' and boasted that he had been a galley slave to provoke compassion. The aldermen banished him for vagrancy, using threats while begging and not having received communion since he had returned from Spain.[18]

While individual accidents of life played a part, processes of social degradation were often driven by more general conditions. Debts sometimes led craftsmen to leave,[19] while ups and downs of employment and wages for structural and cyclical reasons could at times push workers below the poverty line.[20] Estienne Dubois resided in Cambrai for two or three years (until 1599), in Antwerp for six months and settled in Valenciennes (in 1600) where he found a job and housing. But three months later he was under arrest for the theft and resale of clothes and admitted having been 'wrongly advised by poverty'. The *bourats* weaver Ponce Schelppe, accused of stealing small change in a church in Valenciennes, had left Reims eight days previously because he could not find work, and had been equally unsuccessful in finding a job in Tournai where he had stayed for four days. The young bobbinmaker Jean Plu looked for employment in Lille, Mons and Valenciennes. He travelled with his aunt, who allegedly 'convinced him and threatened to kill him if he did not bring anything back'.[21] These thefts of money, food or clothes were occasional actions that illustrate the risks of poverty in daily life. Those arrested had their favourite places: the main square, the corn market, churches; their favourite days: Saturday, market day; and their usual receivers: pawnbrokers (*Lombards*), second-hand clothes dealers (*fripiers*) and companions in suffering.[22]

---

[18]   AMV, FF1 10, fols 79v–80, 82.

[19]   See the examples of David Delattre in AMV, FF1 10, fols 142v–143r, 144r and hosiery maker Jehan Dutrieu in AGR, CPE, 1421, reconciliation 27 November 1606.

[20]   Jütte, *Poverty and Deviance*, pp. 27–44.

[21]   AMV, FF1 11, fols 3–4r, fol. 7 and fols 28v–29r.

[22]   Jütte, *Poverty and Deviance*, pp. 151–2. For further details, A. Farge, *Délinquance et criminalité. Le vol d'aliments à Paris au XVIIIe siècle* (Paris, 1974).

Interurban Movements: Textile Workers

Woollen weavers migrated from town to town over a wider manufacturing area, and their trajectories took place in the context of formal and informal urban networks. A first such formal network was formed by a collection of 23 free towns in Artois, Flanders, Hainaut, Picardy and Champagne that mutually acknowledged their textile workers' qualifications.[23] Of course, not all these towns held the same attractions, as some degraded to the status of secondary job markets (such as Douai and Orchies in Walloon Flanders). In addition, as early as the sixteenth century the urban network faced competition from small towns or villages that had recently converted to the production of new draperies, like the villages near Pernes or Saint-Pol in Artois and Le Quesnoy in Hainaut. With the rise of new draperies, a second urban network developed in the second half of the sixteenth century that extended into England, Holland and German towns such as Wesel, Cologne, Frankenthal and Nuremberg. Movement between the Southern Low Countries and these 'foreign' destinations intensified in the 1560s in the wake of the Dutch Revolt and the establishment of Protestant refuges.[24]

Connections between English, Dutch and Walloon towns were maintained by family links and regular departures after the Spanish reconquest of the southern provinces, despite official suspicion towards contacts with 'rebel' or 'heretic' countries. With the practice of Calvinism made impossible in the Spanish Low Countries in 1579, emigrants from Valenciennes peopled the Calvinist refuge of Canterbury from 1567 until late in the seventeenth century.[25] Yet their primary motivation does not seem to have been religious but economic in character, linked to the decline of local woollen manufacturing at the beginning of the seventeenth century. Even if religious motivations did play a role, income opportunities were a crucial consideration. The case of Leiden shows how the growth of its new draperies at the end of the sixteenth

---

[23] M. Vanhaeck, *Histoire de la sayetterie à Lille*, part I (Lille, 1910), p. 46. A bill of the aldermen of Lille gives a list of these free towns in 1573: St-Quentin, Aubenton, Reims, Chalons, Beauvais, Amiens, Abbeville, Montreuil, Péronne in France; Arras, Saint-Omer, Ieper, Diksmuide, Gent, Brugge, Bailleul, Huy, Lille, Douai, Orchies, Tournai, Valenciennes, Cambrai in the Low Countries.

[24] See in particular W. Frijhoff, 'Migrations religieuses dans les Provinces-Unies avant le second Refuge', *Revue du Nord*, 80/326–7 (1998): pp. 573–98; R. Esser, *Niederländische Exulanten im England des 16. und frühen 17. Jahrhunderts* (Berlin, 1996); A. Spicer, *The French-Speaking Reformed Community and their Church in Southampton, 1567–1620* (London, 1997).

[25] R. Hovenden, *The Registers of the Wallon or Strangers' Church in Canterbury*, vol. 5/2 (Lymington, 1894): 32 Valenciennes-born married in the Calvinist church in the period 1591–1600, 41 in 1601–1630, 10 in 1631–1650 and the last one in 1658. Among them was the *sayetteur* Ghislain Gallamar, who left Valenciennes with his family around 1610.

century was fed by immigration streams from Flemish industrial centres such as Hondschoote, Ieper, Bailleul and Lille. This textile worker migration system was maintained by human chains attracted by relatively high wages and supported by the city's recruitment policies.[26]

Were the departures for England or the Dutch Republic permanent? While some settlements had a lasting character, many workers continued to move back and forth between manufacturing centres. Jean Delevigne, *hautelisseur* of Tournai, occasionally worked in Lille and went to England in 1582 for three months. The aldermen of Valenciennes investigated his movements in 1592: he was suspected of being a messenger between the Walloon refuge and the Low Countries. The same suspicion fell on a *sayetteur* of Valenciennes, Pierre Delalleue, who had stayed five weeks in England in 1583 to 'see his sister'.[27] A *sayetteur* and municipal sergeant, Hermès Desnau, born in Ath, who became a new burgher of Valenciennes in 1586, had to leave town because of an allegation of manslaughter in 1598. He went to Arras and then to Lille, where he worked for a say weaver for four months. He later crossed the Channel with an inhabitant of Lille who was on his way back to Norwich, and reached England to join his son, who had settled there six years earlier. In the manufacturing town of Norwich, he met the Walloon and Flemish communities which had successfully introduced the new draperies in the 1560s.[28] He worked there as a *sayetteur* for eight months, but had to leave because he was suspected of spying. Back in Valenciennes in November 1600, he was arrested a few months later for residing in 'an enemy country where reprobate religion is practised' and for returning without remission letters.[29] In 1590, the young Daniel Piètre, a recently engaged 20-year old lacemaker, left Valenciennes for London, where he married in the Calvinist church. His connection with England was a family story: the son of a horse merchant from Valenciennes, Daniel was born during his family's exile in London after his father had been banished by the Council of Troubles in 1568. The family returned home in 1574 after a general pardon and Daniel learned his craft in Valenciennes, where he also attended Catholic school. In 1590, Daniel left London again, this time for Leiden where he stayed with family, worked as a lacemaker and confirmed his Calvinist commitment by celebrating the Last Supper twice. After residing in Leiden for one and a half years, he wanted to

---

26   L. Lucassen and B. De Vries, 'The Rise and Fall of a Western European Textile-Worker Migration System: Leiden, 1586–1700', in G. Gayot and P. Minard (eds), *Les ouvriers qualifiés de l'industrie (XVIe–XXe siècle). Formation, emploi, migrations* (Lille, 2001), pp. 24–9.

27   AMV, FF1 10, fol. 156r and fol. 82r.

28   L. Martin, 'The Rise of the New Draperies in Norwich, 1550–1622', in Harte (ed.), *The New Draperies*, pp. 245–74.

29   AMV, FF1 11, fols 68v–70r, 81r.

return to the Southern Low Countries: he embarked at Flushing for Calais with another inhabitant of Valenciennes who was returning from Middelburg, and they arrived home two weeks later.[30] Their route was the same as the one followed by a *bourat* weaver who left Tournai in 1606 to work in England and the Dutch Republic and returned a year later.[31] These individual stories complement our knowledge of textile-worker migration patterns in late sixteenth-century western Europe. In addition to permanent migrations from the Southern Low Countries to England or to the Dutch Republic, these different manufacturing areas were connected by a system of circular migrations by temporary workers.

Migrant Textile Workers: Living and Working Conditions

Many textile workers thus operated within inter-urban migration networks, and were oriented towards temporary jobs. In order to investigate how urban authorities tried to regulate the presence and activities of this floating workforce, it is necessary first to understand the main living and working conditions that governed their stay in towns, and which were tied in with patterns of housing, hiring and labour relations.

Housing Conditions

Urban housing conditions grew accustomed to population growth and the presence of large numbers of temporary residents. Newcomers could find a place to stay for a few days in the inns of the suburbs and the main streets of the city. Subletting was very common and adapted to weekly or monthly stays, matching the needs of poor migrant workers with those of permanent tenants who were not much richer.[32] Another practice fostered by sixteenth-century urban growth was the building of small, cheap houses gathered in *courées* (backyards).[33] During the golden age of the woollen industry of Valenciennes, owners of plots of land in cul-de-sacs or close to the town walls built rows of small houses to be let. After the 1566 Revolt, 136 small houses for rent were confiscated by the king

---

30   AMV, FF1 10, fols 157, 160, 164, 165v, 183r, 187r.

31   AGR, CPE, 1421, reconciliation, 10 July 1607.

32   The clothmaker Tobie Lefebvre, in the week of his arrival from Cambrai to Valenciennes, immediately found a job at a master's workshop in Rue de le Sauch and a room at a soldier's home in the same street. He was arrested eight days later for omitting to register (AMV, FF1 10, fol. 84).

33   P. Guignet, 'Cours, courées et corons. Contribution à un cadrage lexicographique, typologique et chronologique de types d'habitat collectif emblématiques de la France du Nord', *Revue du Nord*, 90/374 (2008): pp. 29–47.

of Spain from 27 Calvinist owners. One of them, the rich merchant Michel Herlin, had one backyard built up with seven cheap-rent small houses marked in alphabetical order. Even humble owners invested in this popular housing system. A shoemaker owned 19 small houses rented out to poor people on a weekly basis.[34]

This kind of housing often had charitable connections. Herlin was an alderman and a very active steward of municipal poor relief. After the Protestant Revolt, most of the confiscated *courées* were given to Catholic convents – such as the Magdalene Sisters – who used them to accommodate widows and unmarried women. Links between employers and workers were also important. Most lodgers were 'poor saymakers living off their work', clothmakers, linen weavers and shoemakers. In 1568, a merchant carpenter rented out four of his six small houses to sawyers (*scieurs*) in his employ; some of them paid the rent by working for him. In 1600, a master *sayetteur* rented a block of five small houses recently confiscated from a burgher who had left the Low Countries.[35]

It is not easy to establish whether *courée* dwellers were newcomers or sedentary poor people. Where details on occupancy are known, however, the sixteenth-century *courées* of Valenciennes offer a picture similar to that of the parish of St Sauveur in Lille (the *sayetteurs'* parish) at the end of the seventeenth century. In the main streets of the parish, where the workshops were situated, masters and journeymen resided in more or less proportionate numbers. The backyards and secondary alleys close to the walls of the town, however, were characterized by high concentrations of journeymen, poor people and immigrants, and recorded living densities of more than seven occupants per house.[36]

Merchants or independent masters sometimes provided housing for highly skilled craftsmen, as in the case of the bleaching yards for fine linen cloth that were opened in Valenciennes at the end of the sixteenth century by merchants from Cambrai and Cateau-Cambrésis. They bought large plots along the river Scheldt, financed the building and equipment of the bleaching workshops and employed whitsters from Cambrai. In the 1580s and 1590s, during the take-off of fine linen production, linen workers were frequently accommodated by their

---

[34]   Archives départementales du Nord à Lille (ADN), B 12701–12702 and B 12744, registres des confiscations (1568–1574).

[35]   Y. Junot, 'Mixité sociale, habitat et propriété: la paroisse Saint-Jacques de Valenciennes en 1602 d'après un registre de 100e', *Revue du Nord*, 79/320–21 (1997): pp. 413–27; ADN, B 12744, fol. 27, B 12701, fol. 2, B 12702, fol. 62, B 12708, fol. 45v; AMV, *Série comptabilités et impôts, compte de la levée du 100e denier, paroisse Saint-Jacques* (CC), 478, fols 63–4r.

[36]   A. Lottin, *Chavatte, ouvrier lillois. Un contemporain de Louis XIV* (Paris, 1979), pp. 61–75 (source: census of 1686). See also the example of Gillebert Regnart in AMV, FF1 10, fols 79v–80.

employers.[37] Housing became a way to make migrant labour more sedentary, and to control the labour market and wages. It is notable, in this respect, that all foreign people arrested in Valenciennes on suspicion of theft or unlawful travelling at the end of the sixteenth century were active in either the new draperies (*sayetteurs, hautelisseurs*, makers of *bourats, changeants* and velvet, *epeulman*, cloth shearers) or in modest or unskilled crafts (tailors, ropemakers, cobblers, labourers), but never in linen manufacturing.[38] It is a sign that highly skilled workers in the linen industry enjoyed relatively good living and working conditions, with relatively long durations of hiring – which were in fact an exception in textile manufacturing.

Short Durations of Hiring

Guilds' charters are relatively silent about hiring conditions in workshops. The guilds were commonly open to foreigners, including temporary labour. Foreign journeymen (*ouvriers de dehors*) were welcome in most cases, on the condition of presenting a certificate of apprenticeship and paying a small entrance fee. In Lille, immigrant saymakers had to pay two *livres* to be allowed to work (statutes of 1500). In the Valenciennes woollen industry, foreign journeymen could work freely for eight days and then had to pay one *livre* to the guild (1594); immigrant pinmakers were free to work for two weeks, as were hatmakers (1579), and paid half a *livre* after that (1593); immigrant linenmakers had to pay two *sols*, a very modest sum (1587).[39] Newcomers tended to search for work from door to door as soon as they arrived. Luring away each other's workers was forbidden for masters of the same guild, yet it did occur. Rules concerning the end of the working contract were limited. The only provision was that a journeyman had to finish his piece of work at his master's place (charters of the linen weavers of 1474, charters of the fullers of cloth of 1532): he could leave his employer or the latter could give him notice as soon as the piece of work was completed on the loom.

---

[37] For example, Amé Caufourin, linen weaver (*mulquinier*) and whitster (bleacher or *bueur*) born in Cambrai, lived with Pierre Divan, a master whitster in the service of Claude de Hénin (one of the rich merchants who had settled in Valenciennes and was owner of the factory) (AMV, FF1 11, fols 82v–83r).

[38] In our sample of 40 cases in 1590–1593 and 1600–1601 (AMV, FF1 10 and 11).

[39] At the end of the sixteenth century, the nominal daily wage was 30 *sols* (i.e. 1.5 *livres*) for a master carpenter and 16 *sols* for an unskilled journeyman (Junot, *Les bourgeois de Valenciennes*, pp. 215–17).

A characteristic of the new draperies was a very short manufacturing process.[40] Hence journeymen were often employed for very short periods – a couple of weeks or months. Both immigrant and local craftsmen worked on an irregular basis, changing frequently from one employer to another. Women and children displayed the same job turnover patterns as men.[41] These short hirings by different masters were associated with journeys along urban networks connected by common industries: Lille, Tournai, Valenciennes and Mons for the *sayetteurs* and *hautelisseurs*, Valenciennes, Cambrai, Cateau-Cambrésis and Saint-Quentin for the *mulquiniers* or linen weavers. In other words, high turnover in workshops and towns was a corollary of the textile production process, in particular in the new draperies.

Fragmentation in Small Workshops

An important factor contributing to this pattern of high turnover was that textile manufacturing in the towns of the Southern Low Countries took place in small units of production.[42] The output of a cloth workshop depended on the number of looms, but urban regulations restricted the number of looms per workshop (only two looms in Valenciennes' say industry, no more than six for the production of *changeants* in Lille) and prohibited work outside the workshop.[43] It was a paternalistic type of protection against powerful individual manufacturers, aiming to distribute work among a large number of masters. That is why textile production took place in a large number of workshops run by masters who were more or less economically independent. Yet internal divisions existed. At the turn of the sixteenth century in Lille, for example, the *sayetteurs* masters were characterized by a three-tier hierarchy: an upper class of 40 to 50 masters who were the most *'puissantes en faculté'*; an intermediate group of around 2,000 masters of *'petite faculté'* who depended on their daily activities for a living; and a lower group of 200 masters who were too poor to keep their own workshops. These masters-cum-workers were needy and worked

---

[40]   H. van der Wee, 'Structural Changes and Specialization in the Industry of the Southern Netherlands, 1100–1600', *Economic History Review*, 28 (1975): pp. 203–21, and P. Chorley, 'The "draperies légères" of Lille, Arras, Tournai, Valenciennes: New Materials for New Markets?', in M. Boone and W. Prevenier (eds), *La draperie ancienne des Pays-Bas. Débouchés et stratégies de survie (14e–16e siècles)* (Leuven/Apeldoorn, 1993), pp. 151–9.

[41]   See the examples in AMV, FF1 11, fols 28v–29r and FF1 10, fol. 58v.

[42]   M. Howell and R.S. Duplessis, 'Reconsidering the Early Modern Urban Economy: The Cases of Leiden and Lille', *Past and Present*, 94 (1982): pp. 49–84.

[43]   Vanhaeck, *Histoire de la sayetterie*, pp. 90–115.

for independent masters for wages or else had to migrate, and they shared the everyday life and poverty of the masses of journeymen.[44]

These large numbers of masters – not to mention journeymen – in precarious positions permanently tried to balance worker mobility with downward pressure on wages. Textile workers were usually paid for piecework, hence the obligation to finish the piece before leaving a master – except for fullers, who were paid by the day. Wages were not fixed: the list of piece rates codified in the charters of the sergemakers of Valenciennes (1534) was an exception in local guild regulations. Consequently, master and journeyman set wages directly. Fluctuations in wages and information about them were the prime motivators of labour mobility between towns.[45] As a growing supply of labour and intensifying inter-urban competition pushed down wages, the prospect of better pay became the main reason invoked in workers' testimonies for switching masters and changing towns. Masters of small workshops were in a precarious position: they often had to pay journeymen for their work and buy the raw materials, so they had to sell their output immediately to pay their dues. They had insufficient reserves to survive a temporary slump in sales. As observed by the masters of the Lille *sayetterie* in 1603, several masters were too poor to employ journeymen, and were forced to 'beg for their bread' and to 'pawn their clothes'.[46] The precarious conditions of textile workers in turn restricted opportunities for setting up one's own business by new masters who did not have the capital required, which explains why some continued to work as journeymen after acquiring the master's grade.

In any case, the particularities of the textile production system fostered the existence of a large segment of floating workers who moved from town to town according to employment and wages. In this pattern of itinerant textile labour, personal and institutional links between workers and employers seem to have been very weak.

---

[44]   Lottin, *Chavatte*, pp. 57–8 (source: AM Lille, Affaires Générales, box 1171, d. 9).

[45]   For a general economic synthesis on the Low Countries, see H. van der Wee, 'Industrial Dynamics and the Process of Urbanization and De-Urbanization in the Low Countries from the Late Middle Ages to the Eighteenth Century: A Synthesis', in Wee (ed.), *The Rise and Decline*, pp. 307–81 (in particular pp. 327–56).

[46]   Vanhaeck, *Histoire de la sayetterie*, II, pp. 98–101 (source: AM Lille, Affaires Générales, box 1162, d. 1).

Repression, Control, Exclusion or Inclusion: Which Public Action?

How did urban authorities attempt to regulate the presence and activities of
a large floating population? Confronted with these various forms of mobility,
urban authorities were prepared to redefine their fields of activity in order to
fulfil their missions: to uphold law and order, to take care of the poor and to
protect the manufacturing system. But how did interactions between the social
order, access to municipal poor relief and the masses of textile workers living
near the poverty line shape public action towards temporary workers?

Access to Poor Relief

Textile manufacturing was closely linked to poor relief. High production levels
in manufacturing often coincided with high levels of relief dependence. After
the crisis in the light cloth industry in Tournai due to the troubles of the early
1580s, the aldermen petitioned King Philip II to revive the new draperies.
They explained that 'foreigners arrive daily to make woollen cloth in the city
in return for small change', which was beneficial for economic recovery. They
requested the establishment of a usury-free pawnshop, like a *Mont-de-Piété*, to
assist the poor.[47] Recovery was rapid and the *hautelisse* production reached a
peak around 1615. Over the same period, average municipal spending on poor
relief more than doubled, from 9,546 *livres* per year in 1593–1600 to 15,193 in
1611–1615 and 23,605 in 1616–1620.[48] In Lille, relief expenditure followed
a similar expansion from 29,938 *livres* per year in 1593–1600 to over 34,462
in 1611–1615 and 60,441 in 1616–1620 – likewise in a context of increasing
production levels.[49] Because wages in urban woollen manufacturing were so low,
workers' living conditions often depended on access to poor relief. How did the
new municipal charity institutes, created from the 1520s onwards (Lille in 1527,
Valenciennes in 1531, Tournai in 1565), regulate their access to relief provisions,
particularly in the case of immigrant workers?[50]

---

[47]   Quoted by L.P. Gachard, *Inventaire des archives des Chambres des Comptes, précédé d'une
notice historique sur ces anciennes institutions* (Brussels, 1845), vol. II, p. 147.

[48]   R.S. Duplessis, 'The Light Woollens of Tournai in the Sixteenth and Seventeenth
Centuries', in E. Aerts and J.H. Munro (eds), *Textiles of the Low Countries in European Economic
History* (Leuven, 1990), pp. 68–9 and AGR, CdC, 40010–40036.

[49]   P. Deyon and A. Lottin, 'L'évolution de la production textile à Lille aux XVIe et
XVIIe siècles', *Revue du Nord*, 49/192 (1967); A. Lottin, *Lille, citadelle de la Contre-Réforme?*
(Dunkerque, 1984), pp. 283–98, 441.

[50]   On the foundation of new municipal charity institutes, see: A. Hocquet, *Tournai et le
Tournaisis au XVIe siècle, au point de vue politique et social* (Brussels, 1906), pp. 387–93; S. Le

The official rules forbade foreigners in transit from begging, but they could stay at the city hospitals for one or two nights before continuing their journey. 'Undeserving poor' such as bandits and professional beggars had to leave town unless they 'got down to work to earn their living'. The 'deserving poor' had to reside in town for one year (in Valenciennes) or two (in Lille) to be eligible for assistance by the *Aumône générale* or *Bourse commune* (municipal charity funds). In Valenciennes it was forbidden to let houses or rooms to unemployed foreigners who were likely to be in need of assistance. When Tournai set up a *Bourse commune* in 1565, the new statute of the poor completed the rules of reception and accommodation of foreigners. There was a ban on settlement by poor immigrants, and it was prohibited to let houses and rooms without the aldermen's permission, or to give board and lodging for more than one night to vagrants or unemployed. New rules of control and traceability, such as the obligation to provide evidence of one's last place of residence and one's reason for departure by a local officer or priest, were designed to ensure a close monitoring of newcomers.

How were these official rules applied to poor migrant workers in practice? Only vagrants were liable to immediate exclusion from municipal charity. The statutes were not very clear about workers who stayed in town for a few months. The stewards of the *Aumône générale* of Valenciennes took action according to circumstances and often did not insist on the conditional length of residence. The statutes of Tournai, which were more realistic, did not even specify any residential criteria: any 'inhabitant' (*manant*) could claim municipal poor relief without delay. As one of the main functions of public charity was to maintain social stability, it could not ignore temporary migrants, who were sometimes exposed to precarious employment and wage conditions. From the end of the sixteenth century onwards, when the contribution of private charity to the *Bourse commune* decreased and expenses increased, municipal authorities raised their charity subsidies to maintain the effectiveness of poor relief. While the rules for the distribution of alms remained the same, in the early seventeenth century the aldermen of Tournai decided to restrict entitlements to relief in order to keep pace with financial resources.[51] In the crisis years of 1609–1610, for example,

Boucq, *Histoire ecclésiastique de Valenciennes* (Valenciennes, 1844), pp. 261–3; X. Renouard, *L'assistance publique à Lille de 1527 à l'an VIII* (Lille, 1912), pp. 139–44; on their administration and organization: R.S. Duplessis, 'Charité municipale et autorité publique au XVIe siècle: l'exemple de Lille', *Revue du Nord*, 59/233 (1977): pp. 193–220; Y. Junot, 'L'Aumône générale de Valenciennes (1531–1566). Ordre public, richesse et pauvreté jusqu'à la veille de la Révolte des Pays-Bas', *Revue du Nord*, 82/334 (2000): pp. 53–72.

51   AGR, CdC, 40030, fol. 138r (1613–1614). The aldermen denounced the 'great excesses in alms giving' which was considered a reason for the idleness of the poor: 'causent que les povres

they mainly gave assistance to 'poor *hautelisseurs* who are *natives* of this city and who are out of work, in order to help them to live in these calamitous times'.[52] Municipal poor relief was more flexible than the statutes prescribed. Aldermen and relief administrators were intent on guaranteeing social control and urban prosperity, and were prepared to go to great financial expense to achieve this.

Workers or Vagrants?

The aldermen's repression mainly hit vagrants, whose image had been depreciating from the late Middle Ages onwards.[53] From the 1520s, the poor laws tended to distinguish the underserving poor ('truans, brimbeurs, brimbesses, vagabonds, gens oyseux et aultres vivans sur l'aumosne des bonnes gens') from the deserving poor ('povres malades et autres indigens non puissans gaigner leur vie', 'povres enffans', 'gens honnestes non coustumiers de brimber'). But this distinction was very theoretical and in practice it was difficult to distinguish vagrants from mobile workers.[54]

How did the aldermen proceed? In the case of poverty-related offences, in order to unmask vagrants the judicial files enlist a whole range of elements constitutive of a migrant's social identity – parents' names, place of birth, completion of apprenticeship, name and address of last employer and landlord, reasons for departure, stages of travel, wages earned.[55] Pierre Vanin, born near Lille, told the aldermen of Valenciennes when he was arrested for theft in 1590 that he was a cloth shearer looking for work. In his first interrogation, he stated he had lived in Cologne. In a second interrogation, the aldermen investigated his supposed stay in Cologne: the duration (eight months), the return itinerary (via Liege and Mons), his employer (a man of the 'German nation' called 'Jean Depret', a resident in 'drapers' street') and his landlord (unknown). When asked whether Cologne had a river, Vanin answered that he had not seen one and then that he did not know ... the scenario of the textile migrant worker broke down. The third interrogation enabled the aldermen to establish that Vanin had not exercised his trade since he was banished from Lille for adultery: he wandered

---

se confians par trop sur (ces distributions) ne se mectent à travailler pour gaigner leur vye'.

[52]   AGR, CdC, 40025, fol. 142v.

[53]   J.P. Gutton, *La société et les pauvres en Europe (XVIe–XVIIIe siècles)* (Paris, 1974), pp. 93–121; B. Geremek, *La potence ou la pitié. L'Europe et les pauvres du moyen âge à nos jours* (Paris, 1987), pp. 13–15.

[54]   P. Sassier, *Du bon usage des pauvres. Histoire d'un thème politique (XVIe–XXe siècles)* (Paris, 1990), pp. 61–70.

[55]   A. Shepard, 'Poverty, Labour and the Language of Social Description in Early Modern England', *Past and Present*, 201/1 (2008): pp. 51–95.

from here to there, had lived in Düren (between Aix-la-Chapelle and Cologne) for a while and had recently earned a living by hauling boats on the River Meuse between Huy and Namur. The rest of the time, he lived on alms.[56]

Aldermen paid particular attention to migrants' skills and their guild affiliations.[57] Did they have a job? Did they know anything about a specific craft? Where had they learned their trade? Had they worked recently? The replies to the aldermen's questions about training, skill and work experience gave a portrait of the defendants. Paul Robay, who was accused of stealing clothes at his employer's farm where he was a thresher, admitted that he did not know any craft and that he was an unskilled worker (*manouvrier*). Eighteen-year old Michel Duterque from Saint-Omer, who had been arrested for attempted theft at Valenciennes market, was clearly identified as a woollen weaver. He had worked as a bobbinmaker at a weaver's workshop in Saint-Omer, and had been apprenticed to a *sayetteur* in Lille for two years. In the case of Gillebert Regnart, an aggressive 38-year old beggar covered in scabs, the aldermen tried to reconstruct his professional past prior to his 13-year long vagrant life. The man had been a *sayetteur* apprentice when he was 16 years old, and had made *changeants* for 10 years in Lille. He told his judges that he 'begged because his work was dead', but the aldermen expelled him from Valenciennes because he lived 'without doing his work' … two opposing visions, yet based on the same marker: work.[58]

The enquiries concerning the skills of workers arrested for theft or vagrancy were closely linked to a growing formalization of guild relations. During the reign of Philip II, guilds were reorganized by the aldermen, with renewal of medieval structures, increase of registration fees and intensification of religious duties. The completion of an apprenticeship and a masterpiece became compulsory requirements for becoming a master – their absence was considered anachronistic and harmful to the good reputation of the town and its manufacture. Guild structures also played a role in implementing and maintaining social cohesion.[59] Apprenticeship featured frequently in resolutions concerning poor relief. The new municipal charity system required poor children to be educated in Sunday schools and to be apprenticed at the age of 15 (Valenciennes 1531, Tournai

---

[56]   AMV, FF1 10, fols 14r, 33v–34, 41, 44r.

[57]   Peter Stabel, 'Social Mobility and Apprenticeship in Late Medieval Flanders', in Bert De Munck, Steven L. Kaplan and Hugo Soly (eds), *Learning in the Shop Floor: Historical Perspectives on Apprenticeship* (New York/Oxford: Berghahn Books, 2007), pp. 158–159.

[58]   AMV, FF1 11, fols 49, 51v, 53v, fols 18v, 20r, and FF1 10, fols 79v–80, 82.

[59]   Junot, *Les bourgeois de Valenciennes*, pp. 184–95.

1565).[60] In Tournai, the *hautelisseurs* were paid from the municipal charity funds for the boarding and training provided. Hence, young textile workers were oriented towards the urban manufacturing system by the joint efforts of municipal authorities and masters: the former aimed to limit begging and to relieve charity finances, while the latter enlarged their labour supply.

Municipal authorities punished those people who deviated from the social norms that underpinned the manufacturing system. Foreigners evading registration and 'professional' vagrants were systematically expelled. In the case of theft or debauchery, banishment was preceded by whipping. But the urban authorities could decide against banishment if an alternative sentence was considered more useful. The Cambrai-born linen weaver and bleacher Amé Caufourin, for instance, was arrested in Valenciennes in 1601 after injuring a woman. The prosecution requested he be expelled and sent to his place of birth – which was the usual sentence for injuring a burgher – but the aldermen chose another sanction – a fine and a pilgrimage – which enabled him to stay in Valenciennes.[61] Caufourin was one of the *mulquiniers*, whitsters, starchmakers and other specialized masters and journeymen who in this period were recruited from the Cambrai area to support the take-off of fine linen production in Valenciennes, an activity considered crucial to the successful redeployment of local textile manufacturing. In other words, urban authorities were rather pragmatic and selective in the implementation of repressive policies – much depended on whether they considered offenders useful to the city or not.

Migrants or Heretics?

The migrations of workers between the Southern Low Countries and the enemies of Spain – England and the Dutch Republic – induced urban authorities to be particularly watchful over returnees from Protestant countries. Crossing the borders between the Southern Low Countries on the one hand, and the Dutch Republic and England, on the other hand, was conditional upon special permission. Yet many migrants avoided the need for passports by using freeways, such as the port of Calais or Cologne. While the Spanish authorities worried that this movement of people would help to spread dissident religious ideas, at

---

[60]   The plan of action was more precise on this point in Tournai: the parish overseers of the poor 'tiendront registres des pauvres enfans en leur quartier pour iceulx faire apprendre quelque stilz, s'ilz sont en âge capable, et de les louer et obliger à demeurer aux mestiers à tel temps qu'il sera advisé, lesquelz recepvoir seront constrainctz les maistres es mestiers de ceste ville' (quoted by Hocquet, *Tournai*, p. 393).

[61]   AMV, FF1 11, fols 82v–83r.

the same time they developed a reconciliation policy to attract people from the other side.

Vigilance over newcomers increased in the 1560s with the wars of religion. The repetition of regulations concerning certificates of Catholicism and housing tickets for foreigners attests to the difficulties encountered in efficiently controlling immigration.[62] It is also illustrative of local authorities' endeavours to monitor migrations that mixed workers, unemployed, war refugees, vagrants, exiles, fugitives and religious dissenters in a context of war and religious schisms. The authorities were particularly anxious to avoid the spread of dissent in provinces that had been implicated in the Protestant revolt. An inhabitant of Tournai was punished for lodging his relatives from Arras without due registration: 'they came from England where they had resided in their youth, living the way heretics do' (1593–1594).[63] Towns were particularly watchful for migrants from the Protestant refuge, not to punish them but to control them in the context of the Spanish reconciliation policy. From 1581 onwards, inhabitants of 'rebel countries' – the Dutch Republic, as well as Flanders and Brabant until the Spanish reconquest of 1584–1585 – could apply for protection and reconciliation if they moved to the domains of the King of Spain, on condition that they observed the Catholic religion and did not support the Prince of Orange. Several types of return have been recorded. Sons of first-generation emigrants who had lived and worked in Holland and Zealand since their childhood called upon their Catholic convictions to return to the Southern Low Countries.[64] The case of people who had recently emigrated to the Dutch Republic, without parents or special permission, 'to travel around' or 'in search of a better life', was more problematical. Jean Desruielles, who had moved from Lille to Holland in 1607, repented the 'infamy' of giving up Catholicism. Noël Brabant, a *bourat* weaver who in 1606 had moved from Tournai to London and Holland, asked forgiveness for the 'youthful indiscretion' that had led him to join the Dutch garrison in Lillo near Antwerp.

The narrative in these reconciliation requests resolutely downplayed the migrants' religious and military involvement. Their accounts relate the moralistic story of the prodigal son, and they received permission to return home. The same leniency was bestowed upon Daniel Piètre when he returned to Valenciennes in 1593 after having lived in London and Leiden, where he had frequented the Calvinist church. Upon his return, he risked a death sentence for crimes against

---

62   Eighteen proclamations in Valenciennes from 1576 to 1586 (AMV, MS 734, *Règlements et ordonnances concernant la ville de Valenciennes*).

63   AGR, CdC, 40010, fol. 42v (in 1593–1594).

64   See the example of Anthoine de Hénin's reconciliation on 20 November 1600: AGR, CPE, 1421.

God and the royal laws. He was advised to plead 'immoral persuasion' and 'pressure' as an apology for leaving and participating in the Last Supper, and to renounce his heresy. His eventual sentence required him to stay in town for one year, during which he was to receive communion and go to confession every month.[65] Heresy was in fact rarely punished at the end of the sixteenth century, except in obstinate cases.[66]

In their investigations, the authorities were more intent on learning about migration patterns than on persecuting itinerant workers. Hence, interrogations of return migrants were focused on identifying contact persons and compatriots they had met in the refuge, and on reconstructing their itineraries. It was simply not viable for the manufacturing towns of the Southern Low Countries to prevent textile workers' circular migrations via England or the Dutch Republic.

Conclusions

At the time of the Dutch Revolt and its aftermath, the control of newcomers and temporary migrants formed part of a policy of social control that was also concerned with poor relief, public health, church attendance and education. Judicial proceedings and poor relief documents show how urban authorities applied different measures of social control to different sections of the floating population. One particular but large group consisted of textile workers moving along specific patterns of circular migration connecting the Southern Low Countries, England and the Dutch Republic. Geographic mobility played an important part in urban authorities' attempts to regulate their labour markets and charity finances: it ensured the smooth running of their textile industry, but implied important financial commitments towards poor relief. As a result, urban authorities were engaged in permanent attempts to balance labour needs with relief capacities. This policy forced them to apply the official line on social order – restrictive towards the poor, vagrants and Protestants – in a pragmatic and flexible way.

---

[65]   AGR, CPE 1421 and AMV, FF1 10, fols 157, 160, 164, 165v, 183r, 187r.

[66]   A. Goosens, *Les inquisitions modernes dans les Pays-Bas méridionaux 1520–1633* (Brussels, 1997), part I, pp. 176–81.

Chapter 5

Local Categories of Residence Redefined: The Former Imperial City of Strasbourg and the Politics of the French Crown (1681–1789)

Hanna Sonkajärvi

In January 1786, Strasbourg's highest royal administrator or *préteur royal*, Gérard, gave a speech before the city magistracy complaining about the complexity of local institutions and practices concerning categories of inhabitants.[1] He was struck, in particular, by the fact that *régnicoles* – subjects of the French king – could be excluded from the urban space. According to the *préteur royal*, the problem was caused by the complexity of the system that regulated the policing of foreigners, with different branches of the urban magistracy remaining responsible for defining the ways in which newcomers were admitted to urban citizenship or residence. His response to this complexity was to propose to the magistracy the establishment of a deputation to work out a reform project.[2]

What is striking about the royal administrator's proposal is that these were purely local considerations, limited to the city of Strasbourg. In 1681, Strasbourg had passed from being an imperial city (*Reichsstadt*) to being a free city under the sovereignty of the French king. Despite the French conquest, the city formed a privileged unit within the *Royaume* right up to the French Revolution. A capitulation treaty accorded by Louis XIV guaranteed the retention of local political institutions and territorial integrity. The population remained divided into three groups: the *Bürger* (those who had citizenship rights), the so-called *Schirmbürger* (those who enjoyed the protection of the city but had no political

---

[1]   Archives municipales de Strasbourg (AMS), AA 2418, n° 2.

[2]   See Vincent Denis, 'Peut-on réformer un "monument de la police"? La réforme de la police de Strasbourg en débat à la fin de l'Ancien Régime, 1782–1788', in Vincent Milliot (ed.), *Les Mémoires policiers, 1750–1850. Écritures et pratiques policières du Siècle des Lumières au Second Empire* (Rennes, 2006), pp. 131–49.

rights)[3] and those who were merely tolerated as inhabitants. This system provided the magistracy with the opportunity to decouple rights of domicile from political, economic or juridical rights. Thus even Frenchmen coming to Strasbourg after the annexation could be regarded as foreigners to the city, despite the fact that they were subjects of the same king.

A German-speaking, Lutheran city, Strasbourg was an important migratory centre, both before and after French annexation. After the French conquest, the magistracy was forced by a royal decree to extend local citizenship rights to Catholics. The annexation of the city was followed by the arrival of a Catholic bishop, the royal administration, the army and the French nobility, and this movement was accompanied by the immigration of Catholic artisans. However, only a minority of Catholic immigrants were subjects of the French king. Most were of Alsatian or German origin and came from regions surrounding the city.[4]

In the course of the eighteenth century, Strasbourg's political autonomy came to be increasingly contested by privileged subjects of the French king, royal administrators and noblemen, who refused to acknowledge the political and juridical supremacy of the Strasbourg magistracy. Thus the differing competencies of the local magistracy and the crown became objects of permanent negotiation. The existence of competing authorities, regulations and interests gave rise to numerous conflicts between the municipal authorities and different groups of foreigners. The immigrant population, in daily interaction with the local inhabitants and authorities, took part in this process of continuous redefinition of local norms and practices.

This chapter explores the effects of migration and the French annexation on local systems of citizenship (*Bürgerschaft*) and residence (*Schirmbürgerschaft*). It demonstrates how the state and the local authorities differed in their interpretations of what constituted a foreigner, and how the magistracy of Strasbourg partly succeeded in defending its own regulations despite pressure from the crown. However, even though the administration and the

---

[3]   The name *Schirmbürger* or *Schirmer* (French: *manant*) was peculiar to northern Alsace and Strasbourg. In other Alsatian and various German towns one finds the same category of inhabitants but differing nomenclature – for instance, *Hintersasse* or *Beisasse*. See Angelika Schaser, 'Städtische Fremdenpolitik im Deutschland der Frühen Neuzeit', in Alexander Demandt (ed.), *Mit Fremden leben. Eine Kulturgeschichte von der Antike bis zur Gegenwart* (Munich, 1995), pp. 137–57.

[4]   Suzanne Dreyer-Roos, *La population strasbourgeoise sous l'Ancien Régime* (Strasbourg, 1969), pp. 117–21; Bernard Vogler, 'La pénétration française en Alsace au XVIIIe siècle à travers les testaments', in *Provinces et états dans la France de l'Est. Le rattachement de la Franche-Comté à la France, espaces régionaux et espaces nationaux* (Actes du colloque de Besançon, 3– 4 October 1977) (Paris, 1979), p. 196.

categorizations of inhabitants might have nominally followed traditional patterns, local categories of residence were subjected to a significant process of redefinition in the course of the eighteenth century. In order to trace these changes, I begin by contrasting local citizenship rights with the *naturalité du royaume*, the 'citizenship' of the kingdom. This is followed by an inquiry into the admission procedures to which new urban *Bürger* were subject in practice. I then look at the diversification process that took place concerning the category of *Schirmbürger*, before turning to the efforts undertaken by privileged inhabitants to undermine the magistracy's monopoly in defining local categories of residence.

Local Citizenship: A System of Rights and Privileges Transcending the *naturalité du royaume*

As an imperial city, Strasbourg had been in a position to define its own criteria for admission to local citizenship rights. While the importance of such rights was declining or had completely ceased in many cities of the kingdom, they continued to exist to a certain degree in some parts of France, especially on the northern and eastern borders of the kingdom (in Lille, Douai, Mons, Ath, Metz and Alsace).[5] Urban citizenship was a juridical category, providing its holder with political, juridical and economic rights in exchange for a moral and fiscal commitment to the community.

In political terms, every Strasbourg citizen – artisan or not[6] – had to adhere to at least one guild[7] and could – at least in theory – gain access to the first rank of the *cursus honorum* of the magistracy at 25 years of age and after 10 years of residence (although, in practice, city politics remained the domain of

---

5   See Philippe Guignet, *Le Pouvoir dans la ville au XVIIIe siècle. Pratiques politiques, notabilité et éthique sociale de part et d'autre de la frontière franco-belge* (Paris, 1990), p. 58; Jean Imbert, 'Les rapports entre l'aubaine et la bourgeoisie en Lorraine', *Annales de l'Est*, 3 (1952): pp. 349–64; Jean Imbert, 'De quelques bourgeoisies voisines: La Bourgeoisie lorraine', in *La Bourgeoisie alsacienne. Etudes d'histoire sociale* (Strasbourg/Colmar, 1954), pp. 495–9; Gaston Zeller, 'Manants d'Alsace, derniers manants de France', in *Mélanges 1945, I. Etudes alsatiques* (Paris, 1946), pp. 111–20; Charles Wittmer, 'Les origines du droit de bourgeoisie à Strasbourg', in *La Bourgeoisie alsacienne*, pp. 49–56.

6   Doctors, lawyers, preachers and others not employed in crafts at all were required to adhere to a guild of their choice.

7   See Sabine von Heusinger, *Die Zunft im Mittelalter. Zur Verflechtung von Politik, Wirtschaft und Gesellschaft in Straßburg* (Stuttgart, 2009).

an oligarchy controlled by a small number of families).[8] Juridically, every citizen enjoyed the privilege that he or she could only be judged by urban tribunals for both criminal and civil cases.[9] However, while the Strasbourg magistracy largely succeeded in conserving its sovereignty in legal matters, royal ordinances did limit citizens' rights, especially regarding religious questions and elements of Roman law related to second marriages and wills.[10] The economic rights attached to urban citizenship remained important until the Revolution. Citizenship and the guilds were the centrepieces of municipal, economic and social life. Only citizens enjoyed the right to exercise their profession freely (provided that they observed the regulations of the profession to which they belonged), while the guilds protected their members against unfair competition and upheld monopolies and privileges. Citizens were also the only inhabitants permitted to acquire real estate in the city, and to use communal pastures. Furthermore, the charitable institutions of the city were reserved for urban citizens.

In return, citizens had a moral obligation to defend the general interests of the urban community. Their most important obligations, however, were of a fiscal nature: they were subject to the *Stallgeld*, which was a direct proportional tax calculated on the basis of a citizen's liquid and fixed assets as reported to the tax administration (the *Herrenstall*) and to the guild to which the citizen belonged. Every new citizen had to swear an oath, binding him or her to remain in the city, their physical presence thus preventing defaulting on communal charges. The obligation to defend the city was abolished as a result of the French annexation and replaced by the obligation to lodge billeted soldiers or to pay a tax for exemption from this duty.[11]

The citizens of Strasbourg, regardless of whether they were *régnicoles* or not, were not subject to the *droit d'aubaine*, the king's right to confiscate the property of foreigners who died on French soil.[12] In the years following the annexation, there was some confusion regarding this question, for instance in the case of Jacob Hoser, who was a citizen of Strasbourg and of Swiss origin. His father,

---

[8]   Paul Greissler, *La classe politique dirigeante à Strasbourg, 1650–1750* (Strasbourg, 1987), pp. 49–72.

[9]   If the cost of the latter did not exceed 1,000 livres. See Georges Livet, 'Une enquête à ouvrir. Justice, police et délinquance dans les villes d'Alsace sous l'Ancien Régime', *Annales de l'Est*, 48 (1998): pp. 361–81.

[10]   Bernard Vogler, 'La vie économique et les hiérarchies sociales', in Georges Livet and Francis Rapp (eds), *Histoire de Strasbourg des origines à nos jours*, vol. 3. *Strasbourg de la guerre de Trente Ans à Napoléon, 1618–1815* (Strasbourg, 1981), pp. 189–90.

[11]   Dreyer-Roos, *La population*, p. 33.

[12]   See Jean-François Dubost, 'Étrangers en France', in Lucien Bély (ed.), *Dictionnaire de l'Ancien Régime, Royaume de France, XVIe–XVIIIe siècle* (Paris, 1996), pp. 518–22.

an emigrant from Augsburg, had been given trading rights in the city as if he were a citizen as early as 1629.[13] It was only in 1678 that the family acquired citizenship rights, under pressure from the Merchants' guild. When Hoser, died in 1701, the royal tax collectors tried to seize his fortune by claiming that he was a Calvinist and born in Geneva. He had been separated from his wife and had no children, so that his business associate Johann Niklaus Herff, a Calvinist citizen of Strasbourg living in Basle, was to inherit his fortune.[14] The *intendant* of Alsace, de la Houssaye, judged that Hoser's possessions could not fall under the *droit d'aubaine* because both Hoser and Herff had become citizens of Strasbourg before the French conquest and, under the city's capitulation treaty, its citizens were not subject to the *droit d'aubaine*.[15] In fact, the formal exemption of Strasbourg citizens from the *droit d'aubaine* was only declared by the highest court of Alsace, the *Conseil souverain d'Alsace*, in 1691.[16] Thus, while the city could refuse to receive the subjects of the king into local citizenship, admission to the Strasbourg burghership made individuals born outside the kingdom (*aubains*) immune to the *droit d'aubaine*.[17]

Access to Local Citizenship (the *Bürgerschaft*)

Religion as a Means of Inclusion and Exclusion

Access to urban citizenship depended not only on a candidate's economic means and familial links but also on his or her social status, profession, religious

---

[13]   AMS, AA 2163.

[14]   On Herff and Hoser's business, see Peter Hertner, *Stadtwirtschaft zwischen Reich und Frankreich. Wirtschaft und Gesellschaft Straßburgs 1650–1714* (Cologne/Vienna, 1973), pp. 347–9.

[15]   Archives du ministère de la guerre à Vincennes (SHAT), A¹1501, n° 335 and n° 336; A¹ 1503, n° 125 and n° 126.

[16]   François Henri de Boug (ed.), *Recueil des édits, déclarations, lettres patentes, arrêts du Conseil d'État et du Conseil souverain d'Alsace, Ordonnances & Règlemens [sic] concernant cette Province* (Colmar, 1775), vol. 1, p. 201, 'Arrêt du Conseil d'État qui exempte les Bourgeois de Strasbourg du Droit d'Aubaine, le 15 décembre 1691'.

[17]   As early as 1662, the French crown had accorded *naturalité* to Catholic foreigners in order to promote the repopulation of Alsace after the Thirty Years' War. However, given that the city of Strasbourg was not part of the French kingdom in 1662, this royal ordinance could not be applied in the former imperial city in a retroactive manner. See Jennifer Ngaire Heuer, *The Family and the Nation: Gender and Citizenship in Revolutionary France, 1789–1830* (Ithaca/London, 2005), pp. 175–6, who confirms that, in 1790, the Strasbourg municipal council still referred to urban citizenship as the means of being recognized as French.

confession and personal connections. Religious and confessional affiliations were the main factors in defining an individual's place in Strasbourg, both before and after the French annexation. The multiconfessional city of Strasbourg therefore constitutes an exception within the French context. Parallels can, however, be found on the opposite side of the Rhine, in the Holy Roman Empire. In numerous German cities, access to local citizenship rights was limited to members of one religion (*Religionsverwandte*).[18] On the other hand, the territory of the Empire also counted important cities such as Augsburg and Mannheim, where Catholics and Protestants coexisted.[19] In Strasbourg, where the dominance of Lutherans over Reformed was transformed, through the French conquest, into a system of apparent equality between Lutherans and Catholics and of limited tolerance of Calvinists, confession played an important role in the process of identifying individuals or groups of individuals as foreigners at the local level.

The diverse confessional and religious groups had distinct legal statuses in the city. Before 1681, only Lutherans and Calvinists (the latter with certain restrictions such as higher fees and ineligibility for municipal offices) were admitted to local citizenship.[20] The capitulation treaty of the city guaranteed the rights of these two communities, but the French annexation opened up urban citizenship to Catholics as well.[21] The interests of the crown and the city with regard to Calvinists seemed to coincide: the latter's access to the *Schirmbürgerschaft* was temporarily barred by a royal decree between 1698 and 1718, and they could apply for burghership only if they could prove a personal wealth that was more than three times higher than that required of Lutherans and Catholics.[22] Jews had no residence rights in the city at all and, even at the end of the eighteenth century, the magistracy refused to give residence rights

---

[18]   Ulrich-Christian Pallach, 'Fonctions de la mobilité artisanale et ouvrière: Compagnons, ouvriers et manufacturiers en France et aux Allemagnes (17e–19e siècles)', *Francia*, 11 (1983): p. 375.

[19]   See Étienne François, *Protestants et catholiques en Allemagne. Identités et pluralisme. Augsbourg 1648–1806* (Paris, 1993).

[20]   On the difficult standing of the Calvinists, see Adolf Maeder, *Notice historique sur la paroisse réformée de Strasbourg et recueil de pièces probantes* (Paris and Strasbourg, 1885, 2nd edn); Hanna Sonkajärvi, *Qu'est-ce qu'un étranger? Frontières et identifications à Strasbourg (1681–1789)* (Strasbourg, 2008), pp. 87–95.

[21]   AMS, AA 2118. The revocation of the Edict of Nantes was never applied to Alsace, since the edict was never introduced there in the first place, Alsace not having been part of the French kingdom: see Christian Pfister, 'L'Alsace et l'Édit de Nantes', *Revue historique*, 160 (1929): p. 225.

[22]   A value of 300 florins (600 livres) for the Lutherans and 1,000 florins (2,000 livres) for the Calvinists in 1665. In 1728 the amount was raised to 500 florins (1,000 livres) for the Lutherans and Catholics and to 1,500 florins (3,000 livres) for the Calvinists: see Dreyer-Roos, *La population*, p. 35.

to the army supplier Cerf Berr, although he had acquired naturalization letters from the French king.[23] The magistracy denied his claim by stating that, even if he were treated like any other subject of the king, the fact that he was a Jew would prevent him from becoming an inhabitant, since the city traditionally did not accept Jews.[24]

In 1686, both the *intendant* of Alsace and the *préteur royal* of Strasbourg received instructions from the secretary of war, Louvois, to reduce the burghership fees required of Catholics to a third of those required of Lutherans.[25] The magistracy responded to this by an equal reduction for the Lutherans and by a general elevation of the minimum fortune required. The following year, a royal ordinance established the *Alternative*, meaning that the offices in the magistracy and the municipal administration were to be filled alternately by Catholics and Lutherans.[26] The *Alternative* was by no means a French innovation and parallels can again be found in the Holy Roman Empire: the case of Augsburg, where parity was introduced as a principle for the distribution of municipal charges between Catholics and Lutherans in 1648, is not without similarities to Strasbourg.[27] In the Alsatian city of Colmar (annexed to France in 1648), the *Alternative* had been introduced by the French crown in 1680.[28] In Strasbourg, the introduction of the *Alternative* triggered, especially during the first three decades of French rule, a wave of conversions to Catholicism among individuals who wanted to become eligible for the municipal offices and enter the ruling oligarchy of the magistracy.[29] In 37 years, from 1681 to 1718, burghership admissions increased by 77 per cent; after 1690, however, the rate of accretion dropped significantly. Whereas until 1730 citizens had made up more than half of the total population, at the end of the eighteenth century they only accounted for about 40 per cent.[30] Citizen status lost its attraction as soon as the Catholic elite had installed itself in the oligarchic magistracy and newcomers saw no chance of entering the municipal offices.

---

[23]   AMS, AA 2380. On the Jews of Alsace, see Freddy Raphaël and Robert Weyl, *Regards nouveaux sur les juifs d'Alsace* (Strasbourg, 1980); Hanna Sonkajärvi, 'Les Juifs à Strasbourg au XVIIIème siècle. Enjeux d'inclusion et exclusion', *Annales de l'Est*, 57 (2007): pp. 297–311.

[24]   AMS, AA 2380.

[25]   SHAT, A¹ 773.

[26]   See Louis Châtellier, *Tradition chrétienne et renouveau catholique dans le cadre de l'ancienne diocèse de Strasbourg (1650–1770)* (Paris, 1981).

[27]   See François, *Protestants et catholiques*.

[28]   See Peter G. Wallace, *Communities and Conflict in Early Modern Colmar, 1575–1730* (Atlantic Highlands NJ, 1995).

[29]   Greissler, *La classe politique dirigeante*, pp. 245–6.

[30]   Dreyer-Roos, *La population*, pp. 48–51.

Despite the crown's efforts to encourage Catholic immigration, and despite the fact that Catholic inhabitants outnumbered Lutherans by 1750, the numbers of Lutheran and Catholic citizens remained very unequal. In 1789, when the number of Catholic citizens was at its peak, 74 per cent of the *Bürger* were still Lutheran, but only 24 per cent were Catholics. In fact, 52 per cent of the Catholics were simple inhabitants without official status.[31]

Catholics also continued to be excluded from certain offices and guilds. Some guilds stuck to their German traditions and refused to acknowledge the status of master if it had been attained in another city of the French kingdom.[32] The influx of francophone and, in particular, Catholic migrants therefore led to the establishment of parallel guild organizations, such as the 'French' and 'German' carpenters, and also to marginalization within some of the guilds.[33] In general terms, the guilds covering traditional crafts were those which offered the most resistance to newcomers.[34]

On the other hand, many of the *régnicole* immigrants also belonged to privileged groups, such as royal administrators, members of the Catholic Church and army officials. For reasons that will be explained in more detail below, these individuals had no interest whatsoever in becoming citizens or joining a guild, as this would have obliged them to pay municipal taxes and, even more importantly, placed them under the authority of the magistracy.

The Accordance of Citizenship Rights in Practice

Citizenship rights could be obtained by hereditary transmission, purchase or marriage. The transmission was free for children of citizens, but only children born after the acquisition of citizenship rights by the father could inherit his

---

[31]   In 1789 there were 25,300–25,700 Catholics in the city and 22,200–22,500 Lutherans (Dreyer-Roos, *La population*, pp. 99–100).

[32]   On the practices of inclusion and exclusion in connection with guilds, see the recent article by Simona Cerutti, 'Travail, mobilité et légitimité. Suppliques au roi dans une société d'Ancien Régime (Turin XVIIIe siècle)', *Annales. Histoire, Sciences Sociales*, 65/3 (2010): pp. 571–611.

[33]   See Hanna Sonkajärvi, 'From German-speaking Catholics to French Carpenters: Strasbourg Guilds and the Role of Confessional Boundaries in the Inclusion and Exclusion of Foreigners in the Eighteenth Century', *Urban History*, 35/2 (2008): pp. 202–15; Françoise Lévy-Coblentz, *L'Art du meuble en Alsace au siècle des Lumières*, vol. 2. *De la paix de Ryswick à la Révolution (1698–1789)* (Saint-Dié, 1985), especially pp. 121–42; Ernst Polaczek, 'Das Handwerk der französischen Schreiner der Stadt Strassburg', *Elsässische Monatsschrift für Geschichte und Volkskunde*, 1 (1910): pp. 321–30.

[34]   Vogler, 'La vie économique', pp. 204–5; Dreyer-Roos, *La population*, pp. 132–4.

status.[35] Those born before had to pay a reduced fee in order to become citizens. When a citizen's status was acquired by purchase, the magistracy tried to ensure that the applicant would not become a burden on the city's charitable institutions. The applicant was therefore required to have a certain amount of property, to exercise a profession that could feed his or her family and to pay the tax for the acquisition of citizenship, called the *Bürgerschilling*.[36]

Admission to the citizenry was not necessarily expensive. The magistracy could decide to admit artists, intellectuals or domestics as a favour, at a reduced rate or even for free. Servants who had served the same *Bürger* or a citizen's widow for seven (later six) consecutive years were admitted free of charge.[37] Members of the nobility were also admitted for a reduced tariff or for free. In the eighteenth century, marriage became the most common way of gaining citizenship: the proportion of new citizens via marriage grew from 39 per cent in 1700 to 68 per cent in 1768. Whereas at the beginning of the century men were the ones to acquire citizenship by marriage, this tendency changed over time and, in 1786, almost all women granted citizen status had married a citizen.[38] Access to citizenship by marriage required explicit permission from the magistracy,[39] but a foreigner to the city who married a citizen and aspired to citizenship either paid the reduced tariff, called the *Alte Bürgerschilling*, or could even be received free of charge.[40]

The restrictions relating to admission provoked various types of abuse, as can be seen from the numerous memoranda dedicated to the reform of both citizenship and *Schirmbürgerschaft*. The constant repetition of the same problems suggests that little changed, despite all these reform projects. Given that the sum of money to be deposited before the magistracy in order to obtain citizenship was high, candidates would often try to borrow the required amount, or they might simply fake the appearance of wealth, presenting certificates from their place of origin that attested their pretended richness.[41] The candidates might also beg or purchase certificates from important public figures in order to be received as citizens free of charge.[42]

These kinds of practices seem to illustrate the importance of socially constructed categories of honour, appearance, reputation and confidence in

---

[35] Greissler, *La classe politique dirigeante*, p. 122.

[36] Dreyer-Roos, *La population*, p. 35.

[37] AMS, AA 2106, n° 10.

[38] Dreyer-Roos, *La population*, pp. 41–3.

[39] AMS, AA 2106, n° 5.

[40] Dreyer-Roos, *La population*, p. 42.

[41] AMS, AA 2106, n° 10.

[42] Ibid.

the social organization of the *ancien régime*. A perfect demonstration of the idea of correspondence between appearance and honour is provided in a 1768 memorandum of the magistracy, which concerns reform of the citizenship requirements. Although the memorandum begins with an exposition of the frauds that people committed in order to simulate an appearance of wealth, it still explicitly states that the magistracy reserved the right to admit persons of dignity or persons whose wealth was of common knowledge without subjecting them to an oath or verification of their economic means.[43] It was equally common practice for servants to be admitted earlier than was legally admissible because the regulations were not always followed to the letter: masters would sign certificates without the years of service having been fully observed.

Additionally, a *bourgeoisie foraine* – a group of citizens who did not permanently live within Strasbourg's territory but who still managed to remain citizens – appears to have existed *de facto*, even though the magistracy took great care not to recognize it officially.[44] The most notable group of such citizens consisted of merchants, who accumulated citizenship rights in various cities in order to do business. However, wealthy merchants and manufacturers often preferred not to purchase citizenship rights in order to avoid having to pay fees for renouncing their previous citizenship in a different city, or in order not to lose the benefits already acquired in their former city of residence. For instance, Étienne Romanet, a Savoyard from Chambery who exercised the trade of *limonadier* in Strasbourg, purchased only *Schirmbürger* status because he already held citizenship in Besançon.[45]

Like other foreigners to the city, the Swiss were obliged to apply for local citizenship if they wanted to reside or do business in Strasbourg. This was demanded of Johann Stähelin in 1691, a *Schirmbürger* in Strasbourg and citizen of Basle who was acting as a merchant without being a citizen or member of a guild. The guild of merchants pressured him to join the guild and to become a citizen even though, according to the alliance treaty between the French crown and the Swiss cantons, any Swiss person had the right to establish himself freely in France and to trade.[46] After having first tried to persuade the magistracy to accept his wife as a member of the merchants' guild in his place,[47] Stähelin finally obtained an exception from the magistracy because he explained that he would have to pay a 10 per cent tax on his inheritance from his father if he gave up

---

43 Ibid.

44 AMS, AA 2220, nº 12.

45 Georges Livet, 'Une page d'histoire sociale. Les Savoyards à Strasbourg au début du XVIIIe siècle', *Cahiers d'histoire*, 4 (1959): p. 141.

46 AMS, AA 2163.

47 AMS, XI 276, fol. 492.

his citizenship rights in Basle.[48] *Schirmbürger* Stähelin thus profited from his status as a citizen of Basle, since he was liberated from the *capitation* in France[49] and gained the benefit of his double affinity, combining privileges as a Swiss merchant with the right to trade in Strasbourg as if he were a citizen.[50]

Schirmbürger and Tolerated Inhabitants

The *Schirmbürgerschaft* was an intermediate category of inhabitants between citizens (*Bürger*) and foreigners to the city (*Fremde*). Every person – with the exception of students – who stayed in the city for more than 14 days was obliged to register at the municipal *Schirmgericht*. This chamber convened four times a week and received candidates to the *Schirmbürgerschaft* after having examined 'leurs pièces ou documents nécessaires comme extraits baptistaires, de mariages, services, ou autres produits pour cet effet.'[51] At this point, the aspirants had to provide a registration fee deposited by a citizen or a *Schirmbürger*.

For the city, the *Schirmbürgerschaft* provided an important means of controlling newcomers. Once a residence permit had been granted, the *Schirmbürger* were obliged to swear an oath and to promise to behave 'en bons chrétiens mariés, et en fidèles sujets du Roy'.[52] They had to recognize the legal sovereignty of the magistracy and promise to keep the *Schirmgericht* informed about their current domicile, as well as pay the *Schirmgeld* tax regularly. *Schirmbürger* could also be subjected to providing housing for billeted soldiers. In return, they had the right to be protected by the city, but they were excluded from communal property. They were equally excluded from the guilds and from charitable institutions, which were reserved for citizens.[53]

The institution of *Schirmbürgerschaft* has been little studied because the protocols of the *Schirmgericht* have not been conserved in the archives. However, some traces of the administrative practices linked to the *Schirmbürgerschaft* can be found in the archives of the *intendant* and of the *préteur royal*. It is therefore

---

48   Ibid., fol. 478; AMS, AA 2163.

49   The *capitation* was a direct tax which was to be paid by subjects of the French king. Had Stähelin become a citizen of Strasbourg, he would have counted as a *régnicole*. Hertner, *Stadtwirtschaft*, p. 34.

50   In 1724, Stähelin's name appeared on a list of Swiss merchants who were allowed to export cash out of France: Archives nationales, Paris (AN), G⁷ 83, n° 100 and n° 102.

51   'Their necessary papers or documents such as certificates of birth, marriage, service, or other items serving this purpose' (AMS, AA 2418, n° 11; AA 2418, n° 25).

52   'Like good married Christians and faithful subjects of the king' (AMS, AA 2418, n° 1).

53   Zeller, 'Manants d'Alsace', pp. 111–13.

possible to establish, from the admission fees in 1750 and 1769, that a difference was observed between 'étrangers', 'régnicoles' and 'enfants d'icy'.[54] Thus, a memorandum from Dreyer, clerk of the *Schirmgericht*, indicates that, from the magistracy's point of view, subjects of the king were not to be treated on equal terms with local inhabitants.[55] Rather, they constituted a special category, set between foreigners and local inhabitants. In fact, it remains unclear whether the term 'enfants d'icy' refers to descendants of the city's inhabitants or to all Alsatians. What the memorandum clearly demonstrates, however, is that the primary line of distinction was not that between national categories of *régnicoles* and *étrangers*.

The status of *Schirmbürger* underwent a process of diversification in the course of the eighteenth century. The French annexation and the growing mobility of the population provoked the introduction of other forms of *Schirmbürgerschaft* alongside the traditional status. The magistracy decided to tolerate a new group of *Schirmbürger* who were temporary workers engaged in manufactories or who exercised liberal arts. These *Temporal-Schirmer* could live in the city for a limited period of time against the yearly payment of a moderate fee. In 1758, for instance, *intendant* Lucé intervened and asked the *préteur royal* to arrange for 500 to 600 canvas-manufacture workers, based on the outskirts of the city, to be exempted from the *Schirmbürgerschaft* even if they spent their nights in the city.[56] The practice of the *Temporal-Schirm* thus provided the magistracy with a flexible, non-codified means of keeping track of immigrants.

When the magistracy decided to abolish the *Temporal-Schirm* in about 1778, the growing number of inhabitants who did not pay any fees and who were not registered were grouped under the administrative heading of *simples domiciliés*. Suzanne Dreyer-Roos estimates that the number of such inhabitants was 100–200 families in 1697 and about 3,000–4,500 persons in 1789.[57] The magistracy seems to have realized very rapidly that the abolition of the *Temporal-Schirm* did not put an end to the existence of this group of mostly lower-income and highly mobile individuals, and that these people continued to reside in the city. What the abolition did mean, however, was that the magistracy had no means at all of monitoring the number and quality of these individuals. This is why a project for the reintroduction of the *Temporal-Schirm* appeared just a few years after the abolition, around the mid-1780s. The magistracy envisioned a temporary tolerance, notably for workers in the service of royal authorities.[58]

54   Archives départementales du Bas-Rhin à Strasbourg, C 581, n° 109.
55   AMS, AA 2418, n° 11.
56   AMS, AA 2418, n° 8.
57   Dreyer-Roos, *La population*, p. 62.
58   AMS, AA 2419.

The Undermining of Local Citizenship by Privileged Inhabitants

The Strasbourg nobility, who played a rather restricted role in a city dominated by guilds, gained new members after the French conquest and constituted a very heterogeneous group of citizen-nobles, churchmen, military commanders, royal administrators and members of the Immediate Nobility of Lower Alsace (*Directoire de la noblesse de la Basse Alsace*). Except for the citizen-nobles, all escaped the magistracy's jurisdiction – often their entire households, including servants.[59] The citizen-nobles, or *Constoffler*, were part of the urban patriciate,[60] but since 1482 they had always been in the minority within the different bodies of the magistracy. They were organized into two groups – *Zum Hohensteg* and *Zum Mühlstein* – which represented their interests alongside the 18 guilds of the city. Special political functions were accorded to the nobles: the representative function of *Stettmeister* and one-third of the seats in the Senate and the different secret chambers of the magistracy.[61] The highest official honours were reserved for the noble *Stettmeisters*; but the *Ammeister*, or real administrative chief, was a commoner.

A second and growing group of noble residents consisted of members of the Immediate Nobility of Lower Alsace. This imperial nobility or *Reichsritterschaft* had capitulated to the French king in 1680, before the annexation of Strasbourg, and had obtained extensive privileges. They lacked political rights in the community because they were not citizens, but they had their own jurisdiction. Letters patent issued by Louis XIV in 1681 entitled them to hear civil cases involving any of its members, up to a value of 500 livres, while appeals were to be handled by the *Conseil souverain d'Alsace*. In 1756, there were 24 members of this *Directoire de la noblesse de la Basse Alsace* in Strasbourg.[62]

The French conquest also brought with it French administrators and military commanders who resided in Strasbourg. Overall, the nobles constituted about 1 per cent of the city's population.[63] In 1704, there were 70 noble households

---

[59]   See Hanna Sonkajärvi, 'Un groupe privilégié de domestiques dans la ville de Strasbourg au XVIIIème siècle. Les Suisses portiers d'hôtels', in Bruno Bernard and Xavier Stevens (eds), *La domesticité au siècle des Lumières. Une approche comparative* (Brussels, 2009), pp. 15–23.

[60]   See Ingrid Bátori, 'Das Patriziat in der deutschen Stadt. Zu den Forschungsergebnissen über das Patriziat besonders der süddeutschen Städte', *Zeitschrift für Stadtgeschichte, Stadtsoziologie und Denkmalpflege*, 2 (1975): pp. 1–30.

[61]   Greissler, *La classe politique dirigeante*, p. 80.

[62]   Erich Pelzer, *Der elsässische Adel im Spätfeudalismus. Tradition und Wandel einer regionalen Elite zwischen dem westfälischen Frieden und der Revolution (1648–1790)* (Munich, 1990), p. 126.

[63]   Ibid., p. 10.

in the city; this rose to 97 in 1726 and 112 in 1730.[64] The growth is explained by immigration, since ennoblements were rare in Strasbourg. While the citizen-nobles were of modest income and the richest noble members of the magistracy could not compete in wealth with their bourgeois colleagues, exclusive flair was brought into the city by the bishop and foreign princes establishing residences (*hôtels*) in Strasbourg.

The growing presence of non-citizen nobles affected the logic of the city's way of classifying its inhabitants. The possession of real estate being conditional on citizen status, the magistracy came under pressure to develop other categories of *Schirmbürgerschaft* in order to meet the needs of the growing privileged population, who had no interest in becoming citizens but who wanted to buy houses and to settle in the city. Whereas the citizen-nobles remained attached to the system of the *Bürgerschaft* and contributed to the city's economy by paying the *Stallgeld*, the immediate nobles, the administrators and the military commanders only paid *Real-Schirmgeld*, which was a land tax (*impôt foncier*) linked to the acquisition price of land.[65] Their presence led to continual disputes because they did not always respect the rules set for this category of inhabitants. For instance, the immediate nobility was allowed to buy houses in Strasbourg, but with a prohibition against reselling them to non-citizens without the permission of the magistracy. Furthermore, many of the nobles in Strasbourg claimed to be exempted from the obligation to provide accommodation for military personnel and rented parts of their residences to other people, who then would pretend to be exempted from such obligations as well. A certain number of nobles who did not see any value in being either citizen or *Schirmbürger* simply opted out, claiming that, as subjects of the French king, they had the right to live on the city's territory even without recognizing the magistracy's sovereignty, and thus without paying local taxes.[66] In fact, in 1776, the magistracy counted 29 houses in the possession of non-citizens who did not pay the yearly *Real-Schirmgeld*.[67]

These kinds of problems occurred as early as 1713. In that year, a *sieur* Berquen, who had bought an estate in Ruprechtsau, in the *bailliage* of Strasbourg, demanded an exemption from the *taille réelle* and *droit du manance* (that is, the *Real-Schirmgeld* and the *Schirmbürgerschaft*) on the grounds that the estate in question was an ancient fief of Hanau.[68] The magistracy refused

---

[64] The total number of inhabitants was about 36,000 in 1730: Ingeborg Streitberger, *Der Königliche Prätor von Straßburg, 1685–1789* (Wiesbaden, 1961), p. 381.

[65] Dreyer-Roos, *La population*, pp. 62–3.

[66] AMS, AA 2106 n° 11. See also Dreyer-Roos, *La population*, p. 45.

[67] AMS, AA 2528.

[68] See Georges Livet, 'La monarchie absolue et la bourgeoisie Alsacienne. D'après les fonds notariaux et les registres des Magistrats', in *La Bourgeoisie alsacienne*, pp. 495–9.

because non-citizens were not allowed to buy land without its permission. Berquen unsuccessfully tried to argue that he was a French *citoyen* and that, since the members of the *Directoire de la noblesse de la Basse Alsace* were accorded the right to acquire estates in Strasbourg without becoming citizens, he – as a *commissaire ordinaire d'artillerie* – was just as entitled to do so.[69]

The magistracy also complained about army officers who married citizens and thus gained access to real estate, which could otherwise only be acquired by citizens. In 1781, the magistracy listed six Swiss officers who had married citizens; the list also contains three other officers, two noble ones and one qualified by the magistracy as someone 'qui prétend être noble'.[70] Instead of becoming citizens, the soldiers claimed to be exempt from municipal taxes because they enjoyed Swiss privileges. In 1767, the magistracy was ordered by the crown to demand neither the *vingtième* nor the *capitation* from the Swiss, as long as they did not enjoy any income other than their salaries. Instead, a line was drawn by the crown between persons born on Swiss soil and those who had merely taken up residence in a Swiss canton. The order explicitly stated that Alsatians who had become members of a Swiss canton could not claim these privileges.[71]

On the other side, some Strasbourg citizens argued that, even if they renounced their citizenship rights, they would still have the right to live in the city since they were subjects of the French king.[72] Accordingly, in January 1783, the *préteur royal* of Strasbourg received a memorandum from a certain *sieur* Salzmann, 'conseiller aulique du Prince régnant de Linange-Dabo',[73] who wanted to renounce his citizenship, which, according to him, was 'de pure perte'.[74] Salzmann asked for authorization to be exempted from the oath demanded by the magistracy of everyone who wanted to surrender their *Bürger* status. This oath required the applicant to leave the city within a month. If he or she were to return, they would be considered as a stranger, who must stay in an *auberge* and who was not to have their own house – or, to put it in the magistracy's terms, 'n'aiant ni son propre feu ni sa propre lumière'.[75]

Salzmann asked for an exemption in exchange for his willingness to continue to pay the yearly *capitation* and his quota for the *Conseil souverain* in Colmar and in Lauternec. These taxes were, of course, royal fees, and Salzmann would thus have escaped the municipal taxes. As a consequence, the Grand Senate

---

69   AMS, AA 2206, n° 6.
70   'Pretending to be noble' (AMS, AA 2528).
71   AMS, AA 2616.
72   AMS, AA 2106 n° 11.
73   'Aulic councillor of the count of Linange-Dabo [Leiningen-Dagsburg]' (ibid.).
74   'Of no use' (ibid.).
75   'Having neither his own fire nor his own light' (ibid.).

refused to accord the exemption. Salzmann was scandalized by the fact that, according to the oath that he was obliged to take, he would be treated 'moins favorablement qu'un étranger' if he returned to Strasbourg.[76] He claimed that he had the right to stay in the city, this right being established by the fact that he was a subject of the French king:

> Lorsque la ville de Strasbourg était une ville libre impériale, & que la souveraineté résidait encore dans le Magistrat, la qualité de sujet était réunie à celle de Bourgeois, et il était naturel que tous ceux qui renonçaient au droit de Bourgeoisie cessoient en même tems [sic] d'être sujets, le Magistrat de Strasbourg pouvait donc les regarder avec raison, comme Etrangers & les faire quitter la ville, mais depuis l'heureuse Epoque que le Roi a acquis la souveraineté, un Bourgeois, qui renonce au Privilège de la Bourgeoisie, ne peut pas être regardé comme un simple Etranger, puisqu'en cessant d'etre bourgeois il ne cesse pas d'etre sujet du Roi, & il semble par ces raisons que le Magistrat de Strasbourg n'est point fondé de faire sortir un sujet du Roi d'une ville ou il est né sans d'autres raisons que parce qu'il ne veut plus jouir d'un Privilège; un acte d'autorité pareil ne convient qu'à la Puissance Suprême.[77]

> [At the time when the city of Strasbourg was a free imperial city, and the magistracy still held sovereignty, to be a subject was to be a citizen, and it was natural that all those who renounced their citizenship rights would at the same time cease to be subjects. The magistracy of Strasbourg therefore had the right to consider them foreigners and make them leave the city; but, since the happy era when the king acquired the sovereignty, a citizen who renounces the privilege of citizenship cannot simply be considered as a foreigner because in ceasing to exist as a citizen he does not cease being a subject of the king, and it seems, therefore, that the magistracy of Strasbourg has no firm foundation for making a subject of the king leave the city where he was born without other reason than that he no longer wishes to enjoy the privilege [of citizenship]. An act of such authority is proper to the supreme power alone.]

Salzmann thus explicitly referred to his status as a subject of the king, a status that, according to him, was of higher value than local citizenship. The statements given to the magistracy by the three general advocates – who said that tolerating the presence of Salzmann in the city would imply a re-establishment of the *Temporal-Schirm* – explains the magistracy's insistence on this matter. In fact, the issue was not only that Salzmann wanted to continue living in the city. The magistracy could have tolerated this, just as it did in the case of important

---

[76] 'Less favourably than a foreigner' (ibid.).

[77] Ibid.

personages. Rather, the problem was caused by Salzmann's refusal to take the oath, because abandoning the status of citizen without the oath meant not recognizing the legal sovereignty of the magistracy.[78] Naturally, the magistracy had no interest whatsoever in establishing a precedent guaranteed to encourage others to give up their citizen status. In fact, the case of Salzmann was not unique: five other people renounced their citizenship of Strasbourg between 1781 and 1784 while continuing to live in the city.[79]

Conclusion

The city of Strasbourg was a privileged entity which functioned according to its own constitution and political institutions, whose maintenance was guaranteed by the capitulation treaty and the magistracy's monopoly of jurisdiction over the inhabitants. Given that an increasing number of people were escaping this very jurisdiction, the defence of civic autonomy became an issue that was negotiated and redefined in everyday actions that led to significant modifications regarding local categories of residence.

Clearly, the French state and the local authorities had different interpretations of what constituted a foreigner. The state defined the foreigner by birth outside its borders, whereas, for cities, definition of who was foreign offered an important means of differentiation within the community. Even though a growing proportion of inhabitants remained outside the local citizenship system, and even though this system experienced a certain diversification during the eighteenth century, the population of Strasbourg remained divided into the three groups of *Bürger*, *Schirmbürger* and inhabitants without rights or protection until the French Revolution.

Religion was an important means of differentiation. It provided for a partial exclusion of Calvinists, in which the interests of the city and the crown seem to have coincided. Even though Catholics had access to local citizenship after the French annexation, this did not automatically mean that they were treated on the same footing as Lutherans in everyday life. This was most notably not the case in guild life, where arguments based on religion often coincided with economic interests. Religion also proved an effective means of excluding Jews from residence rights in the city. The magistracy even refused to acknowledge the letters patent accorded by the crown that should have assimilated one Jew to the *régnicoles*.

---

[78] Ibid.

[79] Dreyer-Roos, *La population*, p. 45.

However, even though categories of residence nominally remained the same after 1681, their boundaries shifted and the meanings accorded by different individuals to the *Schirmbürgerschaft* changed over time. This chapter has demonstrated how the Strasbourg categories of residence were contested and gradually undermined by different individuals and groups who did not want to recognize the legal authority of the magistracy or who were not prepared to pay local taxes. In these disputes, the argument of *naturalité* was used, but what in the end seems to have weighed more in conflicts with the magistracy were the social status and privileges of the person in question, and the status of those individuals who backed his or her claims.

PART II
Instruments of Regulation:
Policies and Policing

Chapter 6

Who Is Not Welcome?
Reception and Rejection of Migrants in Early Modern Italian Cities

Eleonora Canepari

This chapter focuses on the reactions of Italian urban authorities towards migrant workers and on the connections between newcomers' integration and their reputations from the sixteenth to eighteenth centuries. The analysis of ordinances and other institutional sources shows that regulatory interventions did not target immigrants because of their foreignness. Rather, ordinances dealing with migrants can be divided in two categories. The first was concerned mainly with urban resources; in these ordinances, migrant workers were seen as either competitors for local resources or potential contributors to the local economy.[1] The second targeted unsettled migrant groups, lumped together under the label of vagrants. The chapter concentrates on these two main concerns of early modern Italian city authorities vis-à-vis immigrants.

In the context of early modern Italian cities, foreignness is not a useful concept to understand migration policies. The approach that implies a strong difference between immigrants and native inhabitants has exerted a great influence on the historiography of migrations: many studies have concentrated on chain migrations and on migrant communities, thereby – explicitly or implicitly – considering migrants as distinct or isolated groups.[2] Yet recent

---

[1]   On labour migrations and labouring poor in early modern Europe see, among the others, Joseph Ehmer, 'Worlds of Mobility. Migration Patterns of Viennese Artisans in the 18th Century', in Geoffrey Crossick (ed.), *The Artisan and the European Town* (Aldershot, 1997), pp. 172–99; Catharina Lis, *Social Change and the Labouring Poor: Antwerp, 1770–1860* (New Haven CT, 1986); Catharina Lis and Hugo Soly, *Poverty and Capitalism in Pre-Industrial Europe* (Brighton, 1979); Jan Lucassen, *Migrant Labour in Europe, 1600–1900: The Drift to the North Sea* (London, 1987).

[2]   This approach is strongly influenced by the Chicago School and its 'ecological' theory of the urban space. In 1928 Louis Wirth described the city as the place of anonymity and urbanism as a fragmented life style, opposed to the community. Urban space was thus

historiography no longer takes for granted the opposition between immigrants and native inhabitants of cities,[3] while migration *per se* is increasingly seen as a normal experience in everyday life.[4] Many scholars have argued that a migrant's 'settledness' – being a permanent resident of the city – was more important for urban authorities than their foreignness.[5] The great variety in factors that influenced migration streams – such as place of origin, distance covered, occupation, age at migration, kind of migration (temporary, seasonal, definitive etc.) – made it impossible to delineate a category of immigrants as much as it was impossible to clearly identify a category of native inhabitants.

This chapter will highlight the limitations of the concept of 'immigrant' as a target of regulatory interventions together with the variations within this category, and will draw attention to what we believe were the main concerns of migration regulation in early modern Italian cities. In the first part of this chapter we will analyse institutional sources such as ordinances and guild statutes to identify those categories of foreigners who were the main targets of urban migration policies – who was welcome and who was not.[6] For the urban authorities of many Italian cities, the main concern with regard to immigrants was whether they were potential competitors for local resources and/or contributors

---

supposed to be an environment where newcomers encountered a difficult if not impossible integration, following an 'adjustment process' upon which a large part of the American sociological literature has focused. Louis Wirth, 'Urbanism as a Way of Life', *American Journal of Sociology*, 44 (1938): pp. 1–24.

[3]   Bernard Lepetit, 'Proposition et avertissement', in Jacques Bottin and Donatella Calabi (eds), *Les étrangers dans la ville: minorités et espace urbain du bas Moyen âge à l'époque moderne* (Paris, 1999), pp. 1–15.

[4]   Jan Lucassen and Leo Lucassen (eds), *Migration, Migration History, History: Old Paradigms and New Perspectives* (Bern, 1999); Leslie Page Moch, *Moving Europeans: Migration in Western Europe since 1650* (Bloomington, 2003).

[5]   Angiolina Arru, 'Il prezzo della cittadinanza', *Quaderni storici*, 91 (1996): pp. 157–71; Angiolina Arru, Joseph Ehmer and Franco Ramella, 'Premessa', *Quaderni storici*, 106 (2001): pp. 4–23; Angiolina Arru and Franco Ramella (eds), *L'Italia delle migrazioni interne. Donne, uomini, mobilità in età moderna e contemporanea* (Rome, 2003); Eleonora Canepari, 'Immigrati, spazi urbani e reti sociali nell'Italia d'antico regime', in Paola Corti and Matteo Sanfilippo (eds), *Storia d'Italia – Annali, Migrazioni* (Turin, 2009), pp. 78–107; Eleonora Canepari, *Stare in compagnia. Strategie di inurbamento e forme associative nella Roma del Seicento* (Soveria Mannelli, 2008); Simona Cerutti, Robert Descimon and Maarten Prak, 'Premessa', *Quaderni storici*, 89 (1995): pp. 281–6.

[6]   Early modern Italian cities refer to foreigners as *forestieri*. This word comes from the Latin *fòris, fòras*, which means 'outside'. *Forestiero* therefore signifies someone who is outside, who comes from outside. In modern Italian, *forestiero* has become *straniero*, a word whose etymology can be traced back to the Latin *extraneus*, like the English word 'stranger'. Early modern sources always refer to foreigners as *forestieri*, and never as *stranieri*.

to the local economy. The link between urban resources and the reception or rejection of migrants was very strong: foreigners were often well accepted when they were deemed to contribute to the local economy (e.g. merchants, temporary workers upon whom many early modern urban economies depended, pilgrims etc.) but rejected if they were deemed useless.

The other major concern of regulatory interventions was migrants' local reputation and stability: the urban authorities were more concerned about unsettledness and transience than about foreignness. We will use the example of Rome to show how vagrants and other unsettled groups were constantly targeted by ordinances that aimed to expel all those deemed unproductive and potentially dangerous. Personal relations of migrants were key to urban authorities' evaluation of their settledness: newcomers' ability to build a good local reputation was considered essential for their 'integration' in the city.

Migrant Workers, Merchants and Urban Resources in Milan and Rome

Early modern Italian cities were traditionally relatively open towards immigrants: local citizenship was no prerequisite for access to a number of important urban resources such as the labour and product markets or the welfare system.[7] Nevertheless, migration policies often depended on the urban context and migrants' profile: a rich merchant was not an unskilled worker, and a welcome reception could easily switch to rejection depending on the type of migrants involved.

Merchants in particular were usually very welcome, and even actively attracted by means of tax exemptions and other fiscal privileges. Such was the case in Genoa, for instance, a commercial and port city where the presence of merchants was considered to increase commerce and wealth.[8] Merchants were rarely interested in acquiring citizenship, which was not a requirement for tax exemption, as their presence in the city was mainly temporary. In fact, the city

---

[7]   An example of local immigration laws is discussed in this volume in the contribution by Anne Winter.

[8]   Gabriella Rossetti, 'Le élites mercantili nell'Europa dei secoli XII–XVI: loro cultura e radicamento', in Gabriella Rossetti (ed.), *Dentro la città. Stranieri e realtà urbane nell'Europa dei secoli XII–XVI* (Naples, 1999), pp. 327–36. On Genoa: Edoardo Grendi, 'Traffico portuale, naviglio mercantile e consolati genovesi nel Cinquecento', *Rivista storica italiana*, 3 (1968): pp. 593–629; Giacomo Casarino, 'Stranieri a Genova nel Quattro e Cinquecento: tipologie sociali e nazioni', in Donatella Calabi and Paola Lanaro (eds), *La città italiana e i luoghi degli stranieri (XIV–XVIII secolo)* (Rome, 1998), pp. 137–50; and, in the same volume, Ennio Poleggi, 'La topografia degli stranieri nella Genova di antico regime', pp. 108–20.

government promoted their trade but not their long-term residence or their citizenship. For instance, merchants would be subjected to a special tax after two months of residence, the *avaria capitis*: a good reason for traders to carry out their commerce quickly.

Highly skilled artisans were another group of immigrants who were often well received in early modern Italian cities. Their know-how of new production techniques was highly desirable, especially in woollen or glass manufacturing.[9] Special licences were issued to attract immigrant artisans and with them new knowledge, techniques and products. In 1567, for instance, Donato Baldesi from Florence applied to the *Conservatori* of Rome to import the techniques of silk working,[10] while in 1640 Francesco Darduini, a Venetian artisan, received a licence to introduce the art of glass working to Rome.[11]

These examples concern the elite of the workforce: highly skilled artisans able to introduce new technologies, and whose occupational activities therefore represented a valuable resource upon which they could capitalize. Yet most immigrant flows were made up mainly of unskilled and poor workers who often moved on a seasonal and temporary basis, and for whom work primarily was a means for survival. Their reception depended on the city's needs and the management of its resources. They were not necessarily deemed unwelcome since many urban economies depended upon them, in particular for seasonal activities. The city of Brescia, for instance, was heavily engaged in metallurgical production, for which it relied on both manpower and ores extracted from the mineral-rich surrounding valleys.[12] Its metallurgical activities encouraged a permanent flow of workers from the valleys to Brescia, further promoted by tax exemptions and the possibility of owning property – for which only citizens were eligible in some other cities. Conversely, the rejection of immigrants by urban authorities was often the result of endeavours to reserve local resources for inhabitants – both those born locally and established immigrants – and not of a general hostility towards foreigners. Even in these instances, urban governments

---

[9]   Gabriella Rossetti, 'Introduzione', in Gabriella Rossetti (ed.), *Dentro la città*, pp. xiii–xxxiii.

[10]   Archivio Storico Capitolino (ASC), *Camera Capitolina*, credenzone (cred.) 1, tomo (t.) 23. The *Conservatori* headed Rome's municipal government.

[11]   ASC, *Camera Capitolina*, cred. 6, t. 1.

[12]   Giorgetta Bonfiglio Dosio, *L'immigrazione a Brescia fra Trecento e Quattrocento*, in *Forestieri e stranieri nelle città basso-medievali* (Florence, 1988), Conference proceedings, Bagno a Ripoli, 4–8 June 1984, pp. 355–72; Paola Lanaro, 'Economia cittadina, flussi migratori e spazio urbano in Terraferma veneta tra basso Medioevo ed età moderna', in Calabi and Lanaro (eds), *La città italiana*, pp. 63–81.

made exceptions for specific categories of immigrants deemed useful for the urban economy.

The ordinances of the city of Milan, called *grida*, provide us with some examples of strong rejection of immigrants: in certain periods the highest authority in Milan, the lieutenant of the king of Spain, forbade all 'foreigners' from entering the city.[13] One of these ordinances, issued in 1593, was explicitly entitled '*Grida* against foreigners due to the dearth'.[14] It starts with the observation that many inhabitants of the State of Milan are suffering from the shortage of wheat and that the great number of foreigners is making the situation worse since they eat the bread that should go to the 'poor citizens'. It therefore stipulates that 'foreigners cannot enter the State of Milan, nor traverse any of its parts, the term foreigners meaning those who were not permanent residents of this State before last year's Michaelmas'. People who needed to enter the State had to apply for a special licence and stay with a 'local' resident. All other foreigners had to leave within eight days.[15] At the same time, some exceptions were made for those deemed useful to the city, such as those 'who come into the State with their livestock for grazing, master carpenters and *resegotti* [sawyers]'. Another exception was made for merchants, who needed to traverse the State to carry out their trade.

Similar concerns about foreigners' impingements on local resources were expressed in the ordinances periodically issued to regulate the fodder harvest that attracted temporary workers. Immigrants were prevented from coming to Milan to work as seasonal workers because they were considered potential competitors for local inhabitants in search of work. Moreover, foreigners were accused of remaining in the State after the fodder harvest. In 1590, one of the *grida* stated:

> In the past, we have noticed that many foreigners who pretend to come for work or to do other operations came into this State with large families, children and wives, and sometimes they remain here many months to the detriment of this State's subjects from whom they take away employment opportunities. Moreover, it is also to the detriment of the poorest subjects since they have to share the charity from pious people with the foreigners, and in general, these foreigners consume the scarce food supplies.[16]

---

13   At this time the State of Milan was part of the Kingdom of Spain.

14   *Grida contra forastieri per causa della penuria*, 27 September 1593, in *Compendio di tutte le gride ... nel governo di D. Juan Fernandez de Velasco & D. Pedro de Padilla ...* (Milan, 1592–1600).

15   The punishments included three years of jail and various corporal punishments.

16   *Grida che prohibisce forastieri l'entrare in questo Stato*, part of *Grida generale sopra le biade*, 11 September 1590, in *Compendio di tutte le gride ... nel governo di D. Carlo d'Aragona* (Milan, 1609).

In an attempt to avoid this, the ordinance imposed corporal punishments (for women and children), jail sentences and fines (for men) for those in breach of immigration restrictions. The *grida* required the collaboration of boatmen and port workers to prevent the entry of foreigners, and anyone denouncing an unauthorized foreigner's entry to the authorities would receive a third of the fines exacted.

What precisely did the ordinances mean by foreigners? As we have seen earlier, foreigners were understood to be people who did not have a permanent residence in the State: no further specifications were provided. Exceptions were made for 'useful foreigners' in the same categories as listed in 1593, but only if they did not bring any family with them – a rule made to prevent the settlement of these immigrants. Though these groups were partially accepted and allowed to enter, foreign porters were 'especially banned' if they were not subjects of the State or if they had no permanent residence since September 1592.

In 1608 and 1648, the same ordinance was re-issued with some modifications. This time, foreigners were accused of taking away the wheat and carrying it with them on their way back.[17] Foreign workers were therefore prevented from entering and from buying fodder and other farm produce.[18] The definition of foreigner was more inclusive here, and defined as 'every person who does not reside permanently in the State with his family, even if he is a native inhabitant'. This detail illustrates once again that cities were not rejecting foreigners because they were not native, but because of concern over the management of scarce local resources, such as food and employment: while some foreigners were rejected as unwelcome rivals, others, like carpenters, were welcomed since they catered to a specific segment of the city's economy.

The same can be said with respect to Rome. Early modern Rome was a cosmopolitan city whose population counted a large percentage of foreigners. Immigrants were attracted to Rome by a range of factors, among which were the presence of the pope, the role of the city as a social welfare centre and its role as the capital of the Pontifical State. Rome was an open city: its major authority – the pope – was often himself a non-Roman; many guilds were founded by immigrants; and the civic nobility was open to people from everywhere. While some Roman ordinances (*bandi*) sought to control their presence on the territory, we never find interdictions on foreigners entering the city or the

---

[17]   *Grida generale sopra le biade dell'anno 1608*, 14 July 1608, in *Compendio di tutte le gride ... nel governo di D. Pietro Enriquez de Acevedo* (Milan, 1611). We find the same rules against foreigner workers in *Grida generale delle biade*, 27 July 1648, in *Gridario ... D. Luigi de Benavides Carillo* (Milan, 1648–1656).

[18]   The same rules applied to intermediaries and to everyone who bought on behalf of a foreigner.

State. On the contrary, many *bandi* aimed to make sure that Romans did not hoodwink foreigners – especially those who brought food to the city. In 1640, for instance, the *Conservatori* issued an ordinance to fix the price of *stallatico*, a kind of manure, and of overnight stays in inns in order to encourage the arrival of foreigners bringing meat.[19] Other rules sanctioned those innkeepers who charged higher prices to this category of foreigners: in 1644 (as in 1650,[20] 1654[21] and 1675[22]) the *Conservatori* forbade all innkeepers from changing the prices or demanding bribes to the detriment of foreigners coming to sell meat.[23] Some ordinances warned people implicated in the immigration process, like city guards, coachmen and innkeepers, not to take advantage of foreigners coming into Rome.[24] At the same time, however, a *bando* of 1606 prevented all foreigners from taking bread away from the city.[25] The main concern was thus preserving the city's resources for its inhabitants, including not only those born locally but also settled migrants. The guild statutes demonstrate that their main concern was about unsettledness, irrespective of people's geographical origins.

Roman Guilds and Migrant Workers

Roman guilds were very open to foreigners but recorded many difficulties with temporary workers. In the course of their establishment in the sixteenth and seventeenth century, most guilds consisted of non-Roman members and remained open to foreigners.[26] Unlike in many other European cities, urban citizenship was not a requirement for admission to a guild, neither according to the statutes nor in everyday practice.[27] The Blacksmiths and Sword Makers' guild

---

19   Archivio di Stato di Roma (ASR), *Bandi del Governatore*, vol. 410 (1543–1670), 20 October 1640.

20   Ibid., 11 October 1650.

21   Ibid., 22 September 1654.

22   ASR, *Bandi del Governatore*, vol. 411 (1671–1700), 4 December 1675.

23   Ibid., 25 October 1644.

24   Ibid., 10 January 1675.

25   ASR, *Bandi del Governatore*, vol. 410, 30 August 1606. This was issued by the *camerlengo*, the cardinal who managed secular matters when the pope was away from Rome.

26   In 1523, for instance, when the statute of the Tiber's boatmen was published, only one out of 50 members of the guild was Roman-born; in 1622, the statute of the shepherds does not list any Roman (R. Ago, *Economia barocca. Mercato e istituzioni nella Roma del Seicento* (Rome, 1998)), and the same goes for the fruit merchants, whose 1563 statute records the presence of many people from Milan (*Statuto dell'Università dei fruttaroli*, Rome 1563).

27   The case of Antwerp, where burghership was – at least theoretically – required for admission to the guilds, is discussed in Jan De Meester's contribution to this volume.

provides us with a telling example of how they regulated the entry of foreigners as members:

> Every Master of this art coming to Rome to live and practise the job of a sword maker
> must respect our statutes and rules, and he cannot open a new shop or start practising
> the job without having a licence from the Consuls and Masters examiners of this
> guild.[28]

Thus, the Blacksmiths and Sword Makers' guild required that foreigners followed the same rules as Romans: abiding by the statutes and possessing a licence. Whereas this particular guild dedicated a specific paragraph to foreigners in its statutes, in the large majority of the cases we find no such specifications at all: foreigners or Romans are treated the same, which is illustrated by the 1621 statutes of the *Battiloro's* (Goldsmiths') guild:

> We order that no one, Romans or foreigners coming from everywhere, can open a new
> shop if he has not spent two years working with a Master of our guild, and if he has not
> passed the examination by our Prior and Guardians and if he has not promised before
> our notary that he will respect our statutes ... .[29]

In only two cases do we find specific rules set up for foreigners. The first is the 1535 statute of the Butchers' guild, stating that non-Romans have to pay one *fiorino* more than Romans when they enrol.[30] Two centuries later, in 1738, the Jewellers' guild specified the procedures for journeymen to follow if they wanted to become a master, which contain some specifications for foreigners:

> Any worker applying to be admitted in the group of the masters has to respect the
> following rules: first, to be a man of good reputation, who has never been investigated,
> or committed a crime, and that must be proven by a certificate signed by at least three
> master jewellers. If he is a foreigner, he has to provide a magistrate's certificate from his
> home country or from wherever he has previously worked. Second, the new member
> has to prove his apprenticeship period in a master's shop. If he is a foreigner, he has
> to prove that he has been admitted to the Jewellers Labourers' Company and that he
> has worked in a master's shop for at least five years, so that his skill and honesty can
> be attested.[31]

---

28   ASC, *Camera Capitolina*, cred. XI, t. 46, 1690, chapter 35.
29   ASC, *Camera Capitolina*, cred. XI, t. 114, 1621, chapter 10.
30   ASC, *Camera Capitolina*, cred. XI, t. 87, 1738, chapter 9.
31   ASC, *Camera Capitolina*, cred. XI, t. 104, chapter 21.

Like the butchers, the jewellers stipulated that the enrolment fee was higher for foreigners than for Romans, and this time the difference was remarkable: nine *scudi*.[32] To justify this decision, the statute referred to customs in use elsewhere:

> If the new member comes from outside Rome, besides providing the documents listed above he has to pay an enrolment fee of 30 *scudi* [for Romans the fee was 21 *scudi*]. This is because of the example given by other cities in Italy and abroad, where the practice of distinguishing between a 'national' and a 'foreigner' is widespread, and where the fee is very high for the latter.[33]

Roman guilds thus clearly did not prevent foreigners from practising their trade: the strongest 'discrimination' consisted of imposing a higher enrolment fee. Like their city governments, guilds were not concerned about newcomers because of their foreignness: the groups they tried to regulate were not those born outside Rome, but the seasonal and itinerant workers.[34] Many guilds throughout the sixteenth to the eighteenth centuries promoted judicial actions against these groups in order to establish their authority over them and to force them to acquire a licence; peddlers and temporary workers were their usual targets.[35] At the beginning of the eighteenth century, the Carpenters' guild in Mantua requested the civic authorities' support against seasonal workers. Their complaint was aimed against people coming to the city to work during the best months of the year, and returning to their place of origin without paying taxes and thus, unlike the inhabitants of Mantua, contributing little to the local economy.[36]

The main point was thus not whether one was a native Roman or foreigner, but whether one paid taxes and recognized the guilds' authority. If a foreigner respected the statutes and paid his taxes, no rule prevented him from becoming a member. By acting in this way, urban governments and guilds distinguished

---

[32] Nine *scudi* was approximately three months' salary of a servant.

[33] ASC, *Camera Capitolina*, cred. XI, t. 104, chapter 21.

[34] On itinerant workers, see Laurence Fontaine, *Histoire du colportage en Europe* (Paris, 1993).

[35] Angela Groppi, 'Ebrei, donne, soldati e neofiti: l'esercizio del mestiere tra esclusioni e privilegi (Roma XVII–XVIII secolo)', in Alberto Guenzi, Paola Massa and Angelo Moioli (eds), *Corporazioni e gruppi professionali nell'Italia moderna* (Milan, 1998), pp. 533–559; Angela Groppi, '*Une ressource légale pour une pratique illégale. Les juifs et les femmes contre la corporation des tailleurs dans la Rome pontificale (XVIIe–XVIIIe siècles)*', in Renata Ago (ed.), *The Value of the Norm: Legal Disputes and the Definition of Rights* (Rome, 2002).

[36] Carlo M. Belfanti, *Mestieri e forestieri: Immigrazione ed economia urbana a Mantova fra Sei e Settecento (Milan, 1994)*.

between settled, permanent residents on the one hand and unsettled, temporary migrants who were feared as a danger to urban resources on the other hand.[37] Local resources, like charity, work and housing, were not denied to those coming from outside, but to those who were unable to provide evidence of continuous residence in the city. It is telling in this respect that in the Milanese ordinances the term 'foreigner' referred to any non-permanent resident, regardless of his or her geographical origins.

Complicating the position of a foreigner was that his or her past life was unknown. That this could prove problematical is illustrated by the specifications in the jewellers' statute: candidates applying to become a master had to provide information about their past to establish a clean record. For Romans, this was attested by the master jewellers themselves: the candidate was already known to the guild members. Yet this was not possible when the new member was a foreigner, i.e. an unknown person. As we will see in the next paragraph, a major endeavour of migration policies was to control newcomers' movements in the city or state territory, and gathering information on their past lives. These restrictive aims conflicted with the fact that early modern urban economies depended on a permanent inflow of temporary workers, mainly for seasonal economic activities. In other words, urban authorities were disturbed by the presence of unsettled groups, but their concerns conflicted with economic imperatives to allow or even stimulate the inflow of temporary workers.[38] This ambiguity probably explains why ordinances targeting unsettled groups were continuously re-issued: they were largely ineffective, and in cities like Rome the inflow of temporary workers remained high throughout the early modern period.

'People unknown, who come and go as they wish': Unsettled Groups and Urban Authorities

Foreign beggars and vagrants certainly made up the least welcome group of immigrants. In their situation, foreigners were seen as potential criminals and as a problem for law and order. Many *bandi* targeted beggars and vagrants regardless of their geographical origins, forcing them to leave the city within a few days

---

[37]   *Cerutti, Descimon and Prak, 'Premessa'.*

[38]   See the contributions by Jason Coy, Aleksej Kalc and Anne Winter in this volume. On the conflicting interests of urban authorities about migrants see also Anne Winter, Divided Interests, Divided M*igrants: The Rationales of Policies Regarding Labour Mobility in Western Europe, ca. 1550–1914* (London, 2005) GEHN Working Paper no. 15.

after the publication of the ordinance. The standard punishment consisted of three or four years on the galleys, defined as 'forced work'.

The definition of vagrant seems to have been relatively unclear, since the criteria to be classified as vagrant were not precisely determined.[39] By the authorities of early modern Rome, they were often defined as unproductive and unsettled people and amalgamated with other categories of people considered to be sharing the same characteristics. Vagrancy legislation often targeted vagrants alongside *oziosi* ('idlers', meaning the unemployed), beggars, 'charlatans', gypsies and newcomers.[40] In 1568, for instance, an ordinance from Rome's Governor (re-issued in 1608, 1642, 1649 and 1672[41]) ordered not only vagrants and *oziosi* to leave the city within 10 days, but also forbade unemployed foreigners to enter the city. In 1676, another Governor's ordinance targeted a range of groups sharing a condition of unsettledness: vagrants were to be expelled, 'isolated soldiers' to be disarmed and a register was to be created for recording all foreigners entering Rome.[42] Some ordinances ordered vagrants to find a job as an alternative to being expelled from the city; others targeted vagrants and unemployed persons at the same time. Often, these ordinances targeted not only newcomers, but also other categories of unsettled people. In 1564, for instance, one single ordinance strove to eradicate prostitution, revoke gun licences, expel vagrants and prevent innkeepers from taking in foreigners without a passport.[43] In 1622, an ordinance prohibiting Romans from going out in groups of more than three people at night and from buying stolen goods at the same time ordered innkeepers to provide the Governor with lists of their foreign guests.[44]

A link between the dangers represented by these groups and the necessity of keeping track of their movements is established in many ordinances. We have already seen an example in Rome's 1676 ordinance promoting the registration of incoming foreigners. Another example is an ordinance published in Milan

---

[39]   Anne Winter, 'Vagrancy as an Adaptive Strategy: The Duchy of Brabant, 1767–1776', *International Review of Social History*, 49/2 (2004): pp. 249–78.

[40]   Between 1556 and 1672, 28 different vagrancy laws were promulgated by Rome's Governor – in only 12 of those vagrants were the sole category targeted, while the other laws also targeted other unwelcome and unsettled groups: ASR, *Bandi del Governatore*, vols 410 and 411.

[41]   ASR, *Bandi del Governatore*, vol. 410, 6 September 1608, 15 July 1642, 18 January 1649; vol. 411, 6 April 1672.

[42]   ASR, *Bandi del Governatore*, vol. 410, 6 April 1676. The same association between vagrants and soldiers is made in the cited 1642 and 1649 ordinances.

[43]   ASR, *Bandi del Governatore*, vol. 410, 23 September 1564.

[44]   ASR, *Bandi del Governatore*, vol. 410, 7 January 1622.

in 1592, entitled '*Grida* against foreigners'.[45] The preamble asserts that 'most of the crimes in this State are committed by foreigners, who, hoping not to be recognized, can easily perpetrate any offence, however grave'. In order to reduce crimes perpetrated by foreigners, innkeepers were instructed to supply the Magistrate with lists of all their guests. Similar measures were adopted in many Italian cities, and innkeepers in many respects appear to have been the backbone of policies aiming to control the movements and presence of foreigners in the territory. Innkeepers were thus supposed to keep track of their guests, but since these stipulations were continuously re-issued, we can assume that their effectiveness was limited. Yet another way of controlling the people entering the city was the imposition of a *bolletta*, a sort of residence permit for newcomers.

Both for the *bolletta* and inn registries, urban authorities required very specific information on the foreigners in question. A 1633 Milan ordinance orders innkeepers to collect the following details on their guests: day of arrival, first and last name, place of birth, purpose of visit, number and type of arms, horses and servants accompanying them and duration of their stay. According to a 1641 ordinance, the *bolletta* needed to contain the answers to the following questions: Who is the person coming? Where does he come from? Where is he going to? How old is he? What is his stature and the colour of his hair? Does he have a horse or a coach? How many servants does he have with him? Will his stay be brief or long?[46] As we can see, the city government gathered information in order to identify the foreigner – name, stature and hair colour – and to evaluate whether his stay could be a danger or benefit to the State.

Registration requirements like the *bolletta* were rarely adopted before the seventeenth century, and were often justified in the name of law and order: as we saw earlier, the city authorities presented these measures as a way to tackle crime, since foreigners were accused of being the perpetrators of most crimes.[47] Together with the imposition of the *bolletta*, the seventeenth century witnessed a change in the definition of a foreigner, which became more exclusive. In the Milanese ordinances issued until the late sixteenth century, a foreigner was a person without a permanent residence in the State. In 1633, other requirements were added to this definition, such as the length and continuity of residence, the possession of goods or practising a trade. The 1642 *grida*, re-issued in 1647, in turn defined foreigners as people who had not lived in the State of Milan for the

---

45   *Grida contra Forastieri, & specialmente Francesi*, 24 December 1592, in *Compendio di tutte le gride ... nel governo di D. Juan Fernandez de Velasco & D. Pedro de Padilla.*

46   *Grida contra forestieri, vagabondi, & otiosi*, 9 Novembre 1641, in *Gridario ... D. Giovanni di Velasco La Cueva* (Milan, 1653)

47   *Grida generale de' Forastieri*, 9 August 1633, in *Compendio di tutte le gride ... nel governo de D. Fernando cardinale infante* (Milan, 1634).

previous 10 years, thus significantly increasing the length of residence required to be considered local. As we can see, the definition of foreigner was not fixed, and inclusion in this category depended on many factors, not only birthplace. For urban authorities, foreignness above all meant being unknown, and thus potentially dangerous.

Local Reputation and Unemployment

Being settled in the city and having a good reputation was an essential requirement for foreigners to be accepted by the authorities.[48] Some of the Roman ordinances discussed earlier made a clear association between a person's reputation and their status as vagrant. On 24 January 1568, an ordinance stated:

> Everyone from this city, or from anywhere else, who will be identified by two witnesses as a vagrant ... or idle person, meaning someone who cannot live of his gains or his job, even if he has not committed any crime, can and must be imprisoned. Because of his reputation of being a vagrant, judges can torture him, without any other evidence against him.[49]

Other ordinances specified that punishment was to be commensurate to the 'quality of the person and the place where he is found'.[50] Building a good reputation was thus very important, especially in critical situations such as unemployment. Every person who was unable to survive on his own could be labelled and treated as a vagrant. As this applied to both Romans and foreigners, the authorities did not distinguish between them: people identified as vagrants were to leave the city, 'whether they come from other cities or countries, or from this city of Rome'.[51]

In the life of Romans and foreigners, the situation of being unable to survive on one's own resources could be quite a common situation. The *ancien régime*'s economy was an uncertain one, and the working classes were subject to marked fluctuations in demand and supply.[52] Moreover, accidents and illness could

---

[48]   On the importance of local reputation see Sandra Cavallo, *Artisans of the Body in Early Modern Italy: Identities, Families and Masculinities* (Manchester, 2007).

[49]   ASR, *Bandi del Governatore*, vol. 410, 24 January 1568.

[50]   ASR, *Bandi del Governatore*, vol. 410, 13 March 1598. Other examples on 28 October 1590, 6 September 1608, 26 February 1621.

[51]   ASR, *Bandi del Governatore*, vol. 410, 8 October 1621.

[52]   Jean-Yves Grenier, *L'économie d'Ancien Régime. Un monde de l'échange et de l'incertitude* (Paris, 1996); Giovanni Levi, *Inheriting Power: The Story of an Exorcist* (Chicago, 1988).

transform even a young, healthy worker into a person unable to work, and thus a potential vagrant. Temporary or permanent unemployment was a common experience to which people tried to respond by shifting jobs or relying on family help. In that case, families had to be affluent enough to support the unproductive member, and this was not always possible.[53] On 16 November 1624, an ordinance stated that vagrants, Romans or foreigners, 'were not exempted from punishment even if they pretended to live with their father, mother, sister, or other relatives, if the latter were not able to take care of them and provide them with food'.[54] The declaration of a witness about a migrant's good behaviour was thus essential to avoid being classified as a vagrant or 'idle person', and to build a local reputation. A local reputation was a way for permanent immigrants to prove their rootedness in the urban space when temporary unemployment could otherwise push them into the category of persons who were unwelcome.

Concluding Remarks

Urban authorities in early modern Italy did not target foreigners because they were not native. Especially in Rome, ordinances targeting foreigners were issued only against those migrants deemed as unsettled and therefore potentially dangerous. In Rome, no distinctions were made between native inhabitants and foreigners with regard to their entitlements to local resources. In Milan, urban authorities did sometimes discriminate against 'foreigners', but in these cases the latter term was synonymous with 'unknown persons' – and this could equally well refer to Milan-born persons without a permanent residence in the city. Moreover, even the most severe Milanese ordinances made differentiations and exceptions to tolerate the entry of migrants deemed useful. In this respect, the concept of migrant as a well-defined target of a clear policy seems to be anachronistic: early modern cities distinguished between settled and unsettled inhabitants, but

---

[53] On the obligations of families towards household's members, see Angela Groppi, 'Old People and the Flow of Resources between Generations in Papal Rome, Sixteenth to Nineteenth Centuries', in Lynn Botelho, Susannah Ottaway and Katharine Kittredge (eds), *Power and Poverty: Old Age in the Pre-Industrial Past* (Westport CT/London, 2002), pp. 89–106; Angela Groppi, *Il welfare prima del welfare. Assistenza alla vecchiaia e solidarietà tra generazioni a Roma in età moderna* (Rome, 2010); Angela Groppi, 'Il diritto del sangue. Le responsabilità familiari nei confronti delle vecchie e delle nuove generazioni (Roma secc. XVIII–XIX)', *Quaderni storici*, 92 (1996): pp. 305–35; Laurence Fontaine, *Pouvoir, identités et migrations dans les hautes vallées des Alpes occidentales (XVIIe–XVIIIe siècles)* (Grenoble, 2003); Angela Groppi, 'Solidarités familiales et logiques migratoires en pays de montagne à l'époque moderne', *Annales ESC*, 45 (1990): pp. 1433–50.

[54] ASR, *Bandi del Governatore*, vol. 410, 16 November 1624.

not between natives and foreigners, and they differentiated between different categories of migrants on the basis of their purported usefulness.

Throughout their policies, city governments and other urban authorities were particularly concerned about the settledness of their inhabitants, and not about their geographical origins. Therefore, building a local reputation was an essential step in the process of insertion in the social structure of the city. A local reputation was a way for permanent migrants to prove their settledness when unemployment could otherwise push them into the category of unwelcome persons. Being settled and having a good reputation allowed migrants to become a part of the city's social structure: it is by this insertion into the urban body that a foreigner could finally become 'known' to the city and not be a stranger any more.

Chapter 7
Immigration Policy in Eighteenth-Century Trieste

Aleksej Kalc

In the course of the eighteenth century, Trieste was transformed from a small walled-in communal town into a maritime emporium and a modern, rapidly growing urban agglomerate. This process was fostered by policies aimed at promoting international and maritime trade adopted by the Habsburg monarchy at the beginning of the century, when diminishing Venetian sea power and the acquisition of new state territories created favourable conditions for the expansion of trade. Among the basic elements and objectives of the mercantilist policy was the development of ports in the north-eastern Adriatic, which were to become successful commercial metropolises. To this end, the state granted free-port status to Trieste and Rijeka in 1719, which was accompanied by the construction of port facilities, the improvement of road networks and other large-scale changes to support the expansion of domestic and international trade, including administrative reorganization, progressively subjecting the Austrian Littoral to central state authority.[1] It was in this context that the development of the 'new' Trieste as the main access to the sea and a flourishing economic centre of the Habsburg monarchy took off. One of the crucial elements in this process was accelerated demographic development, resulting in a population increase from about 5,000 inhabitants in the mid-1730s to almost 25,000 at the end of the century.[2] The driving force behind this expansion was mass immigration from both the immediate hinterland and more remote continental and Mediterranean areas. This mixture of immigrants from various regions created

---

[1]   Eva Faber, 'Territorio e amministrazione', in Roberto Finzi, Loredana Panariti and Giovanni Panjek (eds), *Storia economica e sociale di Trieste. La città dei traffici 1719–1918* (Trieste, 2003), pp. 21–8.

[2]   Pietro Montanelli, *Il movimento storico della popolazione di Trieste* (Trieste, 1905), pp. 41–2.

a new, ethnically and religiously diverse social fabric, with distinct communities defined by language, religion and culture.[3]

The role of immigration and immigrants as protagonists in the economic, social and cultural transformation occupies a prominent place in the historiographic debate on the emergence and rise of the 'new' Trieste. However, the ways in which these immigrant components were incorporated into the social body of the city have so far not received much attention. Historiography has mainly dealt with the legal and administrative bases of the free-port legal system serving to attract various economic actors and favouring a cosmopolitan social development. Although neither dilemmas nor controversial aspects have been neglected, the policies and attitudes towards immigrants in the form of government incentives have mainly been addressed in connection with elite groups.[4]

The aim of this chapter is to chart the ramifications, contradictions and conflicts of the promotion and regulation of immigration in the free port of Trieste. On the one hand, efforts were undertaken to recruit newcomers considered useful to the emporium and to develop free economic activity and competition. On the other hand, ideal intentions were confronted with the need to balance the influx of immigrants with concerns for economic and social stability. Migration policies therefore constituted an arena of confrontation and negotiation of various public and private interests.

We will examine the guidelines of Trieste's immigration policy, as well as the instruments and criteria used to regulate processes of attraction, inclusion and exclusion. Above all, we will highlight the economic and social considerations that informed regulatory practices, and address the underlying interests with reference to the specific free-port context of Trieste. It should be noted that the development of the 'new' Trieste was heavily promoted and supported from the top, and that the state authorities were strongly involved with its immigration policy via the local administrative bodies: the Commercial Intendancy, succeeded in 1776 by the Government of the Austrian Littoral. As we shall see, the legal basis for this was the special free-port legislation aimed at facilitating the development of a maritime emporium, and the existence of central legislation concerning residential rights, relief entitlements, military conscription and foreigners, that governed the legal status of native-born and

---

3   Marco Breschi, Aleksej Kalc and Elisabetta Navarra, 'La nascita di una città: Storia minima della popolazione di Trieste (secc. XVIII–XIX), in Roberto Finzi and Giovanni Panjek (eds), *Storia economica e sociale di Trieste. La città dei gruppi 1719–1918* (Trieste, 2001), pp. 81–90 and 166–81.

4   Aleksej Kalc, *Tržaško prebivalstvo v 18. stoletju. Priseljevanje kot gibalo demografske rasti in družbenih sprememb* (Koper, 2008), pp. 17–31.

immigrant residents in any given place throughout the Habsburg domains. The most important sources used to study Trieste's immigration policy are those produced by its local police authorities, which played a prominent role in the emporium from the mid-century onwards.

Supporting Growth: Attraction and Consolidation

The population question was at the centre of attention of the political architects of the new Trieste. As a top-down design, the maritime emporium of Trieste was the product of a strategic plan to promote immigration and demographic growth. The guiding principle of the institution of the free port was the establishment of conditions and instruments to promote the influx and settlement of Austrian and foreign entrepreneurs and other productive workers who would contribute to the growth and prosperity of the city. The primary role assigned to Trieste by the mercantilist planners of Vienna was that of a maritime emporium to which the main body of the legal system, established by the free-port patent of 1719 and supplementary laws over the next three decades, was dedicated. The envisaged beneficiaries of free-port privileges were mainly large-scale merchants; but the attraction of various manufacturers and artisans was also part of the objective. The import, storage and exchange of goods were all exempt from customs duties or other taxations in force in the Austrian territories, except for certain nominal contributions. The franchises also included a series of other privileges, such as reduced customs duty on goods in transit, concessions for international fairs and rights to ship and store goods of which the importation was otherwise prohibited. Of great strategic importance for the efficient functioning of the free-port system were continuous improvements to the legal system, aimed at simplifying bureaucratic procedures, facilitating commercial exchanges, accelerating mediation of disputes and guaranteeing the rights and safety of people and property.[5]

Among the legal provisions explicitly aimed at stimulating immigration were status privileges and entrepreneurial freedoms for merchants, manufacturers and artisans who settled to undertake their economic activities in the city. They were allowed to purchase land 'at a fair price' on which to build houses, and were exempt from all civic responsibilities such as military service, guard duty and

---

5   Pietro Kandler, 'Emporio e portofranco', in *Raccolta delle leggi, ordinanze e regolamenti speciali per Trieste pubblicati per ordine della Presidenza del Consiglio dal suo procuratore civico* (Trieste, 1861); Pietro Kandler, *Documenti per servire alla conoscenza delle condizioni legali del Municipio ed emporio di Trieste* (Trieste, 1848); Liana De Antonellis Martini, *Portofranco e comunità etnico-religiose nella Trieste settecentesca* (Milan, 1968), pp. 34–45.

the billeting of soldiers. They were granted immediate state protection against harassment and were also awarded significant personal privileges with respect to certain restrictive city laws. One of the most distinctive legal provisions intended to attract foreign entrepreneurs was immunity, which stipulated that foreign merchants were protected from imprisonment for debts incurred in foreign countries and could escape prosecution for economic offences committed outside the Austrian dominions. Immunity had a positive effect on the growth of commercial exchange in Trieste and the influx of economic agents, yet it was a double-edged sword, attracting not only entrepreneurs seeking to repair their damaged reputations but also criminals attempting to flee from justice. In order to prevent this, immunity was linked to foreigners' status as temporary residents in the city. The law also became more selective,[6] but it continued to create such confusion that, despite repeated clarifications made by the authorities, even in the 1790s many foreigners came to Trieste with false expectations of enjoying immunity.[7]

Another important policy instrument in stimulating immigration was to grant religious freedom in order to encourage non-Roman Catholic merchants, entrepreneurs and artisans of various faiths to settle in the city from the 1730s onwards. Up to the Edict of Tolerance of 1781–1782, Trieste's religious tolerance was exceptional in the context of the fairly intolerant attitudes to religions other than Roman Catholicism that reigned in the Austrian dominions in this period. Although it was not yet a full recognition of religious minorities – which came about later with the granting of community statutes, and did not promote religious equality – it was an important basis for attracting members of the Jewish, Protestant, Orthodox and other faiths, many of whom played a prominent role in the economic development of Trieste.[8]

The regulatory provisions designed to facilitate market access and encourage foreign traders to settle in the city included a guarantee that in case of war they would be able to leave the city undisturbed and to sell or export their goods and movables freely. The law on free entry to the port gave foreigners and Austrian citizens the freedom to enter the city, stay and perform economic activities and leave as they wished. Permanent residents of any social status were also exempt from military service. Moreover, immigrants from other Austrian jurisdictions who were subject to military service had no obligations in this

---

6   Archivio di Stato di Trieste (AST), Cesarea Regia Superiore Intendenza Commerciale per il Litorale in Trieste (CRSIC) 1748–1776, b. 456, 15 June 1755.

7   De Antonellis Martini, *Portofranco*, pp. 38–9.

8   For details, see particularly De Antonellis Martini, *Portofranco*, and Eva Faber, 'Fremd- und Anderssein im 18. Jahrhundert: Eine Variation zum Thema am Beispiel von Triest', *Das achtzehnte Jahrhundert und Österreich*, 12 (1997): pp. 29–58.

regard towards the Trieste authorities. While having to obtain a permit to leave the administrative unit of their origin, these inhabitants were free to leave the city without any permit or other certificate issued by Trieste's administrative bodies. Such bureaucratic exemptions represented a serious obstacle for keeping track of those under military obligation and for monitoring the conscription system, which formed the basis for population statistics. Nevertheless, the administrative bodies of Trieste, in their pragmatism, believed that stricter supervision of individuals under military obligation would hamper immigration and population growth.[9]

The launch of the maritime emporium was plagued by many problems. The long sequence of legal acts and the extension of free-port privileges in the early eighteenth century point towards difficulties in triggering the expansion process. Initially, there was a negative influence from state-run commercial enterprises, which enjoyed monopoly privileges until their collapse in the 1730s. It was only then that trade began to develop on the basis of free-market principles and was encouraged by the Commercial Intendancy, which in 1749 became a local state authority. The Intendancy representatives realized that a more active approach to the promotion of immigration was necessary for economic prosperity. Jewish and Orthodox entrepreneurs and merchants were considered essential actors in the growth of the emporium, and their settlement required encouragement 'by all available means'.[10] The government authorities of Trieste closely monitored the development of the Greek and Serbian communities, their business performance and the possibilities of accelerating their immigration.[11] To this end, they were granted special tax exemptions, while the state intervened to resolve religious disputes between the two Orthodox communities. Since in the initial development phase neither Jews nor Orthodox Christians showed any particular interest to settle in Trieste, the government applied considerable effort toward inducing their migration from the Republic of Venice.[12]

The efforts aimed at establishing a colony of Armenian entrepreneurs offers one of the clearest examples of Trieste's active policy to attract wholesalers. In the 1760s, there were active endeavours to achieve this by taking advantage of the emigrations spurred by the persecution of the Armenian population in Persia.

---

9   Archivio Generale del Comune di Trieste (AGCT), Capitanato Circolare, b. 20, 31 August 1787.

10   Loredana Panariti, 'Il dannato commercio: Trieste nel XVIII secolo', *Metodi e ricerche*, 2 (1998): p. 123.

11   AST, CRSIC, b. 55, 1756, p. 80.

12   De Antonellis Martini, *Portofranco*, pp. 126–40; Roberto Finzi, 'Trieste perché', in Roberto Finzi and Giovanni Panjek (eds), *Storia economica e sociale di Trieste. La Città dei gruppi 1719–1918* (Trieste, 2001), pp. 54–5; Kandler, 'Emporio e portofranco', pp. 180–81 and 190–93.

In 1769, an Armenian priest was installed in Trieste at government expense to perform his pastoral duties and thereby attract Armenian entrepreneurs and convince individual Oriental travellers to settle in Trieste. In the following years, after the arrival of a group of monks in the context of an agreement between the authorities of Trieste and the Mechitarist Church of Constantinople, rules regulating the settlement of Armenians and other immigrants wishing to join the Mechitarist Congregation were issued, providing them with the greatest religious freedoms of all the non-Roman Catholic religious communities.[13]

While special free-port privileges were aimed at wholesalers, manufacturers and artisans, the new economic reality of Trieste fostered the influx of other occupational and social groups who also enjoyed the freedom to settle and work in the city. Yet the economic structures of demand and supply for goods and services did not always evolve in a balanced way. Some occupations, such as tailors, tended to multiply beyond viability, attracted by the prospects of demand from the port traffic, but rendered vulnerable by its instability. Other sectors, necessary both for domestic and external markets, were never fully developed or simply did not exist. There was a growing need to attract and retain certain occupations to ensure the survival of sectors particularly sensitive to cyclical fluctuations. Interventions in this context were attuned to individual cases and perceived needs, and could range from providing financial grants for setting up new businesses, free work premises, advance payments or donations for overhead costs, and rewards for success or diligence to financial support for companies in difficulties. In exceptional cases, the authorities would even ensure protection from competition. Because these forms of assistance *ad personam* were generally awarded in exchange for public services, such as the occupational training of poor children, they were mostly financed by local welfare funds.

Daily police reports offer insight into the practicalities of such individual support policies. In 1764, the government and the Mercantile Exchange, as part of their efforts to consolidate the spinning and weaving trades, issued a decree to attract skilled workers to train the poor in order to dissuade women and children from the habit of begging.[14] To retain the services of a sailmaker who planned to leave due to a shortage of orders, the authorities awarded him an annual prize for five years in exchange for which he had to take in an apprentice from the orphanage.[15] A sealmaker was given free work premises on the condition that

---

13   AST, CRSIC, b. 3, p. 38; De Antonellis Martini, *Portofranco*, pp. 145–9; Eva Faber, 'Il problema della tolleranza religiosa nell'area alto-adriatica nel secondo Settecento', in Filiberto Agostini (ed.), *Veneto, Istria e Dalmazia tra Sette e Ottocento. Aspetti economici, sociali ed ecclesiastici* (Venice, 1999), pp. 108–9.

14   AST, CRSIC, b. 489, 8 May 1764, 1 September 1764.

15   AST, CRSIC, b. 488, 1764, p. 1, 15 October 1764.

he provided a poor young man with accommodation and training.[16] A maker of knives and surgical instruments from Germany was allocated free work premises for a period of five years in addition to a three-year rent subsidy.[17] An expert in ivory and tortoiseshell work was paid 600 *liras* from the funds of the foundling home and orphanage as an incentive for starting a business. He also received a rent subsidy; in return he was to take under his roof four boys and two girls from the orphanage and train them in his trade.[18] To ensure a constant supply of books, a bookseller was 'cordially invited' not to leave the city and was ensured 'support and protection' against the unfair competition of travelling booksellers.[19] A poultry breeder with sufficient capital for a constant supply of chicken meat, found after a long search, was granted a free sales concession for five years and assurance that during this period no potential competitors would be allowed to settle in Trieste.[20]

Among artisans special attention was paid to construction workers. Building the new city and port infrastructure provided extensive employment opportunities for both skilled and unskilled workers, attracting workers from a wide area and other centres of construction. As the construction labour market was subject to cyclical fluctuations, builders and stonecutters – whose occupations were mobile by nature – were easily attracted elsewhere during periods of work shortage. The authorities of Trieste monitored the masters of these trades and endeavoured to retain a contingent of this labour force to remain available for new impetuses to urban expansion.[21]

As long as the free port did not offer sufficiently firm economic structures and development perspectives, it was not easy to convince entrepreneurs or other productive workers to move to Trieste. As a result, some leniency was required in the evaluation of the qualifications of people coming to settle in the city. A good example is that of public brokers. In the early 1750s, among 12 patented brokers only a few could be said to possess indisputable professional expertise and to enjoy the full confidence of merchants. Many were ruined entrepreneurs, exiled from Treviso and Venice for theft of public money, bankruptcy or

---

16   Biblioteca Civica di Trieste (BCT), Archivio Diplomatico (AD), Atti di Polizia (AP), 3 April 1771.

17   Ibid., 23 July 1771.

18   AST, Cesareo Regio Governo per il Litorale in Trieste 1776–1809 (CRG), b. 102, Giornali di Polizia (GP), 25 November 1779.

19   BCT, AD, AP, 25 May 1771.

20   Ibid., 9 July 1770.

21   AST, CRG, b. 102, GP, 10 March 1781.

other severe economic offences.[22] A certain Carlo Pellegrini, of the Orthodox religion, was awarded the title of public broker only because three Orthodox public brokers had to be appointed and the 'third person to fulfil the required number was missing'.[23] Tolerance in accepting foreigners is also evident in many other situations, as is clearly illustrated by the case of Venetian deserters who were provided accommodation in the city on the sole condition of having an occupation and the ability to practise it successfully.

Given such casuistry the best that can be said regarding immigration selectivity is that it was applied pragmatically. If the authorities considered a certain economic activity necessary for the city, and if potential immigrants seemed to have good prospects for success, no obstacle would prevent their settlement. The attraction of large-capital ventures was undoubtedly the prevailing aspiration, but the city also welcomed those with specific skills who would take advantage of the free-port benefits. When it came to the particular interests and urgent needs of the city, the authorities paid little or no attention to the professionalism of individuals, their history or moral integrity.

In Search of an Equilibrium between Liberty and 'Good Order'

The previous section outlined the directives and instruments used to promote the economic and demographic growth of the maritime emporium of Trieste. At times the liberal immigration policies required to build the 'new' Trieste ran into conflict with other needs and interests that called for restrictive and regulatory measures. In the 1770s the excessive expansion of certain modest occupations triggered a long legal debate on the question of whether to adopt restrictive measures or maintain the state-designed policies promoting free immigration. The principle of *laissez faire* did not seem to work according to expectations; in the early 1770s the expansion of retail shops and occupations catering for the daily needs of the urban population led to neither price reductions nor improvements in service; but it did promote economic insecurity for the workers involved. This issue was connected with the increasing seasonal presence of Grison shoemakers, who came to Trieste in months of peak traffic, and with the growing numbers of Jewish and Greek food retailers. The presence of the Grisons led to reductions in service prices, which then sky-rocketed after their departure as local artisans sought to compensate for their losses. Local shoemakers called upon the authorities to either force the Grisons to settle in the city or prevent

---

[22]   Ugo Tucci, 'Una descrizione di Trieste a metà del Settecento', *Quaderni giuliani di storia*, 1/2 (1980): p. 105.

[23]   AST, CRSIC, b. 546, 1751, p. 18.

them from practising their craft. Catholic food retailers also objected to the large number of Jewish and Greek shopkeepers and accused them of unfair competition, demanding a 'proportional limitation' of the number of food retail shops in order to 'avoid abuse and great damage caused by unlimited freedom'.[24]

Some in Trieste's government circles acknowledged the protesters' arguments, stating that the service crafts and retail trades (i.e. those catering for the local population) had always been and would remain in the local domain as they represented local resources. Unlike wholesale and commercial crafts, aimed at export, the retail and service crafts depended on population size. Without encouraging a corporative or monopolist spirit, much less by implementing *numerus clausus* or expelling foreign artisans, their numbers needed to be harmonized with local needs determined by population size. Foreigners wishing to pursue these activities would have to settle in the city. In this way, both the free-port principles of free initiative and the right of the local population to practise service activities would be satisfied.[25]

The central government authorities did not agree with such viewpoints. Imperial orders issued in the 1770s prohibited any kind of differentiation and restriction in the fields of crafts and professions. All activities were to be 'treated according to the principle of freedom', which served as the basis for the growth of the Trieste emporium.[26] The access to crafts and trades, whether permanent or seasonal, thus remained free in principle. The government emphasized this every time one or another group called for protective measures against competition. Prohibiting certain economic activities or conceding any right of precedence was regarded, by the central authorities at least, as a violation of the principles and legislation of the free port.

Yet restrictive actions regarding occupational activity did exist. They were part of the general norms of the 'good police', introduced in the 1750s to ensure security, morality, quality of service and public order. The basic criterion for all categories was *onestà* – 'honesty'. Each newcomer intent on settling in the city was obliged to register with the police and to prove his or her moral integrity by credentials or proper behaviour, which the authorities monitored at the beginning of their stay. Another important aspect was possession of occupational skills, and above all self-sufficiency – or rather the possession of the means necessary for practising one's occupation. Typically, a newcomer would

---

24   BCT, AD, AP, GP, 13 and 14 September 1770, 9 August 1772, 10 September 1773, 1 March 1774, 13 June 1775, 22 July 1775.

25   BCT, AD, AP, 13 and 14 September 1770, 22 July 1775.

26   Ibid., 29 November 1773; 1775, p. 45.

obtain a residence permit after a probationary period during which the police checked their actual professional qualifications.[27]

Registration with the police and acquisition of a formal permit was required even for temporary residence and for performing any kind of work. In these cases, the authorities were concerned predominantly with ensuring that artisans' activities were in compliance with technical and security regulations. The acquisition of a residence permit was also dependent on the type of work and the economic conditions in the city. When conditions were unfavourable for performing certain services, or certain trades were over-represented, applications for residence permits could be rejected to prevent social disintegration. A good example is the case of a Jewish dressmaker, Sareda Udine, who arrived in Trieste in 1778 when the forced departure of many poor Jews from Venice caused concern that Trieste would be flooded by 'hundreds of rag dealers and tailors'. Because many tailors and dressmakers in Trieste were already poor, Sareda Udine's occupation was not considered one that would ensure a living. For this reason, her application was rejected. Those whose ability to make a living was not recognized, apart from finding a more suitable job, had only one possibility for settling in the city: a guarantee from a legal resident to support the newcomer financially in case of need.[28]

In practice, the measures remained relatively liberal. In a first phase, the main reason was a relative tolerance dictated by the need to promote the growth of the emporium. After Trieste's take-off, the increasing vigour of the city and the arrival of large numbers of newcomers in turn hampered the implementation of public order regulations. Telling in this respect were repeated edicts urging immigrants and the local population to adhere to the regulations, as 'due to false interpretation of the free-port laws everyone thought that they were allowed to open a shop or practise any kind of profession without registering with the police beforehand and proving their integrity'.[29] The obligation of newcomers to legalize their activities and status through registration was implemented with great difficulty, and in fact remained largely ineffective.

In the approach of the Austrian state regarding the regulation of immigration, there was an overall preference for the principle of free entry over putting up *a priori* obstacles, despite the numerous legal and administrative provisions for selection. The selective measures that were propagated pertained solely to the maintenance of public order and social stability. Their aim was to protect the city against 'needless', 'socially burdensome', 'indecent' and potentially dangerous

---

27   AST, CRG, b. 102, GP, 31 December 1779.
28   BCT, AD, AP, 1 August 1778.
29   BCT, AD, AP, 8 January 1775.

groups and individuals – concerns that mainly involved the lower strata. They were focused in particular on two social phenomena connected with poverty and status ambiguity. The first was that of professional beggars and delinquents, i.e. those entering the city with the intention of making a living by begging and petty crime. The second was that of the working poor, who by accidents of life or economic downturns could be pushed below the line of subsistence and whose social status therefore fluctuated between acceptance and illegality. This was a large unskilled labour force, often seasonal, that consisted of apprentices, journeymen and workers as well as household servants in between jobs.

As migration rates proliferated, further measures for the preventive control and selection of unwanted newcomers, such as beggars, persons of dubious moral character and those unable to work, were set up in the 1750s; yet they proved ineffective – mainly because the borders of the city were very permeable. Immigrants who arrived by sea evaded the obligation to apply for a residence permit and undergo a hearing with the police. Many boatmen allowed them to disembark at uncontrolled locations.[30] And given that from the mid-1750s the city no longer had its wall and gates, it was even easier to avoid bureaucratic procedures when entering the city by land: newcomers would avoid control simply by keeping off the main roads. For these reasons, and also to ensure that sufficient workers flowed into the city, the focus was not on guarding physical entry or on prohibiting the immigration of lower social strata. The police rather concentrated on retroactive strategies of monitoring the immigrant population and expelling unwanted individuals who were considered harmful to the social fabric.

In the implementation of these retroactive selective strategies, many outcomes were possible. Beggars and newcomers without a profession were in principle expelled: Austrian subjects were sent to their place of origin; foreigners were escorted to the state border or put on ships heading for their country.[31] If they had a profession or had been able to earn a living previously, however, they might be allowed to stay for a certain period of time, during which they had to find employment; in that case they had to register with the police and acquire a residence permit. If they subsequently failed to submit evidence of employment, they were expelled as vagrants.[32] People whose occupation was insufficient to make a living were treated in the same way: they were given the opportunity to find an adequate source of income within a certain period of time, while priority was given to those who had family in Trieste.[33] People who

---

[30]   AST, CRSIC, b. 7, 11 and 12 December 1757, 7 May 1759; b. 548, 14 March 1795.

[31]   BCT, AD, AP, GP, 1 December 1775.

[32]   Ibid., 14 January 1772.

[33]   Ibid., 1 December 1775.

did not practise their trade or did not work regularly and were suspected of 'wicked' behaviour were liable to expulsion unless someone offered to vouch for them. The authorities tended to be more severe towards female immigrants than towards men, especially if they were alone and single: because in their case unemployment was associated not only with begging and vagrancy but also with potentially 'indecent behaviour' (i.e. prostitution), young single women were expelled comparatively more rapidly.[34] Many young men in turn sought shelter in Trieste to avoid military service.[35] According to the conscription legislation introduced in the 1770s, male migrants from Austrian provinces had to carry a special permit issued by their conscription office. If they were unable to produce one on demand they were to be sent back home or, after 1778, to the army; but in Trieste this does not appear to have been taken very seriously.[36]

The police tried to improve the system of control over foreigners and the procedures of expulsion by introducing several auxiliary measures, such as the obligation for innkeepers to register their guests with the police (late 1760s), for employers to register their apprentices and journeymen (mid-1770s) and for landlords to keep a record of their tenants (1790s).[37] In emergency situations such as war, as in the 1790s, restrictions on immigration were extremely rigorous, yet they were relaxed completely as soon as possible.[38] In the adjustment of regulatory measures, the police played a leading role. The sources display a rich casuistry that illustrates the centrality of the concern for public order in decisions to accept or reject foreigners, borne out by lists of expelled people and permanently exiled recidivists. At the same time, there are many indications that illegal residence in the city was widespread, that undocumented newcomers could relatively easily find accommodation and avoid police control either through guile or with help.[39] Despite stricter approaches to security questions, the bodies responsible for the monitoring of immigrants and the expulsion of unwanted outsiders failed to keep pace with the social reality of Trieste.

---

[34]   Ibid., 12 July 1771; AST, CRG, b. 101, GP, 18 December 1779.

[35]   Pierpaolo Dorsi, 'Libertà e Legislazione: Il rapporto del barone Pittoni sullo stato della città di Trieste e del suo Territorio (1786)', *Archeografo Triestino*, 49 (1989): p. 149.

[36]   BCT, AD, AP, 12 March 1771; AST, CRG, b. 101, GP, 15 September 1778, 18 February 1779.

[37]   BCT, AD, AP, GP, 1 and 5 October 1768; AST, CRG, b. 101, 27 August 1778; b. 103, 23 January 1783; b. 547, 9 July 1794; BCT, AD, Sicurezza Pubblica (SP), 27 June 1794.

[38]   AST, CRG, b. 549, 18 September 1796, 23 August 1798.

[39]   Aleksej Kalc, 'Tržaško podeželje in policijski red iz leta 1777: Kratek sprehod med črko in stvarnostjo', *Annales. Annals for Istrian and Mediterranean Studies*, 18 (1999): p. 280; Finzi, 'Trieste, perché', pp. 429–30.

Social control and immigration regulation was most effective with regard to immigrants who were non-Roman Catholics, especially Jews – many of whom were poor. Often their own communities contributed to this success as they were worried by the prospect of having to care for disabled or impoverished co-religionists. Not only were they encouraged to cooperate in immigration regulation, but the Jewish community was required by law to prevent the arrival of co-religionists considered non-beneficial to the development of trade.[40] Although principles of solidarity sometimes prevailed, community institutions played an important regulatory role in ensuring the careful checking of newcomers' qualifications and assets. In 1778, when many impoverished Jews were forced to emigrate from Venetian territories, the heads of the Jewish community in Trieste themselves called upon the state authorities to restrict their freedom of immigration. Precise procedures and criteria for the acceptance of Jewish newcomers were drawn up and a committee was established to verify the professional and social suitability of applicants.[41]

Decisions on acceptance and expulsion were also tied in with Austrian legislation with regard to *Heimatrecht* – a status of legal residence which also determined one's right to poor relief. The distinction between 'locals' with *Heimatrecht* and 'aliens' without such a legal residence was an intricate matter in Austrian law,[42] which was complicated even further in the case of Trieste by its free-port legislation and privileges. Many of the exact conditions under which an immigrant could become a 'local' of Trieste – and thus no longer liable to expulsion – remain unclear. The available evidence suggests that in Trieste, as elsewhere in the country, the interpretation of the concepts of 'locals' and 'aliens' depended on individual circumstances – the exercise of discretion by competent authorities and individual officers played a major role, regardless of written rules.

---

[40]   De Antonellis Martini, *Portofranco*, pp. 107–8.

[41]   AST, CRG, b. 96, 8 January 1783; b. 101, GP, 20 and 27 May 1778; b. 172, 22 July 1785. See also Faber, 'Fremd- und Anderssein', pp. 38–9, 57.

[42]   In-depth analysis of the problem in Harald Wendelin, 'Schub und Heimatrecht', in Waltraud Heindl and Edith Saurer (eds), *Grenze und Staat. Paßwesen, Staatsbürgerschaft, Heimatrecht, und Fremdengesetzgebung in der österreichischen Monarchie (1750–1867)* (Vienna, 2000), pp. 173–230. See also Sylvia Hahn, 'Inclusion and Exclusion of Migrants in the Multicultural Realm of the Habsburg State of Many Peoples', *Histoire sociale/Social History*, 66 (2000): pp. 317–19.

Powers and Interests: Apprentices and Porters

Trieste's immigration and incorporation policies represented, as we have seen, a pragmatic compromise between the logic of the market economy and the need to maintain public order and social stability. They were also an arena of conflict and negotiation between different political and economic interests, as well as between principles and pragmatism. This situation is well illustrated by the cases of apprentices and porters.

As far as apprentices were concerned, the government administration tried to give priority to the training of local youth with an eye to the benefit of the local and state economy. This aspiration ran into conflict with masters' preference for immigrant apprentices: the latter tended to pay for their training, while local apprentices were poor and had to be provided for, and their parents could prove meddlesome. Master artisans legitimized their preference for immigrant apprentices by their need to compensate for the unfair competition that resulted from Trieste's lax economic regime. In addition, closed communities such as the Grisons and the Greeks hired only apprentices and journeymen from their regions of origin for various cultural and religious reasons associated with economic strategies in their home communities. Hence when a rule was introduced that obliged masters to give priority to local orphans when taking on apprentices, this did not have the desired effect despite the authorities' call on 'the public interest'. The matter was complicated by the fact that many foreign apprentices left town after completing their training, which conflicted with the authorities' endeavour to expand the local skill base.

Confronted with a growing number of impoverished and unemployed local children and orphans, by the middle of the 1770s several officers promoted a rule that would oblige artisans, manufacturers and retailers to hire apprentices from Austrian regions only, and from Trieste in particular. Opinions on this scheme were divided: even the Mercantile Exchange administration, an important motor behind Trieste's free-trade policy, expressed contrasting views when asked for advice on the matter by the authorities. There were few objections to the idea of subjecting master artisans to this obligation, for similar rules of preference existed in other cities too. Yet with regard to retailers, the issue was more complex. On the one hand, they did not have any of the direct free-port privileges of the wholesalers. Yet, on the other hand, because retail was free, Trieste's retailers did not enjoy the same protection and hence were not subjected to the same obligations as in cities where this activity was the exclusive domain of burghers. In the end, the principle of freedom prevailed and the issue continued to be dealt with case by case, in the mild and ineffective way of persuasion.[43] The only response to the problem of growing unemployment among local youth came from the managers of the city welfare funds, who established an annual grant scheme to finance the apprenticeship of 12 local boys.[44]

More concrete measures were developed with regard to the fluctuating mass of porters. Since loading, unloading, transporting and storing goods were among the port's principal activities, the growth of shipping ultimately depended on the number and efficiency of porters, who represented Trieste's most significant labour force. Together with other unskilled workers, they belonged to the economically and socially most fragile segments of the urban population. Only a very small minority was in permanent employment, typically in large warehouses, and receiving regular pay. The vast majority were free or market porters who were employed on a day-to-day basis and whose employment opportunities fluctuated together with the ups and downs in maritime traffic. Although the labour market of Trieste's docks attracted a lot of seasonal migrants, many settled down on a permanent basis and relied on dockwork as their prime source of income. The continuous expansion of the emporium encouraged their absorption into the city's social fabric, but growing numbers struggled to survive when traffic was low and work was scarce. Late arrival of ships due to bad weather and rough sea jeopardized the livelihood of many porters in wintertime, and could force them to resort to crime to support their families. In addition, offenders against public order sometimes presented themselves as porters in order to avoid police controls.[45]

These problems gave rise to a government initiative for the introduction of a register of porters designed to monitor and control this labour force. Its purpose was to regulate the number of porters in accordance with employment possibilities, in order to avoid dramatic increases in the number of poor during periods of low port traffic. The scheme envisaged that porters would have to register with the Mercantile Exchange administration and that only those enlisted there were allowed to offer their services. The plan also proposed a system of set tariffs and worker classification, stipulated the responsibilities of foremen and laid out rules for their relations with employers.[46] Although the register was drawn up promptly, the system failed because Trieste's wholesalers invoked the free-port legislation to refuse to set tariffs for porters' services. The need to regulate porters' activities resurfaced in the mid-1770s, when a new plan

---

43   BCT, AD, AP, GP, 19 September 1769, 8 January 1775, 21 February 1775, 4 April 1775.

44   AST, CRG, b. 545, 15, 17 and 25 February 1792, 10 March 1792, 12 June 1792; b. 548, 13 June 1795.

45   BCT, AD, AP, GP, 2 December 1774.

46   BCT, AD, AP, 30 August 1768; GP, 20 January 1769, 18 April 1769.

envisaged the employment of temporary workers from Friuli and Istria during seasons when demand for porters was high, while stipulating that local residents would have priority over seasonal migrants and that permanently employed porters would continue to be selected freely. Again wholesalers displayed their reluctance to accept any such intervention, partly out of concern that it could lead to a shortage of porters.[47]

The situation remained unchanged until 1792 when wholesalers finally agreed to the implementation of the system, shortly after a temporary shortage of porters had led to the tripling of their wages.[48] After long preparations and difficult negotiations, at the beginning of 1793 a rule book for porters finally came into force.[49] It is no coincidence that this occurred at a time when war dictated and legitimized the tightening of security measures against external threats and potential unrest within the country. The introduction of a porters register and procedures for checking candidates' integrity provided the police with instruments to filter out unwelcome applicants and to prevent the profession being passed into unauthorized hands.[50] Caution was all the more necessary in an open city like Trieste.

However, the system gradually lost its initial rigour and economic interests again prevailed over concerns for social control and societal stability. In practice, the authorities proved relatively flexible and took care not to make registration too difficult in order to avoid shortages of porters and concomitant wage increases. The development of the emporium went before everything else, and with it the interests of entrepreneurial elites. The policy compromise adopted by the government with regard to the porters' registry is a case in point. While maintaining the principle of registration and regulation, the government adjusted the original plan to wholesalers' interests and instructed the police to carry it out in such a way that 'would not cause the market to suffer from deficiency of such an important labour component'.[51]

Concluding Remarks

The immigration policies of the 'new' emporium of Trieste formed part of a broad scheme designed to stimulate the expansion of the free port. Privileges and freedoms in the spheres of religion, taxation, justice, employment and economic

---

47   BCT, AD, AP, GP, 9 May 1774, 19 December 1774.

48   AST, CRG, b. 546, 27 December 1792.

49   AST, CRG, b. 547, 27 June 1794.

50   AST, CRG, b. 545, 8 October 1792, 7 December 1792.

51   AST, CRG, b. 545, 15 December 1792.

activity were mobilized in order to attract valuable newcomers. In the initial phase of free-port development, diplomatic initiatives and special instruments such as immunity played an important role, while the establishment of a legal normative framework and the administration of justice were also important prerequisites for successful trade and for attracting leading economic groups. At the same time, norms aimed at filtering and controlling the inflow and activities of newcomers were generally implemented in function of the development and expansion needs of the emporium. Prosecuted merchants, fugitives and 'dubious characters' could, in this respect, count on the help of 'friends' in the city. An emblematic witness to this is a police note to a residence permit application stating that: '[The] certificates of integrity of so many traders and townspeople do not prove anything. It is well known how easy it is to issue such certificates in Trieste, especially to save an offender.'[52]

Legal actions aimed at the regulation of immigration and integration can be schematically divided into two categories. The purpose of positive actions was to complement, differentiate and stabilize Trieste's socio-economic layout, predominantly by various *ad personam* measures. In accordance with the main directives of Trieste's economic policy, restrictive measures tended to avoid interference with the principle of free competition and sought mainly to protect the city against unproductive, violent and poor people who were considered a burden on society or a threat to public order. However, even in the case of the 'low population', regulative practices did not so much concentrate on filtering immigrants proactively, but rather on expelling unwanted and bothersome individuals retroactively. One of the main reasons for this was to prevent labour shortages, which the city often encountered. Access to immigrant workers was therefore restricted only very exceptionally, for instance when impoverished farmers from the territory of Trieste were given priority employment in public works after a period of harvest failure.[53] Similarly, resident porters were awarded preferential employment over temporary migrants in order to alleviate the negative side effects of the fluctuating demand for port labour.[54] Yet not even the regulation of porters developed into a restrictive or selective instrument: regulation was exercised only loosely, allowing the continued presence of many non-registered porters.[55] Trieste's immigration control system functioned as an adjustable mechanism, managed by the police according to the fluctuating needs of emporial development. Its devices operated in different domains together with other legal and administrative instruments, while 'in the field' there was

---

52   BCT, AD, SP, 27 December 1793.
53   BCT, AD, SP, 27 December 1793.
54   BCT, AD, AP, GP, 18 December 1774.
55   AST, CRG, b. 547, 27 June 1794.

plenty of room left for discretion and negotiation. In the last instance, the central authorities and in most cases Trieste's merchant elite had the final word on the emporium's immigration policy.

Chapter 8

Urban Police and the Regulation of Migration in Eighteenth-Century France

Vincent Milliot

After 1750, urban growth in France posed difficulties on a scale never previously encountered in the domains of provisioning, maintaining public health and keeping law and order.[1] Torn between pragmatically accepting openness or reverting to closure, urban authorities from the end of the seventeenth century accumulated regulations which sometimes revived earlier measures, but increasingly became more innovative. Reorganizing or renewing measures aimed at managing populations and their movements played an important part in a more general move to transform urban police forces.

Wanting to better monitor population movement may have been an aim common to policy makers in urban police forces, but the latter were quite diverse. In Old Regime France, there was no countrywide policing system: diversity was the norm.[2] The situation of the Parisian police force, with its Lieutenancy under the strict control of the monarchy from 1667 onwards, was an atypical case.[3] Depending on the province or town, other players invested with policing powers need to be considered: municipal magistracies, parliaments, *intendants*, governors and the military, the latter particularly in border zones. Beyond this institutional diversity, the policies put into action to manage phenomena of geographical mobility, the tensions influencing them and the motivations behind their transformations during the Enlightenment all invite investigation.

---

[1]   Bernard Lepetit, 'La population urbaine', in Jacques Dupâquier (ed.), *Histoire de la population française, vol. 2. De la Renaissance à 1789* (Paris, 1988), pp. 81–93.

[2]   Jean-Luc Laffont, *Policer la ville. Toulouse, capitale provinciale au siècle des Lumières* (doctoral thesis, University of Toulouse II Le Mirail, 1997); Catherine Denys, *Police et sécurité dans les villes de la frontière franco-belge au XVIIIe siècle* (Paris, 2002).

[3]   Marc Chassaigne, *La Lieutenance générale de police de Paris* (Geneva, 1975 (Paris, 1906)); Alan Williams, *The Police of Paris 1718–1789* (Baton Rouge/London, 1979); Vincent Milliot, *Un policier des Lumières, suivi de Mémoires de J.C.P. Lenoir, ancien lieutenant général de police de Paris* (...), Seyssel, 2011.

The openness typical of urban societies may explain early regulatory measures aimed at monitoring movement. Throughout the eighteenth century, these inherited frameworks were progressively weakened, particularly as a result of the 1720 plague outbreak and the economic and social ills which swelled the ranks of the vagrant population. More fundamentally though, their evolution may mark progressive changes in both the principles and practices upholding public safety. Ultimately, the range of attitudes adopted towards monitoring mobility in towns may well be key to understanding the forms of 'living together' in communities and the modalities of a new urban order.

The Weakening of Traditional Monitoring Procedures

With different nuances from province to province, measures for obtaining information on *étrangers*, or outsiders (migrants in the wide sense of the word: those not native to the town, rather than the country), were implemented early on.[4]

Traditional Forms of Monitoring Mobility in Towns

Initially, the forms of monitoring mobility involved the surveillance of particular sites such as entrances to the town and lodgings. Such surveillance was therefore primarily a measure of bourgeois self-regulation, for it relied on the policing responsibilities of landlords, who were required to declare their clients, and mobilized a number of municipal officers or neighbourhood representatives.[5] For the authorities, it was a matter of eliminating potential troublemakers or any individual likely to incur additional expenditure for local finances and aid institutions.

In larger towns, the flow of traffic rendered filtering at entrance points uncertain. Royal legislation, copied eventually by urban authorities, moved the point of monitoring to lodgings, putting the onus on those providing accommodation, whether commercially or as private hosts.[6] In most towns, the chief role in this monitoring of population movement was held by municipal officers like the *dizeniers* or their equivalents, with the notable exception of Paris from 1667 onwards. In Toulouse, the *dizeniers* were to keep informed of the identity of all persons living within their area and keep a running census of the population. The latter initially served for taxation purposes, but also allowed the

---

[4]   Marie-Claude Blanc-Chaléard, Caroline Douki, Nicole Dyonet and Vincent Milliot (eds), *Police et migrants. France 1667–1939* (Rennes, 2001).

[5]   Laffont, *Policer la ville*.

[6]   Bibliothèque Nationale de France (BnF), Mss Joly de Fleury 185.

identification of outsiders and suspects. The *capitouls*, or municipal officers of Toulouse, hesitated on several occasions during the eighteenth century between a central monitoring system at the police registry and one where local officers played an essential role.

In the 1670s, identical measures existed in Bordeaux, Besançon and Lille for example, but not all towns advanced at the same speed. The degree of precision required varied from a register to a simple handwritten list on a loose sheet, as in Besançon, while there were probably also oral declarations. From 1673, Bordeaux landlords were asked to keep double copies of their registers, one of which was to be lodged each month at the *jurade*, the magistrates' office.[7] But in Paris, the need to keep double registers only came into force in 1708, when police inspectors were officially appointed for the surveillance of landlords.

Implemented earlier in some towns than others, the principles for monitoring were thus quite similar, retaining relatively loose frameworks up to the end of the reign of Louis XIV. Yet both the challenge of circumstances in the eighteenth century and a general process of reflection within elite government circles on rationalization and consistency in administrative practices would then accelerate change.

The Challenge of Circumstances

The plague of 1720 during the Regency period sparked off new developments in procedures applied to monitoring mobility in towns.[8] Social problems also brought their pressure to bear. Changes to the *police des étrangers*, or outsiders' police, followed the intermittent rhythm of royal legislation aimed at fighting vagrancy, desertion and begging. The transformations which began to affect certain parts of the urban police from this time onwards can be seen as so many experiments in putting principles defined by royal legislation into practice, particularly when they echoed the aims of urban elites.

In many towns, the Marseilles plague had provisionally modified forms of monitoring, sometimes initiating more durable change. Toulouse shows how the epidemic typically led to the reinforcement of checks at entrances to the town, but also provided an opportunity for reflection on the implementation of new measures. The decision to keep a register of *étrangers* was made in 1720, while the degree of precision expected from travellers' declarations increased.[9] In Bordeaux in the early 1720s, the way the *police des étrangers* was viewed changed,

7   Vincent Denis, *Une histoire de l'identité. France, 1715–1815* (Seyssel, 2008).

8   Jean-Noël Biraben, *Les hommes et la peste* (Paris, 1976).

9   Archives municipales de Toulouse, FF 635; Laffont, 'La police des étrangers à Toulouse sous l'Ancien Régime', in Blanc-Chaléard et al. (eds), *Police et migrants*, p. 300.

and their surveillance became key to the preservation of public safety. In all, the impact of the plague, in the administrative context of a move toward rational, standardized procedures for monitoring population movement, marked a distinct change in the manner of viewing and organizing urban police forces.

Apart from the plague, the second theme which contributed to the evolution of measures for monitoring mobility was the fight against begging. Royal legislation on the matter was particularly abundant: between 1700 and 1784, an average of one act every four years.[10] Beyond the different modalities of clamping down on vagrancy – from deportation to penal colonies between 1718 and 1720, to forced labour in the *dépôts de mendicité* or poor houses in the 1760s – regulatory texts insisted strongly on keeping records of high-risk groups and presenting written proof of identity as well, crucially, as of work. The royal declaration of 18 July 1724 on beggars and vagrants recommended the systematic registration of this population type on entry into hospices. It also made provision for the centralization of information obtained via the creation of a central register held at the *Hôpital général de Paris* in order to keep better track of second offenders.[11] The country-wide project was abandoned shortly afterwards, but its range of techniques for registration and written identification could be put to local use in the surveillance of lodgings which, now more than ever, were key in monitoring mobility.

Urban authorities did not systematically adopt the measures of royal legislation on monitoring outsiders. However they did debate the issues, for example when a crisis or riot revived the spectre of the social danger represented by paupers, testing the organization of local police forces. From the mid-eighteenth century, there were propositions for a radical reorganization of the monitoring of transients. The *Mémoire sur la réformation de la police de France* (1750) by Alexandre Guillauté, lieutenant of the *prévôté* of Île de France and *Encyclopédie* contributor, was a good example. The author conceived a perfected system for permanent registration of the population and the partition of urban space, going so far as to assign numbers to apartments, staircases and houses to facilitate administrative identification of whereabouts.[12] Guillauté stated that his system aimed to solve problems of concealed or false identity. The generalized record would allow welfare to be organized on a rational basis and thus banish begging once and for all. The information collected was to be held in a centralized file managed in Paris by the Lieutenancy General of Police.

---

[10]   Christian Romon, 'Mendiants et policiers à Paris au XVIIIe siècle', *Histoire, économie et société*, 2 (1982): p. 268.

[11]   BnF, Mss Joly de Fleury 36, Déclaration du 18 juillet 1724.

[12]   M. Guillauté, *Mémoire sur la réformation de la police de France, soumis au roi en 1749*, ed. J. Seznec (Paris, 1974).

The Chaos of Anonymity

Like a good number of senior police officials, Guillauté focused on movements taking place across units of housing, and thus on lodgings which served as a form of *abcès de fixation* or containment area in the minds of moral observers and those responsible for law and order alike.[13] In a 1722 letter, Commissioner Nicolas Delamarre spoke of monitoring furnished rooms as one 'of the most important parts of the police' as far as public safety was concerned.[14]

The denunciation of categories of the population likely to frequent lodgings was part of a well-entrenched tradition of hostility towards beggars dating from the sixteenth century. What was new were the solutions proposed by authors with experience in keeping law and order: efficient population records and reliable identification of individuals. This relied on building knowledge of the population, based on written information entrusted to specialists, whereas monitoring had hitherto been founded on mutual knowledge and face-to-face encounters.[15] The goal was not so much to prevent population movement but to adapt the policing apparatus to new, heavier responsibilities due to increased population traffic. In a geographically mobile society, the problem facing the police was that of its insertion within the community, and of its legitimacy in intervening within regulatory systems which no longer functioned smoothly, even if it meant creating new ones.[16] The obsession with administration and policing focused less on geographical mobility as such than on the risks of social disaffiliation and disintegration.

Faced with the lack of clear distinctions within a mobile population, the role of the police was to provide a means of creating order which took the form of operations involving registration, classification and identification. Among the institutions able to collect information on individuals, apart from the army or the *maréchaussée*, the authorities invested with policing powers took charge of

---

13   Turmeau de la Morandière, *Police sur les mendiants, les vagabonds, les joueurs de profession, les intriguants, les filles prostituées, les domestiques hors de maison depuis longtemps et les gens sans aveu* (Paris, 1764).

14   BnF, Mss Joly de Fleury 185, fol. 207, Letter dated 23 January 1722; see *La Police de Paris en 1770. Mémoire inédit composé par ordre de G. de Sartine sur la demande de Marie-Thérèse*, ed. A. Gazier (Paris, 1879), p. 77ff.

15   Gérard Noiriel, 'Les pratiques policières d'identification des migrants et leurs enjeux pour l'histoire des relations de pouvoir. Contribution à une réflexion en longue durée', in Blanc-Chaléard et al., *Police et migrants*, pp. 115–32.

16   David Garrioch, *Neighbourhood and Community in Paris, 1740–1790* (Cambridge, 1986); David Garrioch, 'The People of Paris and their Police in the Eighteenth Century: Reflections on the Introduction of a "Modern" Police Force', *European History Quarterly*, 24 (1994): pp. 511–35.

the task, simply because the police, as the accountants of public order, considered the correct arrangement of social taxonomies to be the foundations of the proper organization of society. Such operations could be entrusted to intermediaries, as was the case for trades with the guilds, or else taken on directly by the police and its agents and offices. The registration of trades without guilds, or street vendors, when Sartine was magistrate (1759–1774) is revealing from this point of view.[17]

Under Lenoir's leadership (1776–1785), the Parisian police laid claim to a sort of monopoly on social taxonomy applying to all, in the name of the royal sovereignty and paternalistic power of the king, which it was responsible for putting into practice. For Lenoir, the police were the depository of a regal monopoly on the hierarchical classification of individuals, which only organized social living could enable. But by the latter half of the century, such measures were no longer accepted so easily, as inherited classifications or those provided by the authorities were potentially seen as impositions from on high. The very lively controversy surrounding the episode of the 1776 guild reform illustrates the conflicts which developed around this question.[18]

Obviously, urban authorities had neither the human nor financial resources to make Guillauté's police ideal a reality or to carry out its requirements, let alone the ideological project of someone like Lenoir. Moreover, on such matters there was no unanimous agreement, either at the King's Council or in urban magistracies. Yet the thoughts of administrators at different levels suggest it is worth questioning the circulation of a certain number of proposals and the convergence or degree of local originality in policies followed in the towns with the aim of ensuring more efficient 'public safety'.

Characteristics and Dynamics of the Transformation of Urban Police Forces

All over the kingdom to some extent the development of monitoring outsiders tended to modify the definition of the police, becoming the driving force behind transformations. This situation did not imply uncritical adoption of Parisian solutions, so strong was the wish to defend local political balances. The scale and modalities varied in relation to the size of the urban bodies and authorities locally in charge of the police; and multiple measures were introduced aiming to solve identical problems. Three points in particular appear to characterize this movement. The first is the increased attention paid to written proceedings, and

---

[17]   Jeffry Kaplow, *Les noms des rois. Les pauvres de Paris à la veille de la Révolution* (Paris, 1974), ch. 2; Steven L. Kaplan, 'Réflexions sur la police du monde du travail, 1700–1815', *Revue historique*, 261/1 (1979): pp. 17–77; Erica-Marie Benabou, *La prostitution et la police des moeurs au XVIIIe siècle* (Paris, 1987), p. 291; see Archives Nationales (AN), Y, register Y 9508.

[18]   Steven L. Kaplan, *La fin des corporations* (Paris, 2001), ch. 5.

their greater formalization. Next, monitoring officers can be seen to become more specialized and professional. The last point is the territorialization of monitoring forces: the increasingly well-defined link between controlling space and monitoring populations.

The Role of Written Records

From the end of the seventeenth century, the regular upkeep of landlords' registers was at the heart of surveillance measures of outsiders. The development led to turning accommodation professionals into the 'natural allies' of the police.[19] This collaboration relied on recourse to an official, written document in preference to any other sort, and in preference to traditional forms of identification via the neighbourhood or pre-established networks of connections. It also relied on police officers submitting to the rigours of standardized forms and copying norms that could not be modified at their convenience. The authorities kept a watch on standardization to avoid imprecision. Consideration of models for registers had an effect on the related records, slips and various forms which were then used for keeping more or less centralized registers and files.

The improvements wrought on the administrative task of registration were applied slowly and unevenly, according to the zeal of the monitoring officers. In 1779, in one of his circulars, Lenoir was still recommending commissioners to send neater entries of landlords' records to the *Lieutenance Générale*.[20] However, what is noteworthy is the steady increase in requirements which came to the fore quite soon in certain towns. While attention was paid to the standardization of monitoring tools, there was also a tendency to double up to facilitate the activities of the different surveillance officers. Everywhere, the growing link between the ratification of information contained in the register and the promotion of new monitoring officers was the visible mark of the specialization of increasingly hefty police mechanisms.

A Move toward Specialized, Professional Monitoring Officers

The strengthened surveillance of outsiders in towns led to a clearer hierarchy in the different stages of monitoring. This policy required a greater involvement of officers in direct contact with lodgings, their conversion to the generalized use of written documents and thus the promotion of new professional skills. Such a goal was achieved either by renovating traditional municipal institutions or

---

[19]   AN Y 13728, Letter from Lenoir, 20 March 1778.
[20]   AN Y 13728.

by introducing new heads, the commissioners, whose remit was superimposed on that of the municipal officers who, now deemed too inefficient, began to lose their privileges. The modalities of these transformations defined styles of police reform, characterized by different degrees of rupture or compromise with the usual practices and views of municipal police forces. The size of towns, their geographical position and functions and the nature of the protagonists contributing to change all played a part.

The case of Lille illustrates the clean break model: 32 district commissioners were created as early as 1686 to combat begging, particularly by outsiders to the town. Their number was subsequently decreased to 20 in 1709, this time as part of the re-division of urban space leading to the definition of new 'police' districts.[21] But even in the towns where a relatively clean break was chosen, hesitations emphasize the fact that the neighbourhood police did not disappear in one go. The magistrates would in fact have been wrong to deprive themselves of a close and complex network, or to force change at the risk of provoking strong opposition. Toulouse offers a case of a compromise sought between promoting new monitoring powers, increasing the policing requirements imposed on municipal officers and aiming to keep the traditional organization which was felt to need rationalizing.[22] Without disappearing altogether, the institution of the *dizeniers* was modified little by little, between 1760 and 1770, as the skills of office bearers were verified and their tasks repeatedly honed. Finally, there were also cases where efforts made to better monitor outsiders led first to the revival of duties which had become more or less obsolete, rather than the creation of new authorities. Valenciennes and Besançon in the late 1760s offer an example of this kind of 'reverse' evolution which preserved neighbourhood self-regulation.

The size of the towns obviously affected the scope of the means employed for resolving common problems and giving concrete form to similar political leanings. Nowhere else did the specialization of mechanisms and the sophistication of monitoring measures reach the same level as in the capital.[23] While the police decree on public safety dated 20 May 1667 mentions checks on lodgings as one of the primary functions of Châtelet commissioners, in reality from d'Argenson's time (1698–1713) the Parisian system was developing what was in fact a specialist corps of 40 inspectors created by the edict of 1708. Posted to districts to work alongside the commissioners, their specific tasks were daily checks on landlords and collecting registers. From these duties they progressively took responsibility for monitoring migrants and outsiders, following the

---

21   Denys, *Police et sécurité*, pp. 51–60 and pp. 344–53.

22   Laffont, *Policer la ville*, p. 303.

23   Daniel Roche, *Humeurs vagabondes. De la circulation des hommes et de l'utilité des voyages* (Paris, 2003), p. 376; Milliot, *Un policier*, pp. 143–269.

express wish of the Lieutenant General of Police, anxious to have forces at his disposal which were relatively free from any tutelage but his own. Once the new institution had stabilized, in around 1740, the distribution of tasks on site and the doubling up of checks carried out by the two types of officers lasted until the nineteenth century. The kind of active police work involved with keeping law and order, which had once been the remit of inspectors, could now be taken on by a few commissioners using new, reputedly efficient practices.[24] This on-site specialization found a counterpart in the organization of the departments of the Lieutenancy, particularly from Berryer's time (1749–1757) on. The monitoring of hotels and rented rooms was the remit of the sixth bureau of the Lieutenancy, which was responsible for 'public safety'.

These reforms of varying intensity all moved in the direction of specializing mechanisms and centralizing data. All show the rise in power of individuals trained in techniques for keeping records, originating from military, legal or prison institutions and lending their skills to population monitoring. On occasions, the initiative for reforms came from beyond the town authorities. The influence of the military hierarchy made itself felt in Lille and Dunkirk in the appointment of the clerk in charge of the declaration of outsiders. In Bordeaux, the *intendant* played a major role. In Paris, the King's Council, the Department of the King's Household and the Lieutenants General of police occupied the front stage.[25] The question is to know to what extent their propositions could be communicated through to town authorities or, in other cases, endorsed by powerful regulatory bodies like the parliaments. Agreement was not always unanimous. The implementation of new administrators and officers to carry out centralized monitoring of mobile populations, generally associated with a concern to keep records of the entire population of the town, required a subtle shift in the balance of local political power in order to succeed.[26] The development of urban police forces, approached here via the transformations in the monitoring of outsiders, illustrates a much larger move towards autonomous, specialized and professional police services.

---

[24]   Romon, 'Mendiants'; Milliot, *Un policier*, pp. 252–269.

[25]   Jean-Lucien Gay, 'L'administration de la capitale entre 1770 et 1789. La tutelle de la royauté et ses limites' *Mémoires de la fédération historique de Paris et de l'Ile-de-France* (1956): pp. 299–370, (1957–1958): 283–363, (1959): 181–247, (1960): 263–403, (1961): 135–218.

[26]   Outside the French kingdom, Brussels offers an example of police reform encountering resistance from a magistrate. See Catherine Denys, 'Les projets de réforme de la police à Bruxelles à la fin du XVIIIe siècle. Police et contrôle du territoire dans les villes capitales (XVIIe–XIXe siècle)', *Mélanges de l'école française de Rome, Italie et Méditerranée (MEFRIM)*, 115/2 (2003): pp. 807–26.

Paris, Lille, Bordeaux, Toulouse, as well as Lyon or Grenoble, capital cities, border towns, ports and military strongholds, trading and manufacturing towns: all the towns affected by the transformation of their police forces were cities where intense geographical mobility required stricter monitoring procedures. In addition, control of population movements led to refinements in the partition of space.

The Territorialization of Monitoring

In the view of heads of urban authorities under the Old Regime, there was a link between the size of towns and the ability of officers charged with 'public safety' to monitor space and populations. Their efficiency in the domain of law and order, traffic or aid was determined more exactly by the division of space into units of territory which were sufficiently well calibrated to allow proper administration.[27]

The situation in Paris once more illustrates the pattern for reforms breaking with old institutions. The new 1702 police districts aimed to take over from inherited territorial structures either by destroying them or leaving them practically devoid of substance, so that the municipal districts disappeared in the face of the new administrative subdivisions.[28] A creation of this sort did not modify the spatial practices of the population all at once, but it did remove the old institutional, bourgeois dimension from neighbourhood organizations.[29] A similar reform was carried out in Lille in two stages, in 1686 and 1709. In 1686, the new district commissioners were introduced within the traditional territorial organization. By contrast, the 1709 reform overturned the partition of the town and imposed the division into 20 new police districts. In Bordeaux, during the 1740s, projects were developed with similar views. An overhaul of the districts along geometrical lines was considered.

The inadequacy of police partition at times became patently obvious in the eyes of the administration when a crisis put it to the test. In Besançon, the subsistence riots which broke out in 1740 were at the origin of the creation of another police commission and a new division of urban space, which was enlarged to include suburbs. The creation of 10 police districts in Lyon in 1745 also came

27   Bibliothèque multimédia d'Orléans, J.C.P. Lenoir (1732–1807), *Mémoires, t. 12, De la police judiciaire et administrative*, Mss 1422, fol. 859.

28   Robert Descimon and Jean Nagle, 'Les quartiers de Paris, du moyen âge au XVIIIe siècle: évolution d'un espace pluri-fonctionnel', *Annales ESC*, 5 (1979): pp. 956–83.

29   Robert Descimon, 'Les barricades de la Fronde parisienne. Une lecture sociologique', *Annales ESC*, 2 (1990): pp. 397–422; Robert Descimon, 'Milice bourgeoise et identité citadine à Paris au temps de la Ligue', *Annales ESC*, 4 (1993): pp. 885–906.

about after disturbances caused by workers in the silk industry in the summer of 1744.[30] Yet the new territorial framework with its clearly geometrical intent, did not really seem to replace the finer mesh of the 30 or so *penonnages* which remained the principal policing and administrative units.[31] Unlike the situation in Lyon, magistrates sometimes preferred to reclaim former structures, as was the case in Valenciennes, without giving up entirely on hopes of modernization and adding extra police requirements.

Such plans and changes may be seen to illustrate the impact of the Parisian model. Several of those putting forward plans, both in France and abroad, made explicit reference to it.[32] But when Lenoir, the Lieutenant of Police, was approached to support a report on police reform in Strasbourg, he gave a measured response. In his view, each system of urban police should take the customs, climate and particular character of the inhabitants into account. For police operations in the provinces to copy Paris would, he explained, run the risk of 'committing grave errors'.[33] It could not have been better put: the transformation of urban police did not conform to a centralized, standardizing plan stemming solely from government circles, but rather relied, in nearly every case, on compromises forged between several protagonists.

Towards a New Urban Order?

The appearance of new police mechanisms associated with innovative monitoring procedures was not without consequences for the socio-political

---

[30]   Ordonnance de police du 15 juillet 1745, Archives Municipales de Lyon (AML), BB 414, 1; Stéphane Nivet, *La police de Lyon au XVIIIe siècle: l'exemple de la police consulaire puis municipale* (Mémoire de DEA, Université Jean Moulin Lyon 3, 2003), pp. 14, 151; Olivier Zeller, 'Géographie des troubles et découpages urbains à Lyon (XVIe–XVIIIe siècles)', in *Actes du 114e Congrès National des Sociétés Savantes* (Paris, 1989), pp. 43–59.

[31]   In 1747 the Lyon consulate ordered a detailed map of districts and *penonnages*. See AML, 3 S 693, C. Jacquemin, *Plan géométral et proportionnel de la ville de Lyon* (1747), 46x59, 1/62000ᵉ.

[32]   Brigitte Marin, 'Compétences territoriales et transformations urbaines à Naples au XVIIIe siècle: la nouvelle *strada della marina* entre volonté monarchique et prérogatives municipales', in *Pouvoirs publics (État, administration) et ville en France, Italie, et Espagne de la fin du XVIIe siècle à la fin du XVIIIe siècle, LIAME*, 5 (January–June 2000): pp. 83–98; Brigitte Marin, 'Administrations policières, réformes et découpages territoriaux (XVII–XIXe siècle)', in *Police et contrôle du territoire dans les villes capitales (XVIIe–XIXe siècle), MEFRIM*, 115/2 (2003): pp. 745–50; Catherine Denys, Brigitte Marin and Vincent Milliot (eds), *Réformer la police. Les mémoires policiers en Europe au XVIIIe siècle* (Rennes, 2009).

[33]   Archives Municipales de Strasbourg, AA 2508, Copie de la lettre de Mr Le Noir, à Mr Lautour, le 3 octobre 1780. My thanks to Vincent Denis for this reference.

compromises which provided the basis for law and order, but were weakened by increasing, generalized mobility. Faced with the scope of the proposed modifications, populations and certain protagonists within the authorities were liable to protest, so that their acceptance depended on the prudence with which promoters put their ideas into practice.

Tension Brought on by Innovation

Awareness of the need to adopt exceptional measures to keep law and order in a moving urban society was particularly sharp in Paris and towns where the imperatives of military security were strong. The sense of urgency did not help to organize the reception of new measures in a diplomatic way. After being annexed to France, Lille experienced the rapid accumulation of a set of measures which appeared to endanger the policing powers of the magistrate and broke with traditional means of control. The military command's appointment of a clerk to declare outsiders in 1739, with the aim of having him prepare a general census of the population of Lille to help the identification of non-natives, may have been the last straw. Launching an operation which made people fear some sort of new taxation measure during the crisis of winter 1740 moved the population to rise against the clerk, who was too foreign to the local police and their ways.

At the beginning of the eighteenth century, the Chamber of Justice of 1716 and the legal action filed against the Parisian police inspectors appointed by Lieutenant General d'Argenson showed that, in the eyes of the population, certain innovations were not legitimate despite their supposed efficiency.[34] The plaintiffs of 1716–1720 belonged to stable elements of district populations: officers, members of the bourgeoisie, masters of trades (including landlords and innkeepers). They denounced the corruption and unlawful status of the Lieutenancy's new officers engaged in active police work, as well as the taxes they charged for the exercise of their functions. Criticism was not limited to a protest against taxes, but rather targeted the new policing measures themselves: visits and searches at all hours, without regard for Sundays or holidays, violence and impertinence, secrecy and concealment instead of the normally public nature of local policing. The accusation took on a moral character: the inspectors were not known to the public, they came from the lower echelons of society and were not familiar with the law. Between the lines of such accusations, the public expectations for the police force are clear: roots in the neighbourhood,

---

[34]   Paolo Piasenza, 'Juges, lieutenants de police et bourgeois à Paris aux XVII et XVIIIe siècle', *Annales ESC*, 4 (1990): pp. 1189–215; Patrice Peveri, 'L'exempt, l'archer, la mouche et le filou. Délinquance policière et contrôle des agents dans le Paris de la Régence', in Laurent Feller (ed.), *Contrôler les agents du pouvoir* (Limoges, 2004).

visibility and services.[35] In Paris, only the Châtelet commissioners had claim to such legitimacy and were able to live up to the expectations of the population, in the same way as in other towns the role might go to municipal officers and local dignitaries. Like a classic conflict of remit or precedence between officers, the Parisian crisis confronted two ways of understanding policing practices.

Such conflicts are significant for at least two reasons. They emphasize, firstly, that within police institutions which were not stable, contradictions and confrontations were developing. The second significance is less institutional and more directly socio-political in nature. The establishment of a professionalized policing model according to modalities which were both similar yet specific to each town, and were inspired in more than one case by a military template, was in fact opposed to the traditions of bourgeois self-regulation – whether the latter were still strong or else weakened depending on the case. However, more and more often throughout the century, it also met with the magistrates' own modernizing aims. The substitution of commissioners for municipal officers, the promotion of police inspectors in Paris, the new divisions of urban territory nevertheless led to an undeniable turnaround. The new protagonists in charge of policing were no longer there to represent the interests of the inhabitants to the urban authorities, but to check and monitor the population reporting recorded discrepancies to the authorities.

Such transformations would not be considered without a significant gain in return. For Guillauté, organizing absolute social and spatial transparency under the aegis of the police would lead to the disappearance of the *basse police* and its much disparaged spying – in a word, to a raising of moral standards. For Lenoir, it was the ever more precise formalization of administrative police practices, and therefore the increased professionalism of officers, which was to lower risks of unlawfulness. In any case, the extent of the projected or actual break should not be exaggerated. The example of Paris shows that neither the inertia nor the flexibility of the practices characterizing the ways police administrations worked should be ignored.

The Flexibility of Policing Practices

The analysis of infringements to legislation on furnished rooms and lodgings in Paris in the eighteenth century shows that by far the most common offence, making up about half of the infractions throughout the century, concerned the

---

[35]   BnF Mss FF Joly de Fleury 185, fol. 242ff: *Mémoire pour plusieurs particuliers tenans hôtels … contre les inspecteurs de police …*, undated.

poor keeping of landlords' registers.[36] Neither these figures nor the reiteration of rules concerning the keeping of registers, nor even the grand-scale summary of infractions of 1777, constitute proof of the inability of the police to monitor mobility and ensure obedience to the law.[37] Rather, if the expansion of the commercial side to providing lodging is kept in mind, it would suggest persistent police preoccupation with those spaces which functioned as receptacles for populations in movement. The role played by the Lieutenant General in launching clampdown operations, including for this type of basic infringement, shows that the concern was shared in high places.[38] It was not only limited to the ordinary tasks of police commissioners and inspectors within their districts. Poor keeping of registers was not considered a minor infringement. Far from being lax, prosecutions on the contrary show a will to accustom the public to written administrative norms. Nevertheless difficulties encountered in communicating the need to use new identification procedures to the general public need to be taken into account.

Qualitatively, the nature of register-keeping infringements ranged from simple negligence to deliberate fraud. Some people who provided lodgings on an occasional basis committed involuntary fraud without wishing to break the law. Such cases simply show that despite legislation, declaring provision of lodging was not obvious in cases close to traditional forms of hospitality. It can be assumed that police tolerance in these cases was reasonably strong, the commissioner being content more often than not to collect information informally to ascertain who was visiting or staying with whom. Even without a register, the commissioner was aware of lodgers' place of residence, date of arrival in the district, reputation and morals. The commissioner knew his world, remembered minor infringements and potential sexual offences; but he was far from writing down or prosecuting all of them. Knowing how to turn a blind eye without being fooled was a condition for working efficiently and gaining public approval.

The case of 'illegal' landlords lacking signs, registers and any declaration of their activity, located in particular in the Saint-Denis, Saint-Germain and Saint-Benoît districts during the 1760s, was slightly different. Within this single category of offenders, whom the police considered highly suspicious, a number of different practices coexisted. On occasion, underground accommodation

---

[36]   Out of 545 infringements recorded between 1718 and 1780 there were 265 cases of poor keeping of registers; Vincent Milliot, 'La surveillance des migrants et des lieux d'accueil à Paris du XVIe siècle aux années 1830', in Roche, *La ville promise*, pp. 54–5.

[37]   BnF recueil Z Le Senne 167 (25), Ordonnance de police ... du 26 juillet 1777.

[38]   Nearly 60 per cent of the cases for the 1760–1765 period related to regulations on rented rooms brought by the Lieutenant of Police concern landlords' poor or absent registers.

did indeed go hand in hand with the development of shady activities aiming to escape police detection.[39] However other reports suggest a lowly type of landlord looking for extra income by offering shabby, cluttered accommodation for the night. Police raids sometimes revealed clusters of such shelters in one street, in an alley where low-paid workers might take in casual labourers, water haulers or floor scrubbers.[40] Through the snippets of interrogations included in reports it appears that in such places migrant or trade networks probably grew, helping people from the same geographical area or similar jobs to find accommodation. In this context, it was neither usual nor necessary to have recourse to police procedures based on written identification of individuals and the logic of rational administration. The police were caught between the necessity of applying regulations and awareness of the economic fragility of the small-time landlords who generally also had another occupation.[41] The preference was for lowering the tariff of fines according to their 'capabilities' well under the decreed levels in order to retain the educational value of the penalty. When indulgence appeared to have exhausted its educational virtues, the police were ready to return to repression.[42]

The greater or lesser speed with which commissioners intervened with a landlord in trouble over one aspect or another of the regulations is a good measure of the levels of tolerance of the police in applying the law. In theory, from 1708 onwards, landlords' registers were subject to a dual monitoring system: daily by the inspector and monthly by the district commissioner. This system, which took advantage of the stabilization of the body of inspectors in the 1740s, was to allow late and irregular entries of clientele to be detected quickly. However, certain reports made to police hearings in the mid-1800s – which, in order to emphasize the gravity of the offence, made reference to the duration of an infringement in correct keeping of the register – show delays ranging from three days to three years. The majority of cases concern delays of between one and two years! The reports thus suggest that the commissioners, who had the administrative means for keeping track of irregular landlords, were well aware of the offenders.[43] This clearly emphasizes the existence of a period of verbal admonishment, which may have been quite long, before issuing a summons to the hardened offender and setting more serious proceedings into motion leading to prosecution and a published sentence which would damage

---

[39] AN Y 9468, Audience du 19 juillet 1765.

[40] AN Y 9467, Audience du 15 février 1765.

[41] BnF, Mss Joly de Fleury 185, fols 85–92, 'Auberges et chambres garnies de Paris', enquête des commissaires sur les logeurs, octobre 1721.

[42] AN Y 9466B, Rapport du commissaire Belle, novembre 1764.

[43] AN Y 9449A, Rapport du commissaire Demortain, janvier 1748.

the landlord's reputation. It is perhaps quite a good illustration of the idea of preventative rather than punitive policing, or the ability to weigh the letter of the law to ease its application. However, beyond a certain degree of seriousness in the proceedings, or a second offence, it became difficult for a commissioner to turn a blind eye.[44]

Restoring a rationale dictating either a repressive or a tolerant attitude was never easy. The attitude adopted depended on fine balances within the neighbourhoods and districts which the commissioner needed to understand; it depended on the importance of local dignitaries and personalities, the balance of possible needs for protection and the pressure exerted by the police hierarchy. In theory, each district was likely to come up with its own configuration. In the latter half of the eighteenth century, the intensification of arrivals and departures in the capital and the dissolution of territorial solidarities modified the conditions for obtaining a balance.[45] The Parisian police attempted as far as possible to take the place of the missing intermediaries. However, unable to effectively master all movements and the networks enabling them, the police applied themselves to targeting their interventions more accurately and obtaining the consensus of the established fringe of the population on the use of their reformed methods.

A New Urban Order and Exclusion

The surveillance of lodgings in the eighteenth century in Paris and throughout the kingdom was considered central to clamping down on begging, vagrancy and prostitution – offences which proliferated in the mobile fringes of the population. This concern led police authorities to refine the nomenclature of suspects and order types of accommodation in relation to their presumed danger. Most observers pointed to the same target. Social danger was first identified with a refusal to work rather than mobility itself: 'gens sans aveu, workers without work, good-for-nothings with no trade', all of them 'dangerous characters who, forced to leave their home province, come to hide in Paris hoping to get off free'.[46] Monitoring policy was increasingly closely targeted in the latter half of the eighteenth century: it was aimed at 'high-risk' groups. The police received the probable approbation of the population in such matters, since they were responding to an increased need for public 'safety' at a time of generalized change in urban society.

---

44   AN Y 9461A, Rapport du commissaire Bouquigny, juin 1760.
45   David Garrioch, *The Making of Revolutionary Paris* (Berkeley, 2002), chs 10–11.
46   BnF, Mss Joly de Fleury 1803, fols 6–7.

The intense clampdown on beggars and prostitutes, particularly in Paris under Sartine and Lenoir, offers a final example.[47] The royal declaration of 1764 and the October 1767 decree on the *dépôts de mendicité*, or poor houses for beggars, gave rise to a dizzying increase in arrests. The clampdown on prostitution in rented rooms showed clear progress, going from 14 per cent of prosecutions between 1718 and 1752 to 32 per cent between 1760 and 1780. During Lenoir's second term in office (1776–1785), more than half of the reports on infringements to regulations on rented rooms presented by commissioners to the Chamber concerned this type of offence. This took place without public revolt despite the solidarity which the working classes were reputed to show towards the destitute.[48] 'Resistance' did exist, but a more moderate use of police and military forces in particular after the riots of 1750 may explain the relative calm.[49] In 1777, a circular from Lenoir invited commissioners to take additional precautions to avoid popular unrest when launching a campaign for arresting beggars.[50] Was the cause of unrest really due to compassion for the poor, or rather to indignation caused by the spectacle of unlawful behaviour and violence, no matter who its victims? Like other authors of his time, Mercier assimilated rented rooms with a type of poverty and vice, places where concealed identity, disguise and social opacity were rife. They were perfect places for 'police kidnapping', an indubitable form of unlawful behaviour which took advantage of anonymity.[51] Its condemnation led to a feeling of ambivalence: the unlawful behaviour of the police was denounced, but the need for such actions could not really be denied. It was condemned in the name of the subject's rights, whether rich or poor. However, it suggested that enlightened opinion, which rarely champions the masses, would be willing to swap the efficiency of the repressive measures of the police for the old community regulation which had been destroyed by the growth of the city, as long as certain rights were guaranteed and police activities were properly supervised. The main losers in the evolution were therefore recent migrants finding it hard to enter the urban employment market, who were

---

[47]   Milliot, 'La surveillance', 21–76 ; Romon, 'Mendiants', 259–95.

[48]   Arlette Farge, 'Le mendiant, un marginal? Les résistances aux archers de l'Hôpital dans le Paris du XVIIIe siècle' in *Les Marginaux et les exclus dans l'histoire* (Paris, 1979), *Cahiers Jussieu*, 10/18, pp. 312–28.

[49]   Arlette Farge and Jacques Revel, *Logiques de la foule. L'affaire des enlèvements d'enfants, Paris 1750* (Paris, 1988); Christian Romon, 'L'affaire des enlèvements d'enfants dans les archives du Châtelet (1749–1750)', *Revue historique*, 3 (1983): pp. 55–95.

[50]   AN AD+ 1032, pièce 15 and AN Y 12830, 19 août 1777.

[51]   Louis-Sébastien Mercier, *Le Tableau de Paris (1781–1789)*, ed. J-C. Bonnet (Paris, 1994), ch. 337.

inadequately looked after by community networks in a context of weakened solidarity and sociability.

The Parisian police force may have tried, towards the end of the eighteenth century, to combine modes of intervention based on long-term presence in the districts and recognition of the mediating skills of its officers, with more functional, 'de-territorialized' styles of intervention.[52] From 1760 onwards, the fight against infringements to the legislation on renting furnished rooms shows that certain offences, such as the poor keeping of registers, were still prosecuted within the districts by the officers assigned there. Under this system, settlements were possible, all the more so since there were a number of professionals among the minor dignitaries and respectable shopkeepers. Conversely, the rapidly developing hunt for illegal landlords or prostitutes in rented rooms was due to commissioners or inspectors working in several districts at once, some of whom – like Commissioner Hugues, from 1760 to 1780 – specialized in the area. The intervention of officers who themselves were 'outsiders' to the district was usual in the context of police patrols, but now tended to become more frequent and systematic in clamping down on certain offences. However, the 'outsider' status of public forces had, in the past, justified a number of rebellious acts and speeches to officers who did not come from the district and were thus not recognized as lawful. It was as though the relationship established between the public and the active police forces which had aroused so much reticence in the Regency period had begun to change by the end of the eighteenth century. The neighbourhood seemed more ready to give its silent support, outside the old community frameworks of social regulation, to the fight against 'debauchery', which itself may have changed, now that more recently arrived prostitutes walked the streets and the spectre of poverty haunted public speeches and policies as well as the town squares.

Concluding Remarks

Although they were not the same, and were not based on the sole reference to a supposed 'Parisian model', urban 'police' forces in France under the Old Regime nevertheless faced similar challenges. The growing mobility of populations, well before the development of the railway, was one of them, obliging administrators of all sorts to reflect on the modalities of social monitoring and how to adapt them to new contexts. The nature of the responses provided throughout the

---

[52]   Vincent Milliot, 'Saisir l'espace urbain: la mobilité des commissaires au Châtelet et le contrôle des quartiers de police parisiens au 18e siècle', *Revue d'Histoire Moderne et Contemporaine*, 50/1 (2003): pp. 54–80.

century of the Enlightenment – from the move towards professional, specialized monitoring agents and the promotion of written records to the new division of urban spaces – profoundly modified the balance of traditional policing powers and the meaning of their action within the social body.[53] The will to transform urban police forces may be seen as one aspect of a more general tendency towards the standardization and administration of men and things. In many ways, it contributed towards defining a repertoire of methods which in future would become systematic. But such a 'laboratory', over and above anything else, challenges any teleological reading of the birth of state police apparatuses, and invites investigation of the circulation of ideas and practices, keeping in mind their constant adaptations to socio-political realities and the local institutional balances which underlie the compromises upon which social order is based.

Translated by Susan Nicholls

---

[53]   Catherine Denys, 'De l'autorégulation sociale au contrôle policier, la naissance de la police moderne dans les villes du nord de la France du XVIIIe siècle', in Pedro Fraile (ed.), *Modelar para gobernar. El control de la poblacion y el territorio en Europa y Canada. Una perspectiva historica* (Barcelona, 2001), pp. 99–109.

PART III
Crossing the Lines:
Begging and Poor Relief

PART III

Chapter 9
Magistrates, Beggars, and Labourers: Migration and Regulation in Sixteenth-Century Ulm

Jason P. Coy

During the mid-sixteenth century, southern Germany began to experience repeated waves of famine and epidemic disease, along with frightening economic depression, mass impoverishment and rural landlessness. Ulm, a free imperial city in the region, had grown rich on long-distance trade in textiles during the late Middle Ages, but fell into a steady decline in the sixteenth century as the regional economy faltered.[1] As the city's economic situation worsened, the admission rates of new citizens declined since, it was no longer attractive to propertied immigrants capable of purchasing citizenship (*Bürgerrecht*). Accordingly, during the 1500s Ulm's population growth stalled and the number of citizens began to contract.[2] However, the city continued to draw a steady stream of impoverished outsiders from its extensive rural hinterland and beyond, migrants hoping to find work or alms in the city. In the face of this sobering situation, Ulm's town council intensified its efforts to control migration, issuing new edicts and carrying out exhaustive procedures intended to regulate the flow of poor migrants into the territory.

---

[1] For the economic situation in southern Germany in the late sixteenth century, see Tom Scott, *Society and Economy in Germany, 1300–1600* (Bristol, 2002), pp. 254–5. See also David Sabean, *Power in the Blood: Popular Culture and Village Discourse in Early Modern Germany* (Cambridge, 1984), pp. 6–9.

[2] Most of Ulm's tax rolls have not survived, so it is difficult to establish its sixteenth-century population precisely. According to the most recent estimates, it appears that the city had between 9,200 and 11,300 residents in the decades before 1550, and the local population peaked in the 1580s with somewhere between 16,500 and 21,000 inhabitants. By 1600 the figure had dropped to between 11,300 and 19,000. See Annemarie Kinzelbach, *Gesundbleiben, Krankwerden, Armsein in der frühneuzeitlichen Gesellschaft. Gesunde und Kranke in den Reichsstädten Überlingen und Ulm, 1500–1700* (Stuttgart, 1995).

Despite these official efforts, the city's craftsmen relied upon the cheap labour supplied by migrants from the countryside; and the local magistrates, an oligarchic group drawn from Ulm's leading patrician and mercantile families, could not afford to prohibit migration entirely. Consequently, the Ulmer authorities classified would-be migrants according to their apparent suitability for work and their respectability, provisionally admitting those able to secure steady employment and who appeared to be both obedient and upright. Those who could not or would not find work, on the other hand, were labelled 'beggars' and 'vagrants' and ruthlessly driven from the city.[3] Likewise, migrants who had been admitted but subsequently lost their jobs or misbehaved faced expulsion.

This examination of the selection and expulsion of newcomers in sixteenth-century Ulm will demonstrate that the regulation of migration in this south German city, one whose experience was similar to other imperial city-states in the region, was based not only on economic considerations but also on moral ones. Analysis of these regulatory efforts will also elucidate their role in defining inclusion in the urban community, as the local authorities determined which migrants were acceptable and which were to be expelled, enacting in the process definitive changes in newcomers' social status. The flow of migrants into the city during this troubled era overwhelmed the local magistrates' meagre manpower resources and they proved incapable of identifying and punishing many of the unwanted newcomers who entered. Nevertheless, the public punishment of troublesome migrants who fell foul of the authorities demonstrates the authorities' efforts to police the boundary between inclusion and exclusion in Reformation-era Germany.

The animosity towards the wandering poor that the Ulmer authorities displayed in their regulatory policies echoed the fear and mistrust of impoverished migrants that was prevalent throughout early modern Europe. Across the continent, respectable, settled society associated the alien, able-bodied poor with epidemic disease, social disruption and moral decay. The marked rise of vagrancy, a consequence of the economic disruption of the period, often led to the development of a distinction within European poor laws between the 'deserving' and 'undeserving' poor. In the Holy Roman Empire, the Imperial Diet at Lindau (1497) codified the principle that each community should care for its own indigenous poor. The Reformation, emphasizing the sanctity of work and the secularization of poor relief, accelerated these developments in Protestant territories like Ulm. According to Martin Luther, writing in 1528, 'every town and village should know and be acquainted with its own poor,

---

[3]   For concise treatment of the history of Ulm during the sixteenth century, see Hans Eugen Specker, *Ulm. Stadtgeschichte* (Ulm, 1977).

listing them in a register so they can help them. But foreign beggars ought not be tolerated without a letter or seal, for there is far too much roguery among them'.[4] The first Protestant city to enact a Lutheran model of poor relief was Wittenberg, which issued a code in 1521 that outlawed all begging within the city in favour of providing for the 'worthy' poor from a community chest.[5]

Ulm's first comprehensive poor law dates from before the Reformation, but as the city moved towards adopting Protestant worship after 1526, its regulations gradually came to resemble the Lutheran ordinance from Wittenberg. By the time the city formally joined the Protestant camp, its treatment of the poor adhered closely to the Lutheran model adopted by other south German city-states. Thus, Ulm's *Almosenordnungen* of 1528, which was reissued in 1581, drew a firm distinction between the worthy poor, local indigents who could not work owing to age or infirmity, and the unworthy poor, able-bodied, foreign beggars. According to the Ulmer magistrates, the former should be tolerated and aided from the community chest, while the latter should be driven from the city, a distinction that shaped the regulation of migrants throughout the century.[6]

An influential advice book for 'housefathers' from the 1550s, written by Caspar Huberinus, a Lutheran pastor well known in the area around Ulm, reveals the widespread mistrust of the wandering poor that informed these policies:

> One finds many foul rogues who wander the countryside and beg from town to town. The poor people are up to their ears in these vagrants ... who take up begging not out of necessity, but rather out of idleness, and what someone will not give them, they take it themselves, stealing it, and becoming in the end shameless vagabonds, foul rogues, swindlers, traitors, thieves, robbers and murderers. In the end, no villainy is too great. ... Just as a man should not trust a robber who creeps from town to town, so one should not trust a man who has no nest, and must wander about ... .[7]

Huberinus's assertion that impoverished migrants posed a dangerous threat to settled society and that they begged out of 'idleness' was echoed in sermons

---

[4] Martin Luther, Foreword to *Liber Vagatorum* (Wittenberg, 1528).

[5] See Robert Jütte, *Poverty and Deviance in Early Modern Europe* (Cambridge, 1994), pp. 105–8, 145–7.

[6] Stadtarchiv Ulm (StAU) A 2002, *Ordnung des neu aufgerichteten Almoskastens* (1528); StAU A 4176/1, *Almosenordnungen* (1581).

[7] Casparum Huberinum, *Jesus Syrach. Spiegel der Haußzucht genannt, Sammpt einer kurtzen Außlegung für die armen Haußväter und ir gesinde, wie sie ein Gottselig leben gegen meniglich sollen erzeigen. Darinnen der Welt lauff begriffen und wie sich ein ieglicher Christ in seinem beruff und in der Policey ehrlich und löblich solle halten* (Nuremberg, 1552/1587).

and printed tracts throughout the period, helping to shape the regulation of migrants in German territories like Ulm, where amid hard times unemployment was increasingly considered a moral failure and indigence a criminal offence.

Regulation and Classification: The Migrants' Ordinance

Influenced by traditional attitudes towards the wandering poor and by Lutheran notions of poor relief, Ulm's town council drew strong distinctions in its legislation among the labouring poor, classifying them according to their ability to earn their own bread. Accordingly, in their edicts the local authorities categorized some migrants as 'pious, good, and tolerated here', and others as 'good-for-nothing' – the latter presumed to be a drain on the poor chest.

As the chapters in this volume demonstrate, throughout early modern Europe migrant workers were essential to the craft economy. In the cities of southern Germany, young men and women from rural areas provided crucial temporary and seasonal labour in the markets, households and workshops of nearby cities and towns.[8] Male villagers often found work in urban marketplaces and warehouses or served as wage labourers in craft workshops, particularly in the late sixteenth century as the guilds closed ranks and opportunities to attain the rank of master diminished.[9] Female migrants usually found work as domestic servants while they saved up enough money to marry.[10]

In Ulm, this rural labour force was essential to the urban workshop economy, and temporary workers constantly flowed into the city from the countryside in search of wages. Ulm's town council administered an extensive territory known

---

[8]   For the economic role of migrant workers in early modern Germany, see Christian Pfister, 'The Population of Late Medieval and Early Modern Europe', in Bob Scribner (ed.), *Germany: A New Social and Economic History, 1450–1630* (London, 1996), pp. 55–8. See also Merry E. Wiesner, *Working Women in Renaissance Germany* (New Brunswick NJ, 1986), pp. 83–92, for the function of female migrant workers. According to Pfister, most migrant workers during this period were from rural cottager families. While they changed their place of residence frequently in search of jobs (particularly those working in domestic service), they usually only migrated during their youth and within the orbit of the nearest large town.

[9]   On the liminal position of journeymen and apprentices, who increasingly worked for wages in guild workshops without any hope of become masters themselves and who had a place in the guild establishment without enjoying citizenship rights, see Merry E. Wiesner, 'Gender and the Worlds of Work', in Scribner (ed.), *Germany: A New Social and Economic History*, pp. 224–6.

[10]   Of the migrant workers who applied for residency in Ulm during the period 1550–1559 and whose employment can be determined, some 50 per cent were hired as domestic servants. Of these domestics, females outnumbered males by about two to one. See Kinzelbach, *Gesundbleiben, Krankwerden*, pp. 59–63.

as the *Ulmer Herrschaft* that was comprised of a trio of market towns and dozens of farming villages. Most of the migrants working in the city came from this large rural hinterland. Fortunate migrants were able to secure employment in the city's workshops and households soon after they arrived, usually through acquaintances from home already working in Ulm. Those without skills or connections, however, were forced to wait each morning in a corner of the marketplace to be hired as day labourers. Too poor to purchase citizenship, migrant workers were retained or discharged according to local economic conditions, but always made up a large part of the city's population. Concerned with the disruptive potential of these outsiders, the Ulmer authorities sought to select them according to their economic potential and moral suitability, barring the unsuitable and carefully regulating the activities of those they admitted through an array of detailed ordinances.

The local magistrates' efforts to systematize the selection and regulation of migrants were part of the surge in civic legislation that swept the empire in the late Middle Ages. In Ulm, the earliest edicts pertaining to migrants date from the late fifteenth century.[11] Beginning in the 1490s, these ordinances sought to control the daily life of resident aliens, regulating how they sought work, married and even socialized. In 1527, amid the fervour of the early Reformation, the town council issued a comprehensive legal code that collected and expanded upon these late medieval ordinances. The result of this Reformation-era codification was a detailed and highly restrictive legal code known as the Migrants' Ordinance (*Ordnung der Beywoner halben*), first issued in 1527 and reissued in 1581.

The central concerns of the Migrants' Ordinance were fiscal and moral, and it provided detailed provisions for evaluating prospective migrant workers' economic utility and respectability. In order to protect the solvency of the civic poor chest, the council sought to exclude unemployed migrants, complaining that 'in lean years, this city, and in particular the honourable council's common citizens, have spent too much on handouts from the civic grain stores, the hospital, the orphanage and the poorhouse'.[12] While the city's workshops and storehouses relied upon a steady stream of cheap labour from the countryside, migrants were permitted to reside in Ulm only as long as they had stable employment. The council justified this policy in the language of Lutheran piety:

> according to the word and command of God, no one is to be idle. Therefore, each must earn and win his bread by the sweat of his brow. So must each day labourer, not afflicted with bodily infirmity, and without steady employment, wait on the market

---

[11]   See Carl Mollwo (ed.), *Das rote Buch der Stadt Ulm* (Stuttgart, 1905). See also Eberhard Naujoks, 'Ulm's Sozialpolitik im 16. Jahrhundert', *Ulm und Oberschwaben*, 33 (1953): pp. 88–98.

[12]   Preamble to StAU A 3785, *Ordnung der Beywoner halben* (1527/1581).

each morning for work ... . Those who do not find work should return after midday
and wait again. Those who do not do this, and do not earn wages, but rather appear
too many times to be idle, should be expelled from the city and not tolerated here as
residents any longer.[13]

Since the regulatory activities of Ulm's magistrates were based on the stark
distinction between 'useful' migrants and 'useless' ones, verifying the employment
status of prospective resident aliens was a crucial component of the authorities'
disciplinary efforts. As soon as migrants found work, they had to appear before
the council with their prospective employer and apply for official permission to
reside in the city as resident aliens. Furthermore, the citizen hoping to employ
the migrant had to testify that he would support the worker, even if he or she fell
ill, without the aid of the *Spital* or the poorhouse. Married applicants also had
to bring along their spouse and report 'truthfully, how many children they had,
along with their ages'. The council mandated that the town scribe (*Stattschreiber*)
was to record all of this information, and further decreed that migrant workers
had to swear an oath that if they were discharged by their employer, or left his
employ, they were to report to the authorities and then leave the city with their
spouse and children within eight days. Furthermore, each resident alien accepted
by the council was required to appear before the authorities each year with his or
her family to renew these vows, or else leave the city immediately.

Once the migrant worker gained official permission to reside within the
walls of Ulm, the regulation of their daily existence only intensified. Shut out of
civic politics, these resident aliens nonetheless were required to pay taxes and to
serve on the fire brigade. The council sought to control the activities of migrant
workers to a remarkable extent, proclaiming that they were not allowed to keep
dogs and that they were to remain at work, summer and winter, from the tolling
of the work-bell in the morning until it rang in the evening, with an hour break
from 11 to 12. Resident aliens were not allowed to drink alcohol outside their
own homes on workdays and were specifically barred from entering taverns or
gambling during the workweek. Migrant workers were allowed to drink toasts
on holidays, but the council commanded that they were not to consume more
than a single measure of wine at a sitting. The local authorities also made it
illegal for young apprentices or journeymen to assemble after dark, a law aimed
at curtailing boisterous night-time festivities.[14] Any deviation from the rules laid
out in the Migrants' Ordinance called for expulsion, and resident aliens who fell

---

13   StAU A 3785, *Ordnung der Beywoner halben* (1527/1581).
14   StAU A 3681, *Vorhälte und Rüfe*, fols 183–4 (1560), 296–7 (1574), 299 (1574).

ill, took poor relief, married without permission or violated the law were to be driven from the territory.[15]

By punishing errant migrant workers, the Ulmer authorities sought to provide order in a time of disruption and anxiety. In an attempt to ensure stability and uphold morality in the territory, the local magistrates purged society of threatening migrants judged in terms of their economic value and moral respectability. As analysis of Ulm's legislation demonstrated, the local magistrates and citizenry had sought since the late Middle Ages to keep the city financially solvent by excluding unemployed migrants and penniless beggars from the territory. After mid-century, as the city's economic situation worsened, the local magistrates redoubled these efforts in an attempt to shore up civic finances.[16] Meanwhile, the urban craft household was under increasing financial strain, as markets contracted and the purchasing power of wages plummeted after 1550. Thus, efforts to rid the city of unemployed migrants can be viewed as a shared effort by Ulm's magistrates and its citizenry to spare the city the expense of feeding foreign paupers. Accordingly, the council stringently enforced the Migrants' Ordinance in an attempt to rid the civic commune of migrants who appeared to be work-shy or to be a potential drain on the poor chest.

A case from the summer of 1590, involving a day labourer named Hanns Weiler, provides a useful example. Weiler was banished from the territory for life for squandering his wages and for 'bad housekeeping' after the council learned that his wife and five small children were relying upon support from the municipal poorhouse.[17] According to the Migrants' Ordinance, making use of any sort of public support was grounds for expulsion. This was especially the case in dealing with a spendthrift like Weiler, who reportedly kept a disorderly household rife with drinking and debauchery. Banishment was a prominent feature of Ulm's disciplinary policies during the sixteenth century, and all sorts of residents, including citizens, were expelled from the city for a wide range of offences. Whereas banished citizens could gain eventual readmittance after lodging appeals with the town council, migrants like Weiler lacked the legal

---

15   StAU A 3785, *Ordnung der Beywoner halben* (1527/1581). For background on this legislation, see Andreas Baisch, 'Die Verfassung im Leben der Stadt, 1558–1802', in Hans Eugen Specker (ed.) *Die Ulmer Bürgerschaft auf dem Weg zur Demokratie* (Ulm, 1997), pp. 197–203; Specker, *Ulm. Stadtgeschichte*, p. 64.

16   For the fiscal pressures facing the early modern state, and its efforts to harness the productive household for taxation, see David Sabean, *Power in the Blood*, pp. 200–213. For Ulm's *Steueramt* and tax structures, see Adolf Kölle, 'Ursprung und Entwicklung der Vermögenssteuer in Ulm', *Württembergische Vierteljahrshefte für Landesgeschichte*, 7 (1989): pp. 1–24; Kurt Rothe, *Das Finanzwesen der Reichsstadt Ulm im 18. Jahrhundert* (Ulm, 1991).

17   StAU A 3530, *Ratsprotokolle*, Nr. 39, fol. 386 (14 July 1587).

rights granted by citizenship and generally faced lifelong banishment from the city and its hinterlands. Furthermore, while citizens were usually only banished after committing serious crimes, migrants could be expelled simply for resorting to public assistance or being discharged by their employer. Once banished, convicts who returned without the town council's permission risked corporal punishment for violating the terms of their sentence if the authorities found them in the city or the Ulmer territory.

In another interesting case from December 1588, one that serves here as the exception that proves the rule, a maid named Anna Schmidin, a villager from Rietheim in the Duchy of Württemberg, actually avoided expulsion for adultery because of her value as a servant. Her record states that despite becoming pregnant after an adulterous encounter with a young weaver's apprentice – the sort of scandalous offence that usually called for immediate banishment – she was pardoned owing to her 14 years in service. Although the authorities had shown remarkable leniency, they were careful to include the warning 'that she should make sure that the authorities do not receive any further complaints about her, or else she would face a serious punishment' in their official verdict, to deter further misbehaviour.[18]

Despite the council's surprising lenience in Anna Schmidin's case, migrants who offended the city's strict Lutheran morality usually faced serious punishment, especially in instances of sexual misconduct. Facing repeated waves of famine and disease in the decades after 1550, the Ulmer authorities sought to avert God's wrath by punishing vice within their domain. In February 1589, for example, the authorities in Geislingen, a hillside town in Ulm's territory, wrote to the council about how to proceed in the case of a young farmhand imprisoned for such misbehaviour. The local authorities reported that the migrant labourer, Hanns Frey, from the Franconian village of Rieden, had been jailed after he 'engaged in all manner of indiscipline [*unzücht*] with a young girl [*Döchterlin*]'. Worse yet, 'he had previously promised marriage to another harlot [*diern*]'. The magistrates instructed the authorities in Geislingen to use humiliation to curb Frey's disruptive promiscuity. He was to be released, after paying his prison expenses and hearing a stern warning about his behaviour, and ordered to 'stand two Sundays in a row before the Church wearing the violin', a heavy wooden collar used to inflict pain and humiliation on miscreants.[19]

The local authorities deemed cases of adultery involving migrants even more threatening, since they disrupted marriage, an institution considered the very bedrock of a Christian polity by the Lutheran clergy and the municipal

---

[18]   StAU A 6590, *Strafbuch 10*, fol. 33 (23 December 1588).
[19]   StAU A 6590, *Strafbuch 10*, fol. 51 (10 February 1589).

government alike. Thus, in July 1567, a young migrant named Wolff Hünoldt from Leutkirch, a village in the Allgau, found himself facing the Ulmer magistrates while working for a local miller. According to the court, Hünoldt had 'impregnated Anna Baürenmüller, the natural daughter of his master ... and had taken her virginity'. The justices banished the errant migrant from the territory, ordering him to stay 5 miles away from its borders for life. They also commanded Hünoldt to take his wife and child with him, the first indication that this was an adulterous affair and a potential explanation for the severity of his sentence.[20] The public punishment of wayward migrants like Wolff Hünoldt served to present and to protect the social hierarchy by highlighting distinctions between acceptable, pious behaviour and culpable, scandalous misbehaviour.

The council also demonstrated its power through rare displays of mercy, sparing suitably contrite migrants the rigors of justice. Thus, in rare cases, banished migrant workers were able to secure pardons and permission to return to the territory after expulsion, but only after years of persistent appeals to the council for clemency. One such instance, from May 1570, involved an unruly apprentice named Enderlin Schreiber who, like Anna Schmidin, hailed from the village of Rietheim. Schreiber had been imprisoned in Leipheim, a town in the Ulmer territory, for stealing two pieces of *golschen* cloth from his employer and running off with them to Ulm, where he sold them and gambled away the proceeds. Noting that his father had arranged a settlement with his employer, the authorities in Ulm ordered him released, but imposed a series of stringent controls on him. Schreiber was ordered to refrain from drinking wine outside his master's house, was not allowed to entertain companions there and, above all, was precluded from gambling. These restrictions seem to have kept Schreiber in check for a long while, but 20 years later, in the spring of 1590, he was in custody again in Leipheim, this time for 'wantonly squandering a great deal of money, uttering unseemly insults against the mayor of Leipheim himself, and for all manner of culpable activity'. The Ulmer magistrates ordered him to be released, making him swear that he would leave the territory and not return unless he was pardoned. It did not take long for the troublemaker to petition the court to have his sentence lifted, and in May and June 1590, he submitted a pair of unsuccessful appeals. Finally, on 6 July, a third supplication did the trick, and the authorities allowed him to return to Leipheim, warning Schreiber about his disobedience and ordering him once again to refrain from wine drinking and companionship – this time outside his own house – and from any sort of

---

[20] StAU A 3530, *Ratsprotokolle*, Nr. 30, fols 425, 429 (11 July 1567).

gambling. The authorities also threatened him with serious punishment if he overstepped these bounds.[21]

Enderlin Schreiber provides a striking example of how the regulatory efforts of the Ulmer council served to enact changes in the social status of migrants. In his dealings with the authorities, confrontations ranging over two decades, his social status was transformed repeatedly by the court: he went from migrant, as an apprentice, to resident, as a householder in Leipheim, to vagrant, as a banished criminal, and back to resident, as a pardoned offender living under a form of house arrest. Thus, in their regulation of this migrant's unruly behaviour the Ulmer magistrates repeatedly demonstrated their power not only to recognize, but also to enact changes in social position.

Regulation and Exclusion: The Beadles' Ordinance

Regulating the activities of the migrant workers they permitted to live in the town as resident aliens was not the Ulmer council's sole concern; driving out the unemployed paupers they classified as vagrants was also central to their regulatory efforts. The Ulmer authorities had feared the incursions of 'sturdy beggars' since the Middle Ages, and they employed a variety of measures in an attempt to bar penniless outsiders from the city, mirroring the practices of rulers throughout early modern Europe. In an attempt to purge the foreign poor, the council's agents summarily expelled unemployed outsiders caught begging or squatting in the town, driving them out without trial or record. The earliest surviving legislation issued by the council, for example, dating from the 1420s, proclaims its intention to rid its territory of vagabonds, characterized as arsonists, thieves and robbers.[22] Like other German cities, by the 1490s the local magistrates had declared all unlicensed begging illegal, and proclaimed that foreign beggars were only allowed to remain in the city for a single night. Vagrants, once turned away from the city, would only be readmitted after a month's absence.[23] As a 1491 mandate makes clear, it was not a specific crime that prompted the magistrates

---

[21] StAU A 3530, *Ratsprotokolle*, Nr. 31, fol. 565 (17 May 1570); StAU A 6590, *Strafbuch 10*, fol. 273 (1 April 1590; 8 May 1590; 26 June 1590; 6 July 1590).

[22] Mollwo (ed.), *Das rote Buch*.

[23] StAU A 2001, fols 46–53 (1492–1493). These laws remained in effect throughout the period and were officially renewed in 1586 and again in 1601: see StAU A 4396, *Hauß Ordnung der Armen Sonder Siechen* (1586/1601). See also Specker, *Ulm. Stadtgeschichte*, pp. 105–6. The city council of Nuremberg, having 'been informed often and emphatically, fully and credibly that some beggars and beggaresses live a life without fear of God, even lives that are unseemly and unbecoming', had already enacted similar regulations in 1478. See Christoph Sachsse and Florian

to drive these impoverished migrants from the city, but rather their marginal status in the local social order. Proclaiming their determination to rid the town of vagrants, the council asserted that 'many foreign and useless people linger here in Ulm, who should be outside the city rather than inside'.[24]

Reflecting Lutheran norms, the Ulmer authorities redoubled these efforts after the Reformation. A mandate read aloud to the citizenry in August 1544, for example, illustrates the council's attitudes towards the wandering poor, characterizing them as 'tramps and vagrants, who create many nuisances and evil deeds, and everyday lie before the gates, and many of whom steal into the city'.[25] In another edict, from 1555, the council ordered its officials to apprehend and punish all such 'foreign vagrants, sturdy beggars, and other idlers' found in the territory.[26] A 1586 version of the mandate also made it illegal for any of the council's subjects to provide housing or charity to any 'discharged soldiers, vagrants, sturdy beggars and all other dissolute, loose and good-for-nothing riff-raff'.[27] The council also stepped up its efforts to monitor the poor, reiterating in 1528 their ban on begging 'in the city, before the city, before or under the city gates, in or before the churches, in the taverns or other houses, whether by day or night', and ordering the beadle to enter the dwellings of the resident poor each month to inspect 'how they keep house, what sort of work they do, how they are deficient and how they are ailing'. Any 'useless beggars' or 'dishonourable people' discovered during these monthly rounds were to be punished, serving as an 'example and illustration' for the rest.[28] In this edict, Ulm's magistrates reveal the logic behind their efforts to enforce the migration statutes they issued. Given the deficiencies inherent in sixteenth-century policing, including the lack of adequate manpower and the rudimentary nature of record keeping, the local authorities proved incapable of keeping all unwanted or unsuitable migrants from settling in the city. Thus, they sought to identify and arrest as many as they could through random sweeps, using public punishment to make an 'example' of the unlucky ones they apprehended, hoping to deter the rest and to demonstrate their determination to regulate migration into their domain.

Tennstedt, *Geschichte der Armenfürsorge in Deutschland. Vom Spätmittelalter bis zum Ersten Weltkrieg* (Stuttgart, 1980), pp. 64–6.

[24]   See StAU A 3669, fol. 101 (1491).

[25]   StAU A 3872, *Rufes bettlens halben* (15 August 1544).

[26]   StAU A 3688, fol. 21, 11 May 1551. See also A 3688, fols 23 (1563), 27 (1586), 32 (1590).

[27]   StAU A 3688, 11 April 1586.

[28]   StAU A 2002, *Ordnung des neu aufgerichteten Almoskastens*, 1528; StAU A 4176/1, *Almosenordnungen* (1581).

After mid-century, as official law enforcement increased throughout the empire, the punishment of vagrants in Ulm intensified dramatically. Despite the local magistrates' increasing determination to rid their domain of vagrants, however, they faced a rising tide of illegal immigration as southern Germany experienced a prolonged economic depression. While Ulm had long attracted a steady flow of migrant workers from the surrounding countryside, the number of penniless vagabonds seeking refuge in the city increased amid the famine and disorder that afflicted southern Germany during the late sixteenth century. Defying the council's efforts to bar them, impoverished migrants from Ulm's hinterlands and beyond continually drifted into the city as prices rose and poverty spread. As we have seen, many of the poor migrants who entered Ulm found work and registered as resident aliens with the beadle, settling down as servants or day labourers. Those unable or unwilling to find work, however, were denied such residency and increasingly risked being identified as vagrants and expelled by the local authorities. Throughout the century, many of these unfortunates were apprehended and driven away without formal sentence during the periodic mass round-ups of beggars (usually street urchins) carried out by the council's patrolmen. Turned out of the city, they disappeared from the judicial record, joining the floating population of unemployed, rootless wanderers teeming on Germany's roads.

While the Ulmer authorities were able to expel the unwanted migrants they identified as vagrants, their ability to police their sprawling territory was in fact rather limited. Even the area just outside Ulm's gates was difficult to control, and the squalid shanty towns that sprawled there remained semi-lawless zones patrolled sporadically by the town watch. Vagrants refused entry into the city camped in these settlements – in orchards, brick ovens and barns – looking for a chance to slip into the city where they could find alms or bread. Throughout the period, the Ulmer authorities struggled to police this liminal zone just outside their gates. In a typical mandate from 1586, for example, the council ordered measures to be taken against 'the good-for-nothing rabble before the gates'.[29] Thus, official efforts to rid the city of unwanted outsiders began at the city gates, the frontier between the ordered urban community and the disordered zone before the city; and the Ulmer council concerned itself with monitoring and controlling the boundaries of the city, excluding and expelling undesirables. In carrying out these efforts, the town council relied upon an imposing curtain of walls that ringed the city and marked its physical boundaries. These walls were punctuated with a series of gate-towers, themselves protected by guardhouses and checkpoints manned by watchmen and scribes who sought to monitor and

---

[29]   StAU A 3530, *Ratsprotokolle* Nr. 38, fol. 760 (n.d., 1586).

control access to the city. The gates of Ulm were central to the local authorities' efforts to control access to the city as well as the terminus of their efforts to exclude and expel those they deemed disorderly or dangerous, but beyond these boundaries, the town council's ability to regulate the movement of migrants diminished with distance. Thus, while the magistrates' sentences often ordered expelled migrants to leave the territory, their power to enforce these verdicts was in practice usually limited to policing residence within Ulm's walls.

While the town council's efforts to expel vagrants remained sporadic before mid-century, during the 1550s the local authorities augmented these informal procedures with more systematic official prosecution and bureaucratic procedures. By mid-century the local magistrates felt overrun by hungry outsiders: in 1552, a year of warfare and anxiety in the territory, the council issued a mandate excoriating vagrants, stating that 'daily investigation and inquiry shows that the number of foreign and alien beggars here in this city ... grows everyday'.[30] Ulm's magistrates sought to counter this threat through more rigorous law enforcement, and on 16 August 1559 they issued new instructions to the town's beadles, the officials appointed to police vagrants and the undeserving poor.[31] This detailed piece of legislation provided the blueprint for an aggressive new policy aimed at closing the city to foreign vagrants. The council instructed their beadles to patrol the entire city each day, searching for 'all beggarly people, local or foreign, but especially foreign'.[32] When alien paupers were identified, the beadles were ordered to interrogate them, noting 'what they are called, where they are from, and when and through which gate they had entered the city'. Hoping to preclude troublesome vagrants from re-entering the city, the Ulmer authorities ordered their officials to make foreign vagrants swear not to beg in the city again, escort them to the gate through which they had entered and expel them. After turning out the vagrant, the beadle was ordered to instruct the clerk stationed at that gate to record the information he had collected and to remain vigilant, an attempt to create a watch-list so that the expellees could not gain access to the city again.

Despite these measures, the flow of migrants and visitors through the town gates overwhelmed the gatekeepers, and many of the vagrants the beadles ousted slipped back into the city after being expelled. Thus, the 1559 Beadles' Ordinance also addressed disobedient vagrants who broke their expulsion oath and returned to the city after being banished. The new procedures instructed the beadle to apprehend illegal returnees, lock them in the *Narrenheuslin*, a

---

30   StAU A 3672, fol. 246 (15 February 1552).

31   StAU A 3693, *Der Zwayer Bettelvögt Ordnung* (1559).

32   The alien, able-bodied poor increasingly aroused the anxieties of magistrates across Europe during this troubled period: see Jütte, *Poverty and Deviance*, pp. 165–6.

cage-like holding pen on the marketplace, and send a written report to the Lord
Mayor. Once the mayor ordered these offenders released, the beadle was to expel
them again through the gate they had used to enter the city. This time, however,
the beadle was instructed to warn vagrants that if they ever returned they would
be 'worthy of the honourable council's punishment', in essence threatening
them with corporal punishment. This time, after the expulsion the beadle was
to admonish the gate's clerk and order him to pay closer attention. The Beadles'
Ordinance even deals with incorrigible vagrants 'found begging here for the
third time', who were to be incarcerated in the tower for questioning, after which
the 'honourable council would judge them according to their guilt and punish
them'.

Most of the Ulmer authorities' efforts to rid the territory of the penniless
migrants they labelled vagrants took the form of mass roundups of beggars
and tramps in the city or in the settlements of the Ulmer territory. While these
operations, invariably ending in summary expulsion, usually went unrecorded,
a few examples survive in the official record. In June 1552, for example, the
council ordered the beadle to round up and expel all unemployed outsiders
from the city immediately.[33] In another case, from the winter of 1588, 'six
good-for-nothing tramps and beggars' were arrested in Geislingen and brought
in chains to Ulm for sentencing after trying to pass several counterfeit copper
coins, stealing and 'doing other bad things'. The dizzying array of hometowns
associated with these illegal migrants gives a sense of the distances covered by
the wandering poor in search of sustenance: Jorg Dreher and his wife hailed
from Esslingen in Württemberg; Afra Deüblerin was listed as the wife of Jorg
Herlin from Hanbach in Franconia; Hainrich Traub was from the alpine hamlet
of Oberstdorf in Bavaria; Davidt Mair from Balzhausen, also in Bavaria; and
Agatha Visherin was from Schalkstetten, a village near Geislingen that was part
of the Ulmer territory. The Ulmer authorities released the vagrants without
requiring them to pay their prison expenses, since they were penniless, and
compelled them to swear an oath that they would 'immediately leave the city,
cross the Danube Bridge, and go four miles away from the territory, and would
never return again'. Before expelling them, the magistrates also warned them
that if they did not keep their pledge, they would suffer a serious punishment.[34]

Destitute migrants from among the 'worthy' poor – those who were aged or
sick or pregnant and thus incapable of earning their own bread – could expect
to be admitted (at least temporarily) to the *Spital* for convalescence. If the
authorities ascertained that a pauper's claims to such support were fraudulent,

---

[33]   StAU A 3671, fols 270–71 (3 June 1552).
[34]   StAU A 6590, *Strafbuch 10*, fol. 32 (20 December 1588).

however, the swindler often faced harsh punishment. In one such case from January 1590, a wandering pauper from Augsburg named Lienhart Menhofer was arrested in Langenau, a town in the Ulmer territory, along with 'several other tramps' and transported to Ulm for sentencing. The authorities had found a fraudulent 'Bettelbrief', a document issued by some territorial or municipal authority certifying that the bearer had some ailment that entitled him or her to alms, in Menhofer's possession. Worse yet, the authorities recognized him, and charged that he had 'begged here many times before, had been jailed and had been punished with expulsion', a clear violation of the Beadles' Ordinance. The magistrates released him, making him swear that he would leave the city, the territory and stay 6 miles from its borders, an indication of their frustration with the incorrigible beggar. Before driving him from the city again, they warned him that he would face serious punishment if he ever returned.[35]

The archival records from Ulm demonstrate that in practice sixteenth-century authorities, lacking modern police forces or advanced bureaucratic technologies, proved unable to enforce their ambitious edicts consistently. Consequently, many poor, unemployed migrants slipped into the city, seeking work or charity, as the Ulmer magistrates frequently complained in their own council minutes. Yet while an unrecorded number of these impoverished migrants were summarily expelled by the council's patrols, the unruly or the incorrigible faced public punishment. In the course of this troubled century, over 300 migrants labelled vagrants suffered public expulsion at the hands of the Ulmer authorities.[36]

In order to deal with these intractable offenders, the council turned to violent correction, sometimes ordering several punishments in tandem, compounding expulsion with public humiliation and pain. In sixteenth-century Ulm, this usually took the form of exposure at the pillory, sometimes in leg-irons, before being whipped out of town. These expulsion rituals took place in the crowded open spaces of the city. The pillory and the *Narrenheuslin* both stood in prominent places in the city's central marketplace; and the hangman whipped expellees along prescribed routes that twisted from the *Rathaus*, Ulm's political and ceremonial heart, through the crowded streets of the town to the gate-towers that marked the civic boundaries. Thus, these highly public expulsions provided a visual display of the council's determination to regulate inclusion in its domain and to expel the unwanted migrants it identified as vagrants. In May 1553, for example, a beggar named Lorenz Wech and known as 'Ganßer', from the

---

[35] StAU A 6590, *Strafbuch 10*, fol. 227 (19 January 1590).

[36] For the role of public expulsion in efforts to deal with vagrancy in sixteenth-century Ulm, see Jason P. Coy, *Strangers and Misfits: Banishment, Social Control, and Authority in Early Modern Germany* (Leiden, 2008).

distant Franconian village of Pfaffenhofen, was arrested for unlicensed begging 'in violation of the honourable council's ordinance' and for public drunkenness. Questioned by the authorities, Wech admitted that he had already been in the tower and the *Narrenheuslin* twice before, and that he had sworn never to beg in the city again, a promise he had broken repeatedly. The exasperated magistrates also maintained that this time he had 'squandered the alms he had collected, using them to become excessively drunk on wine'. They banished Wech from the territory for life, again, and this time ordered the hangman to flog him through the city gates as a painful and humiliating reminder not to return.[37]

Like magistrates throughout the empire, the Ulmer authorities sometimes resorted to more gruesome physical violence in their attempts to control unruly vagrants, using mutilation as a retributive punishment. Mutilation, which in Ulm usually meant boring or cutting off the convict's ears, not only served to cause pain but also permanently marked the victim as an outsider and criminal, making future identification easier if he or she ever returned.[38] Given the relative weakness of the council's policing capabilities, and the strong economic pull that Ulm exerted on the surrounding countryside, it is not surprising that despite such violent penalties, many of the desperate people the high court expelled subsequently returned to the city.[39] A banishment sentence from January 1586, for example, bears the following marginalia: 'Expulsion of Vetterin from Lonsee, who has been cast out many times before for begging, but every time has come back again', betraying the authorities' growing frustration with controlling intractable offenders like her.[40] Local prosecution records indicate that Vetterin was not alone, and that in the course of the sixteenth century the Ulmer authorities punished over 20 per cent of the vagrants they banished for subsequently returning illegally, proving that many offenders – facing the hardship and hunger that plagued the dispossessed poor – chose to risk returning to Ulm.

As this examination of the Ulmer council's attempts to bar the wandering poor – migrants they classified as vagrants – from their domain has illustrated, after mid-century the local authorities sought to use new bureaucratic procedures and violent expulsion to exclude newcomers who could not or would not earn their keep. The council evaluated migrants carefully and attempted to bar those

---

[37]   StAU A 3530, *Ratsprotokolle*, Nr. 22, fol. 311b (15 May 1553).

[38]   For the role of these sorts of degrading physical punishments in attempts to control vagrancy in early modern Europe, see Jütte, *Poverty and Deviance*, pp. 161, 165.

[39]   Robert Jütte has pointed out that throughout early modern Europe the expulsion of the alien poor proved an ineffective solution to the vagrancy problem, as it merely served to shift the problem to other jurisdictions. See Jütte, *Poverty and Deviance*, p. 167.

[40]   StAU A 3530, *Ratsprotokolle*, Nr. 38, fol. 491b (24 January 1586).

they deemed to be 'useless' or 'dangerous' – and especially the unemployed, alien poor – from residing within the city's walls. Using expulsion, the local authorities removed 'unworthy' migrants from the community, both physically and socially, by punishing them as vagrants. Thus, Ulm's magistrates worked to mark and to regulate the spatial and social boundaries of the territory, classifying and expelling unwanted migrants.

Conclusion

The Ulmer council, ruling a city-state that drew its economic lifeblood from commerce, remained responsive to the concerns of the urban guildsmen, who relied upon a steady flow of migrants from the city's rural hinterland and beyond for cheap labour. However, in a time of alarming economic decline, failed harvests and recurrent epidemics, they carefully selected and regulated these outsiders in an attempt to protect the property of the citizenry and respectability of the community. Thus, the local magistrates classified and monitored migrants, allowing a lucky few to enjoy conditional status in the city, as resident aliens, while trying to rid the city of the rest, presented as vagrants and beggars and excoriated as thieves and parasites.

By allowing productive and pious migrants who submitted to the council's regulatory regime to reside within the city walls as resident aliens, the local authorities ensured that the city's hunger for cheap labour was satisfied. Meanwhile, by publicly expelling the destitute, disorderly and disobedient migrants they apprehended, Ulm's magistrates sought to deter the ones who evaded arrest from settling in the city. These expulsions also served to demonstrate to the citizenry their rulers' determination to regulate migration and to bar unwanted newcomers from the city. Thus, while the outmanned authorities proved unable to regulate the flow of migrants effectively, and many paupers slipped into the city illegally, official migration policies met the citizenry's need for wage labourers from the countryside and demonstrated the council's authority to police inclusion in the urban community.

Through their regulatory activities, based on careful classification and selection, Ulm's magistrates did not so much identify vagabonds or differentiate between vagrants and migrant workers as 'create' them. Through their verdicts and public punishment rituals, the council actually enacted dramatic changes in social status, transforming would-be migrants into either accepted residents or expelled vagrants. By punishing unwanted or unruly migrants in performative penal acts, and casting them out on the roads, the authorities excluded them from respectable, settled society, relegating them to the ranks of the desperate, rootless wanderers who ranged along the roads of the empire, drifting from town to town in search of refuge.

Chapter 10

Regulating Urban Migration and Relief Entitlements in Eighteenth-Century Brabant

Anne Winter

Poor relief was essentially a local affair in early modern Europe. Every parish, village or city organized and financed its own relief provisions, permeated by the general principle that each local community should look after its own poor. Yet determining who belonged to the 'own poor' was no straightforward affair in a world characterized by increasing spatial mobility and growing relief burdens – developments that were tied in with the spread of wage dependency throughout early modern Europe. The spread of wage dependency made poor relief ever more vital as a means to overcome periods of unemployment or to complement low wages.[1] At the same time, it also generated growing levels of labour mobility, as more and more unemployed or underemployed had to look elsewhere to find a job.[2] The combination of pressured but localized relief resources and increasing mobility fostered growing contention over the costs and gains of migration in towns and villages. The ensuing tensions were particularly pertinent in early modern cities because the latter had a disproportionately large share of their inhabitants and economy dependent on wage labour, generally harboured a denser and more varied array of relief institutions than the surrounding countryside and recorded comparatively high migration and turnover rates.

According to De Swaan, the localized basis of relief provisions was a fundamental weakness that jeopardized both the stability and efficiency of premodern poor relief. Because places with relatively generous relief provisions attracted poor immigrants – especially in periods of crisis – local relief funds were repeatedly 'eaten away' by outsiders. The result was that early modern poor relief was haunted by a geographical free-rider problem that could only

---

[1]   Olwen Hufton, *The Poor of Eighteenth-Century France* (Oxford, 1974), p. 20; Catharina Lis and Hugo Soly, *Poverty and Capitalism in Pre-Industrial Europe* (Brighton, 1979), passim.

[2]   Leslie Page Moch, *Moving Europeans: Migration in Western Europe since 1650*, 2nd edn (Bloomington/Indianapolis, 2003), pp. 3–4, passim.

be surmounted with the introduction of regional and eventually national social provisions.[3] Yet, urban authorities were no passive onlookers. Many studies have evoked how urban authorities sought to safeguard local relief provisions by refusing entry to destitute immigrants, by barring non-locals from relief access or by forcefully removing alien 'beggars' and 'vagrants'.[4] Unfortunately, the definition of 'unwanted' newcomers is often treated as self-evident in these cases, while the contradictions and effectiveness of restrictive migration policies are rarely addressed.[5] This contribution, in contrast, starts from the contention that the criteria for branding certain migrants as 'unwanted' were extremely vague and malleable. They were subject to varied interpretations and potentially conflicting interests.[6] A poor worker might for instance be considered unwelcome by those competing for or contributing to relief provisions, but valued as a cheap labour supply by local employers. In addition, scholars like Lis, Soly and van Leeuwen have stressed that poor relief was not necessarily or merely a charitable institution, but that relief policies were often manipulated by employer and elite interests to sustain a labour reserve army, to subsidize wages and/or to maintain social stability.[7] Refusing immigrants entry or access to relief could however frustrate employers' attempts to enlarge the local labour supply or jeopardize social stability. The implication is that restrictive migration or relief policies could at times run into conflict with this 'logic of charity'.

---

[3]   Abram de Swaan, *In Care of the State: Health Care, Education, and Welfare in Europe and the USA in the Modern Era* (Oxford, 1988), pp. 30–41.

[4]   Marc Boone, 'Les villes de l'espace flamand au bas Moyen Age. Immigrations et migrations internes', in Stéphane Curveiller and Laurent Buchard (eds), *Se déplacer du Moyen Âge à nos jours* (Calais, 2009), pp. 99–112; Maria B. Roes, 'Unwanted Travellers: The Tightening of City Borders in Early Modern Germany', in Thomas Betteridge (ed.), *Borders and Travellers in Early Modern Europe* (Aldershot, 2007), pp. 87–112.

[5]   Although Jean-Pierre Gutton concedes that he feels 'uncomfortable to find a convenient boundary' to distinguish migrant workers from 'real vagrants': Jean-Pierre Gutton, *L'état et la mendicité dans la première moitié du XVIIIe siècle. Auvergne, Beaujolais, Forez, Lyonnais* (Lyon, 1973), p. 188.

[6]   For critical reflections on the meaning of the concept of vagrancy, see for instance: Leo Lucassen, 'A Blind Spot – Migratory and Travelling Groups in Western European Historiography', *International Review of Social History*, 38/2 (1993): pp. 209–35; Xavier Rousseaux, 'L'incrimination du vagabondage en Brabant (14e–18e siècles). Langages du droit et réalités de pratique', in G. Van Dievoet, P. Godding and D. Van Den Auweele (eds), *Langage et droit à travers l'histoire. Réalités et fictions* (Leuven/Paris, 1989), pp. 150–1; Anne Winter, 'Vagrancy as an Adaptive Strategy: The Duchy of Brabant, 1767–1776', *International Review of Social History*, 49/2 (2004): pp. 249–78.

[7]   Lis and Soly, *Poverty*, pp. 90–96, 116–29, 194–214; Marco H.D. van Leeuwen, 'Logic of Charity: Poor Relief in Preindustrial Europe', *Journal of Interdisciplinary History*, 24/4 (1994): pp. 589–613.

So far, the varied and potentially conflicting nature of concerns regarding migrants' relief entitlements has been insufficiently recognized. Nor has it been given the centrality it deserves in the analysis of early modern urban migration policies. As a consequence, our understanding of the *why* and *how* of the varied policy options towards newcomers and their relief claims remains cloudy at best. Those studies that do address the interrelationship of local migration and relief access policies have focused mainly on the Settlement Laws of England and Wales[8] – which I believe were not so much an exception as a specific case of a more general, shared and recognizable set of concerns, interests and conflicts that shaped the contours of local migration policies, and in particular urban migration policies, throughout early modern Europe.[9] This chapter will build upon the insights of these studies to examine the causes and consequences of urban policies towards migrants and their relief entitlements in relation to conflicts over the distribution of the associated costs and gains. When, how, why and by whom were certain immigrants given relief, others merely tolerated and others forcefully expelled? And to what extent did these policies allow urban authorities to overcome the geographical free-rider problem identified by De Swaan?

Although the empirical focus of this chapter is on the Duchy of Brabant in the eighteenth century, the historiographical and conceptual framework guiding the analysis lends a broader relevance to the case study. I will argue that migration policies were the outcome not only of specific social and economic contexts, but also of conflicts and power relations between different interest groups, and were constantly adapted in order to deal with problems in their enforcement. The paradoxes and conflicts of interests identified as governing local migration policies in eighteenth-century Brabantine cities offer insights that are relevant to other early modern urban settings as well. To develop the

---

8   For a recent survey, see: K.D.M. Snell, *Parish and Belonging: Community, Identity and Welfare in England and Wales, 1700–1950* (Cambridge, 2006), pp. 85–6. Rare studies addressing these issues in continental settings are Dirk van Damme, 'Onderstandswoonst, sedentarisering en stad-platteland-tegenstellingen: evolutie en betekenis van de wetgeving op de onderstandwoonst in Belgie (einde achttiende tot einde negentiende eeuw)', *Belgisch Tijdschrift voor Nieuwste Geschiedenis*, 21/3 (1990): p. 483–534; Sylvia Hahn, 'Migrants and the Poor Law System in Late Habsburg Empire Cities', in Mat Berglund (ed.), *Sakta vi gå genom stan – City Strolls* (Stockholm, 2005), pp. 121–34; Marco van Leeuwen, 'Amsterdam en de armenzorg tijdens de republiek', *NEHA Jaarboek*, 59 (1996): pp. 132–61; Joke Spaans, *Armenzorg in Friesland, 1500–1800. Publieke zorg en particuliere liefdadigheid in zes Friese steden ...* (Hilversum, 1997), pp. 207–17; Anne Winter, 'Caught between Law and Practice: Migrants and Settlement Legislation in the Southern Low Countries in a Comparative Perspective, c. 1700–1900', *Rural History*, 19/2 (2008): pp. 137–62.

9   This point is developed explicitly in Winter, 'Caught'.

argument, I will first discuss some of the conceptual assumptions underlying the analysis based on existing literature, and then sketch the historical background to the case study, before engaging in a discussion of the empirical materials.

Conflicting Interests and Varied Outcomes

Central to the argument developed in this chapter is the contention that the ways in which newcomers and their potential relief claims were dealt with, in early modern cities as much as in present-day society, was an inherently contentious matter, shaped by conflicts of interests and power relationships. In theory, employers had an interest in stimulating immigration with an eye to putting pressure on wages. Relief payers, from their part, had an interest in avoiding immigration to keep relief expenses in check. In practice, however, the interests of employers and relief payers vis-à-vis immigration varied according to the profile of newcomers. The arrival of elderly, disabled, child-burdened or other vulnerable households likely to be in acute need of relief was likely to alarm those concerned about local relief provisions, but it did comparatively little to rouse the spirits of employers seeking to expand their labour supply. The immigration of young, single and trained workers, in contrast, was generally more valuable for employers and comparatively less daunting from the perspective of relief payers.[10]

The outcome of these opposing interests was therefore often a compromise in the form of a selective migration policy and/or a selective relief policy. *Selective migration policies* were at play when urban authorities accepted or even welcomed the influx of productive or valuable newcomers while trying to repel migrants with comparatively high relief needs. A typical example is the attempts of the magistrate of fourteenth- and fifteenth-century Bruges to attract wealthy merchants and skilled artisans by granting them special privileges while expelling needy or unruly vagrants whose presence was deemed 'harmful to the town and the community'.[11] *Selective relief policies* aimed to exclude (recent) newcomers from relief schemes, for instance by making access to them conditional on certain residential criteria (such as three or 10 years of residence), work-related requirements (e.g. membership of a guild), birthplace or other criteria of local belonging. We find examples of this in the stipulation that Jewish newcomers in Frisian cities were excluded from public relief provisions in the requirement to

---

[10]   For a further discussion, see Anne Winter, *Divided Interests, Divided Migrants: The Rationales of Policies Regarding Labour Mobility in Western Europe, c. 1550–1914* (GEHN Working Paper no. 15, London, 2005).

[11]   Boone, 'Les villes', pp. 99–112.

have been resident for a number of years in order to have access to the Hospital of Saint Sixtus in late sixteenth-century Rome, or in the fact that resident aliens lost their right to stay in sixteenth-century Ulm when they appealed to the communal chest.[12]

While selective migration and relief policies can best be understood as the outcome of conflicting interests in favour of and against immigration, the degree of selectivity remained a bone of contention between the stakeholders involved. The main reason is that differentiation between productive and unproductive workers was never straightforward: even young, healthy workers could be in need of assistance in case of illness, accidents or family expansion, while workers with families could also be useful to employers. Especially in tight labour markets, employers therefore had a stake in removing as many barriers to immigration as possible. To the extent that poor relief functioned as a wage subsidy, moreover, employers had reasons to ensure that their workers enjoyed access to relief provisions. These endeavours sometimes brought them into direct conflict with relief administrators, who aimed to restrict the number of relief recipients. In the booming port town of seventeenth-century Amsterdam, for instance, powerful employer groups successfully avoided the introduction of any selective relief policies out of concern that these would hinder the immigration 'of all types of workmen and sailing people (...) the wheat is mixed with the chaff and we leave the cleansing to the harvest's Lord'.[13] Likewise, textile manufacturers in eighteenth-century Leiden complained that existing migration restrictions with regard to 'unproductive' migrants were limiting the influx of useful workers.[14] Silk tycoons in eighteenth-century Lyon, in contrast, battled with royal authorities to reserve the city hospitals for local silk workers in temporary unemployment rather than having to accept the riff-raff of useless vagrants arrested by the *Maréchaussée*.[15] Depending on the structure of local labour markets, the migration or relief policies advocated by employers could therefore range from tolerant to restrictive. Their influence on actual policies in turn depended on the power relations with other parties concerned, from local

---

[12]   Jason P. Coy, 'Earn Your Penny Elsewhere: Banishment, Migrant Laborers, and Sociospatial Exclusion in Sixteenth-Century Ulm', *Journal of Historical Sociology*, 20/3 (2007): pp. 285–6, 288; Angela Groppi, 'Old People and the Flow of Resources between Generations in Papal Rome, Sixteenth to Nineteenth Centuries', in Lynn Botelho, Susannah Ottaway and Katharine Kittredge (eds), *Power and Poverty: Old Age in the Pre-Industrial Past* (Westport/London, 2002), p. 92; Spaans, *Armenzorg*, pp. 249–50.

[13]   Cited by Leeuwen, 'Amsterdam', p. 153.

[14]   Ibid., p. 152.

[15]   Jean-Pierre Gutton, *La societé et les pauvres. L'exemple de la généralité de Lyon, 1534–1789* (Paris, 1970), pp. 458–62.

relief administrators to central authorities. On the whole, migration and relief policies were therefore often more liberal when labour demand and employment rates were on the rise, and more stringent in economic downturns.[16]

At the same time, many intricacies hindered the practicability of selective migration and relief policies. Purely economic or financial considerations were at times overruled or supplemented by political concerns for societal stability, or by religious, cultural or sanitary considerations.[17] Even when a compromise was struck between the various interest groups and stakeholders involved, control and enforcement of selective regulations were no simple matter in a time of limited police control, inadequate administrative means and a varied array of decentralized and semi-autonomous relief institutions. National or regional legislation could further limit the autonomy of urban authorities to devise migration policies at their own discretion. Reciprocal relations with other local authorities – for instance migrants' places of origin – could also limit their room for manoeuvre. Depending on the economic and political context, the power relationships involved and the profiles of migrants in question, then, there were many possible policy outcomes. These outcomes tell us something about the nature and strength of the different interests involved. Analysing them helps to deepen our understanding of the politically contentious context within which early modern urban migrations took place. By exploring policies and conflicts pertaining to urban migration in Brabant during the second half of the eighteenth century, this chapter aims to trace the limits and possibilities of selective migration and relief policies in practice, and to gauge their impact on the lives and decisions of urban migrants.

Cities and Relief in Eighteenth-Century Brabant

The Duchy of Brabant was one of the provinces of the Southern Low Countries, which for most of the eighteenth century were part of the Austrian Habsburg domains. Made up more or less of today's provinces of Antwerp, Flemish Brabant and Walloon Brabant, it was one of the core provinces of the Austrian Netherlands, both in political and economic terms. While some central institutions existed at the 'national' level and Austrian interference was on the rise in the second half of the century, the provinces of the Southern Low Countries enjoyed a large degree of regional autonomy, with separate legal systems and their own judicial and political councils. Although Brabant had

---

[16]   Leeuwen, 'Amsterdam', pp. 150–53; Mary Lindemann, *Patriots and Paupers: Hamburg, 1712–1830* (Oxford, 1990), pp. 49–65.

[17]   Winter, *Divided Interests*, pp. 7–18.

had a strong urban tradition since the late Middle Ages, the first half of the eighteenth century was a phase of urban decline in both absolute and relative terms, with many urban industries dwindling in the face of declining domestic demand, heightened protectionism in neighbouring countries and increased imports. During the second half of the century, however, cities started to grow again in numbers – although in relative terms urban growth was still surpassed by an even greater expansion of the rural population.[18]

The underlying basis of this re-urbanization process of the second half of the eighteenth century has been identified with an increased demand for non-agricultural goods and services by urban and rural elites, driven by an agrarian upswing and the proliferation of commercial networks, which helps to explain why most growth was concentrated in small and middle-sized market towns.[19] For the poorer sections of the Duchy's population, however, the eighteenth century was a period of impoverishment and increasing vulnerability, as proletarianization joined demographic growth to marginalize rural livelihoods.[20] Urban growth was therefore a story of both push and pull. While net flows from the countryside to towns had come to a virtual standstill and were even reversed during Brabant's urban crisis of the first half of the century, growing numbers of rural inhabitants again started to migrate to towns and cities after 1750.[21]

The growing intensity of urban immigration in a period of proletarian impoverishment in turn placed urban concerns over the relief entitlements of newcomers high on the agenda. Poor relief in Brabantine cities was in the hands of a varied assortment of clerical, private and secular institutions, subject to a greater or lesser extent of centralization or supervision by urban authorities. The latter were endowed with a legal and moral duty to relieve their 'own poor' by means of the parochial resources of the Tables of the Holy Spirit if no other assistance was available. Both private and public relief institutions generally had access to steady revenues from independent capital bases derived from legacies

---

[18]   Paul M.M. Klep, *Bevolking en arbeid in transformatie. Een onderzoek in Brabant, 1700– 1900* (Nijmegen, 1981), pp. 97–104; Herman van der Wee, 'Industrial Dynamics and the Process of Urbanization and De-Urbanization in the Low Countries from the Late Middle Ages to the Eighteenth Century: A Synthesis', in Herman van der Wee (ed.), *The Rise and Decline of Urban Industries in Italy and in the Low Countries (Late Middle Ages–Early Modern Times)* (Leuven, 1988), pp. 358–70.

[19]   Bruno Blondé, *Een economie met verschillende snelheden. Ongelijkheden in de opbouw en de ontwikkeling van het Brabantse stedelijke netwerk, ca 1750–ca 1790* (Brussels, 1999), pp. 25–32 and passim; Paul M.M. Klep, 'Urban Decline in Brabant: The Traditionalization of Investments and Labour (1374–1806)', in Wee (ed.), *The Rise and Decline*, pp. 261–86.

[20]   Lis and Soly, *Poverty and Capitalism*, pp. 188ff.

[21]   Klep, *Bevolking*, p. 63.

and bequests, and traditionally enjoyed a large degree of self-sufficiency.[22] As growing impoverishment increased overall pressure on relief provisions in the course of the eighteenth century, however, many charitable institutes were confronted with growing financial deficits, especially in cities. As a result, subsidies by local or central authorities, ultimately derived from taxes, came to play a greater role in the financing of urban relief institutions, raising the awareness of the 'poverty problem' among elites and middle classes.[23]

Urban authorities in eighteenth-century Brabant did not have complete discretion when dealing with migrants' entitlements. There was a fairly consistent case law in the Duchy that went back to a ducal decree of 1618 fixing relief entitlements in the place of birth, and transferring them to the place of residence after three years of stay. According to the same decree, married women followed the settlement of their husbands, and children that of their father.[24] The logical complement was that every pauper *had* a 'settlement', i.e. the place where he or she could/should turn to for assistance. This responsibility of local communities towards the maintenance of their 'own poor' was acknowledged by law and sometimes enforced in court.[25] While legal provisions stipulated that migrants were to be removed to their settlement if they became chargeable, fragmentary local evidence demonstrates that out-resident relief sometimes functioned as an alternative for removal: instead of being sent back, some migrant paupers received relief from their place of settlement while living elsewhere.[26] Decisions over migrants' relief entitlements therefore had repercussions for at least two local communities, that of residence and of origin. Both could, and increasingly did, challenge each other in court over their respective relief responsibilities

---

[22]   Paul Bonenfant, *Le problème du pauperisme en Belgique à la fin de l'ancien régime* (Brussels, 1934), pp. 153–248.

[23]   Bonenfant, *Le problème*, pp. 134–44; Catharina Lis, 'Sociale politiek in Antwerpen, 1779. Het controleren van de relatieve overbevolking en het reguleren van de arbeidsmarkt', *Tijdschrift voor sociale geschiedenis*, 2 (1976): pp. 154, 160–61; Eric Vanhaute, 'De armenzorg op het Antwerpse platteland, 1750–1850. Onderzoek naar een instelling tijdens de scharniereeuw', in *Machtsstructuren in de plattelandsgemeenschappen in België en aangrenzende gebieden (12de–19de eeuw)* (Brussels, 1988), pp. 653–6.

[24]   Bonenfant, *Le problème*, pp. 116–17; Remi Albert du Laury, *La jurisprudence des Pays-Bas autrichiens établie par les arrets du Grand Conseil, de sa Majesté Imperiale et Apostolique, resident en la ville de Malines, auxquels sont ajoutés quelques decrêts portés au Conseil privé de Sadite Majesté* (2 vols, Brussels, 1761), vol. 1, pp. 286–9.

[25]   See Winter, 'Caught', pp. 144–6.

[26]   Selective evidence of out-resident practices can be found for instance in A. Verhalle, *Peilingen naar armoede en armenzorg in het Brugse Vrije van 1770 tot 1789* (Ma thesis, Katholieke Universiteit Leuven, 1964), pp. 68–9, 205; and in the archives of the Openbaar Centrum voor Maatschappelijk Welzijn te Antwerpen (OCMWA), Kamer van Huisarmen (KH), 872.

towards migrants. Simple as the 1618 decree may seem at first sight, it left ample room for discussion, interpretation, negotiation and adaptation.[27] This chapter will explore how urban authorities used this room to deal with mounting challenges of growing immigration and rising relief expenses in the second half of the eighteenth century.

Searching for empirical evidence on urban policies towards immigrants and their entitlements in eighteenth-century Brabant is not straightforward. So far, three main bodies of sources have been explored. Legal sources, such as local and regional rulings and decrees, provide a first perspective on the prescriptive dimension of migration policies. Yet these sources often tell us little about implementation in practice, and give very few indications on underlying motives and expectations. The second main body of sources explored consists of judicial sources relating to disputes and litigation over relief entitlements. While they are better suited to shed light on underlying motives and conflicts of interest, they reveal only a tip of the iceberg. Formal litigation was slow and costly: many discussions and negotiations must have taken place in a more informal manner. Thirdly, administrative sources emanating from both local authorities and relief institutions yield valuable information on the more informal ways in which migrants' relief entitlements were dealt with in practice: assembly notes sometimes give elaborate accounts of policy problems and objectives, extant letters can lay bare the intricate bargaining processes which sometimes took place between place of origin and of residence, while pauper distribution lists can tell us more about who was helped by whom.

Because opportunities for systematic research into these often fragmentary sources are limited and in any case far beyond the possibilities of an individual researcher, my explorations so far have been guided mainly by prior familiarity with certain archival funds and by the degree of detail in existing inventories. Although the harvest has therefore been disparate and uneven, the collected materials yield important insights into some of the dynamics, interests and conflicts underlying urban migration regulation in eighteenth-century Brabant. These can be grouped under three main headings, which correspond to the three main strategies or instruments employed by urban authorities to deal with the challenges of growing immigration levels and increasing pressures on relief resources: local immigration laws, inter-parish agreements and campaigning for comprehensive reform.

---

[27]   Particularly intricate interpretation problems for instance arose in the case of live-in servants, soldiers, widows, foundlings, repeated moves and so on: Archives Générales du Royaume (AGR), Conseil Privé Autrichien (CPA), Cartons, 1285/B. See also: Bonenfant, *Le problème*, pp. 126–34.

Local Immigration Laws and the Warranty System

One of the most obvious and ubiquitous responses by local authorities to deal with migration and its associated challenges consisted of devising new legislation or reinforcing existing regulations on the modalities of immigration and settlement. Local immigration laws proclaimed between the 1740s and 1780s in both large and small settlements, often sanctioned by royal consent, were very similar in content and form. Their main thrust was to make an immigrant's possibility to settle down conditional upon providing a financial security towards the parochial relief institutions. This warranty was generally fixed at 150 guilders, which was the equivalent of more than 200 days' wages of an unskilled labourer.[28] The sum was not necessarily required in cash from the immigrants themselves. In practice it was often guaranteed by their parish of origin by means of an *acte de garant* or *borgbrief* ('surety letter').[29] This was a document issued by the poor relief administrators of a particular parish, by which they acknowledged responsibility for the bearer's relief and pledged to reserve the required sum on the parish funds to that effect. The practice can be traced back at least to the seventeenth century, but became increasingly common in the eighteenth century.[30]

By requiring newcomers to provide a *borgbrief*, local authorities tried to avoid potential relief responsibilities towards immigrants in the future: *borgbrieven* overruled the three-year residence rule, and in principle ensured that the bearers remained at the charge of their parish of origin if they ever needed assistance. Financial warranties and *borgbrieven* – equivalents to which were also in use

---

[28]   See for instance Rijksarchief te Leuven (RAL), Kerkarchief Brabant (KA Brabant), 2.492; 23.307; 23.954; 33.947; 34.438; Rijksarchief te Antwerpen (RAA), Kwartier van Arkel, 53, fols 8–10. Etienne Scholliers, 'Prijzen en lonen te Antwerpen en in het Antwerpse (16e–19e eeuw)', in C. Verlinden (ed.), *Dokumenten voor de geschiedenis van prijzen en lonen in Vlaanderen en Brabant, vol. 2* (Bruges, 1965), pp. 660–1045, cites 13 stivers (20 stivers in one guilder) as the average day wage for an unskilled mason's helper in the 1750s and 1760s.

[29]   Bonenfant, *Le problème*, pp. 117–18; Herman Coppens, 'Een arme eend in de vreemde bijt. Het overheidsoptreden tegenover binnenlandse migranten in de regio Antwerpen tijdens het late ancien régime (ca. 1550 ot 1790)', *Taxandria*, 81 (2009): pp. 147–55; FJ Nooyens, 'De borgbrieven', *Ons Heem*, 3 (1947): p. 142.

[30]   As in the case of English certificates, the origins of the practice of demanding *borgbrieven* can be traced to the late medieval practice of demanding securities or warranties from newcomers whose reputation or means were unknown to local authorities: Philip Styles, 'The Evolution of the Law of Settlement', *University of Birmingham Historical Journal*, 9/1 (1963): pp. 34–43. See also Winter, 'Caught', pp. 144–5.

in England and Holland[31] – were clearly developed by local authorities as a bottom-up device to deal with the paradox of growing spatial mobility and localized relief resources. Their prominence in local legislation confirms that migrants' relief entitlements were a crucial consideration in local migration policies in this period. These were in turn often assisted by measures targeted directly at monitoring immigration, like surveillance at the city gates, control over landlords and inns, and the demolition of pauper dwellings.[32]

Yet in practice the warranty system had many defects. First of all, it required stringent control mechanisms to ensure that all new residents provided a surety or *borgbrief*: if newcomers without a warranty succeeded in settling down unnoticed, they became chargeable to their new place of residence after three years.[33] Secondly, because local authorities were never obliged to provide their emigrants with *borgbrieven*, important social and regional differences existed as to their frequency and use. Although it is impossible to establish the social profile of *borgbrief* holders in the absence of any systematic research into the matter, they probably consisted – as in England – of a relatively 'employable' subset of migrants: risking the future liabilities which the issuing of a *borgbrief* entailed made little sense in the case of particularly vulnerable and poor migrants who were unlikely to find a job elsewhere.[34] Furthermore, the many collections of warranties in the local archives of what is now the province of Antwerp attest to their frequent use in northern parts of the Duchy,[35] while

---

[31]   C.A. Davids, 'Migratie te Leiden in de achttiende eeuw. Een onderzoek op grond van de acten van cautie', in H.A. Diederiks (ed.), *Een stad in achteruitgang. Sociaal-historische studies over Leiden in de achttiende eeuw* (Leiden, 1978), pp. 146–92; Leeuwen, 'Amsterdam'; Styles, 'The Evolution'.

[32]   Bonenfant, *Le problème*; G. Dalle, *De bevolking van Veurne-ambacht in de 17de en 18de eeuw* (Brussels, 1963), pp. 84–8; Lis, 'Sociale politiek', p. 157.

[33]   Hence fraudulent practices could arise whereby out-parish relief was given secretly to sojourners long enough to have them acquire a new settlement. Cf. RAA, Kwartier van Arkel, 53, fols 8–9: 'For example, when a village notices that one of their residents is likely to soon become chargeable, it often happens that this village tries to send out this resident to another village, where it provides him secretly with some relief from time to time, with which he can live quietly, until the three years necessary to acquire a new settlement have elapsed, after which he is abandoned, and left to the charge of his new place of residence.'

[34]   Byung Khun Song, 'Agrarian Policies on Pauper Settlement and Migration, Oxfordshire 1750–1834', *Continuity and Change*, 13 (1998): pp. 378–9.

[35]   Virtually all municipal and church archives in today's province of Antwerp hold relatively large collections of (mostly incoming) certificates. See the series *Oud Gemeentearchief* and *Oud Kerkarchief* in RAA and the many source publications by H. Delvaux in the genealogical journal *De Vlaamse Stam* in the 1970s.

in the south they appear to have been less common.[36] Indications of the use of immigration policies cum warranty systems in the eighteenth century were found for most of the major cities in the northern half of Brabant, like Antwerp, Turnhout, Lier and Mechelen, but so far not for their southern counterparts like Brussels or Leuven. In addition, while villages south of Mechelen often required *borgbrieven* from newcomers at the time of their arrival, in the Campine area they appear to have demanded them only if and when sojourners married and established a household.[37]

These differences in local practice could cause serious inconveniences. The joint village officers of the *kwartier* of Arkel to the south of Antwerp, for instance, pleaded in 1776 for the abolition of warranties because the lack of enforceability and uniformity in the issuing of *borgbrieven* had led to 'much confusion and costly litigation': some towns and villages had stopped providing them, while other authorities still requested them from newcomers. The lifelong – and even intergenerational – responsibilities which *borgbrieven* implied, they explained, had made many local authorities increasingly reluctant to provide them. The cities of Antwerp, Mechelen and Lier had by then abolished them altogether. This had resulted in an uncertificated group of paupers being 'transported from one village to the next without support or mercy', who 'have nothing to expect but death by hunger'.[38] It was probably no coincidence that the largest cities in the region had turned their backs on the warranty system. While providing *borgbrieven* to their own emigrants created important future liabilities, the 'return' was less easily realized: for obvious reasons, controlling newcomers was more difficult in large cities than in villages.[39]

Next to issues of control and enforcement, other problems could complicate the restrictive objectives of urban immigration laws of the period. While such policies helped to reduce future relief expenses, they could frustrate the interests of urban employers: given that warranties were not always readily obtainable,

---

[36]   Or in any case very differently archived: certificates are only very sporadically found in the communal and church archives of present-day Brabant and the Brussels region. See for rare instances: RAL, KA Brabant, 24.672; 23.666; 23.100; 25.899; 26.859; 28.085; 30.678.

[37]   RAA, Oud Gemeentearchief Arendonk, 4280. The certificates kept in these archives often explicitly refer to the occasion of marriage, and often state responsibility for half of the possible relief costs incurred by the couple's future children, and sometimes one quarter of the costs of their future grandchildren. See for example RAA, Oud Gemeentearchief Arendonk, 4555.

[38]   RAA, Kwartier van Arkel, 53, fols 1–10.

[39]   Similar considerations were also relevant in the observed decline in the use of certificates in England and Holland after mid-century: Ethel M. Hampson, 'Settlement and Removal in Cambridgeshire, 1662–1834', *Cambridge Historical Journal*, 2/3 (1928): p. 286; Leeuwen, 'Amsterdam', p. 150; Snell, *Parish and Belonging*, p. 99.

requiring newcomers to provide one could hinder the influx of immigrant labour. Several high-rank judicial officers of the Austrian Netherlands pleaded against the use of warranties in the second half of the eighteenth century exactly because they represented a barrier to labour mobility, and therefore harmed the interests of commerce and agriculture.[40] In other words, the warranty system implied a trade-off between economizing on relief expenses on the one hand and enlarging the local labour supply on the other hand, and could therefore generate conflicts of interests between relief administrators and employers at the local level. This is illustrated by a petition to the central authorities by three employers from the small town of Vilvoorde, who in 1767 requested an exception to the new migration regulations issued by the town council a few months earlier. These regulations required, in line with other local immigration laws of the time, all 'foreigners' to provide a warranty of 150 guilders to the Table of Holy Spirit. The three employers – a tanner, cloth dyer and manager of a sawmill – argued that these new regulations 'hindered them in the choice of their workers'. They requested that their workers be exempt from the requirements and allowed 'to work freely in their enterprises as before'. Initially turned down, the request eventually succeeded in securing exceptions from the warranty rule for the tannery workers. To defend their decision, the central authorities agreed that 'a strict interpretation of the ordinance could ... hinder Buchet [the tannery owner] in the choice of his workers': given 'the acclaimed utility [of the tannery] for the Low Countries, we think that these considerations which pertain to the public good, have priority over the particular well-being of a Table of the Poor'.[41] The Vilvoorde request is exceptional in that local disputes over migration policies were seldom played out in such an explicit and formal matter. At the same time it is illustrative of how strong employer interests could clash with those primarily concerned about relief expenses. While employers rarely undertook formal petitions to this effect, more informal ways of lobbying probably hindered an indiscriminate enforcement of immigration restrictions, or in any case mitigated the stringency with which they could be put into practice.

Restrictive migration policies and warranty practices, then, were probably the commonest *normative* response of both village and town authorities to the menace of increasing relief responsibilities towards destitute newcomers in eighteenth-century Brabant, much as in England and Holland. Yet several problems limited the usefulness of these policies in practice, especially in large cities. Varying local practices, a growing reluctance to provide warranties, and limited means of policing and administrative control *a priori* prohibited any

---

[40]   AGR, CPA, Cartons, 1283: Avis des fiscaux du Grand Conseil 5 August 1750. See also Bonenfant, *Le problème*, pp. 118 n. 2, 124.

[41]   AGR, CPA, Registres des consultes, 458, fol. 150.

general enforcement of entry conditions, while employer interests could strive actively or passively to mitigate their restrictive aims in practice.

Inter-Parish Agreements, Negotiations and Conflicts

As an alternative to individual warranties, which were sometimes difficult to enforce, inter-parish negotiations offered more comprehensive scope for settling some of the intricacies of migrants' relief entitlements. From the eighteenth century onwards, local authorities in the Austrian Netherlands increasingly concluded bilateral or multilateral agreements on migrants' relief entitlements with other local authorities, which in fact amounted to establishing collective warranties. The 'Concordat of Ypres' (1750), for example, represented a voluntary agreement between different West Flemish cities and villages to employ birthplace as the sole criterion for determining a person's settlement, rather than the three-years' residence clause provided for in national legislation.[42] A similar arrangement was later established, and nationally sanctioned, in the *Waasland* region in the east of the County of Flanders.[43] The advocates of the birthplace criterion argued that it would simplify the confusion and litigation arising from settlement disputes, and would prevent fraudulent practices whereby migrants were secretly subsidized by their place of origin long enough for them to acquire a new settlement.[44]

Local authorities did not necessarily adhere to one sole definition of settlement in their inter-parish relationships. On the contrary, several appear to have maintained different types of settlement arrangements with distinct local authorities. The city of Antwerp, for instance, concluded separate agreements with the town of Lier (1760) and the village of Gierle (1770) to use the birthplace criterion in their reciprocal settlement arrangements, while it endorsed the three-year residence criterion in a bilateral agreement with the town of Turnhout (1770), and agreed with the suburban village of Ekeren in

---

[42]   *Plakkaten van Vlaanderen*, V, p. 38, 46. Also: Bonenfant, *Le problème*, pp. 118–23; Damme, 'Onderstandswoonst', pp. 494–5.

[43]   *Recueil des ordonnances des Pays-Bas Autrichiens* (ROPBA), série 3, IX, pp. 72–4. The ways in which the move towards multilateral settlement agreements in these *rural* areas was also tied in with transformations in the agricultural labour market is a subject that I will be exploring together with Thijs Lambrecht of the University of Ghent in future publications. On the failed attempt to establish such an agreement in the Campine region, see Coppens, 'Een arme eend', pp. 160–75.

[44]   See note 33.

1778 that mutual costs for sojourners would be relieved on a fifty-fifty basis.[45] That the varying nature of these bilateral agreements was based mainly on ad hoc cost-benefit calculations may be illustrated by an internal memo from the 1730s concerning the settlement arrangements to be followed in relation to the French city of Lille: here, the Antwerp overseers advised the city to endorse the principle of residence rather than that of birth, as they estimated that there were considerably more Antwerp-born living in Lille than Lille-born living in Antwerp.[46]

It is difficult to establish how widespread such bilateral and multilateral arrangements were, but they were probably rather the exception than the norm. They were likely to be established only between communities engaged in a relatively intense exchange of population, as the administrative effort engaged in setting up and maintaining the agreement was considerable. Most of the agreements found were indeed either between major urban centres – such as Antwerp, Mechelen, Turnhout and Lier – or between a city and its rural hinterland, as was the case for instance in Antwerp and Turnhout.[47] While intense correspondence over individual cases demonstrates that the enforcement of these agreements was not always straightforward, they nevertheless appear to have instilled sufficient sense of obligation and trust to support the development of out-resident relief practices from at least the 1760s onwards, with people living in one place but receiving their relief from another.[48]

Inter-parish agreements over settlement had many advantages over the warranty system, especially for cities. They also protected local relief provisions from encroachments by newcomers, but they did not require individual control measures. In fact, by establishing clarity over relief responsibilities, these agreements generally removed or mitigated the need for entry control, especially when relief entitlements remained fixed in one's birthplace. Stimulating labour mobility was indeed one of the objectives explicitly mentioned by the supporters of the 'Concordat of Ypres' in Flanders, which guaranteed absolute freedom

45   And many more arrangements existed with other local authorities: Bonenfant, *Le problème*, 124–5; E. Geudens, *Le compte moral de l'an X des hospices civils d'Anvers* (Antwerp, 1898), p. CII; Eva Pais-Minne, 'Weldadigheidsinstellingen en sociale toestanden', in *Antwerpen in de achttiende eeuw. Instellingen, economie, cultuur* (Antwerp, 1952), pp. 162–3. See also OCMWA, KH, 866, fols 108, 115, 221.

46   OCMWA, KH, 866, fol. 108.

47   For Turnhout's 'perpetual warranty' agreement with the surrounding countryside, see Nooyens, 'De borgbrieven', pp. 143, n. 6.

48   Evidence of out-resident practices in Antwerp in OCMWA, KH, 872.

of movement between municipalities endorsing the birthplace criterion.[49] Obviously, propagating the birthplace criterion had evident advantages for urban authorities. It allowed immigration to take place without having to bear the associated relief costs. But as much as the birthplace criterion favoured cities where immigrants outnumbered emigrants, it was to the disadvantage of communities with migration deficits: the latter remained liable for the relief costs of long-absent residents. Hence opportunities for urban free-riding in this respect were limited by the consensual nature of inter-parish agreements: if parties felt that they were systematically disadvantaged by a given arrangement, they simply pulled out.[50] While inter-parish agreements provided better ways for urban authorities to deal with migrants' relief entitlements than unilateral migration restrictions, then, their consensual basis rendered them too fragile an instrument to systematically shift migrants' relief costs to other communities.

Neither the existence of legal stipulations and warranties nor the development of bilateral agreements was robust enough to prevent evasions of relief responsibilities. There are several indications that parishes resorted to unlawful removals of pauper migrants by force or intimidation, without reference to legal rules or agreements. It is difficult to assess the scale on which either lawful or unlawful removals took place. The cases eventually brought to court are likely to have been only the tip of the iceberg. Yet in qualitative terms they appear to have been targeted mainly at the most vulnerable groups of migrants, like pregnant or widowed women, whose (potential) relief requirements were deemed particularly costly. Thus, 'under the threat of beatings', local officers pressured 44-year-old Elisabeth Van Dijk into leaving the town of Herentals in 1742. At the time of her expulsion, she had lived in Herentals for 16 years and had recently lost her husband. She was driven out around the same time as 27-year-old Elisabeth Bodenberghs, recently widowed and eight months pregnant – in the words of the Herentals authorities, 'urgently time to remove her so that the future child would not become chargeable to the town' – and 42-year-old Maria Lembrecht, who could think of no other reason for her removal than 'that her

---

49   AGR, CPA, Cartons, 1283: Avis des *conseillers-fiscaux* du Grand Conseil, 5 August 1750; Request of the Brugse Vrije to the Empress, 16 May 1757; Letter of the Council of Flanders to the Conseil Privé, 1 October 1757.

50   As happened with the concordat of Ypres: cracks in the multilateral arrangements emerged by the 1770s when a number of communities petitioned for the right to pull out from the arrangements and place themselves again under the general residence rule. Requests to pull out of the arrangement were invariably granted, so that by the 1780s most of the convention had evaporated: ROPBA, série 3, XI, p. 123; AGR, CPA, Cartons, 1284/A, Actes concernant la mendicité en Flandres, 1776.

husband ... had recently died and had left her with a child'.[51] We know about these cases because the authorities of the women's place of origin, the village of Geel, took the case to court – but not all paupers were able to rally this kind of support. Other evidence of removals can sometimes be found in local correspondence or accounts, as when we encounter a detailed invoice of the costs incurred by the urban wagoner to transport insane Maria Anna Marloy from Mechelen to Antwerp in a cart.[52] Yet many removals probably went unrecorded, as suggested by the – admittedly dramatic – outcry of the *kwartier* of Arkel quoted above on the existence of an uncertificated group of paupers being 'transported from one village to the next'.[53] These observations echo the fate of paupers who were the subject of informal and unlawful removals on the other side of the Channel, and are a powerful reminder that the normative guidelines and provisions are only part of the story.[54]

Lobbying for Comprehensive Legal Reform

The observed limitations of the settlement system as it existed in late eighteenth-century Brabant formed the background to a campaign for more comprehensive legal reform in the domain of settlement legislation, in which the city of Antwerp took the lead. As inter-parish agreements had proved too weak as a basis on which to establish the birthplace criterion, the city magistrate hoped that an obligatory law at the central or provincial level could establish what inter-parish agreements had failed to do. In the course of the second half of the eighteenth century, the town council repeatedly requested the regional and central authorities to install the birthplace as the only lawful place of settlement. Their official line of argumentation was one of juridical and administrative simplicity. They maintained that the birthplace criterion would put an end to the confusion, conflict and costly litigation occasioned by the ambiguity of existing settlement legislation: 'That by adopting the right of birth ... one prevents a great number of difficulties, because birth is certain and therefore not subject to long examinations and intricate arguments. Residence, in contrast, depends on several facts which are often very difficult to prove.'[55] Yet as in the case of

51   Rijksarchief te Anderlecht, Raad van Brabant, Procesdossiers Steden, 712.

52   OCMWA, KH, 866, fol. 115.

53   RAA, Kwartier van Arkel, 53, fols 1–10. See above, note 38.

54   Steve Hindle, *On the Parish: The Micro-Politics of Poor Relief in Rural England, c. 1550–1750* (Oxford, 2004), pp. 250–54. See also Leeuwen, 'Amsterdam', p. 150.

55   AGR, CPA, Cartons, 1284/A, Mémoire contenant les raisons démonstratives ..., 18 June 1779.

the bilateral agreements discussed earlier, cost-benefit considerations were an important if not crucial factor. For a city like Antwerp, which attracted more migrants than it sent out, the birthplace rule was the easiest way to safeguard urban charitable provisions from 'foreigners who flock here from all over the place, due to the liberty beggars enjoy to run from one city to the other ... to settle down with their children in the place where charity is most abundant'.[56]

The Antwerp authorities' repeated requests to install the birthplace rule as the one and only criterion for relief access were, however, systematically blocked by higher authorities, who argued that existing legislation was sufficiently clear and that the three-year residence criterion was well established by Brabantine case law.[57] The main governmental council moreover considered Antwerp's proposal at odds with 'humanity and reason'. In this, it followed the argument of the Grand Conseil de Malines – the highest judicial authority of the Austrian Netherlands – which declared that it would be a sign of 'inhumanity to chase away a citizen who succumbed to poverty, often in his old age, from the place where he would have contributed many years towards local taxes and levies, and where he would have earned the pity and kindness of his fellow citizens, to send him and his misery away to his place of birth where no one would know him'. In other words, when a migrant had given the best of his years in a particular place, it was only just that he be relieved by that local community if and when he fell on hard times.[58]

After repeated failed attempts to have the birthplace rule adopted by law, the Antwerp authorities subsequently resorted to their second-best strategy. In 1779 the city magistrate gained royal approval for an extensive immigration monitoring scheme. This was based on a very strict interpretation of existing legislation and enabling the expulsion of all immigrants who did not carry a warranty.[59] A memo on the first page of the 'residence-book' initiated in the same year illustrates the main objective of these measures. It recorded a whole list of humble occupations, from buttonmakers to diamond mill turners, that 'were not to be accepted for residence'. Nor were 'all persons coming here with

---

56   AGR, CPA, Cartons, 1284/A, Letter of Warnot in name of the Antwerp Magistrate, 18 June 1779.

57   AGR, CPA, Consultes, 475, fols 218–29.

58   AGR, CPA, Cartons, 1283, *Letter of the Grand Conseil de Malines*, 09 October 1750; 1284/A, *Letter of the conseiller-fiscal of Brabant*, 12 July 1779; Consultes, 475, fols. 218–29.

59   AGR, CPA, Cartons, 1284/A, *Letter of Cuylen in name of the Antwerp Magistrate*, 31 December 1780; *Extrait du protocole*, 20 January 1781; *Interpretatie van de ordonnantie van den 30 october 1779*.

a family and with insufficient means of subsistence, or who in the least case of illness, misfortune, or idleness are to become chargeable to the poor'.[60]

Failing to have the birthplace criterion installed, the city authorities thus opted for a reinforcement of traditional restrictive migration policies against families with children and other poverty-prone newcomers. It is telling in this respect that the (often temporary) immigration of young, fit and single migrants – the largest group of newcomers in this period – does not appear to have met much opposition.[61] Yet, as before, this strategy of selective immigration quickly ran up against its limits. Already in 1781 the Antwerp magistrate complained about the many problems faced in their efforts to 'get rid of poor strangers'. This had resulted in situations in which they had no choice but to give them some relief. After all, they observed, 'they are still humans, and for as long as they are under our eyes, we cannot let them perish'.[62] Although much of this is rhetoric, their laments do illustrate how consistent attempts to restrict migrants' relief entitlements in times of great need could clash with the minimal moral responsibilities necessary to maintain social stability. Yet however gloomy the picture they drew, Antwerp's repeated requests for having the birthplace criterion installed continued to be rejected by the central authorities.[63] Further legislative activity in the domain of settlement legislation had to await the discontinuities of the French Revolution.[64]

The main goal of Antwerp's migration policy in this period – both in its campaign for the birthplace rule and subsequently in its reinforcement of selective entry conditions – was the protection of its local relief resources. It is interesting to note that there are no signs of employer protest against Antwerp's renewal of restrictive immigration policies like there were for instance in Vilvoorde. On the contrary, while employer influence in domains of social policy was manifestly large in late eighteenth-century Antwerp, they did not make use of this political power to oppose restrictive migration policies.[65] This can be explained by the city's specific pattern of labour market segmentation: due to unenviable working

---

60   Stadsarchief Antwerpen (SAA), Vierschaar, V177.

61   On the characteristics of Antwerp's immigration patterns in the second half of the eighteenth century, see Anne Winter, *Migrants and Urban Change: Newcomers to Antwerp, 1760–1860* (London, 2009), pp. 79–85.

62   AGR, CPA, Cartons, 1284/A, *Letter of Cuylen in name of the Antwerp Magistrate*, 31 December 1781. Similar laments and complaints are reiterated in later years: AGR, CPA, Cartons, 1283, *Memoire of the Antwerp Magistrate*, 14 May 1783.

63   AGR, CPA, Cartons, 1283, *Suppression de la mendicité à Anvers*.

64   Bonenfant, *Le problème*, pp. 249–556; Winter, 'Caught', pp. 148–9.

65   On the influence of employer interests on Antwerp's relief policies in this period: Lis, 'Sociale politiek', pp. 152–160.

conditions and a lack of skill, very few migrants worked in the production of lace and textiles.[66] Yet these were the city's most important export industries and the lucrative domain *par excellence* of its most powerful tycoons.[67] The virtual absence of migrants in their trades, then, explains why these entrepreneurs took little interest in opposing immigration restrictions, but instead concentrated their efforts on augmenting the supply of cheap, skilled and disciplined child and female labour from the ranks of the impoverished Antwerp population and on mobilising relief as wage subsidies.[68]

While the Vilvoorde request discussed earlier illustrated the potential conflict of interest between employers wanting to remove barriers to immigration and relief administrators aiming to protect local relief provisions, the Antwerp example alerts us to the fact that employers could in certain situations have an interest in restricting immigration and migrant relief entitlements too – as in the case of eighteenth-century Lyon referred to in the beginning of this chapter. The Vilvoorde/Antwerp contrast therefore highlights the importance of contextualizing local labour markets in order to adequately interpret migration policies and the associated interests of stakeholders. When most of their workers were immigrants, as in port towns relying on a large supply and turnover of relatively unskilled labour, employers had reasons to lobby against entry and relief restrictions for newcomers. Yet in situations where they employed mainly local-born workers, as in proto-industrial textile industries requiring a steady supply of relatively skilled labour, employers could have strong incentives to reserve relief provisions for their own, local, workers – especially when relief provisions functioned as *de facto* wage subsidies as in the cases of eighteenth-century Antwerp and Lyon.

---

[66] While no less than 32 per cent of Antwerp-born men and 70 per cent of Antwerp-born women were engaged in the lace and textile industries, the respective proportions among their immigrant counterparts were only 11 and 24 per cent. Migrants' comparative avoidance of these trades appears to have been attributable both to a lack of necessary skills and to the unenviable working conditions in these sectors, where children, women and the elderly were paid pittances for long working hours. The implication was that migrants were relatively unimportant as a source of labour supply to local textile entrepreneurs – although migrants made up around 27 per cent of Antwerp's total active population, they supplied only 10 per cent of the workforce engaged in the production of textiles and lace: Winter, *Migrants*, pp. 79–85.

[67] Lis, 'Sociale politiek', pp. 152–60; Catharina Lis, *Social Change and the Labouring Poor: Antwerp, 1770–1860* (New Haven, 1986), pp. 6–16; Alfons K.L. Thijs, *Van werkwinkel tot fabriek. De textielnijverheid te Antwerpen (einde 15de–begin 19de eeuw)* (Brussels, 1987), pp. 180–85, 215–18, 370–80, 392.

[68] Lis, 'Sociale politiek', pp. 152–6.

Conclusions

The question of migrants' relief entitlements was a crucial concern of urban migration policies in eighteenth-century Brabant. While the specificities of national and regional settlement legislation no doubt constituted an important mediating factor, I believe that the associated interests and tensions were common to all early modern urban contexts facing high immigration levels in a time of growing pressure on localized relief provisions. Underlying these tensions was an uneven distribution of the (collective) costs and (private) gains of immigration, and a trade-off between economizing on local relief expenses and increasing the local labour supply, which often pitted the interests of relief administrators against those of employers.

The range of immigration policy instruments identified and explored for eighteenth-century Brabantine cities is illustrative of the policy options available to other cities confronted with similar challenges – and their respective limits. Selective relief policies, aimed at excluding newcomers from access to local relief provisions, could only be practised up to a point that moral or political concerns for social stability dictated that pauper migrants 'cannot be left to perish' – as the Antwerp authorities emphatically expressed it. Selective migration policies, aimed at preventing the entry of unwanted or costly newcomers, were in turn particularly difficult to enforce in large cities, as they required an intensive monitoring of immigrants with only limited administrative and coercive means, and could clash with pro-immigration employer interests as in the Vilvoorde case. Hence, attempts to restrict newcomers and/or their relief entitlements could run counter to a 'logic of charity' in which labour market regulation and the maintenance of social stability were also important functions of poor relief provisions. The Antwerp case, where local employers were happy to go along with heightened immigration restrictions, reminds us that this 'logic of charity' could at the same time vary considerably according to the structure of local labour markets.

The Brabant material offers revealing examples of how urban authorities tried to overcome these deficiencies, conflicts and paradoxes by means of inter-parish negotiations and agreements. This attests to local dynamism in trying to devise new solutions to old problems. Yet the consensual nature of bilateral or multilateral agreements could not prevent attempts to bend or circumvent the rules, or the materialization of conflicts within and between local communities, which multiplied as the stakes and concerns associated with migrants' entitlements increased in the course of the eighteenth century. Together with the observation that the Antwerp authorities eventually resorted to lobbying for national reform, the observed limits of both bilateral bargaining and unilateral discretion lends support to De Swaan's argument that the contradictions between localized relief provisions and geographical mobility could eventually be overcome only by 'national' initiatives.

Yet while national action may well have provided the only *structural* solution to the observed problems and paradoxes, this does not mean that cities were passive victims of De Swaan's geographical free-rider problem. Within the limits set by their means of enforcement, cities were engaged in permanent attempts to regulate immigration flows as well as newcomers' relief entitlements in accordance with shifting power relations between urban interest groups. Although the degree of success of the various policy responses explored was limited and uneven, the economically most vulnerable migrants were probably among those most likely to suffer their negative effects. The memo to the Antwerp 'residence book' as well as the studied court cases all indicate that the selective measures in place were targeted primarily at migrants in vulnerable phases of their life cycles, such as elderly people or single mothers, who were most likely to be subjected to informal evictions or formal removals. Further research is needed, however, to gain better insight into the frequency of removals and their impact on the experiences and strategies of migrants themselves.

Chapter 11

Rough Lives: Autobiography and Migration in Eighteenth-Century England

Tim Hitchcock

The history of poverty and the family privileges the unadventurous and stay at home. In an English context, and in the work of scholars such as Paul Slack, Steve Hindle, Joanna Innes and Lynn Hollen Lees, we are possessed of wonderful analyses of the workings of the institutions of charity, of the Old Poor Law and, at least tangentially, the experience of the settled poor.[1] This literature has charted the unusual evolution of the uniquely comprehensive system of taxation, redistribution and settlement that characterized English poor relief following the passage of the Old Poor Law at the beginning of the seventeenth century.[2] But the bureaucratic nature of the precocious English system, and the extent to which it privileged the 'deserving poor', has naturally led its historians to overemphasize the experience of people who fitted within the system's cosy categories and were able to access its resources.[3] A pension list records all the grey-haired men and women of the parish, its ill-starred children and broken families, but is silent about the casual poor, the wandering peddler and unsettled drunk. Even the hundreds of thousands of settlement examinations that litter English archives – mini-biographies demanded by magistrates in exchange for

---

[1] Paul Slack, *From Reformation to Improvement: Public Welfare in Early Modern England* (Oxford, 1999); Steve Hindle, *On the Parish? The Micro-Politics of Poor Relief in Rural England, c. 1550–1750* (Oxford, 2004); Joanna Innes, 'The State and the Poor: Eighteenth-Century England in European Perspective', in John Brewer and Eckhart Hellmuth (eds), *Rethinking Leviathan: The Eighteenth-Century State in Britain and Germany* (Oxford, 1999), pp. 225–80; and Lynn Hollen Lees, *The Solidarities of Strangers: The English Poor Laws and the People, 1700–1948* (Cambridge, 1998).

[2] 43 Elizabeth, c.7.

[3] A notable exception to this emphasis on the settled poor can be found in the growing literature on unmarried motherhood, whose objects of study were significantly migratory and socially dislocated. See for example Lisa Forman Cody, *Birthing the Nation: Sex, Science, and the Conception of Eighteenth-Century Britons* (Oxford, 2005); and Tanya Evans, '*Unfortunate Objects': Lone Mothers in Eighteenth-Century London* (Basingstoke, 2005).

alms – tend to reflect the lives of those whose migratory peregrinations have come to a natural halt.

The people who might be termed 'successful' beggars and mendicants – those able to secure an adequacy from begging and other pauper professions, who were able to travel without too much hindrance or trouble – are largely absent from the records, and ignored by historians. To ask for broken victuals at a kitchen door, to walk unmolested through a town or a village, to sleep in a barn or even to be warned off or moved on by a constable leaves no record. It is the failed migrant and incompetent beggar who leaves the most indelible trace. And yet, as Patricia Fumerton has recently suggested, it was precisely the unsettled poor, the migratory and vagrant poor, who most fully characterized and influenced late seventeenth- and eighteenth-century English society. Fumerton has convincingly argued that the experience of mobility was central to the cultures of most working people, and that this experience of geographical and cultural deracination led to a particular cast of mind and notion of individuality that formed a significant fragment of a modern 'self'.[4] In other words, for Fumerton, travel and migration were normal aspects of the lives of the majority population. This chapter aims to explore the experience of successful beggars and pauper migrants in an attempt to rebalance our view of the experience of plebeian men and women in the eighteenth century – to refocus our attention from the system of poor relief and regulation as seen from the perspective of the parish clerk, to that of the seasonal migrant and hardened beggar.

The Caveats of a Legal System

On the face of it, the ever growing body of case law associated with the Act of Settlement and the dense blanket of English vagrancy laws that evolved in parallel would appear to militate against successful migration and unsettled beggary. The settlement laws identified the parish responsible for each individual on the basis of a complex hierarchy of birth, apprenticeship, and marriage. The system was first legislated in 1662 (13 & 14 Car. II c.12) and was then made much more workable by acts in 1691 (3 William & Mary c.11) and 1697 (8 & 9 William III c.30), allowing migrant paupers to present a 'settlement certificate' that evidenced their legal relationship to their home parish. Throughout the eighteenth century, thousands of certificates – and appeals, petitions and weighty judgements by weightier judges sitting in Quarter Sessions or at the

---

4   Patricia Fumerton, *Unsettled: The Culture of Mobility and the Working Poor in Early Modern England* (Chicago, 2006).

Court of King's Bench – were created in order to regulate both migration and the allocation of responsibility for pauper relief. Most contemporary commentators certainly believed that settlement effectively handcuffed labourers and their families, and acted as a significant disincentive to migration.[5]

It is clear that some people did find their lives turned upside down by this system. And although we do not have a clear statistical measure of the number of paupers 'removed' each year, the survival of over 2,000 'removal orders' among the manuscript sessions papers for Middlesex and the City of London between 1690 and 1799, reflects a system that worked, as does the level of legal costs expended in pursing settlement cases and reported to Parliament. In a large and poor London parish such as St Botolph Aldgate, for instance, with a population of around 12,000 people and an economy centred on the used clothing trade, the costs of making the settlement system work ran to an average £58 a year in the mid-1770s.[6]

The legislation relating to vagrancy appears equally robust and coherent. From 1700 onwards the county (or the city in the case of incorporated towns like London or Exeter) was responsible for removing individual vagrants. Most counties developed sophisticated systems, frequently run by independent contractors, dedicated to transporting a vagrant flood from county to county. In Middlesex the vagrant's cart could be seen trundling across the county twice a week, first northward and then southward.[7] The legal position was codified in 1714 and again in 1744, and throughout the century rewards were offered for arrest, and severe punishments stipulated. At the beginning of the century, and according to the law, two shillings could be earned by any constable willing to arrest a vagrant, rising to five shillings and even 10 shillings for the arrest and prosecution of an 'incorrigible rogue'. The law also laid out periods of hard labour, with public whippings for all vagrants.[8]

This legal system, like the system of settlement, did have an impact. In the mid-1770s, for instance, Middlesex committed an average of 531 vagrants to

---

[5]   Most famously Adam Smith, *An Inquiry into the Nature and Causes of the Wealth of Nations* (1776; Everyman edn, 1910), i, p. 128. For a survey of the workings of the settlement system and of elite attitudes towards it, see J.S. Taylor, 'The Impact of Pauper Settlement 1691– 1834', *Past and Present*, 73 (1976): pp. 42–74.

[6]   Parliamentary Papers, 'Second Report. Reported by Thomas Gilbert, Esq. 21 May 1776', p. 293.

[7]   For details of the arrangements in Middlesex see the 1757 contract between James Sturgis Adams and the county. London Metropolitan Archives, Middlesex Sessions of the Peace, Sessions Papers, 1757, MJ/SP/1757/07.

[8]   Although there were some 26 acts relating to vagrancy passed between 1700 and 1824, the two most significant pieces of legislation were 13 Ann c.26 and 17 George II. c.5.

a House of Correction each year.[9] Most of these vagrants were settled in the county, and it is much less clear that this number was being forcibly removed to a distant parish or condemned to hard labour, imprisonment and whipping, as the law demanded. But it still means that one or two people a day found themselves directly affected.

These legal provisions for both vagrancy and settlement, however, contained a range of caveats and exceptions, both legal and cultural, which effectively permitted a large number of men and women to live on the roads and in the interstices of a growing urban and industrial world.[10] In both the 1714 and the 1744 Vagrancy Acts, the categories of individuals that made up the definition of a 'vagrant' were explicitly listed:

Patent gatherers, or gatherers of alms, under pretence of loss by fire, or other casualty ...

Collectors for prisons, gaols or hospitals ...

Fencers and bearwards ...

Common players of interludes ...

All persons who shall for hire, gain or reward act, represent or perform, or cause to be acted ... any interlude, tragedy, comedy, opera, play, farce or other entertainment of the stage, or any part ... not being authorized by law ...

All minstrels, jugglers ...

All persons pretending to be Gypsies, or wandering in the habit or form of Egyptians; or pretending to have skill in physiognomy, palmistry, or like crafty science, or pretending to tell fortunes, or using any subtle craft to deceive and impose ... or playing or betting at any unlawful games or plays ...

All persons who run away and leave their wives or children, whereby they become chargeable ...

---

9   Parliamentary Papers, 'Second Report. Reported by Thomas Gilbert, Esq. 21 May 1776', p. 291.

10   The survival of an increasing number of 'pauper letters' from the 1780s onwards reinforces the impression of eighteenth-century England as a society in which migration was commonplace. For a comprehensive collection of one county's letters see Thomas Sokoll, (ed.), *Essex Pauper Letters, 1731–1837* (Oxford, 2001), Records of Social and Economic History, ns, 30.

All petty chapmen and pedlars wandering abroad not being duly licensed or otherwise authorized by law ...

All persons wandering abroad and lodging in alehouses, barns, outhouses, or in the open air, not giving a good account of themselves ...

All persons wandering abroad and begging, pretending to be soldiers, mariners, seafaring men, or pretending to go to work in harvest ...

All other persons wandering abroad and begging shall be deemed rogues and vagabonds ...[11]

It was precisely this list that was then incorporated into handbooks for magistrates and parish officers, and endlessly reproduced for the rest of the century.[12] At one level the occupations enumerated in the Act simply describe the intolerable, but it can equally be read against the grain. For everyone 'pretending' to be a gypsy, a fortune teller or possessing a skill in physiognomy, with its implication of a false claim to professional authority, many others were perceived as legitimate claimants to be gypsies, fortune tellers and readers of physiognomy. Making a distinction between an 'authorized' chapman or peddler and the unauthorized variety required a nicety of judgement that was beyond most early modern magistrates. As one beggar remarked in his 1745 autobiography, he adopted the guise and profession of a rag-gatherer precisely because 'this branch of travelling is a very safe one, for it is neither obnoxious to the laws against strolling, nor to those of buying or selling without license'.[13] And while 'lodging in old houses, barns, outhouses' seems a clear enough talisman of a vagrant, the large body of evidence suggesting that the barns and outhouses of most pubs and alehouses, farms and larger businesses, were readily available for such rough sleeping, suggests that this was a sign that had become de-coupled from the state it was thought to signify.[14]

---

[11]   A Bill Intituled, An Act to amend and make more effectual the Laws relating to Rogues, Vagabonds, and other idle and disorderly Persons and to Houses of Correction (1744), 17 George II. c.5, pp. 2–3.

[12]   See for example, Richard Burn, *The Justice of the Peace and Parish Officer* (18th edn, London, 1797), iv, pp. 410–11.

[13]   C.H. Wilkinson (ed.), *The King of the Beggars: Bampfylde-Moor Carew* (Oxford, 1931), p. 17.

[14]   For sleeping rough in London see Tim Hitchcock, *Down and Out in Eighteenth-Century London* (London, 2004), ch. 2.

Of all the categories that this list incorporates, the last is perhaps most telling. Those 'pretending' to be soldiers and sailors are listed along with the rest, but in this instance a further provision was added:

> Provided always, That this Act ... shall not extend ... to soldiers wanting subsistence, having lawful certificates from their officers ... or to mariners or seafaring men licensed by some testimonial ... or to any person or persons going abroad to work at any lawful work in the time of harvest, so as he, she or they carry with ... them a certificate in writing ...[15]

What we are left with is a system that not only clearly impacted on the lives of tens and thousands of paupers over the course of the century, but one that also possessed an ambiguity and flexibility that a knowing individual might exploit. By examining the handful of published vagrant autobiographies that record eighteenth-century lives, the remainder of this chapter will attempt to navigate a path between legal precept, bald statistics and personal narrative.

The use of autobiographies as social historical evidence is, of course, fraught with difficulties – all the more so when the authors were paupers hoping to earn a few pence from the stories, or religious converts retailing the details of youthful sin to contrast mature redemption. But at least some details of all the accounts provided by the autobiographies used here can be confirmed through alternative sources. And while each narrative conforms to a series of different generic conventions (picaresque novel, conversion narrative, sentimental journey), none of these genres obviously excludes descriptions of arrest and punishment of the sort experienced by vagrants. Indeed, the dominant generic convention of the century – the picaresque novel – would seem to invite and demand narrative emphasis on conflicts with authority. [16]

The Adventures of Mary Saxby

Mary Saxby was born in London to poor parents in 1738. After the death of her mother, and her father's remarriage, she ran away from home at the age of 11:

> I was forced to creep under bulks, or any where, to hide myself from the watchmen; and as soon as day broke, I went into the markets to pick up rotten apples, or cabbage-stalks; as I had nothing else to support nature. At length ... [I went] ... into the country

---

[15]   A Bill Intituled, p. 3.
[16]   Hitchcock, *Down and Out*, ch. 7.

... I can recollect sitting in a black-smith's shop, and holding my feet in my hands, to get some warmth into them. One night, I crept under a hovel for shelter, and there came an old beggar-man to lie down; seeing a child by herself, he asked me where I came from? ... Poor as he was he had pity on me; and gave me a piece of fat bacon, which I ate, without bread as greedily as if it had been the finest food.[17]

She later fell in with 'a poor travelling woman, who had three daughters [who] washed, combed and fed me, and took as much care of me as if I had been her own'. For the next few years, through her early teens, Mary made a living singing ballads in partnership with the youngest daughter of her protector, 'singing in alehouses, at feasts and fairs, for a few pence and a little drink'. Eventually, the two fell in with a 'gang of gypsies', whom the two girls joined. In the succeeding years Mary Saxby cohabited with one of the men, learned a gypsy 'cant' and 'was every way like them, excepting in colour'. At this point, however, being proposed as the 'second wife' to a member of the group, Mary struck off on her own:

I travelled as far as Dover in Kent, with a very little to support me; stopping, at times, to ask for a bit of bread, to keep me from starving. When I reached the coast, I met with a woman who sung ballads, which was a profitable trade in those parts; and she took me into partnership, till we had some words and separated. ... A vessel was, at this juncture wrecked near Sandwich; and the cargo consisting of checks and muslins, was sold cheap; which afforded opportunity to me, and many more, to get clothed for a trifle. Soon after this, having made myself clean and smart, I joined company with a decent woman, who had some small children. ... she sold hardware.[18]

For the next 20 years Mary lived what she herself described as a 'vagrant' existence. She cohabited with at least three different men, married one of them and had a slew of illegitimate children. She earned her living first as a ballad singer and seller, and later as a seasonal harvest worker and unlicensed peddler. She lived for many years with groups who identified themselves as Gypsies, who moved about the country, setting up temporary tent encampments. In this generation of mobility she was subject to the force of law only once, and in her own recollection clearly blamed the incident on her own *naiveté*. After a long stay in hospital in London, she 'set out and went into Kent, to pick hops':

Out of Kent, I went into Essex; where they would not suffer any one to travel without a licence, except they could give a very good account of themselves. I, not knowing the

---

[17]   Mary Saxby, *Memoirs of a Female Vagrant Written by Herself* (London, 1806), p. 6.
[18]   Ibid., p. 11.

rules of the country, sung ballads in Epping market. In the course of the day, I became acquainted with a middle-aged woman, who looked like a traveller; and we went to sleep together at an alehouse. For this I soon smarted; as she proved to be a common woman, though I did not know it. Being in her company, and having been seen with her in the market, the constable came in the night, obliged us to leave our bed, and secured us till morning; when we were taken before a justice, who committed us both to Bridewell, ordering us both to be repeatedly whipped.[19]

Mary had fallen in with an identified woman of poor repute, and had failed to acknowledge 'the rules of the country'. But even in this solitary instance of punishment, the treatment she received was, in her own estimation at least, relatively mild:

> The keeper heard my story very candidly; and I believe he was a good man. Observing my youth and inexperience, he pitied me; and remonstrated with the woman for drawing me into a snare. We were to be confined there six weeks, without any allowance. She was a good spinner; and he made her work, and give me half her earnings. As to being whipped, I knew little but the shame of it; for he took care not to hurt me.[20]

By her own account, Mary was never subject to a bastardy examination, despite her multiple illegitimate births (which legally ensured that her children were the responsibility of the parish in which they were born).[21] She was never 'moved on', or subject to legal harassment after the one unfortunate incident in Epping Forest. And although she frequently begged for her bread, this did not result in further punishment. Her greatest self-confessed fear was the unwanted attention of the men who listened to her ballads and assumed that she was sexually available. On the one occasion, however, on which she was actually subjected to an attempted rape, the incident was taken up by the local authorities and serious (though unsuccessful) endeavours were made to bring the perpetrators to justice.

Mary and her by then legally sanctioned husband finally came to rest in Stony Stratford, Buckinghamshire, in the early 1780s, and with some difficulty

---

[19]   Ibid., p. 14.

[20]   Ibid., p. 14.

[21]   A 'bastardy examination' in which the mother of the child confirmed the identity of the father was a legal requirement. In theory, an expectant mother was obliged to submit to an examination 40 days before the birth. Most examinations, however, took place after the birth. These examinations can contain extensive details about the father, and the sexual relationship that initiated the pregnancy. Tim Hitchcock and John Black (eds), *Chelsea Settlement and Bastardy Examinations, 1733–66* (London, 1999), London Record Society 33, pp. viii–ix.

established a legal settlement by virtue of renting a part of a house.[22] But even later in life she continued to travel long distances to undertake harvest work and to perform the services of an unlicensed peddler to the more isolated communities of midlands.

The image of eighteenth-century society that emerges from Mary's religious autobiography and conversion narrative is one which is willing to encompass a substantial migratory minority. In sharp contrast to the legal precepts that fill both statute and common law, there is little sense of outrage or anxiety about begging, unlicensed peddling, Gypsies or fortune tellers.[23] In part, Mary Saxby's experience suggests that the fragment of the lives recorded in the archives of crime and social policy are atypical and narrowly selective. When Mary Hyde, a seasonal worker and regular migrant, was examined by the Middlesex Justice Samuel Bever in 1756, she patiently explained her circumstances:

> She is about 35 years of age. ... She hath a mother now living and married to George Floyd in the parish of Dawley in ... Shropshire, with whom [she] hath for fourteen or fifteen years past resided and lived with them in the winter season and hath usually come every year to or near London to work in the summer season, and hath constantly about Michaelmas gone to the said parish of Dawley aforesaid, of her own home. And should have done the same at Michaelmas last had she not been afflicted with sore eyes. And [she] hath lately been discharged out of St Georges Hospital, blind and incurable.[24]

As a result of her blindness she was temporarily exposed in the role of a vagrant, but this came at the end of a period of 14 years, during which she apparently progressed across the length of the country twice a year without hindrance.

---

[22]   Saxby, *Memoir*, p. 26.

[23]   In recent scholarship on identity, autobiography and plebeian culture, the creation of a distinctly 'modern' narrative self has been charted. James Amelang has explored the world of European non-elite autobiography, and discovered a distinctive worldview. In a similar way, historians of the Atlantic world have posited the existence of a working-class consciousness arising through the interactions of voluntary and forced migration, trade, commerce and simple movement. But, what has not been substantially explored is the inter-relationship between domestic legal restrictions and that growing unsettledness that seems ever more central to the cultures of non-elite English men and women. See James S. Amelang, *The Flight of Icarus: Artisan Autobiography in Early Modern Europe* (Stanford CA, 1998); Peter Linebaugh and Marcus Rediker, *The Many-Headed Hydra: The Hidden History of the Revolutionary Atlantic* (London, 2000); David Feldman, 'Migrants, Immigrants and Welfare from the Old Poor Law to the Welfare State', *Transactions of the Royal Historical Society*, 6th ser., 13 (2003): pp. 79–104.

[24]   Hitchcock and Black (eds), *Chelsea Examinations*, no. 308.

Armed with a vagrant's pass her progress homeward would have been equally unmolested.

The King of the Beggars

A vagrant's pass, a soldier's or clerk's certificate, the ability to give a 'good account' of oneself, a useful service and non-threatening demeanour seem in most cases enough to prevent the migratory poor from attracting unwanted attention. It is the sheer variety of guises, however, in which one could legitimately wander the roads of England that is remarkable. This variety is reflected in perhaps our most complete (though difficult) eighteenth-century vagrant narrative – the picaresque autobiography of Bampfylde-Moore Carew, the 'King of the Beggars'.

The two editions of Carew's autobiography, published in 1745 and 1749, contain a complex amalgam of literary invention and bald description. Much of the information contained in the first edition is verifiable from other sources, and certainly many of Carew's encounters with the law, and career as a transported vagrant, certainly are. But other elements seem at best unlikely. The second edition, bowdlerized and embellished by its editor Robert Goadby, is much further from an autobiographical narrative – and much more a literary concoction created in response to the contemporary evolution of the picaresque novel.[25] Nevertheless, Carew's account remains a valuable historical document, and one which seems to reflect powerfully on both how contemporaries viewed the migratory and unsettled, and also on the workings (or otherwise) of the vagrancy laws.

Born in Bickleigh, near Tiverton, in 1693, Bampfylde-Moore Carew fell into a vagrant mode of life at school when he and two companions joined a band of Gypsies. For the next 30 years he lived a begging, vagrant life, spending the majority of his time (interspersed with voyages to Newfoundland) roving through the south-west of England begging for a living. Eighteenth-century readers of this autobiography were probably most struck by the shams and guises that Carew adopted in his ever more elaborate attempts to prise a few pence from the communities through which he passed. And there is little doubt that he could count himself among the small number of 'professional' beggars who worked the streets and roads of Britain. But the range and variety of disguise

---

[25]   For an account of the evolution of these texts and supporting scholarship on Carew's life see Wilkinson (ed.), Carew, 'Introduction'; Gwenda Morgan and Peter Rushton, *Eighteenth-Century Criminal Transportation: The Formation of the Criminal Atlantic* (Basingstoke, 2004), pp.78–85; and M.A. Nooney, 'The Cant Dictionary of Bampfylde-Moore Carew: A Study of the Contents and Changes in Various Editions' (MA thesis, University of Florida, 1969).

and account that Carew uses to justify his vagrancy also acts as a clear census of legitimate reason for travelling, and justifications for begging. The *Life and Adventures of Bampfylde-Moore Carew, the Noted Devonshire Stroller and Dog Stealer* is a ribald tale of how to sin against agreed standards of behaviour; but in the process of transgressing those standards, Carew effectively illuminates them.

Early in his wandering career Carew takes on the guise of a Gypsy, and returns to it on several occasions during the next three and a half decades. Armed with a skilfully forged series of passes, he repeatedly pretends to be a shipwreck sailor: 'The news-papers which they constantly and carefully perused, continually furnished them with some melancholy and unfortunate story fitting for their purpose.'[26] At other times, Carew took on the character of a 'Grazier dwelling in the Isle of Sheepy in Kent, whose grounds were overflowed and whose cattle were drowned.'[27] He travelled as a rat-catcher: 'On the outside of his coat he always wore a large buff girdle, stuck thick with the largest and most terrible rats he destroyed, which served as a badge or ensign of his profession'; and a rag-gatherer, dressed in 'an old red Soldier's coat, ... a counterfeit sore on his right hand, and ... his beard ... very long, pretending he had been disabled in the Flanders wars ... Crying, *rags for the ragman, rags for the ragman.*'[28] At other times, Carew pretended to be a 'ragged old clergyman' turned out of his parish as a result of a religious dispute.[29] He was a lunatic on licence from Bedlam, a cripple, a match seller, a seller of 'songs and little two-penny histories, *Tom Thumb, Jack the Giant-Killer*, and such other little romances.'[30] He pretended to be a Quaker on several occasions; and regularly cross-dressed, begging with a borrowed child on his hip for verisimilitude.

In a text that rapidly becomes dull through repetitive renditions of one disguise after another, the boundaries of legitimate begging and migration are rapidly set. If you could 'give a good account of yourself'; if you were useful; if you were a Gypsy; or woman and child; if you sold a commodity that people wanted to buy; if you could demonstrate a disability or a tragic accident; or simply a real need to be in one place over another – movement was relatively unhindered, and uncomplicated.

The remarkable thing about Carew's 30-year vagrant career is that despite being 'famous' as the 'king of the beggars' (he was described as 'a most notorious

---

[26] Wilkinson (ed.), *Carew*, p. 30.

[27] Wilkinson (ed.), *Carew*, p. 14.

[28] Wilkinson (ed.), *Carew*, pp. 16–17.

[29] Wilkinson (ed.), *Carew*, p. 19.

[30] Wilkinson (ed.), *Carew*, pp. 19–21.

common vagrant' in the records of the Exeter Quarter Sessions[31]), despite being widely believed to lead a gang of impostors and frauds, and despite committing a series of serious criminal acts (he was a serial deserter from the army and navy), Carew was only punished on a handful of occasions – prior to his transportation to Maryland in 1739. The first of these appears to have dated to around 1724, when he appears in the records of the combined house of correction and workhouse at Exeter for the first time. In Carew's explanation, he was 'Committed to Bridewell as a vagrant and impostor' when, after having been mistaken for a local malefactor, he was discovered on examination to be the 'famous' Bampfylde Carew. But after two weeks in chains, the justices sitting in Quarter Sessions simply 'turn'd it off with a joke, respectively bowing to him, and expressing great joy in seeing a man who had rendered himself so famous and of whom the world so loudly talk'd ... Without any trial they there fore discharged him.'[32]

On two later occasions in the late 1720s and 1730s he was apprehended and whipped: first at Great Torrington, where the mayor's wife was tricked into providing relief, only to discover her error and fly into a self-righteous rage; and the second time at Chard, where a dispute about the ownership of two dogs led to Carew's persecution by a local Justice of the Peace (JP).[33]

Carew's final run-in with the law – as recounted in the first, more reliable edition of his life – occurred at Exeter and resulted in transportation to North America. In Carew's account, his predicament was the result of ill-luck and poor judgement. On visiting one local magistrate with whom he had an excellent relationship, a fellow justice, who knew Carew and had vowed vengeance on him after a previous encounter, happened to be visiting:

> as ill-luck would have it, in comes Justice Lethbridge, ... he therefore now secured Bampfylde and sent him to St Thomas's Bridewell near Exeter. After two months confinement there he was brought up to the Quarter Sessions held at the Castle, where justice Beavis was Chairman, to whom he [Carew] used some abusive and opprobrious language, and the Justice ordered him seven years transportation.[34]

---

[31]   Devon Record Office, QS 1/18 Order Book, 1734–1745, Easter 1739, pp. 105–7. Quoted in Morgan and Rushton, *Eighteenth-Century Criminal Transportation*, p. 81.

[32]   Wilkinson (ed.), *Carew*, pp. 38–40. For an excellent piece of scholarship tracing aspects of Carew's career in the local records of Devon see Morgan and Rushton, *Eighteenth-Century Criminal Transportation*, pp. 78–85.

[33]   Wilkinson (ed.), *Carew*, pp. 115–16, 131–2.

[34]   Wilkinson (ed.), *Carew*, pp. 134–5.

The remarkable element of this story is not Carew's punishment or his professional character as a vagrant and beggar, but that he appears to have avoided any minor or substantial punishment for the vast majority of the more than 30 years spent on the roads of south-west England. His eventual punishment was not a result of his vagrant and begging habits, or even his undoubted forgery of official documents (in the form of a Justice's pass, among several others items), but his notorious character in combination with his inability to keep his mouth shut in court. Like most able-bodied men and women, Carew appears to have been free to travel and migrate as he wanted, regardless of the blanket of laws and regulations which supposedly policed just this sort of thing. Despite Carew's claims to have perfected his many disguises, and the work he purports to invest in his many hard-luck stories, it is difficult to believe that a figure of his sort could escape censure and suspicion. The fact that he appears to have done so reflects more on the apparent tolerance of eighteenth-century communities than on Carew's inherent skills. If we turn to other, less substantial narratives, this same sense of a freedom of movement in the face of apparent legal obstacles emerges again and again.

Disguise, Skill and Bad Luck

When John Harrower set out from home in search of work in December 1773, he carried almost no cash. Instead he hawked knitted stockings in exchange for accommodation, food and money. Although technically this meant that he fell under the heading of an 'unlicensed pedlar' and therefore subject to arrest and punishment,[35] he travelled unmolested from Lerwick in the Shetland Islands to Leith, and on to Newcastle and then to Portsmouth, begging free passage on a coaler on his way to London. The last three days of his journey to London from Portsmouth were undertaken on foot through some of the most travelled, crowded and rigorously policed parishes of southern England. In his own words, he was 'like a blind man without a guide, not knowing where to go'. His accent, if not his clothing and manner, must have marked him out as a member of the unsettled poor, but nevertheless he came across little but good cheer and friendliness from the people he met on the way.[36]

A few years later, Israel Potter reproduced the last leg of Harrower's journey from Portsmouth to London in more difficult circumstances. A prisoner of war,

---

[35] Richard Burn, *The Justice of the Peace, and Parish Office* (15th edn, 1785), ii, 'Hawkers and Pedlars', pp. 391–8.

[36] Edward Miles Riley (ed.), *The Journal of John Harrower: An Indentured Servant in the Colony of Virginia, 1773–1776* (Williamsburg VA, 1963), pp. 3–14.

he escaped from a prison ship at Spithead and proceeded directly towards the capital, where he hoped the anonymity of a great city would protect him from re-capture. As a man on the run, dressed in a naval outfit, he stood out in the agricultural parishes of Sussex, but he nevertheless proceeded with remarkably little trouble. His first encounter after finally securing his escape was with 'an old man ... tottering beneath the weight of his pick-ax, hoe and shove, clad in tattered garments', with whom Potter rapidly struck a deal. He traded his navy 'pea-jacket, trousers, &c.' for the man's Sunday suit. Dressed in less attention-grabbing attire, Potter made rapid progress: 'I travelled about 30 miles that day, and at night entered a barn ... for I had not money sufficient to pay for a night's lodging'. In order to further justify his vagrant presence on the roads, the following day he fashioned a crutch and pretended to be a cripple. This allowed him to progress through towns along the way 'without meeting with any interruption'. He hitched a lift with 'an empty baggage wagon, bound to London', and again slept in a barn, unmolested, on the following night. It was only on the third day that he met with any trouble. At Staines he was arrested and thrown into the roundhouse, but not on account of his vagrant behaviour or faked lameness. Instead, he was arrested because his shirt (which he had refused to part with when he exchanged clothes with the elderly labourer), 'exactly corresponded with those uniformly worn by his Majesty's seamen', and 'not being able to give a satisfactory account of myself', he was 'made a prisoner of, on suspicion of being a deserter from his Majesty's service'. He escaped a second time, and was soon mending chairs on the streets of London, an occupation he pursued in combination with outright begging, for the next 40 years.[37]

Although from a relatively comfortable background, Charlotte Charke also travelled through the English countryside, and occasionally attracted the censorious attentions of the authorities. Charke fell within the terms of the Vagrancy Act, at least between 1746 and 1754, when she made a precarious living as a 'strolling player' in the South-West. In this capacity she fell within the definition of the 'Common players of interludes, and all persons who shall for hire, gain, or reward, act, represent, or perform ... any interlude, tragedy, comedy, opera, play, farce or other entertainment of the stage ...'.[38] But, like the other individuals discussed above, her single run-in with the law resulted from ill-luck rather than the effective implementation of a legal precept. At Minchinhampton in Gloucestershire she (cross-dressed as a man), along with one companion, was arrested for vagrancy as part of an attempt to 'apprehend all persons within the limits of the act of Parliament'. According to her autobiography, this policy was

[37]   Israel Potter, *Life and Remarkable Adventures of Israel R. Potter*, ed. Leonard Kriegal (Providence RI, 1824, New York, 1962 edn), pp. 27–32.

[38]   Burn, *Justice* (15th edn, 1785), iv, p. 335.

implemented by an 'ignorant blockhead' who 'carried his authority beyond legal power' and who apparently did so in order to solicit bribes from his victims. The resulting night in gaol, and appearance at the Quarter Sessions, caused a local uproar in which various factions within the town appear to have been at loggerheads. Charke's landlord and the Lord Mayor intervened repeatedly on her behalf, and she was eventually released, having spent a long night in a holding cell entertaining her fellow prisoners with renditions of 'all the bead-roll of songs in the last act' of Gay's *Beggar's Opera*.[39]

Unhampered Wandering

Like Saxby and Carew, Potter, Harrow and Charke were able to largely avoid the attentions of the systems intended to control internal migration, and to quietly meld into the constant stream of men and women who populated the roads of England.

When Carl Philipp Moritz undertook his travels 'chiefly on foot' in 1782, he fully reported the unusualness of a 'gentleman' travelling in this way, and by the end of his journey believed:

> that, in England, any person undertaking so long a journey on foot, is sure to be looked upon as either a beggar, or a vagabond, or some necessitous wretch, which is a character not much more popular than a rogue.[40]

But he also noted with real surprise how differently parish and town officers treated travellers by comparison to their German equivalents:

> It strikes a foreigner as something particular and unusual, when, on passing through these fine English towns, he observes none of those circumstances, by which the towns in Germany are distinguished ... no walls, no gates, no sentries, nor garrisons. No stern examiner comes here to search and inspect us, or our baggage; no imperious guard here demands a sight of our passports: perfectly free and unmolested we here walk through villages and towns, as unconcerned, as we should through an house of our own.[41]

---

[39]   Charlotte Charke, *A Narrative of the Life of Mrs Charlotte Charke*, ed. Robert Rehder (London, 1755, 1999 edn), pp. 109–12.

[40]   Carl Philipp Moritz, *Travels of Carl Philipp Moritz in England in 1782*, ed. P.E. Matheson (1795, London, 1926 edn), p. 152.

[41]   Moritz, *Travels*, p. 114.

The heavy coins and letters of introduction secreted in Moritz's pockets no doubt contributed to the warmth of his welcome and the ease of travel, but the general point remains that despite the Vagrancy Acts and settlement laws, movement through the English countryside, and Britain more broadly, was largely unregulated. Of course, the security of a nation state delineated by watery boarders (however complex its internal configuration) undoubtedly helped. But the contrast with Britain's European neighbours remains stark.

Nor is this a story solely about the countryside, where the rarity of travellers bringing news and a peddler's packet might be expected to generate a cautious welcome. If we return for a moment to the figures for vagrant removal from Middlesex for the 1770s, the extent to which western Europe's largest city was also remarkably welcoming becomes more apparent. The average figure of 531 vagrant removals per year between 1772 and 1774 equates to around one and a half people a day. Because the City of London is almost completely surrounded by the county of Middlesex, this figure also includes the majority of vagrants arrested in the centre of London as well as in its burgeoning suburbs. With a population in the 1770s of between 750,000 and 800,000, the number of actual arrests and removals begins to feel remarkably small.[42]

In part, this conclusion must be the result of the many loopholes built in to the Vagrancy Acts. These Acts allowed justices to issue a certificate that permitted a vagrant:

> to pass the next and direct way to the place where he is to repair, and to limit so much time only, as shall be necessary for his travel thither; and in such case pursuing the form of such licence, he may for his necessary relief in his travels, ask and take the relief that any person shall willingly give him.

Even contemporaries felt that this formed a simple 'licence to beg', and certainly presented a small barrier to a wandering life.[43] And although 'pretending to go to work in harvest' certainly fell within the Acts, this provision too was relatively simple for either a legitimate (or indeed roguish) traveller to circumvent:

> this shall not extend to any person going abroad to work at any lawful work in the time of harvest so as he carry with him a certificate signed by the minister and one of

---

42   There was a difference between London and other parts of the country, however. In the whole of Wales during these same three years only 42 people (an average of 14 a year) were reported as having been sent to a House of Correction on a charge of vagrancy. Parliamentary Papers, 'Second Report. Reported by Thomas Gilbert, Esq. 21 May 1776', p. 293.

43   Burn, *Justice* (15th edn, 1785), iv, p. 342.

the churchwardens or overseers where he shall inhabit, that he hath a dwelling place there.[44]

In the early nineteenth century, James Dawson Burn's mother certainly felt that the vagrancy and settlement legislation posed little obstacle to her own travel arrangements. In around 1810 he accompanied his mother to the Mansion House in London, where she lied to the Lord Mayor:

> My mother took the whole of the children into her charge, and made application at the Mansion House for a pass to Hexham, in Northumberland, as a soldier's widow, which she had no difficulty in obtaining; with this pass we visited nearly all the towns and villages on the east coast of England between London and Newcastle-upon-Tyne. As my mother preferred taking the journey at her ease, and her own time, she frequently had the benefit of the cash that the overseers would have had to pay for sending us forward in a conveyance, and at the same time she had the advantage of the intermediate relieving officers, who were often glad to get clear of us at the expense of a shilling or two.[45]

Concluding Remarks

There is no doubt that large numbers of men and women fell foul of the English vagrancy and settlement laws, and that huge efforts and substantial resources were dedicated to their implementation. The thousands of vagrancy and settlement examinations, certificates, removal orders and passes that litter English archives are testimony to this. But this does not imply that the eighteenth-century state (either national or parochial) was successful in regulating migration. The apparent contradiction between the findings of most demographers – that up to 40 per cent of people born in even rural parishes disappeared within a generation – and the belief expressed by historians of social policy that domestic migration was subject to severe restriction can only be resolved by assuming that the legal provisions designed to prevent casual migration just did not work.[46] The evidence of pauper autobiographies suggests that while the unlucky and the ill-informed, the positively recalcitrant and obviously vicious might find themselves subject to the full and painful obloquy of the law, it required a certain wilfulness.

---

[44]   Burn, *Justice* (15th edn, 1785), iv, p. 343.

[45]   James Dawson Burn, *The Autobiography of a Beggar Boy*, ed. David Vincent (London, 1978), p. 58.

[46]   For a recent survey of the literature on 'movers and stayers' see Hindle, *On the Parish*, pp. 304–5.

Many well padded eighteenth-century commentators deplored the workings of the Acts of Settlement and the Vagrancy Laws as impositions on the lives and liberties of English men and women. Most famously, Adam Smith complained with apparent bitterness that: 'There is scarce a poor man in England of forty years of age, I will venture to say, who has not in some part of his life felt himself most cruelly oppressed by this ill-contrived law of settlements.'[47] But the evidence of the autobiographical literature surveyed here is that he was wrong, and that many people wandered the roads and byways of Britain without substantial let or hindrance.

---

[47]   Smith, *Wealth of Nations*, i, p. 128.

PART IV
Comparisons and Conclusions

Chapter 12
Cities, States and Migration Control in Western Europe: Comparing Then and Now

Leo Lucassen

On 1 May 2004 eight eastern European countries, among them Poland and Hungary, became members of the European Union (EU). This meant that labour migrants, provided that they were granted a work permit, could be legally employed in other EU countries.[1] Employers immediately asked for these permits on a large scale, especially in those sectors of the labour market where native workers were hard to get – mainly in agriculture, construction, cleaning and low-skilled manufacturing. Three years later, most European states lifted the work permit condition and the movement of Poles, Hungarians and others was completely liberalized. At the same time, Rumania and Bulgaria entered the EU and from then on their citizens, like the Poles in 2004, could work legally provided they had a work permit.[2] As the decision to liberalize the migration of these groups was taken by states, cities had to go along with the national rules and – in contrast to the early modern period – had few instruments left to regulate their movements.

This situation has led to much discontent at the local level as – largely temporary – migrants from eastern Europe sometimes cause social problems, ranging from illegal housing to violence and alcohol abuse, which are hard to solve. At the same time this category of migrants seldom poses any direct financial

---

[1]   Already before 2004 Poles with a German passport (partly 'ethnic' Germans living in the western part of Poland) had free entrance to the EU. Poles without such a privileged position could only work as illegal immigrants: Cathelijne Pool, 'Open Borders: Unrestricted Migration? The Situation of the Poles with a German Passport in the Netherlands as an Example of Migration after Accession to the European Union', in Anita Böcker, Betty de Hart and Ines Michalowski (eds), *Migration and the Regulation of Social Integration* (Osnabrück, 2004), pp. 203–12.

[2]   At the moment of writing (summer of 2010) this restriction has not yet been lifted in the Netherlands and other western European countries. Rumanians and Bulgarians will have to be admitted free entrance to the labour market ultimately in 2014.

problems because they are almost completely excluded from the benefits of the welfare state. Only those who settle down more or less permanently and work for a long uninterrupted period can gradually enter the social security system. As the bulk of eastern Europeans, mainly Poles, have only temporary jobs and regularly return to their country of origin, they contribute to the welfare state without profiting from it.

This state of affairs contrasts sharply with the preceding mass immigration of former guest workers and their families from outside the EU, especially Turks (in Germany and France), Algerians (in France) and Moroccans (in France, Belgium and the Netherlands), and of migrants from former colonies. For different reasons these migrants were allowed to settle down permanently and to bring over their family members as well as marriage partners for their children. For the former guest workers this resulted in a mass settlement in the 1980s and 1990s, predominantly in large cities throughout western Europe.[3] Although economically speaking the timing was rather unfortunate, in the midst of a long recession following the oil crisis of the early 1970s the liberal democracies had few opportunities to refuse them entrance.[4] Whereas migrants from (former) colonies were allowed in for political and imperial reasons, guest workers had built up both social and legal rights. Moreover, for both categories restrictive immigration policies often produced the opposite effect: many tried to beat the ban, whereas those already present stayed on for fear of finding the door closed next time if they left.

If we restrict ourselves to labour migrants, which by the way includes many colonial migrants, the recent past in western Europe therefore offers us two different models:

1. The first one could be described as the 'Golden Cage'. As states could not refuse mass immigration because of unanticipated embedded social and legal rights, immigrants and their descendants obtained the same social, economic and often also political rights as nationals. This includes their incorporation into the welfare state. This model discouraged them from leaving, at least at first, because it would mean giving up these rights.
2. In the contrasting 'Tantalus Torment' model, migrants are allowed to enter (or leave) a high-wage 'paradise' at all times, but do not have access

---

[3]   Leslie Page Moch, *Moving Europeans: Migration in Western Europe since 1650* (Bloomington IN, 2003), pp. 189–96; Leo Lucassen, David Feldman and Jochen Oltmer, 'Drawing Up the Balance Sheet', in Leo Lucassen, David Feldman and Jochen Oltmer (eds), *Paths of Integration: Migrants in Western Europe (1880–2004)* (Amsterdam, 2006), pp. 283–96.

[4]   James F. Hollifield, *Immigrants, Markets, and States: The Political Economy of Postwar Europe* (Cambridge MA, 1992).

to the benefits of the welfare state. Movement is predominantly governed by the labour market and only those who are able to find a permanent job for years without interruption gradually acquire access to the benefits of the welfare state.

In both models cities are the major destination of these foreign migrants, but urban authorities have little or no power to regulate their entry. Regulation is predominantly the result of decisions taken at the central state level, whether through national legislation and bilateral agreements with other states or through international agreements.

At first sight the contrast with the situation in early modern cities in western Europe is considerable.[5] Central authorities in most early modern states were preoccupied with the religious identity of their subjects, which occasionally led to forced expulsions – as in the case of Jews and Muslims in sixteenth-century Spain and Huguenots in late seventeenth-century France – or to more or less voluntary emigration of religious minorities, like Protestants from the Southern Low Countries at the end of the sixteenth century.[6] This preoccupation with religious minorities stands in sharp contrast with states' lack of interest in mundane patterns of labour migration, both internal and external, which in a quantitative respect were much more important but also less conspicuous.[7]

At the local level the situation was quite different. With most urban populations unable to reproduce themselves until the end of the eighteenth

---

[5] This also explains the lack of systematic temporal comparisons of the relationship between migration and poor relief. Exceptions are Lynn Hollen Lees, *The Solidarities of Strangers: The English Poor Laws and the People, 1700–1948* (Cambridge, 1998); David Feldman, 'Migrants, Immigrants and Welfare from the Old Poor Law to the Welfare State', *Transactions of the Royal Historical Society*, 13 (2003): pp. 79–104; Anne Winter, 'Caught between Law and Practice: Migrants and Settlement Legislation in the Southern Low Countries in a Comparative Perspective, c. 1700–1900', *Rural History*, 19/2 (2008): pp. 137–62. See also Andreas Gestrich, Lutz Raphael and Herbert Uerlings (eds), *Strangers and Poor People: Changing Patterns of Inclusion and Exclusion in Europe and the Mediterranean World from Classical Antiquity to the Present Day* (Cambridge and New York 2011).

[6] For an overview, see Klaus J. Bade, Pieter C. Emmer, Leo Lucassen and Jochen Oltmer (eds), *The Encyclopedia of migration and minorities in Europe. From the 17th century to the present* (Paderborn/Munich, 2007).

[7] In the Dutch case, between 1600 and 1800 refugee migration only consisted of one-quarter of the total immigration from abroad. See also Jan Lucassen and Leo Lucassen, 'The Mobility Transition Revisited, 1500–1900: What the Case of Europe Can Offer to Global History', *Journal of Global History*, 4/4 (2009): pp. 347–77; Jan Lucassen and Leo Lucassen, *The Mobility Transition in Europe Revisited, 1500–1900: Sources and Methods* (International Institute of Social History Research Paper 44, Amsterdam, 2010).

century, especially in northern Europe, urban authorities realized that they depended on immigration.[8] At the same time, however, they were wary of destitute and unproductive migrants, especially in economically bad times. The fear that migrants would become dependent on local poor relief was crucial for the way migration policies were devised.[9] Cities therefore developed elaborate rules and mechanisms to regulate migration. 'Foreigners' was defined much more narrowly and concerned all those who came from outside the city walls, irrespective of distance. Religion did play a role, and could lead to the exclusion of religious minorities (especially Jews), but the economy and concerns about poor relief were key.

As I will demonstrate in this chapter, local policies in early modern Europe have a lot in common with national policies in the twentieth and twenty-first centuries, as local relief provisions were gradually taken over by the (national) state from the end of the nineteenth century. As a result, nation states were confronted with dilemmas with respect to foreign migrants somewhat similar to those encountered in early modern cities. Early modern local and modern national migration regulations therefore show a difference in scale but not so much in principle.

This raises two questions which I will explore in this chapter. First of all I will test the analytical value of the two different models – that of the 'Golden Cage' and the 'Tantalus Torment' – for cities then and states now by looking for structural similarities, notwithstanding the difference in scale. Secondly, I will look more closely at the intermediate transition period of the long nineteenth century, which seems to have created a sort of a vacuum in which cities lost most of their legal tools to regulate migration to the nation state, while the state had not yet taken up its responsibilities in the welfare domain.[10] I will do this by concentrating on the case of the Dutch Republic and the subsequent Kingdom of the Netherlands within its European context.

---

[8]   Lucassen and Lucassen, 'The Mobility Transition Revisited'; Lucassen and Lucassen, *The Mobility Transition in Europe*, pp. 15–29. See also Edward A. Wrigley, 'A Simple Model of London's Importance in Changing English Society and Economy 1650–1750', *Past and Present*, 37 (1967): pp. 46–70; Robert Woods, 'Urban–Rural Mortality Differentials: An Unresolved Debate', *Population and Development Review*, 29/1 (2003): pp. 29–46.

[9]   Leo Lucassen, *Zigeuner. Die Geschichte eines polizeilichen Ordnungsbegriffes in Deutschland 1700–1945* (Cologne, 1996); Keith D.M. Snell, *Parish and Belonging: Community, Identity and Welfare in England and Wales, 1700–1950* (Cambridge, 2006); Feldman, 'Migrants'; Anne Winter, *Migrants and Urban Change: Newcomers to Antwerp, 1760–1860* (London, 2009).

[10]   For this transition period in general, see Maarten Prak, *Republikeinse veelheid, democratisch enkelvoud. Sociale verandering in het revolutietijdvak. 's-Hertogenbosch 1770–1820* (Nijmegen, 1999).

Immigration to Dutch Cities in the Early Modern Period

Before examining early modern urban migration regulations, I will first very briefly sketch the extraordinary impact of migration on Dutch cities, especially in the western coastal part of the current provinces of South and North Holland. Even if we limit ourselves to migrants from other countries it is clear that foreign immigration in the seventeenth and eighteenth centuries was considerable and only slightly below the high level reached in the first decade of the twenty-first century (Figure 12.1).

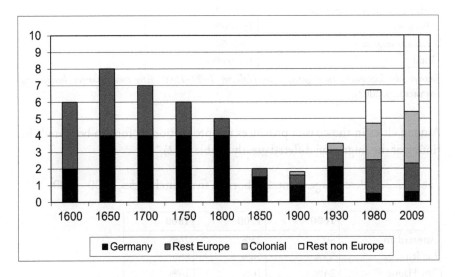

Figure 12.1   Percentage of foreign-born in the Netherlands, 1600–2009

Source: Jan Lucassen and Leo Lucassen, 'The Netherlands', in Klaus J. Bade, Pieter C. Emmer, Leo Lucassen and Jochen Oltmer (eds), *The Encyclopedia of Migration and Minorities in Europe* (Cambridge and New York 2011, pp. 34–43, there p. 35).

As explained above, from the perspective of the largely autonomous towns, *all* migrants from outside its city gates were considered 'foreign' and treated as such. Apart from religious characteristics, human capital was what interested urban gatekeepers most. And this often meant that skilled newcomers from other states, like the Flemish textile workers in Leiden from the end of the sixteenth century onwards, were more welcome than unskilled migrants from nearby villages.[11] Between 1600 and 1800, migrants born outside the Dutch Republic made up almost 50 per cent of all migrants who settled in cities in the provinces of North and South Holland (Table 12.1).[12]

Table 12.1   Origin of migrants in cities in South and North Holland, 1600–1800

Origin	Number
Countryside of Holland	200,000
Rest of Dutch Republic	400,000
Other countries (foreign-born)	600,000
- Refugees	*150,000*
- Labour migrants	*450,000*
Total	1,200,000

Source: Jan Lucassen, *Immigranten in Holland 1600–1800. Een kwantitatieve benadering* (Amsterdam, 2002).

Among cities in the coastal provinces the proportion of foreign-born and the timing of the migration differed greatly (Table 12.2).

Table 12.2   Percentage of foreign-born in five Dutch cities, 1600–1800

	1600	1700	1800
Amsterdam	40%	25%	24%
Leiden	55%	10%	8%
The Hague	24%	10%	14%
Dordrecht	30%	15%	11%
Rotterdam	24%	9%	12%

Source: J. Lucassen, *Immigranten in Holland 1600–1800.*

---

[11]   Leo Lucassen and Boudien de Vries, 'The Rise and Fall of a Western European Textile-Worker Migration System: Leiden, 1586–1700', in G. Gayot and P. Minard (eds), *Les ouvriers qualifiés de l'industrie (16e–20e siècle). Formation, emploi, migrations* (Lille, 2001): pp. 23–42.

[12]   As Erika Kuijpers has rightfully argued, we have to realize that these shares have been based on sources that measure migrants who married in these cities, and thus leave out many more who were already married at arrival or who never married at all. Finally a considerable number of migrants who only stayed temporarily are not included in these numbers: Erika Kuijpers, *Migrantenstad. Immigratie en sociale verhoudingen in zeventiende-eeuws Amsterdam* (Hilversum, 2005).

Amsterdam, which was by far the largest Dutch city in the eighteenth century, with some 200,000 inhabitants, attracted large numbers of foreign migrants during two centuries, whereas the Flemish migration to Leiden, massive between 1590 and 1620, was more of a 'refugee-like' character.[13] The constantly high level of foreign-born in Amsterdam need not be a surprise, as the city was a nodal point of international trade since the end of the sixteenth century, which generated an extensive and varied demand for labour.[14] Low-skilled workers in particular were in great demand to work in the urban industries or as sailors and soldiers for the Dutch East India Company (the VOC). As a result the population of

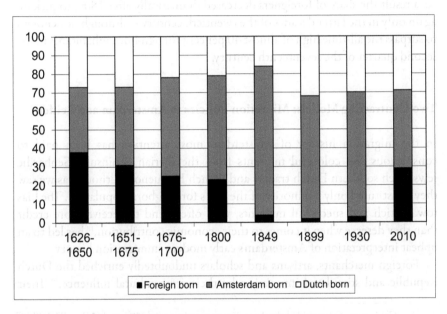

Figure 12.2   Origins of the population of Amsterdam, 1626–2010 (%)

Source: Erika Kuijpers and Maarten Prak, 'Gevestigden en buitenstaanders', in Frijhoff and Prak (eds), *Geschiedenis van Amsterdam*, p. 191; Municipal Statistical Bureau Amsterdam.

---

13   Lucassen and de Vries, 'The Rise and Fall'.

14   Karel Davids and Jan Lucassen (eds), *A Miracle Mirrored: The Dutch Republic in European Perspective* (Cambridge, 1995); Kuijpers, *Migrantenstad*; Jelle van Lottum, *Across the North Sea: The Impact of the Dutch Republic on International Labour Migration, c. 1550–1850* (Amsterdam, 2007); Lotte van de Pol and Erika Kuijpers, 'Poor Women's Migration to the City: The Attraction of Amsterdam Health Care and Social Assistance in Early Modern Times', *Journal of Urban History*, 32/1 (2005): pp. 44–60. See also Jelle van Lottum, 'Labour Migration and Economic Performance: London and the Randstad, c. 1600–1800', *Economic History Review*, 64/2 (2011): pp. 531–70.

Amsterdam increased tenfold within a century, from around 20,000 inhabitants in 1575 to more than 200,000 by 1675.[15]

Given the high death rates of early modern cities, this growth was possible only thanks to massive and continuous immigration. When death rates decreased considerably in the course of the nineteenth century,[16] and natural growth became more important as a source of population increase, the share of Amsterdam-born increased accordingly (Figure 12.2). By that time Amsterdam had, moreover, lost its attractiveness to foreigners as industrial regions in neighbouring countries – the Ruhr area, the British Midlands, eastern France and Wallonia – developed.[17] As a result the share of foreigners decreased dramatically after 1800, to pick up again only in the latter decades of the twentieth century – although not enough to surpass the all-time high of almost 40 per cent foreign-born inhabitants in the second quarter of the seventeenth century.

Two Contrasting Models: Migration Policies in Amsterdam and Leiden

In the migration history of Amsterdam most attention has been paid to conspicuous and colourful migrants from the Iberian Peninsula (Sephardic Jews), rich southern Dutch traders and French Huguenots, although as we saw they constituted only a minority of the city's foreign-born population. The bias toward rich and successful migrants, who often tend to receive more credit than they deserve when it comes to their economic contribution,[18] has led to an upbeat interpretation of Amsterdam's early modern immigration history.

Foreign merchants, artisans and scholars undoubtedly enriched the Dutch Republic and stimulated innovation by their cross-cultural influence.[19] Their

---

[15]   Clé Lesger, 'De wereld als horizon. De economie tussen 1578 en 1650', in W. Frijhoff and M. Prak (eds), *Geschiedenis van Amsterdam, vol. II-1. Centrum van de Wereld, 1578–1650* (Amsterdam, 2004), pp. 103–88.

[16]   Marco H.D. van Leeuwen and J.E. Oeppen, 'Reconstructing the Demographic Regime of Amsterdam 1681–1920', *Economic and Social History in the Netherlands*, 5 (1993): pp. 61–104. For London: Wrigley, 'A Simple Model'.

[17]   Leo Lucassen, *The Immigrant Threat: The Integration of Old and New Migrants in Western Europe since 1850* (Urbana/Chicago IL, 2005).

[18]   As argued by Oscar Gelderblom, *Zuid-Nederlandse kooplieden en de opkomst van de Amsterdamse stapelmarkt (1578–1630)* (Hilversum, 2000). For a counter-argument, see Lesger, 'De wereld'.

[19]   For the concept of cross-community migration, see Patrick Manning, 'Cross-Community Migration: A Distinctive Human Pattern', *Social Evolution and History*, 5/2 (2006): pp. 24–54; and Karen Barkey, *Empire of Difference: The Ottomans in Comparative Perspective* (Cambridge, 2009), p. 33.

arrival helped to establish new merchant networks, extending the traditional Dutch–Baltic–Mediterranean trade system with new networks in the Middle East, Asia and South America,[20] and to develop new financial, banking and trading techniques which contributed to a highly successful economic institutional structure.[21] Antwerp merchants like Coymans, Bartolotti, Calandrini, Quingetti, Isaac le Maire, Dirck van Os and Pieter van Pulle helped Amsterdam to develop into *the* money and capital market of Europe. They also introduced letters of exchange and the bank of exchange, which opened its doors in 1609.[22]

Rich merchants and skilled artisans, however, constituted only a minority of all foreign migrants. The bulk were poor men and women whose hands were much needed to haul, stow and store the goods that were transported to and from Amsterdam, and to refine, improve and finish raw products, like sugar. Others were needed to man the merchant ships as sailors, and large numbers were attracted by a demand for baker journeymen, building workers, peddlers, shoemakers, domestic servants and prostitutes. In short: migration contributed heavily to the growth of Amsterdam's proletariat, concentrated in the poorest quarters of town – near the harbour at the east side of the city.

This was certainly where most migrants from Scandinavia – especially from southern Norway – and north-western Germany ended up. Being Lutherans they experienced some legal discrimination and at least the first generation held on to their own churches, language and networks, often marrying among themselves and living in close proximity to one another. Unlike Jews, they lost their ethnic traits over time. As the research by Erika Kuijpers suggests, however, a considerable number of them ended up in the Amsterdam proletariat,[23] leading to the formation of an underclass without an ethnic marker – an often neglected, because largely invisible outcome of long-term settlement processes.[24]

Regulating Entrance and Settlement

Amsterdam was the only city in the Dutch Republic that resisted the temptation of becoming selective at its gates and barring (poor) migrants from entering.

---

[20]   Jessica V. Roitman, *Us and Them: Inter-Cultural Trade and the Sephardim, 1595–1640* (PhD dissertation, Leiden University, 2009).

[21]   Jan Luiten van Zanden and Maarten Prak, 'Towards an Economic Interpretation of Citizenship: The Dutch Republic between Medieval Communes and Modern Nation States', *European Review of Economic History*, 10 (2006): pp. 111–45.

[22]   Lesger, 'De wereld'.

[23]   Kuijpers, *Migrantenstad*.

[24]   Lucassen, Feldman and Oltmer, 'Drawing Up'.

When the economic tide turned at the end of the seventeenth century, all other Dutch cities decided to prevent the immigration of people who were most likely to become a financial burden for the poor relief system. The once so prosperous textile town of Leiden, for example, whose number of inhabitants quintupled by mass immigration between 1590 and 1670,[25] decided in 1716 that from then on (poor) newcomers had to carry an *act of indemnity* (settlement certificate) issued by their municipality of legal settlement. Expanding industrial centres like Leiden had an extra hard time because economic downturns lead to high unemployment rates, especially among migrants who often did not have large networks of assistance.[26] In 1737 Leiden proclaimed a new decree 'to bar the invasion of foreigners and destitute persons' because too many migrants had settled illegally and had become a burden on the poor relief system. Settlement was reserved for *poorters* (full citizens), who had to fulfil strict conditions, such as carrying an act of indemnity. Inhabitants who housed 'illegal migrants' risked heavy fines, and the so-called masters of the *gebuurten* – Leiden's 130 neighbourhoods – were instructed to track down clandestine immigrants.[27] Admission to the city was only granted when applicants had the necessary papers which guaranteed that others would pay for financial support if needed.

The city council of Amsterdam (at times pressured by the Admiralty, which was in desperate need of sailors),[28] in contrast, argued that immigration restrictions would damage its economic position as it depended on a continuous inflow of low-skilled migrants, not only for the urban economy but also to satisfy the ongoing demand for sailors and soldiers on the ships of the VOC. The latter sent out a million people between 1600 and 1800, half of them born outside the Dutch Republic and most of them enlisted in Amsterdam. The authorities

---

25   Lucassen and de Vries, 'The Rise and Fall'.

26   Elise van Nederveen Meerkerk and Griet Vermeesch. 'Reforming Outdoor Relief: Changes in Urban Provisions for the Poor in the Northern and Southern Low Countries (c. 1500–1800)', in Manon van der Heijden, Elise van Nederveen Meerkerk, Griet Vermeesch and Martijn van der Burg (eds), *Serving the Urban Community: The Rise of Public Facilities in the Low Countries* (Amsterdam, 2009), pp. 135–54, there pp. 151–2.

27   Karel (C.A.) Davids, 'De migratiebeweging in Leiden in de achttiende eeuw', in H.A. Diederiks, D.J. Noordam and H.D. Tjalsma (eds), *Armoede en sociale spanning. Sociaal-historische studies over Leiden in de achttiende eeuw* (Hilversum, 1985), pp. 137–56. See also Kees Walle, *Buurthouden. De geschiedenis van burengebruiken en buurtorganisaties in Leiden (14de–19de eeuw)* (Leiden, 2005); Elise van Nederveen Meerkerk, 'Werkgelegenheid, opleiding en onderstand. De economische aantrekkingskracht van vroegmoderne steden', in Leo Lucassen and Wim Willems (eds), *Waarom mensen in de stad willen wonen, 1200–2010* (Amsterdam, 2009), pp. 103–23.

28   Marco H.D. van Leeuwen, 'Migrants' Entitlements to Poor Relief in the Netherlands, 16th–20th Centuries', paper presented at the workshop 'Migrants, Entitlements and Welfare, 1500–2000: Comparative Perspectives', Brussels, 6–7 September 2010.

realized that this open-door policy put a strain on poor relief funds. Already in the heyday of the Golden Age the large majority of relief recipients were foreign-born. In 1614 90 per cent of the 2,500 families enlisted with the new institution of almoners (*aalmoezeniers*) came from outside the Republic. The main purpose of this institution was to provide second-rate poor relief, much lower than that to which 'locals' were entitled. It was a safety net for immigrants, but one for which they could apply only after three years of residence, and – given its paltry quality – of a deterrent nature. Moreover, most migrants had to be relieved by their church communities, for which the Lutheran and Jewish had great trouble amassing enough funds and often tried to push their co-religionists on to other destinations.[29] Finally, from the end of the seventeenth century onwards Amsterdam developed measures to decrease demands on poor relief funds without deterring labour migrants. District wardens were asked to check the necessary minimal residence requirements to be eligible for poor relief, and conditions for support were tightened.[30]

Given the comparative scope of this chapter it is interesting to note that local welfare arrangements, both in the sending and receiving localities, did exert some influence on migration patterns and that this is not a phenomenon that is specific to twentieth-century welfare states. As has been shown by Erika Kuijpers in her in-depth study of seventeenth-century Amsterdam, small cities and villages in the north-west of Germany often provided their poor inhabitants with travel money to go to Amsterdam in order to spare their own poor relief funds. We are particularly well informed about the policies of Husum, a small town in East Friesland in the north-west of Germany that in the seventeenth century was hit by floods (1634) and warfare. In an attempt to restrict local relief expenses the urban authorities provided hundreds of poor inhabitants with the necessary money to travel to Holland, where work was abundant and wages high. Between 1618 and 1682 over 300 Husum residents – 188 men and boys, 75 women and 57 children – received assistance for their journey to the Dutch coastal provinces, often ending up in Amsterdam.[31] While many found employment, single women with children became dependent on poor relief provided by the city and the Lutheran Church. For many of them the availability of poor relief in Amsterdam, modest as it may have been, constituted an important pull factor.[32]

---

[29]   Robert Cohen, 'Passage to a New World: The Sephardi Poor of Eighteenth-Century Amsterdam', in L. Dasberg and J.N. Cohen (eds), *Neveh Ya'kov: Jubilee Volume Presented to Dr. Jaap Meijer* (Assen, 1982), pp. 31–42. See also Roitman, *Us and Them*.

[30]   Leeuwen, 'Migrants' Entitlements'.

[31]   Kuijpers, *Migrantenstad*, p. 63.

[32]   Ibid., p. 66. See also van de Pol and Kuijpers, 'Poor Women's Migration'.

The open-door policy did not prevent increasing tensions between established residents and outsiders. Already from the second half of the seventeenth century Amsterdam-born workers such as building workers and carpenters complained about foreign competition, while in some instances textile workers refused to work together with Hamburg journeymen.[33] As a result the position of migrant workers deteriorated and most of them found themselves locked in the secondary segment of a dual urban labour market, with less job security and lower wages – a pattern that was also present in other Dutch cities and which bears resemblances to the positions of low-skilled immigrants today.[34]

It is interesting to note that cities that practised the system of acts of indemnity gradually realized the downside of their defensive immigration policy: it also meant that they had to provide their own citizens who left town with such declarations. In 1785 Leiden's overseers observed that they issued more of these settlement certificates than they received, and therefore proposed abolishing the whole system altogether. Moreover, some textile manufacturers feared that the restrictive system hindered the immigration of skilled workers. Although the city council did not change its policies, the Protestant and Catholic institutions of outdoor relief stopped producing acts of indemnity.[35]

The example of Leiden also shows that urban poor relief provisions, combined with neighbourhood support networks, could act as a brake on migration. A well-known contemporary, Johannes le Francq van Berkhey, observed around 1770 that his co-citizens were reluctant to leave even in times of mass unemployment, and attributed this to Leiden's strong neighbourhood networks and its relief system. It is tempting to draw a parallel with allegedly immobilizing effects of the Old Poor Law in England,[36] but it may also have been related to Leiden's economic reorientation in this period, which made it less dependent on textile production and therefore offering new job opportunities to its inhabitants.[37]

To establish the comparative analytical value of the two models presented in the introduction of this chapter, the cases of early modern Amsterdam and Leiden offer two interesting configurations. Whereas Leiden shows similarities with the 'Golden Cage' model, Amsterdam to some extent represents an early version of the 'Tantalus Torment' model. Just like eastern European labour

---

[33]   Nederveen Meerkerk, 'Werkgelegenheid'; based on Ad Knotter and Jan Luiten van Zanden, 'Immigratie en arbeidsmarkt in Amsterdam in de 17de eeuw', *Tijdschrift voor sociale geschiedenis*, 13 (1987): pp. 411–12.

[34]   Nederveen Meerkerk, 'Werkgelegenheid'; Arend W. Odé, *Migrant Workers in the Dutch Labour Market Today* (Amsterdam, 1996).

[35]   Davids, 'De migratiebeweging'.

[36]   Lees, *The Solidarities*, pp. 29–30.

[37]   Ibid.

migrants *now*, migrants in Amsterdam *then* were free to enter during the entire period because the urban authorities realized that a constant stream of migrants was necessary to satisfy the port city's massive demand for labour. Imposing restrictive measures would harm the attractiveness of Amsterdam, and providing immigrants with some poor relief during brief periods of economic downturn was accepted as a necessary evil – yet their relief entitlements stood at a much more modest level than those of citizens or long-term residents. As in the case of Poles and Rumanians today, only after a long period of contributing to the local economy did a gradual entrance into the urban relief system become possible.

The case of Leiden – which is representative of most other Dutch cities (and by the way also of most other western European settlement regimes)[38] – bears more resemblances with the 'Golden Cage' model, in which immigration became restricted when the economic situation deteriorated. As with the oil crisis of 1973, which marked the end of guest worker recruitment policies, proactive policies to attract skilled immigrants ended. New migrants were accepted only when they were expected to contribute and could present a relief certificate issued by their municipality of settlement. In other words, what we see is a variant of the English (Old) Poor Law system and the German and Austrian *Heimat* principle. This insured receiving authorities against having to pay for newcomers' potential relief needs: if they did become chargeable, either the migrants or their relief bills could be sent back to their parish of settlement. In both cases sending or receiving municipalities became golden cages which could restrict the mobility of their residents.[39]

Finally it is interesting to note that, as in modern times, restrictive regimes created their own 'illegals' – as we saw in the case of Leiden. People who lost their entitlements altogether, for whatever reason, became the target of exclusionary practices and even persecution – most visible in the case of people labelled as 'Gypsies' or 'vagrants'.[40] People with unclear identities or lacking declarations of former parishes were considered a potential threat to local poor relief systems and subject to monitoring practices by both urban and rural authorities.

---

[38] Winter, *Migrants*, p. 65.

[39] Although scholarly opinions about the alleged immobilizing effects of the Poor Law range widely: Lees, *The Solidarities*, pp. 47–9; George Boyer, *An Economic History of the English Poor Law, 1750–1850* (Cambridge, 1990).

[40] With huge differences through time and space: Lees, The Solidarities, p. 353; Leo Lucassen, *Zigeuner. Die Geschichte eines polizeilichen Orndungbegriffes* (Cologne, 1996); Leo Lucassen, 'Between Hobbes and Locke. Gypsies and the Limits of the Modernization Paradigm', *Social History*, 44/4 (2008): pp. 423–41.

The Rise of the National State and the 'Long Vacuum'

With the rise of the nation state and the concomitant shift of indirect to direct rule, the state gradually took an interest in the question of who left or entered its territory.[41] Already in the early modern period this formed part of the competences of the territorial state – as is witnessed by the expulsion (or reception) of religious refugees or practices such as the French *droit d'aubaine*[42] – but this right was enforced only incidentally and was often thwarted by overlapping jurisdictions. This changed with the French Revolution.

Although many French revolutionaries associated passports with oppressive *ancien régime* practices and were afraid that a passport system could lead to a tyrannical police state, the failed attempt of Louis XVI to flee his kingdom with a false passport in June 1791 motivated the revolutionary regime to issue passports both to French citizens wishing to travel in France or abroad and to foreigners who entered France.[43] Barely a year later, in March 1792, an act was adopted which can be considered the birth of the modern passport system.[44] From then on states started to use passports to control and monitor movements of their own citizens or of foreigners.

Passports could be used either to keep potential emigrants in or to keep potential immigrants out. In the first half of the nineteenth century this monitoring practice – in use from France to Russia, with the exception of the United Kingdom – was motivated by political considerations. Fear of foreign revolutionaries and of opponents from within was widespread. At the same time, passports could be refused to one's own citizens out of mercantile motives to prevent them from leaving. German states, for example, considered emigration as a loss and tried to prevent it.[45] Finally, authoritarian states with severe

---

[41]   John Torpey, *The Invention of the Passport: Surveillance, Citizenship and the State* (Cambridge, 2000); Jane Caplan and John Torpey (eds), *Documenting Individual Identity: The Development of State Practices in the Modern World* (Princeton NJ, 2001).

[42]   Simona Cerutti, 'A qui appartiennent les biens qui appartiennent à personne? Citoyenneté et droit d'aubaine à l'époque moderne', *Annales. Économies, sociétés, civilisations*, 62/2 (2007): pp. 355–86; Peter Sahlins, *Unnaturally French: Foreign Citizens in the Old Regime and After* (Ithaca NY/London, 2004).

[43]   Leo Lucassen, 'A Many-Headed Monster: The Evolution of the Passport System in the Netherlands and Germany in the Long Nineteenth Century', in Caplan and Torpey (eds), *Documenting Individual Identity*, pp. 235–55; M. de Hartoy, *Histoire du passeport francais. Depuis l'antiquité jusqu'à nos jours* (Paris, 1937), pp. 39–52.

[44]   Torpey, *The Invention*.

[45]   Nancy L. Green and François Weil (eds), *Citizenship and Those Who Leave: The Politics of Emigration and Expatriation* (Urbana/Chicago IL, 2007).

restrictions on labour migration, like Russia, tried to use internal passports to prevent serfs from moving to cities and to at least regulate peasant migration.[46]

In the course of the nineteenth century most states became much more liberal when it came to the freedom of movement and the crossing of international borders, which is exemplified by the abolition of passports in most western countries between the mid-1850s and the mid-1860s. Yet this liberalization did not apply to Russia or the Ottoman Empire. Nor did it preclude other systems of control and monitoring, like the strictly regulated seasonal labour migration of Russians from Polish areas into Prussia.[47] In general, however, one can say that the period 1850–1914 did away with many of the restrictions that were imposed in the wake of the French Revolution.

This new period of free international and internal movement left cities in western European countries in limbo. With the establishment of the national state, cities had lost much of their former power to regulate migration. Internal migrants had become fellow citizens of the national state and therefore could not be refused entrance or settlement in the city. The power to stop migrants at the gates had shifted to the national border. At the same time the national state had not (yet) established a nation-wide system of poor relief, so that the settlement of internal migrants put urban authorities in a difficult position: they were not insured against the risk of having to pay for newcomers' relief needs.

This vacuum, during which cities had lost the power to decide who was admitted yet poor relief systems were still local in character, led to intense discussions about the basic principles of relief systems in many western European countries. The result was that the existing rules – a continuation of *ancien régime* poor laws – gave receiving municipalities, often cities, the right to refuse poor relief to newcomers. In some cases, such as in Germany, poor (internal) migrants

---

[46]   Jeffrey Burds, *Peasant Dreams and Market Politics: Labor Migration and the Russian Village, 1861–1905* (Pittsburgh, 1998); Boris B. Gorshkow, 'Serfs on the Move: Peasant Seasonal Migration in Pre-Reform Russia, 1800–61', *Kritika: Explorations in Russian and Eurasian History*, 1/4 (2000): pp. 627–56; Peter Kolchin, *Unfree Labor: American Slavery and Russian Serfdom* (Cambridge MA, 1987); David Moon, 'Peasant Migration, the Abolition of Serfdom, and the Internal Passport System in the Russian Empire, c. 1800–1914', in David Eltis (ed.), *Coerced and Free Migration: Global Perspectives* (Stanford CA, 2007), pp. 324–57.

[47]   Klaus J. Bade, '"Preussengänger" und "Abwehrpolitik". Ausländerbeschäftigung, Ausländerpolitik und Ausländerkontrolle auf dem Arbeitsmarkt in Preussen vor dem Ersten Weltkrieg', *Archiv für Sozialgeschichte*, 24 (1984): pp. 91–162; Corrie van Eijl and Leo Lucassen, 'Holland beyond the Borders: Emigration and the Dutch State, 1850–1940', in Nancy L. Green and François Weil (eds), *Citizenship and Those Who Leave*, pp. 156–75; Lucassen, 'A Many-Headed Monster'. For attempts to monitor European migrants to the United States see Aristide Zolberg, *A Nation by Design: Immigration Policy in the Fashioning of America* (New York/Cambridge MA, 2006).

could even be refused the right to settle or to marry.[48] As the urbanization process intensified and large numbers of country dwellers flocked to cities, these old poor laws came increasingly under pressure. Especially in the United Kingdom the criticism of the poor laws was further strengthened by liberals who considered them a hindrance to the proper functioning of the labour market.

The result of these epochal changes was that in most countries poor relief systems were fundamentally restructured. We are best informed about the English situation, where the New Poor Law of 1834 introduced strict rules combined with workhouses to deter workers from applying. Furthermore it reduced the possibilities of municipalities sending back migrants to their parish of settlement. This liberalization of the labour market via the restructuring of the poor relief system was adopted by other countries in various guises as well. Thus, the power to regulate migration by excluding newcomers on the basis of poor relief melted away. In all western European countries poor relief legislation was changed so as to facilitate migration to (industrial) cities. Major landmarks in this development were – apart of the British New Poor Law (1834) – the German *Freizügigkeits* legislation (1867/1871) and the revision of the Dutch Poor Law of 1854 in 1870, which finally abolished the 1818 Law of Domicile which had obliged the parish of origin to pay for poor relief, even when someone resided elsewhere.[49] Belgium closed ranks with a fundamental shift in 1891.[50]

Although one of the intentions of the new poor relief legislation was to shift the burden to receiving cities and stimulate mobility, especially to urban areas,[51] the effects differed from country to country, but also internally. Moreover, the new principle could even have unexpected immobilizing effects. As Peter Lindert and George Boyer have argued with respect to the English New Poor Law, policies toward the poor in the rural south-east depended on a mix of local economic interests and the configuration of political power.[52] Where landed interests held the upper hand, for example in the south-east, rates of poor relief

---

[48]   Andreas Gestrich, Steven King and Lutz Raphael (eds), *Being Poor in Modern Europe* (Bern, 2006); George Steinmetz, *Regulating the Social: The Welfare State and Local Politics in Imperial Germany* (Princeton NJ, 1993).

[49]   For the Netherlands, see Annemarie Cottaar, *Kooplui, kermisklanten en andere woonwagenbewoners. Groepsvorming en beleid, 1870–1945* (Amsterdam, 1996), p. 140; Marco H.D. van Leeuwen, *Bijstand in Amsterdam, ca 1800–1850. Armenzorg als beheersings- en overlevingsstrategie* (Zwolle/Amsterdam, 1992), p. 169.

[50]   Winter, 'Caught between Law and Practice', p. 149.

[51]   Steven Hochstadt, *Mobility and Modernity: Migration in Germany, 1820–1989* (Ann Arbor MI, 1999).

[52]   Boyer, *An Economic History*; Peter H. Lindert, *Growing Public: Social Spending and Economic Growth since the Eighteenth Century* (Cambridge, 2004), pp. 75–7.

were relatively high, which prevented the poor from leaving to work in urban industries.

A similar mix of interests, but in an urban context, has been shown for Amsterdam, where local elites used poor relief to prevent the poor from *leaving* the city and thus they reserved a much needed labour reserve.[53] The financial-commercial elites realized that a certain labour reserve was vital for the functioning of the labour market. The poor relief system made it unattractive to leave for other places where it was more difficult to get support. As Marco van Leeuwen has argued, poor relief, as part of social politics, was a means to buy off the poor, to keep them quiet and prevent unrest.[54]

Both the English and the Amsterdam cases show that it is too simple to speak of a void or vacuum with cities, or municipalities in general, without the means to regulate migration – and the national state disinterested or impotent in this matter. It is true that the share of rural to urban migrations more than doubled in the nineteenth century[55] and that cities could no longer refuse migrants; but through the manipulation of poor relief systems[56] authorities could still influence who was to move and who was to stay.

From the end of the nineteenth century onwards welfare benefits became more generous and universal, but at the same time a new dividing line became visible between natives and foreigners which would have a huge impact on migration controls, both at the state and the city level.

The National State, Welfare and the Birth of the Foreigner

Some 20 years ago the French historian Gérard Noiriel dubbed the nineteenth century as the emergence of the *tyrannie du national*, which turned the concept of foreigners, defined as citizens from other nation states, into a 'master status'.[57] An important stimulus in this process, which reached its highest point in the twentieth century, was the gradual realization in western Europe that the national state had to take some form of responsibility to reduce risks for

---

[53] Leeuwen, *Bijstand*, p. 190, 237.

[54] Ibid., pp. 161–2. See also Lindert, *Growing Public*, 74.

[55] The share of cityward migrations in the total cross-community migrations in Europe increased from an average of 15 per cent in the period 1650–1800 to some 40 per cent in the nineteenth century. Lucassen and Lucassen, 'The Mobility Transition Revisited'; Lucassen and Lucassen, *The Mobility Transition in Europe*, p. 104, Table 9.3.

[56] See also Winter, 'Caught between Law and Practice'.

[57] Gérard Noiriel, *La tyrannie du national. Le droit d'asile en Europe (1793–1993)* (Paris, 1991).

its taxpaying citizens. One of these risks, apart from sickness and old age, was unemployment. From the early modern period onwards this risk had been partly covered by guilds and mutual funds and arrangements of artisans. For many poor and unskilled people such insurance schemes were simply too costly, so that they had to rely on various forms of private and public poor relief.

As populations increased and urbanization and industrialization proliferated, states felt increasing pressure to go beyond the liberal functions of a watchman state. The pressure to act was built up further by the gradual democratization process and the fear of revolution and anarchy. A consequence of widening the vote was that some form of redistribution of wealth had to be implemented.[58] The social legislation initiated by the conservative government of Bismarck in Germany at the end of the nineteenth century is well known.[59] Other countries, like England and the Netherlands, were less precocious; but there also the state, in close cooperation with denominational private initiatives, slowly became more active in the social domain,[60] for example by contributing to unemployment provisions.

These first steps on the long and winding road to the welfare state had crucial consequences for the regulation of international migration. This became clear in France at the end of the nineteenth century, for instance, when preferential treatment of nationals on the labour market was enforced to some extent.[61] Another example is Prussia, which did not allow Russian Poles who worked in agriculture in the eastern provinces of the German empire to settle and devised a rotation system ('Karenz)' which obliged these migrants to return to Russian Poland at the end of each year, only to return a few months later. Furthermore these migrants were only allowed to work in the eastern provinces.[62] More relevant to our argument is the much less known practice by Prussian border authorities of demanding written proof of nationality of Dutch workers who moved en masse to the booming Ruhr area after 1870. Such written proof of nationality, issued by Dutch provincial governors,[63] was the equivalent of early modern settlement certificates,[64] now issued by national instead of local

---

[58]   Daron Acemoglu and James A. Robinson, *Economic Origins of Dictatorship and Democracy* (Cambridge, 2006).

[59]   Steinmetz, *Regulating the Social*.

[60]   Lindert, *Growing Public*.

[61]   Gérard Noiriel, *Le creuset français. Histoire de l'immigration, XIXe–XXe siècles* (Paris, 1988), pp. 278–89.

[62]   Lucassen, *The Immigrant Threat*, pp. 51, 59–61.

[63]   Eijl and Lucassen, 'Holland beyond Borders', p. 161; see also Lucassen, 'A Many-Headed Monster', pp. 249–50.

[64]   Winter, 'Caught between Law and Practice', p. 144.

governments. In both cases they gave a guarantee to the receiving community that the potential costs of poor relief were covered.

These preliminary international skirmishes at the end of the nineteenth century paved the way for a much more fundamental and rigorous *tyrannie du national*, when the liberal watchman state was finally buried in the aftermath of World War I in response to mounting pressures from the labour movement to grant universal suffrage and provide unemployment insurance.[65] One of the consequences of this expansion of state activities was that the category of 'foreigner' or 'alien' became key to policies not only concerning the crossing of national boundaries, but also concerning entry to the labour market.[66]

The reintroduction of passports in 1914 therefore marked the final breakthrough of a process that had already started with the issuing of nationality certificates in the second half of the nineteenth century. An instructive example is that of the Netherlands. Authorities at the national level, especially in the departments of Justice and Labour, wanted to prevent foreign workers from crowding out nationals, who then had to be paid unemployment benefits. At the same time, however, policy makers and employers realized that the labour market was too segmented simply to replace foreign workers with unemployed nationals. Moreover, there was a great reluctance to give up the laissez-faire ideology, while there were (justified) fears that German authorities would retaliate against Dutch workers in Germany if life were made too difficult for Germans in the Netherlands.[67] The result was the introduction of a new principle that is still in force: the entrance of foreign workers was made conditional on the state of the national labour market, and employers had to prove that no national supply was available. In the 1920s many exemptions were made, especially for Germans, but the legal framework was flexible and the screws could be tightened when the economy deteriorated, as happened in the 1930s.[68] In other countries similar acts were put into action which did not differ materially from local (urban) regulations of the early modern period.

---

[65]   Marcel van der Linden, 'The National Integration of European Working Classes (1871–1914): Exploring the Causal Configuration', *International Review of Social History*, 33 (1988): pp. 285–311.

[66]   Lucassen, Leo, 'The Great War and the Origins of Migration Control in Western Europe and the United States (1880–1920)', in Anita Böcker, Kees Groenendijk, Tetty Havinga and Paul Minderhoud (eds), *Regulation of Migration: International Experiences* (Amsterdam, 1998), pp. 45–72.

[67]   The importance of the principle of reciprocity has been rightly stressed by Corrie van Eijl, *Al te goed is buurmans gek. Het Nederlandse vreemdelingenbeleid 1840–1940* (Amsterdam, 2005).

[68]   Leo Lucassen, 'Administrative into Social Control: The Aliens Police and Foreign Female Servants in the Netherlands, 1918–1940', *Social History*, 27/3 (2002): pp. 327–42.

The development of national immigration policies in other European countries varied according to their economic situations. In France agriculture and industry yearned for foreign workers, and large-scale recruitment schemes for bringing in Poles and Italians were put in place until the economic crisis of the 1930s. Germany represents the other extreme, with towering inflation and unemployment rates in the early 1920s and a weak economy until a Keynesian spending policy was implemented by the Nazi government in the 1930s. One of the consequences of the bad economic situation was that even descendants of Germans who lived in eastern Europe, who for ethno-national reasons were considered to belong to the German people, were refused entry to the 'mother country'. This was not only because they were considered necessary as a national bridgehead in the east, but also because of the expected welfare costs.[69]

The Role of Cities in Implementing National Regulations

Although in most countries during the 1920s labour migrants were welcome and were granted work permits easily, the principal differentiation between nationals and non-nationals was there to stay and had major implications for both bureaucratic institutions and foreigners alike. Especially the formation of specialized departments to deal with aliens within local police forces and registration authorities are of interest to ascertain the relative autonomy of cities with regard to the regulation of foreign migration.[70] That national regulations were implemented differently from town to town has been stressed by many studies.[71] Due to the sometimes wide discretionary powers granted to the executive urban branches, especially the police forces, the execution of national policies could vary considerably and sometimes even hamper the aims of the national state.[72] A good example is the lenient way the Amsterdam police dealt with Jewish refugees in the 1930s. Although national restrictive policies defined Jewish migrants as unwanted *per se* and thereby made their stay illegal,[73] the

---

[69]   Jochen Oltmer, '"To Live as Germans among Germans": Immigration and Integration of "Ethnic Germans" in the German Empire and the Weimar Republic', in Lucassen, Feldman and Oltmer (eds), *Paths of Integration*, pp. 98–115.

[70]   And in some countries, like France, also of colonial subjects: Clifford Rosenberg, *Policing Paris: The Origins of Modern Immigration Control between the Wars* (Ithaca NY/London, 2006).

[71]   For the Netherlands, see Marij Leenders, *Ongenode gasten. Van traditioneel asielrecht naar immigratiebeleid, 1815–1938* (Hilversum, 1993).

[72]   Leo Lucassen, 'Bringing Structure Back In: Economic and Political Determinants of Immigration in Dutch Cities, 1920–1940', *Social Science History*, 26/3 (2002): pp. 503–29.

[73]   Corrie van Eijl, 'Tracing Back "Illegal Aliens" in the Netherlands, 1850–1940', in Marlou Schrover, Joanne van der Leun, Leo Lucassen and Chris Quispel (eds), *Illegal Migration and*

Amsterdam head of police often turned a blind eye to the presence of illegal Jewish refugees and *de facto* refused to put this highly discriminatory policy into practice.[74]

This relative autonomy was never entirely lost, although it varied greatly through space and time. Well-known examples today are the hesitations at the local level in many European countries to tackle the problem of illegal residents. Often they are left in peace, and even supported, because it does not suit local interests – either economically or for reasons of public safety – to rout these migrants. For political reasons, however, some cities sometimes pursue a very tough line, as recent examples in Italy show.

Finally, urban institutions could also play an unexpected role in stimulating the emigration of national citizens. Thus in the Netherlands during the 1920s and especially the 1930s, unemployed nationals were forced to accept jobs in Germany – where the economic situation was more favourable – on the penalty of losing their benefits.[75]

Conclusion

The art of comparison is to guard oneself from the temptation of easy parallels, while keeping an eye open for structural resemblances. It is therefore of utmost importance to be very explicit about the levels of analysis. In this chapter we are interested in the ways in which cities and states in western Europe have regulated (and enforced) migration to and within their territory in the last four centuries. The comparison has focused on cities before 1800 and states after 1800. The underlying assumption was that cities were to a large extent autonomous in their decisions about whom to admit until they lost this prerogative to the modern nation state from the nineteenth century onwards. In this chapter I argue that this shift between the early modern and modern period primarily entailed a difference in scale rather than a structural difference. This conclusion echoes Charles Tilly's analysis of state formation processes in Europe in the last millennium.[76] Both early modern cities and modern states at least had the pretension to regulate migration at their respective borders, and often acted on this when it was deemed necessary. Understanding the regulation of migration before 1800 should therefore focus on the level of cities, whereas for the

Gender in a Global and Historical Perspective (Amsterdam, 2008), pp. 49–51.

[74]   Guus Meershoek, *Dienaren van het gezag. De Amsterdamse politie tijdens de bezetting* (Amsterdam, 1999).

[75]   Eijl and Lucassen, 'Holland beyond Borders', p. 163.

[76]   Charles Tilly, *Coercion, Capital and European States, AD 990–1992* (Cambridge, 1990).

nineteenth and twentieth centuries similar processes can be seen at the level of nation states.

In the early modern period, like today, processes of inclusion and exclusion did not only, or even primarily, take place at the gates. Apart from airports, territorial borders in our modern world are very open, especially when approached by car or train. Once inside, however, migrants are confronted with other gates that govern entrance to work and welfare. In early modern cities, physical gates were omnipresent and better guarded, yet the constant massive movement of people in and out of towns made a waterproof system impossible. As in our own days, institutions inside the city walls were at least as important for the regulation of migration. In both cases the bottom line is that insiders (or the established)[77] have preferential rights compared to outsiders, however they are defined. These rights materialize primarily with respect to labour market activities and welfare entitlements. When we apply these three dimensions of migration regulation – territorial, labour market and welfare – to the comparison between early modern cities and modern states the similarities are obvious (Table 12.3).

Table 12.3   Regulating migration in western European cities and states, 1600–2010

	Early modern cities		Nineteenth-century cities		Nineteenth-century states		States in the 20th and 21st centuries	
Type of regime	Open	Closed	Open	Closed	Open	Closed	Open	Closed
Access to territory	F	R	F	F	PR	R	F	R
Access to labour market	F	R	F	F	F	R	F	R
Access to welfare	R	R	F	R	F	R	R	R

Abbreviations: F: Free; R: Regulated; PR: Partially regulated

In Table 12.3 I make a basic distinction between open and closed regimes of migration regulation. As we have seen, both types existed in each period; the specific policies developed by cities and states determined to what extent and for what kind of migrants access to the various domains was regulated. Open regimes both *then* (cf. the example of Amsterdam) and *now* are indifferent to movements over territorial and labour market borders, and may even erase legal differences between migrants and locals or nationals in this regard. When it

---

[77]   Norbert Elias and John L. Scotson, *The Established and the Outsiders: A Sociological Enquiry into Community Problems* (London, 1965).

comes to entitlements to welfare (or poor relief), however, the line is drawn very clearly. To shield receiving societies from the financial risks of immigration, migrants can penetrate this domain only very gradually. For migrants, open regimes mean that they can profit from job opportunities and wages, while other fruits of society – especially welfare – remain inaccessible. This is what I described as the 'Tantalus Torment' model in the introduction.

Closed regimes are less welcoming and try to regulate migration at all three levels, either because the economy has no need for migrants or because it is feared that poor and destitute immigrants will put a strain on their resources. This is what happened in Leiden and many other western European cities by the end of the seventeenth century. Migrants could settle, but only if and when financial risks were minimized.[78] Most closed regimes, however, were once much more open. Before the 1670s, for instance, Leiden welcomed migrants – as did western European states until the 1970s. After these migrants had settled, however – and when the economy started doing less well – the relevant authorities realized that many of the outsiders had become insiders, and with it a financial burden to welfare systems. Many migrants showed little inclination to leave because by doing so they risked losing their welfare entitlements. Relatively rich cities in early modern Europe remained a better place to live than poverty-stricken rural areas where welfare and job opportunities were sparse. This is why I labelled this configuration the 'Golden Cage' model.

Notwithstanding the structural similarities, we must not close our eyes to differences. In modern welfare states 'embedded' rights are often the result of supranational arrangements and have more consequences than just those pertaining to staying or leaving. States are now part of a higher state system – the European Union – which has introduced yet another scale of sovereignty and political decision making. Furthermore, the content of 'embedded rights' has expanded significantly in the post-war period. As we saw in the case of guest workers from Algeria, Morocco and Turkey, closing the gates in the early 1970s sparked off a huge immigration of family members joining their husbands and parents, reaching levels five times as high as the number who originally arrived as 'guest workers'. Similar family reunion rights were unthinkable in early modern cities. One could therefore say that both the bars and the content of the cage have become much more 'golden' than in the early modern period.

This leaves us with the question of how to understand the intermediate transition period of the long nineteenth century. As Table 12.3 shows this was

---

[78]   Especially German states tended to be very strict and widened these restrictions also to marriages: Piet Lourens and Jan Lucassen, '"Zunftlandschaften" in den Niederlanden um im benachbarten Deutschland', in W. Reininghaus (ed.), *Zunftlandschaften in Deutschland und den Niederlanden im Vergleich* (Münster, 2000), pp. 11–44.

indeed a kind of vacuum. Depending on specific contexts, states did regulate entry to their territory, but only in a very ad hoc manner. Moreover, they were not particularly interested in the domains of welfare and the labour market, which they did not consider their responsibility. Only when states started taking on welfare functions and thinking in terms of a national labour market, beginning with Germany in the 1880s, were similarities with early modern cities restored. In the intermediate period cities were left with few instruments to regulate (mostly internal) migration, namely using poor relief systems to keep out unwanted immigrants or keep in wanted residents. This power to regulate was definitively lost when the state finally took over in the twentieth century. From then on cities could only influence migration by bending national rules via their own urban institutions, for instance by being more tolerant than the rules of the nation state prescribed. One might interpret this as an early modern legacy, but also more generally – and more likely – as part of an inherent tension between central and local levels.

Chapter 13
Conclusions

Leslie Page Moch

Because the introduction to this volume provides a comprehensive analysis of its chapters and themes, I write as a migration historian bystander. It is striking, first of all, that these chapters create a narrative rhythm when taken all together – although they are placed as a group between ascriptive practices of medieval settlements and cities on one hand, and the untrammelled free-market capitalism of the industrial age on the other.

Beginning with Eleonora Canepari, we have an overview of Italian cities in the sixteenth to seventeenth centuries, where a combination of ordinances, proclamations and guild regulations worked to create a specific labour force in such towns as Milan, Siena, Florence and Pisa. They also served to keep beggars, vagrants and Gypsies away; and in Rome to deflect those who cheated pilgrims, the lifeblood of the city. Innkeepers are the backbone of this system – the link between policing forces and the unwelcome. The municipality is key.

With Strasbourg and Hanna Sonkajärvi's research, the state and religious confession muddy the waters – or complicate regulation – as the French crown insists on the welcoming of Catholics to this Protestant town, an imperial city before Louis XIV's aggression took hold. Here the question of confession and competing levels of authority come into the picture of this study that covers a century, and so we see state and local authority at odds where there is putative equality between Protestants and Catholics (although both agree that Calvinists are not to be borne) – but social distinctions are such that the bishop himself suggests intermarriage as a way to help Catholics find a social place.

Jan De Meester emphasizes the fate of craft guilds in Antwerp in a relatively short period of prosperity and – foreshadowing concerns in later chapters – detects fractures within guilds as small masters and guilds lost clout in comparison with big entrepreneurs. As in Strasbourg, Burgher status was at stake. De Meester makes a more general conclusion: that it was not guild policy that worked to the detriment of small masters, but rather decisions made on an ad hoc basis under the pressure of changing conditions.

Ulrich Niggemann moves to a longer view of guilds and newcomers by comparing several German cities with London, primarily as Huguenot artisans entered in the last half of the seventeenth century, when they were persecuted in seventeenth-century France. Yet Niggemann eschews confessional explanations for anti-Huguenot actions (as well as anti-state explanations), focusing instead on what one could call the 'moral economy' of the guild that is fundamentally opposed to a competitive marketplace. In addition, he shows that in the case of the English, tensions within the guilds belie the internal stresses of a modernizing labour force.

The volume moves south and forward to the eighteenth century with Aleksej Kalc's study of Trieste after it was named a free port of the empire by Vienna in 1719. Designed for merchant capitalism, the port developed inclusive measures that positively welcomed those who could develop commerce while attempting to keep out those who would be a drag on the economy, but welcomed a diversity of confessions and nationalities. At the same time, Vincent Milliot shows, the cities of France were reining in their welcome to newcomers and supervising cities more closely – at least in the writings and organization of policing bodies. In order to control the usual suspects (beggars, vagrants and prostitutes), written records and specialization increased while, as in sixteenth- and seventeenth-century Italy, innkeepers were the key to the supervision of mobile people; innkeepers were also the objects of higher police organization, since their failures at record keeping constituted the most frequent lapse.

With Yves Junot's study of the towns of Artois, Flanders and Hainaut in the sixteenth century we get our first close look at those who were considered anathema to urban society: the vagrants, wandering soldiers, heretics and immoral men and women who were questioned by Aldermen. They show us both the lifeways of people who lived on the margins of society and how they were defined by the cities in what is now northern France during a chaotic age. Jason Coy's study of Ulm in roughly the same period shows rough treatment of the 'study beggar' and vagrant – or the migrant worker defined as one of these – in an era of simultaneous economic decline and what Coy calls a 'surge in civic legislation'. The Lutheran model for good behaviour written into in the Migrants' Ordinance was a demanding one, with carefully delineated rules for seeking work and taking a drink. Beadles kept a close watch – at least the rules were tight and the punishments of the holding cage and public humiliations were draconian. There were repeat offenders, but they paid a high price.

Tim Hitchcock begs to differ – that is, he makes the case that in eighteenth-century England there was a culture of mobility among the poor, dramatically illustrated by the fact that 40 per cent of parishioners did not stay around for demographic historians' family reconstitution exercises. His literate, clever men and women who peddled and sang their way around the country managed to avoid trouble most of the time, despite England's famous Vagrancy Act and Settlement Laws.

In her magisterial chapter, Anne Winter observes that neither these very Settlement Laws, nor the English Poor Laws of the seventeenth century distinguish England from the continent, but rather demonstrate a 'specific case of a more general, shared and recognizable set of concerns, interests and conflicts' that shaped local policies toward migrants. She demonstrates that legal, judicial and administrative sources reflect these concerns, and highlights the tensions between the desire for a viable and competitive labour force, on one hand, asnd one free of those who would draw on public funds for relief, on the other – using the contrasting tales of eighteenth-century Antwerp and Vilvoorde.

This collection seems to tell a tidy tale, then; but, related like this, a welter of interesting differences are masked that are worth interrogating. The greatest is differences in where the tensions lie within municipalities: in some cases they are among the guilds; in others among municipal authorities; in still others with the larger state or empire. The times that trigger change also vary: the period under study is in some cases a point of tension and decline in resources (sixteenth-century Ulm or Southern Low Countries); in others a changing point in state relations (when Strasbourg and Lille came under French rule). The varied structural situations trigger a series of questions.

Is it true that in periods of decline those who restrict migration (as in Winter's thinking) have the upper hand, while in periods of expansion it is the employers who have it? Changes in the confessional mix highlight what difference confession makes (in Ulm, for example) – or does not (Huguenots in London). Can we discern the circumstances under which confession is not a point of contention? This would seem to be most useful.

Regulations come from myriad sources: public proclamations, the grand senate of Strasbourg, the Mason's guild of Antwerp, police *memoires*, beadles' directions, migrants' ordinances and vagrancy acts – in short the legal, judicial and administrative sources parsed out by Anne Winter. Are these distinct from one another in systematic ways?

One can pose a similar question about marginal people. That is, outside the usual marginals – beggars and vagrants – of whom cities were most leery, how did the identity of those defined as pariahs change?

The tensions between municipalities and larger units – the government in Vienna or Paris – expand in the eighteenth century and will only be resolved, in some cases, in the nineteenth century. How do these vary? Finally, it is well known that in a general way policing has become more effective since the sixteenth century – and took a great leap forward in the eighteenth century. Is this the case in the history of the regulation of migration? Is the end of this story the point at which state power was increased, and city power so negligible that regulation was no longer necessary? To pose the question a bit differently: What was the significance of cities tearing down their walls, as they finally did?

Enough questions. I turn to ways in which to move forward, knitting the findings in these studies together. If the question to be addressed is how early modern cities regulated migration, setting in motion a search for the dynamics of urban policies – however ad hoc or reactive they may have been – then perhaps answers could be more systematized by aligning themselves along a number of axes. Some of this may involve attaching to some rather tired general historical narratives – but also refreshing them. For example, the questions of confession can be linked to histories of the Reformation and Counter-Reformation. These tales of regulation can also be related to types of cities – key ports like Trieste and Amsterdam, the textile cities or inland trading centres.

As a migration scholar, I am a bit uneasy with regulating migration without attention to migrants themselves, and so I suggest that they might be included in two ways. First, the cities in question can be tied to findings about the geographies of historical migrations, attending to the migration systems that animated early modern Europe. Finally, there is space between urban rulings and enforcement to seek out the strategies on the part of migrants themselves in response to regulation, both the evasive and proactive behaviour on the part of people on the road that is perceived by Hanna Sonkajärvi and emphasized by Tim Hitchcock. This sort of suggestion can only be ventured because this set of studies has paved the way for a complete and comprehensive history of the relationship between the city and migrants in the early modern period.

Bibliography

Primary Sources (By Chapter)

Chapter 2 – Jan De Meester

Manuscript sources
Rijksarchief, Antwerp, *Fonds Antwerpen*, 39.
Stadsarchief, Antwerp, *Gilden en Ambachten*, 4001, 4055, 4267, 4268.
Stadsarchief, Antwerp, *Privilegekamer*, 661, 914, 915, 918, 2213–2216.
Stadsarchief, Antwerp, *Tresorij*, 1702.
Stadsarchief, Antwerp, *Vierschaar*, 142–153.

Printed primary sources
Recueil des ordonnances des Pays-Bas, série 2, 8 vols (Brussels: Goemaere, 1910–1978).

Chapter 3 – Ulrich Niggemann

Manuscript sources
Geheimes Staatsarchiv Preußischer Kulturbesitz, Berlin-Dahlem, *I. HA Rep. 122*, 7bI no 1; 7bII no 6, no 8, no 10, no 13; 14 no 1; 16 no 1 vol. I, vol. III; 18c vol. I, vol. II, vol. V; 27 no 1 vol. I.
Hessisches Staatsarchiv, Marburg, *Best.* 5 no 15464; 17f no 586.
Landeshauptarchiv von Sachsen-Anhalt, Magdeburg, *Rep. A*, 13 no 465.
The National Archives, Kew, Surrey, *PC* 2/70, 2/71, 2/73, 2/75; *SP* 29/431, 31/5.
Niedersächsisches Hauptstaatsarchiv, Hannover, Cal. Br. 8 no 638.

Printed primary sources
Calendar of State Papers, Domestic series, of the Reign of Charles II, ed. F. H. Blackburn Danielle and Francis Bickley (vol. 17, Nendeln: Kraus, 1968).
England's Advocate, Europe's Monitor: Being An Intreaty for help, In Behalf of the English Silk-Weavers and Silk-Throsters ... (London, 1699) [Wing/N2].

Klingebiel, Thomas (ed.), *Die Hugenotten in den welfischen Landen. Eine Privilegiensammlung* (Bad Karlshafen: Verlag des Deutschen Hugenotten-Vereins, 1994).

Mempel, Dieter (ed.), *Gewissensfreiheit und Wirtschaftspolitik. Hugenotten- und Waldenserprivilegien 1681–1699* (Trier: Auenthal-Verlag, 1986).

Mengin, Ernst (ed.), *Das Recht der französisch-reformierten Kirche in Preußen. Urkundliche Denkschrift* (Berlin: Consistorium der Französischen Kirche, 1929).

Seckendorff, Veit Ludwig von, *Teutscher Fürsten-Stat* (Jena, 1754, 1st edn Frankfurt am Main, 1656).

Shaw, William A. (ed.), *Letters of Denization and Acts of Naturalization for Aliens in England and Ireland, 1603–1700* (London: Huguenot Society of London, 1911).

Waller, William C. (ed.), *Extracts from the Court Books of the Weavers Company of London, 1610–1730* (London: Huguenot Society of London, 1931).

Chapter 4 – Yves Junot

Manuscript sources

Archives départementales du Nord, Lille, B 12701–12702; B 12708; B 12744.

Archives générales du royaume, Brussels, *Chambre des Comptes*, 39999–40036.

Archives générales du royaume, Brussels, *Conseil Privé espagnol*, 1420–1421.

Archives municipales, Lille, *Affaires Générales*.

Archives municipales, Valenciennes, FF1 10–11; Série CC, *Comptabilités et impôts, compte de la levée du 100e denier, paroisse Saint-Jacques*; MS 734, *Règlements et ordonnances concernant la ville de Valenciennes*.

Printed primary sources

Gachard, L.P., *Inventaire des archives des Chambres des Comptes, précédé d'une notice historique sur ces anciennes institutions* (Brussels: Hayez, 1845).

Chapter 5 – Hanna Sonkajärvi

Manuscript sources

Archives départementales du Bas-Rhin, Strasbourg, C 581, n° 109.

Archives du ministère de la guerre, Vincennes, A^1 773; A^1 1501, n° 335–6; A^{1}1503, n° 125–6.

Archives municipales, Strasbourg, AA 2106, n° 5, 10–11; AA 2118; AA 2163; AA 2206, n° 6; AA 2220, n° 12; AA 2380; AA 2418, n° 1–2, 8, 11, 25; AA 2419; AA 2528; AA 2616; XI 276.

Archives nationales, Paris, AN, G⁷ 83, n° 100–102.

Printed primary sources
Boug, François Henri de (ed.), *Recueil des édits, déclarations, lettres patentes, arrêts du Conseil d'État et du Conseil souverain d'Alsace, Ordonnances & Règlemens [sic] concernant cette Province* (2 vols, Colmar: Decker, 1775).

Chapter 6 – Eleonora Canepari

Manuscript sources
Archivio di Stato di Roma, *Bandi del Governatore*, vol. 410 (1543–1670), vol. 411 (1671–1700).
Archivio Storico Capitolino, *Camera Capitolina*, credenzone (cred.) 1, tomo (t.) 23; cred. 6, t. 1; cred. XI, t. 46, 1690, chapter 35; cred. XI, t. 114, 1621, chapter 10; cred. XI, t. 87, 1738, chapter 9; cred. XI, t. 104, chapter 21; cred. XI, t. 104, chapter 21.
Statuto dell'Università dei fruttaroli (Rome, 1563).

Printed primary sources
Compendio di tutte le gride, et ordini publicati nella città, & Stato di Milano. Nel governo dell'Ill.mo et Eccellentiss.mo signor don Carlo d'Aragona, duca di Terranuova, &c. governatore del detto Stato, & capitan generale per Sua Maestà catholica in Italia (Milan, 1583–1592, edn 1609).
Compendio di tutte le gride, bandi, et ordini, fatti, & publicati nella città, & Stato di Milano. Nel governo de gli Illustriss. & Eccellentiss. signori Juan Fernandez de Velasco, contestabile di Castiglia, &c. et don Pedro de Padilla, castellano di Milano, &c. luogotenenti, & governatori per Sua Maestà catholica dello Stato di Milano (Milan, 1592–1600).
Compendio di tutte le gride, bandi, et ordini, fatti, & publicati nella città, & Stato di Milano. Nel governo dell'Illustriss. & Eccellentiss. signor don Pietro Enriquez de Acevedo, conte di Fuentes &c. (Milan, 1611).
Compendio di tutte le gride, bandi, et ordini, fatti, & publicati nella città, & Stato di Milano. Nel governo dell'Altezza Sereniss. don Fernando per la gratia di Dio cardinale infante di Spagna &c. governatore dello Stato di Milano, e capitano generale in Italia &c. (Milan, 1633–1634, edn 1634).
Gridario dell'Eccellentissimo signore il sig. don Luigi de Benavides, Carillo, e Toledo, marchese di Fromista, Caracena, conte di Pinto, del consiglio supremo di guerra di S.M., suo governatore, e capitano generale nello Stato di Milano &c. (Milan, 1648–1656).

Gridario dell'Ecc.mo sig.r don Giovanni di Velasco La Cueva, conte di Siruela, del consiglio di Stato della maestà del rè N.S., suo governatore, e capitano generale nello Stato di Milano &c. (Milan, 1653).

Chapter 7 – Aleksej Kalc

Manuscript sources

Archivio di Stato di Trieste, *Cesarea Regia Superiore Intendenza Commerciale per il Litorale in Trieste* (1748–1776), b. 3; b. 7; b. 55; b. 456; b. 488–489; b. 546; b. 548.

Archivio di Stato di Trieste, *Cesareo Regio Governo per il Litorale in Trieste*, b. 96; b. 101–103; b. 172; b. 545–549.

Archivio Generale del Comune di Trieste, *Capitanato Circolare*, b. 20.

Biblioteca Civica di Trieste, *Archivio Diplomatico, Atti di Polizia, Giornali di Polizia*, 1768–1778.

Biblioteca Civica di Trieste, *Archivio Diplomatico, Sicurezza Pubblica*, 1769–1795

Printed primary sources

Kandler, Pietro, *Documenti per servire alla conoscenza delle condizioni legali del Municipio ed emporio di Trieste* (Trieste, 1848).

Kandler, Pietro, 'Emporio e portofranco', in *Raccolta delle leggi, ordinanze e regolamenti speciali per Trieste pubblicati per ordine della Presidenza del Consiglio dal suo procuratore civico* (Trieste, 1861).

Chapter 8 – Vincent Milliot

Manuscript sources

Archives municipales, Lyon, BB 414; 3 S 693.

Archives municipales, Strasbourg, AA 2508.

Archives municipales, Toulouse, FF 635.

Archives nationales, Paris, AN série AD+ 1032, pièce 15; AN série Y 9449A; 9461A; 9466B; 9467; 9468; 9508; 12830; 13728.

Bibliothèque multimédia, Orléans, J.C.P. Lenoir (1732–1807), *Mémoires*, Mss 1421–1424.

Bibliothèque nationale de France, Paris, Manuscripts, Joly de Fleury 36; 185, fols 85–92, 207, 242ff.; 1803, fols 6–7.

Bibliothèque nationale de France, Paris, recueil Z Le Senne 167 (25).

Printed primary sources

Guillauté, M., *Mémoire sur la réformation de la police de France, soumis au roi en 1749*, ed. J. Seznec (Paris: Hermann, 1974).

Mercier, L.-S., *Le Tableau de Paris (1781–1789)*, ed. J.-C. Bonnet (Paris: Mercure de France, 1994).

La Police de Paris en 1770. Mémoire inédit composé par ordre de G. de Sartine sur la demande de Marie-Thérèse, ed. A. Glazier (Paris, Mémoires de la société de l'histoire de Paris et de l'Ile-de-France, 1879, pp. 77ff.).

Turmeau de la Morandière, *Police sur les mendiants, les vagabonds, les joueurs de profession, les intriguants, les filles prostituées, les domestiques hors de maison depuis longtemps et les gens sans aveu* (Paris: Dessain Junior, 1764).

Chapter 9 – Jason Coy

Manuscript sources

Stadtarchiv Ulm, A 2001–2002; A 3530; A 3669; A 3671–3672; A 3681; A 3688; A 3693; A 3785; A 3872; A 4176/1; A 4396; A 6590.

Printed primary sources

Casparum Huberinum, *Jesus Syrach. Spiegel der Haußzucht genannt, Sammpt einer kurtzen Außlegung für die armen Haußväter und ir gesinde, wie sie ein Gottselig leben gegen meniglich sollen erzeigen. Darinnen der Welt lauff begriffen und wie sich ein ieglicher Christ in seinem beruff und in der Policey ehrlich und löblich solle halten* (Nuremberg, 1552/1587).

Martin Luther, Foreword to *Liber Vagatorum* (Wittenberg, 1528; originally published c. 1509).

Chapter 10 – Anne Winter

Manuscript sources

Archief van het Openbaar Centrum voor Maatschappelijk Welzijn, Antwerp, *Kamer van Huisarmen*, 866, 872.

Archives générales du royaume, Brussels, *Conseil Privé Autrichien, Cartons*, 1283, 1284/A, 1285/B.

Archives générales du royaume, Brussels, *Conseil Privé Autrichien, Registres des consultes*, 458, 475.

Rijksarchief, Anderlecht, *Raad van Brabant, Procesdossiers steden*, 712.

Rijksarchief, Antwerp, *Kwartier van Arkel*, 53.

Rijksarchief, Antwerp, *Oud gemeentearchief Arendonk*, 4280, 4555.

Rijksarchief, Leuven, *Kerkarchief Brabant*, 2.492, 23.100, 23.307, 23.666, 23.954, 24.672, 25.899, 26.859, 28.085, 30.678, 33.947, 34.438.
Stadsarchief, Antwerp, *Vierschaar*, V 177.

Printed primary sources
Laury, Remi Albert du, *La jurisprudence des Pays-Bas autrichiens établie par les arrets du Grand Conseil, de sa Majesté Imperiale et Apostolique, resident en la ville de Malines, auxquels sont ajoutés quelques decrêts portés au Conseil privé de Sadite Majesté*, 2 vols (Brussels: Jean Moris, 1761).
Plakkaten van Vlaanderen, 13 vols (Ghent/Antwerp, 1766–1794).
Recueil des Ordonnances des Pays-Bas Autrichiens, série 3, 15 vols (Brussels: Goemaere, 1867–1942).

Chapter 11 – Tim Hitchcock

Manuscript sources
London Metropolitan Archives, *Middlesex Sessions of the Peace, Sessions Papers*, 1757, MJ/SP/1757/07.

Printed primary sources
Burn, James Dawson, *The Autobiography of a Beggar Boy*, ed. David Vincent (London: Europa Publications, 1978).
Burn, Richard, *The Justice of the Peace, and Parish Officer* (18th edn, London, 1797).
Burn, Richard, *The Justice of the Peace, and Parish Officer* (15th edn, London 1785).
Charke, Charlotte, *A Narrative of the Life of Mrs Charlotte Charke*, ed. Robert Rehder (1755, London: Pickering and Chatto, 1999 edn).
Hitchcock, Tim and John Black (eds), *Chelsea Settlement and Bastardy Examinations, 1733–66* (London, 1999), London Record Society, 33.
Moritz, Carl Philipp, *Travels of Carl Philipp Moritz in England in 1782*, ed. P.E. Matheson, (1795, London: Oxford University Press, 1926 edn).
Parliamentary Papers, 'Second Report. Reported by Thomas Gilbert, Esq. 21 May 1776'.
Potter, Israel, *Life and Remarkable Adventures of Israel R. Potter*, ed. Leonard Kriegal, (1824, New York: Corinth Books, 1962 edn).
Riley, Edward Miles (ed.), *The Journal of John Harrower: An Indentured Servant in the Colony of Virginia, 1773–1776* (Williamsburg VA: Colonial Williamsburg, 1963).
Saxby, Mary, *Memoirs of a Female Vagrant Written by Herself* (London, 1806).

Smith, Adam, *An Inquiry into the Nature and Causes of the Wealth of Nations* (1776, London: Everyman edn, 1910).

Sokoll, Thomas (ed.), *Essex Pauper Letters, 1731–1837* (Oxford, 2001), Records of Social and Economic History, ns, 30.

Wilkinson, C.H. (ed.), *The King of the Beggars: Bampfylde-Moor Carew* (Oxford: Clarendon Press, 1931).

Secondary Sources

Acemoglu, Daron and James A. Robinson, *Economic Origins of Dictatorship and Democracy* (Cambridge: Cambridge University Press, 2006).

Ackhurst, F.R.P. and Stephanie C. Van D'Elden (eds), *The Stranger in Medieval Society* (Minneapolis: University of Minnesota Press, 1997).

Aerts, Erik and John H. Munro (eds), *Textiles of the Low Countries in European Economic History* (Leuven: Leuven University Press, 1990).

Ago, Renata, *Economia barocca. Mercato e istituzioni nella Roma del Seicento* (Rome: Donzelli, 1998).

Amelang, James S., 'Cities and Foreigners', in Donatella Calabi and Stephen Turk Christensen (eds), *Cultural Exchange in Early Modern Europe: Vol. 2: Cities and Cultural Exchange in Europe, 1400–1700* (Cambridge: Cambridge University Press, 2007).

Amelang, James S., *The Flight of Icarus: Artisan Autobiography in Early Modern Europe* (Stanford CA: Stanford University Press, 1998).

Antonellis Martini, Liana De, *Portofranco e comunità etnico-religiose nella Trieste settecentesca* (Milan: Giuffre, 1968).

Arru, Angiolina, 'Il prezzo della cittadinanza', *Quaderni storici*, 91 (1996): 157–71.

Arru, Angiolina, Joseph Ehmer and Franco Ramella, 'Premessa', *Quaderni storici*, 106 (2001): 4–23.

Arru, Angiolina and Franco Ramella (eds), *L'Italia delle migrazioni interne. Donne, uomini, mobilità in età moderna e contemporanea* (Rome: Donzelli, 2003).

Asche, Matthias, *Neusiedler im verheerten Land. Kriegsfolgenbewältigung, Migrationssteuerung und Konfessionspolitik im Zeichen des Landeswiederaufbaus. Die Mark Brandenburg nach den Kriegen des 17. Jahrhunderts* (Münster: Aschendorff, 2006).

Bade, Klaus J., '"Preussengänger" und "Abwehrpolitik": Ausländerbeschäftigung, Ausländerpolitik und Ausländerkontrolle auf dem Arbeitsmarkt in Preussen vor dem Ersten Weltkrieg', *Archiv für Sozialgeschichte*, 24 (1984): 91–162.

Bade, Klaus J., Pieter C. Emmer, Leo Lucassen and Jochen Oltmer (eds), *Enzyklopädie Migration in Europa vom 17. Jahrhundert bis zur Gegenwart* (Paderborn/Munich: Wilhelm Fink Verlag/Ferdinand-Schöningh-Verlag, 2007).

Bade, Klaus J., Leo Lucassen, Pieter C. Emmer and Jochen Oltmer (eds), *Encyclopedia of migration and minorities in Europe. From the 17th century to the present* (Cambridge and New York 2011).

Bairoch, Paul, *De Jéricho à Mexico. Villes et économie dans l'histoire* (Paris: Gallimard, 1985).

Baisch, Andreas, 'Die Verfassung im Leben der Stadt, 1558–1802', in Hans Eugen Specker (ed.), *Die Ulmer Bürgerschaft auf dem Weg zur Demokratie* (Ulm: Kommissionsverlag W. Kohlhammer, 1997), pp. 197–203.

Barkey, Karen, *Empire of Difference: The Ottomans in Comparative Perspective.* (Cambridge: Cambridge University Press, 2009).

Barry, Jonathan, 'Civility and Civic Culture in Early Modern England: The Meanings of Urban Freedom', in Peter Burke et al. (eds), *Civil Histories: Essays Presented to Sir Keith Thomas* (Oxford: Oxford University Press, 2000).

Bátori, Ingrid, 'Das Patriziat in der deutschen Stadt: Zu den Forschungsergebnissen über das Patriziat besonders der süddeutschen Städte', *Zeitschrift für Stadtgeschichte, Stadtsoziologie und Denkmalpflege*, 2 (1975): 1–30.

Belfanti, Carlo M., *Mestieri e forestieri: immigrazione ed economia urbana a Mantova fra Sei e Settecento* (Milan: Angeli, 1994).

Benabou, Erica-Marie, *La prostitution et la police des moeurs au XVIIIe siècle* (Paris: Perrin, 1987).

Biraben, Jean-Noel, *Les hommes et la peste* (Paris: Mouton, 1976).

Blanc-Chaléard, Marie-Claude, Caroline Douki, Nicole Dyonet and Vincent Milliot (eds), *Police et migrants. France, 1667–1939* (Rennes: Presses Universitaires de Rennes, 2001).

Blickle, Renate, 'Nahrung und Eigentum als Kategorien der ständischen Gesellschaft', in Winfried Schulze (ed.), *Ständische Gesellschaft und soziale Mobilität* (Munich: Oldenbourg, 1988), pp. 73–93.

Blockmans, Frans 'Het vroegste officiële ambachtswezen in Antwerpen', *Bijdragen voor de geschiedenis der Nederlanden*, 8 (1953): 161–201 and 237–50.

Blondé, Bruno and Michael Limberger, 'De gebroken welvaart', in Raymond Van Uytven (ed.), *Geschiedenis van Brabant van het hertogdom tot heden* (Leuven: Davidsfonds, 2007).

Blondé, Bruno, *Een economie met verschillende snelheden. Ongelijkheden in de opbouw en de ontwikkeling van het Brabantse stedelijke netwerk, ca 1750–ca 1790* (Brussels: Paleis der Academiën, 1999).

Boes, Maria R., 'Unwanted Travellers: The Tightening of City Borders in Early Modern Germany', in Thomas Betteridge (ed.), *Borders and Travellers in Early Modern Europe* (Aldershot: Ashgate, 2007).

Bonenfant, Paul, *Le problème du pauperisme en Belgique à la fin de l'ancien régime* (Brussels: Académie Royale de Belgique, 1934).

Bonenfant, Paul, 'Les origines et le caractère de la réforme de la bienfaisance aux Pays-Bas sous le règne de Charles Quint', *Revue belge de philologie et d'histoire*, 5 (1926): 887–904; 6 (1927): 207–30.

Bonfiglio Dosio, Giorgetta, *L'immigrazione a Brescia fra Trecento e Quattrocento*, in *Forestieri e stranieri nelle città basso-medievali* (Florence: Salimbeni, 1988).

Boone, Marc, 'Droit de bourgeoisie et particularisme urbain dans la Flandre bourguignonne et habsburgoise (1384–1585)', *Belgisch tijdschrift voor filologie en geschiedenis*, 74 (1996): 707–26.

Boone, Marc, '"Cette frivole, dampnable et desraisonnable bourgeoisie": de vele gezichten van het laatmiddeleeuwse burgerbegrip in de Zuidelijke Nederlanden', in Joost Kloek and Karin Tilmans (eds), *Burger. Geschiedenis van het begrip van de Middeleeuwen tot eenentwintigste eeuw* (Amsterdam: Amsterdam University Press, 2002).

Boone, Marc, 'Les villes de l'espace flamand au bas Moyen Age. Immigrations et migrations internes', in Stéphane Curveiller and L. Buchard (eds), *Se déplacer du Moyen Âge à nos jours* (Calais: Kleinefenn, 2009).

Boone, Marc and Maarten Prak (eds), *Individual, Corporate and Judicial Status in European Cities (Late Middle Ages and Early Modern Period)* (Leuven/ Apeldoorn: Garant, 1996).

Boone, Marc and Walter Prevenier (eds), *La draperie ancienne des Pays-Bas. Débouchés et stratégies de survie (14e–16e siècles)* (Leuven/Apeldoorn: Garant, 1993).

Boone, Marc and Peter Stabel, 'New Burghers in the Late Medieval Towns of Flanders and Brabant: Conditions of Entry, Rules and Reality', in Rainer C. Schwinges (ed.), *Neubürger im Späten Mittelalter: Migration und Austausch in der Städtelandschaft des alten Reiches (1250–1550)* (Berlin: Duncker & Humblot, 2002).

Boucq, Simon Le, *Histoire ecclésiastique de Valenciennes* (Valenciennes: Prignet, 1844).

Bos, Sandra, *'Uyt liefde tot malcander'. Onderlinge hulpverlening binnen de Noord-Nederlandse gilden in internationaal perspectief (1570–1820)* (Amsterdam: International Instituut voor Sociale Geschiedenis, 1998).

Bos, Sandra, 'A Tradition of Giving and Receiving: Mutual Aid within the Guild System', in Maarten Prak et al. (eds), *Craft Guilds in the Early Modern Low Countries: Work, Power and Representation* (Aldershot: Ashgate, 2006).

Bottin, Jacques and Donatella Calabi (eds), *Les étrangers dans la ville. Minorités et espace urbain du bas Moyen Âge à l'époque moderne* (Paris: Editions de la Maison des sciences de l'homme, 1999).

Boumans, René, 'L'évolution démographique d'Anvers (XVe–XVIIe siècle)', *Bulletin statistique*, 34 (1948): 1683–91.

Boumans René, *Het Antwerps stadsbestuur voor en tijdens de Franse overheersing. Bijdrage tot de ontwikkelingsgeschiedenis van de stedelijke bestuursinstellingen in de Zuidelijke Nederlanden* (Bruges: De Tempel, 1965).

Boumans, René and Jan Craeybeckx, 'Het bevolkingscijfer van Antwerpen in het derde kwart der XVIe eeuw', *Tijdschrift voor geschiedenis*, 60 (1974): 394–405.

Boyer, George, *An Economic History of the English Poor Law, 1750–1850* (Cambridge: Cambridge University Press, 1990).

Brandt, Robert and Thomas Buchner, 'Einleitung', in Robert Brandt and Thomas Buchner (eds), *Nahrung, Markt oder Gemeinnutz. Werner Sombart und das vorindustrielle Handwerk* (Bielefeld: Verlag für Regionalgeschichte, 2004), pp. 13–28.

Breschi, Marco, Aleksej Kalc and Elisabetta Navarra, 'La nascita di una città: Storia minima della popolazione di Trieste (secc. XVIII–XIX)', in Roberto Finzi and Giovanni Panjek (eds), *Storia economica e sociale di Trieste. La città dei gruppi 1719–1918* (Trieste: Lint, 2001).

Brett-James, Norman G., *The Growth of Stuart London* (London: Allen & Unwin, 1935).

Brulez, Wilfrid, 'De Handel', in *Antwerpen in de XVIde eeuw* (Antwerp: Mercurius, 1975).

Brulez, Wirlfrid, 'Brugge en Antwerpen in de 15de en 16de eeuw: een tegenstelling?', *Tijdschrift voor geschiedenis*, 83 (1970): 15–37.

Buchner, Thomas, 'Überlegungen zur Rezeption von Nahrung in der handwerksgeschichtlichen Forschung seit dem Nationalsozialismus', in Robert Brandt and Thomas Buchner (eds), *Nahrung, Markt oder Gemeinnutz. Werner Sombart und das vorindustrielle Handwerk* (Bielefeld: Verlag für Regionalgeschichte, 2004).

Burds, Jeffrey, *Peasant Dreams and Market Politics: Labor Migration and the Russian Village, 1861–1905* (Pittsburgh: University of Pittsburgh Press, 1998).

Calabi, Donatella and Stephen Turk Christensen (eds), *Cultural Exchange in Early Modern Europe: Volume 2: Cities and Cultural Exchange in Europe, 1400–1700* (Cambridge: Cambridge University Press, 2007).

Calabi, Donatella and Paola Lanaro (eds), *La città italiana e i luoghi degli stranieri (XIV–XVIII secolo)* (Rome: Laterza, 1998).

Canepari, Eleonora, 'Immigrati, spazi urbani e reti sociali nell'Italia d'antico regime', in Paola Corti and Matteo Sanfilippo (eds), *Storia d'Italia – Annali, Migrazioni* (Turin: Einaudi, 2009).

Canepari, Eleonora, *Stare in compagnia. Strategie di inurbamento e forme associative nella Roma del Seicento* (Soveria Mannelli: Rubbettino, 2008).

Caplan, Jane and John Torpey (eds), *Documenting Individual Identity: The Development of State Practices in the Modern World* (Princeton: Princeton University Press, 2001).

Casarino, Giacomo, 'Stranieri a Genova nel Quattro e Cinquecento: tipologie sociali e nazioni', in Donatalla Calabi and Paola Lanaro (eds), *La città italiana e i luoghi degli stranieri (XIV–XVIII secolo)* (Rome: Laterza, 1998).

Cavallo, Sandra, *Artisans of the Body in Early Modern Italy: Identities, Families and Masculinities* (Manchester: Manchester University Press, 2007).

Cerutti, Simona 'A qui appartiennent les biens qui appartiennent à personne? Citoyenneté et droit d'aubaine à l'époque moderne', *Annales ESC*, 62/2 (2007): 355–86.

Cerutti, Simona, 'Travail, mobilité et légitimité. Suppliques au roi dans une société d'Ancien Régime (Turin XVIIIe siècle)', *Annales. Histoire, Sciences Sociales*, 65/3 (2010), 571–611.

Cerutti, Simona, Robert Descimon and Maarten Prak, 'Premessa', *Quaderni storici*, 89 (1995): 281–6.

Chassaigne, Marc, *La Lieutenance générale de police de Paris* (1906, Geneva: Slatkine Reprints, 1975).

Châtellier, Louis, *Tradition chrétienne et renouveau catholique dans le cadre de l'ancienne diocèse de Strasbourg (1650–1770)* (Paris: Ophrys, 1981).

Chorley, Patrick, 'The "draperies légères" of Lille, Arras, Tournai, Valenciennes: New Materials for New Markets?', in M. Boone and W. Prevenier (eds), *La draperie ancienne des Pays-Bas. Débouchés et stratégies de survie (14e–16e siècles)* (Leuven/Apeldoorn: Garant, 1993), pp. 151–9.

Clark, Peter and Paul Slack (eds), *English Towns in Transition, 1500–1700* (Oxford: Oxford University Press, 1976).

Clark, Peter and David Souden (eds), *Migration and Society in Early Modern England* (London: Hutchinson, 1987).

Clarkson, Leslie A., *The Pre-Industrial Economy in England 1500–1750* (London: Batsford, 1971).

Clay, Christopher G., *Economic Expansion and Social Change: England, 1500–1700* (2 vols, Cambridge: Cambridge University Press, 1984).

Claydon, Tony and Ian McBride (eds), *Protestantism and National Identity: Britain and Ireland, c. 1650–c. 1850* (Cambridge: Cambridge University Press, 1998).

Cody, Lisa Forman, *Birthing the Nation: Sex, Science, and the Conception of Eighteenth-Century Britons* (Oxford: Oxford University Press, 2005).

Cohen, Robert, 'Passage to a New World: the Sephardi Poor of Eighteenth-Century Amsterdam', in L. Dasberg and J.N. Cohen (eds), *Neveh Ya'kov. Jubilee Volume Presented to Dr. Jaap Meijer* (Assen: Van Gorcum, 1982), pp. 31–42.

Colley, Linda, *Britons: Forging the Nation 1707–1837* (London: Pimlico, 1994).

Coppens, Herman, 'Een arme eend in de vreemde bijt. Het overheidsoptreden tegenover binnenlandse migranten in de regio Antwerpen tijdens het late ancien régime (ca. 1550 ot 1790)', *Taxandria*, 81 (2009): 147–55.

Cottaar, Annemarie, *Kooplui, kermisklanten en andere woonwagenbewoners. Groepsvorming en beleid, 1870–1945* (Amsterdam: Spinhuis, 1996).

Cottret, Bernard, *The Huguenots in England: Immigration and Settlement, c. 1550–1700* (Cambridge: Cambridge University Press, 1991).

Coy, Jason P., 'Earn Your Penny Elsewhere: Banishment, Migrant Laborers, and Sociospatial Exclusion in Sixteenth-Century Ulm', *Journal of Historical Sociology*, 20/3 (2007): 279–303.

Coy, Jason P., *Strangers and Misfits: Banishment, Social Control, and Authority in Early Modern Germany* (Leiden: Brill Academic Press, 2008).

Cunningham, William, *Alien Immigrants to England* (London/New York: Cass, 1969).

Cuvelier, Joseph, *Les dénombrements de foyers en Brabant (XIVe–XVIe siècle)* (Brussels: Koninklijke Commissie voor Geschiedenis, 1912).

Dalle, G., *De bevolking van Veurne-ambacht in de 17de en 18de eeuw* (Brussels: Koninklijke Vlaamse Academie, 1963).

Dambruyne, Johan, *Corporatieve middengroepen. Aspiraties, relaties en transformaties in het 16de eeuwse ambachtswezen* (Ghent: Academia Press, 2002).

Damme, Dirk van, 'Onderstandswoonst, sedentarisering en stad-platteland-tegenstellingen: evolutie en betekenis van de wetgeving op de onderstandwoonst in Belgie (einde achttiende tot einde negentiende eeuw)', *Belgisch Tijdschrift voor Nieuwste Geschiedenis*, 21/3 (1990): 483–534.

Davids, C.A., 'Migratie te Leiden in de achttiende eeuw. Een onderzoek op grond van de acten van cautie', in H.A. Diederiks (ed.), *Een stad in achteruitgang. Sociaal-historische studies over Leiden in de achttiende eeuw* (Leiden: Rijksuniversiteit, 1978), pp. 146–92.

Davids, C.A., 'De migratiebeweging in Leiden in de achttiende eeuw', in H.A. Diederiks, D.J. Noordam and H.D. Tjalsma (eds), *Armoede en sociale spanning. Sociaal-historische studies over Leiden in de achttiende eeuw* (Hilversum: Verloren, 1985), pp. 137–56.

Davids, Karel and Jan Lucassen (eds), *A Miracle Mirrored: The Dutch Republic in European Perspective* (Cambridge: Cambridge University Press, 1995).

Denis, Vincent, 'Peut-on réformer un "monument de la police"? La réforme de la police de Strasbourg en débat à la fin de l'Ancien Régime, 1782–1788', in Vincent Milliot (ed.), *Les mémoires policiers, 1750–1850. Écritures et pratiques policières du Siècle des Lumières au Second Empire* (Rennes: Presses Universitaires de Rennes, 2006).

Denis, Vincent, 'Surveiller et décrire: L'enquête des préfets sur les migrations périodiques, 1807–1812', *Revue d'histoire moderne et contemporaine*, 47/4 (2000): 706–30.

Denis, Vincent, *Une histoire de l'identité. France, 1715–1815* (Seyssel: Champ Vallon, 2008).

Denys, Catherine, 'De l'autorégulation sociale au contrôle policier, la naissance de la police moderne dans les villes du nord de la France du XVIIIe siècle', in Pedro Fraile (ed.), *Modelar para gobernar. El control de la poblacion y el territorio en Europa y Canada. Una perspectiva historica* (Barcelona: Publicaciones Universidad de Barcelona, 2001).

Denys, Catherine, *Police et sécurité dans les villes de la frontière franco-belge au XVIIIe siècle* (Paris: L'Harmattan, 2002).

Denys, Catherine, 'Les projets de réforme de la police à Bruxelles à la fin du XVIIIe siècle. Police et contrôle du territoire dans les villes capitales (XVIIe–XIXe siècle)', *Mélanges de l'école française de Rome, Italie et Méditerranée (MEFRIM)*, 115/2 (2003): 807–26.

Denys, Catherine, Brigitte Marin and Vincent Milliot (eds), *Réformer la police. Les mémoires policiers en Europe au XVIIIe siècle* (Rennes: Presses Universitaires de Rennes, 2009).

Descimon Robert, 'Les barricades de la Fronde parisienne. Une lecture sociologique', *Annales ESC*, 2 (1990): 397–422.

Descimon, Robert and Jean Nagle, 'Les quartiers de Paris, du Moyen âge au XVIIIe siècle: évolution d'un espace pluri-fonctionnel', *Annales ESC*, 5 (1979): 956–83.

Descimon, Robert, 'Milice bourgeoise et identité citadine à Paris au temps de la Ligue', *Annales ESC*, 4 (1993): 885–906.

Deyon, Pierre and A. Lottin, 'L'évolution de la production textile à Lille aux XVIe et XVIIe siècles', *Revue du Nord*, 49/192 (1967): 22–33.

Dittrich, Erhard, *Die deutschen und österreichischen Kameralisten* (Darmstadt: Wissenschaftliche Buchgesellschaft, 1974).

Dölemeyer, Barbara, *Die Hugenotten* (Stuttgart: Kohlhammer, 2006).

Dölemeyer, Barbara, 'Rechtliche Aspekte konfessioneller Migration im frühneuzeitlichen Europa am Beispiel der Hugenottenaufnahme', in Joachim Bahlcke (ed.), *Glaubensflüchtlinge. Ursachen, Formen und Auswirkungen frühneuzeitlicher Konfessionsmigration in Europa* (Münster: Lit, 2008).

Dorsi, Pier Paolo, 'Libertà e Legislazione. Il rapporto del barone Pittoni sullo stato della città di Trieste e del suo Territorio (1786)', *Archeografo Triestino*, 49 (1989): 137–85.

Dreyer-Roos, Suzanne, *La population strasbourgeoise sous l'ancien régime* (Strasbourg: Istra, 1969).

Dubost, Jean-François, 'Étrangers en France', in Lucien Bély (ed.), *Dictionnaire de l'ancien régime, royaume de France, XVIe–XVIIIe siècle* (Paris: Presses Universitaires de France, 1996).

Dunn, R.M., 'The London Weavers' Riot of 1675', *Guildhall Studies in London History*, 1 (1973): 13–23.

Duplessis, Robert S., 'Charité municipale et autorité publique au XVIe siècle. L'exemple de Lille', *Revue du Nord*, 59/233 (1977): 193–220.

Duplessis, Robert S., 'The Light Woollens of Tournai in the Sixteenth and Seventeenth Centuries', in E. Aerts and J.H. Munro (eds), *Textiles of the Low Countries in European Economic History* (Leuven, 1990), pp. 66–75.

Duplessis, Robert S., 'One Theory, Two Draperies, Three Provinces, and a Multitude of Fabrics: The New Drapery of French Flanders, Hainaut and Tournaisis, c. 1500–1800', in N.B. Harte (ed.), *The New Draperies in the Low Countries and England, 1300–1800* (Oxford/New York: Oxford University Press, 1997), pp. 130–42.

Ebrard, August, *Christian Ernst von Brandenburg-Baireuth. Die Aufnahme reformirter Flüchtlingsgemeinden in ein lutherisches Land 1686–1712* (Gütersloh: Bertelsmann, 1885).

Eckstein, Nicholas and Nicholas Terpstra (eds), *Sociability and its Discontents: Civil Society, Social Capital, and their Alternatives in Late-Medieval and Early-Modern Europe* (Turnhout: Brepols, 2010).

Ehmer, Josef, 'Worlds of Mobility: Migration Patterns of Viennese Artisans in the 18th century', in Geoffrey Crossick (ed.), *The Artisan and the European Town* (Aldershot: Ashgate, 1997).

Ehmer, Josef and Catharina Lis (eds), *The Idea of Work in Europe from Antiquity to Modern Times* (Farnham: Ashgate, 2009).

Eijl, Corrie van, *Al te goed is buurmans gek. Het Nederlandse vreemdelingenbeleid 1840–1940* (Amsterdam: Aksant, 2005).

Eijl, Corrie van, 'Tracing Back "Illegal Aliens" in the Netherlands, 1850–1940', in Marlou Schrover, Joanne van der Leun, Leo Lucassen and Chris Quispel (eds), *Illegal Migration and Gender in a Global and Historical Perspective* (Amsterdam: Amsterdam University Press, 2008).

Eijl, Corrie van and Leo Lucassen, 'Holland beyond the Borders: Emigration and the Dutch State, 1850–1940', in Nancy L. Green and François Weil (eds), *Citizenship and Those Who Leave: The Politics of Emigration and Expatriation* (Urbana/Chicago: University of Illinois Press, 2007).

Elias, Norbert and John L. Scotson, *The Established and the Outsiders: A Sociological Enquiry into Community Problems* (London: Frank Cass, 1965).

Ennen, Reinald, *Zünfte und Wettbewerb. Möglichkeiten und Grenzen zünftlerischer Wettbewerbsbeschränkungen im städtischen Handel und Gewerbe des Spätmittelalters* (Cologne/Vienna: Böhlau, 1971).

Epstein, Stephan R., 'Craft guilds, Apprenticeship, and Technological Change in Preindustrial Europe', *Journal of Enomonic History*, 58 (1998): 684–713.

Epstein, Stephan R. and Maarten Prak (eds), *Guilds, Innovation, and the European Economy, 1400–1800* (Cambridge: Cambridge University Press, 2008).

Esser, Raingard, *Niederländische Exulanten im England des 16. und frühen 17. Jahrhunderts* (Berlin: Duncker & Humblot, 1996).

Esser, Raingard, '"They obey all magistrates and all good lawes ... and we thinke our cittie happie to enjoye them": Migrants and Urban Stability in Early Modern English Towns', *Urban History*, 34/1 (2007): 64–75.

Evans, Tanya, '*Unfortunate Objects': Lone Mothers in Eighteenth-Century London* (Basingstoke: Palgrave Macmillan, 2005).

Faber, Eva, 'Fremd- und Anderssein im 18. Jahrhundert. Eine Variation zum Thema am Beispiel von Triest', *Das achtzehnte Jahrhundert und Österreich*, 12 (1997): 29–58.

Faber, Eva, 'Il problema della tolleranza religiosa nell'area alto-adriatica nel secondo Settecento', in Filiberto Agostini (ed.), *Veneto, Istria e Dalmazia tra sette e ottocento. Aspetti economici, sociali ed ecclesiastici* (Venice: Marsilio, 1999), pp. 105–23.

Faber, Eva, 'Territorio e amministrazione', in Roberto Finzi, Loredana Panariti and Giovanni Panjek (eds), *Storia economica e sociale di Trieste: La città dei traffici 1719–1918* (Trieste: Lint, 2003), pp. 21–49.

Farge, Arlette, *Délinquance et criminalité. Le vol d'aliments à Paris au XVIIIe siècle* (Paris: Plon, 1974).

Farge, Arlette, 'Le mendiant, un marginal? Les résistances aux archers de l'hôpital dans le Paris du XVIIIe siècle', in *Les marginaux et les exclus dans l'histoire. Cahiers Jussieu* (Paris, UGE, 10/18, 1979): 312–28.

Farge, Arlette and Jacques Revel, *Logiques de la foule. L'affaire des enlèvements d'enfants, Paris 1750* (Paris: Hachette, 1988).

Farr, James R., *Artisans in Europe, 1300–1914* (Cambridge: Cambridge University Press, 2000).

Feldman, David, 'Migrants, Immigrants and Welfare from the Old Poor Law to the Welfare State', *Transactions of the Royal Historical Society*, 13 (2003): 79–104.

Finzi, Roberto, 'Trieste, perché', in Roberto Finzi and Giovanni Panjek (eds), *Storia economica e sociale di Trieste. La Città dei gruppi 1719–1918* (Trieste: Lint, 2001), pp. 13–66.

Fischer, Wolfram, *Handwerksrecht und Handwerkswirtschaft um 1800. Studien zur Sozial- und Wirtschaftsverfassung vor der industriellen Revolution* (Berlin: Duncker & Humblot, 1955).

Fontaine, Laurence, 'Solidarites familiales et logiques migratoires en pays de montagne à l'epoque moderne', *Annales ESC*, 45 (1990): 1433–50.

Fontaine, Laurence, *Histoire du colportage en Europe* (Paris: Albin Michel, 1993).

Fontaine, Laurence, *Pouvoir, identités et migrations dans les hautes vallées des Alpes occidentales (XVIIe–XVIIIe siècles)* (Grenoble: Presses Universitaires de Grenoble, 2003).

François, Étienne, *Protestants et catholiques en Allemagne. Identités et pluralisme. Augsbourg 1648–1806* (Paris: Albin Michel, 1993).

François, Étienne (ed.), *Immigration et société urbaine en Europe occidentale, XVIe–XXe siècle* (Paris: Recherche sur les Civilisations, 1985).

Friedrichs, Christopher R., *The Early Modern City* (London/New York: Longman, 1995).

Frijhoff, W., 'Migrations religieuses dans les Provinces-Unies avant le second Refuge', *Revue du Nord*, 80/326–7 (1998): 573–98.

Fröhlich, Sigrid, *Die Soziale Sicherung bei Zünften und Gesellenverbanden. Darstellung, Analyse, Vergleich* (Berlin: Duncker & Humblot, 1976).

Fumerton, Patricia, *Unsettled: The Culture of Mobility and the Working Poor in Early Modern England* (Chicago: University of Chicago Press, 2006).

Garden, Maurice, 'The Urban Trades: Social Analysis and Representation', in Steve L. Kaplan and Cynthia Koepp (eds), *Work in France: Representations, Meaning, Organization, and Practice* (Ithaca: Cornell University Press, 1986).

Garrioch, David, *Neighbourhood and Community in Paris, 1740–1790* (Cambridge: Cambridge University Press, 1986).

Garrioch, David, 'The People of Paris and their Police in the Eighteenth Century: Reflections on the Introduction of a "Modern" Police Force', *European History Quarterly*, 24 (1994): 511–35.

Garrioch, David, *The Making of Revolutionary Paris* (Berkeley: University of California Press, 2002).

Gay, Jean-Luc, 'L'administration de la capitale entre 1770 et 1789. La tutelle de la royauté et ses limites', *Mémoires de la fédération historique de Paris et de l'Ile-de-France* (1956): 299–370; (1957–1958): 283–363; (1959): 181–247; (1960): 263–403; (1961): 135–218.

Gayot, Gérard and Philippe Minard (eds), *Les ouvriers qualifiés de l'industrie (XVIe–XXe siècle). Formation, emploi, migrations* (Villeneuve d'Ascq: Université Lille 3, 2001).

Gelderblom, Oscar, *Zuid-Nederlandse kooplieden en de opkomst van de Amsterdamse stapelmarkt (1578–1630)* (Hilversum: Verloren, 2000).

Gelderblom, Oscar, 'The Decline of Fairs and Merchant Guilds in the Low Countries, 1250–1650', *Jaarboek voor Middeleeuwse Geschiedenis*, 7 (2004): 199–238.

Geremek, Bronislaw, *La potence ou la pitié. L'Europe et les pauvres du moyen âge à nos jours* (Paris: Gallimard, 1987).

Gestrich, Andreas, Steven King and Lutz Raphael (eds), *Being Poor in Modern Europe* (Bern: Peter Lang, 2006).

Gestrich, Andreas, Lutz Raphael and Herbert Uerlings (eds), *Strangers and Poor People. Changing Patterns of Inclusion and Exclusion in Europe and the Mediterranean World from Classical Antiquity to the Present Day* (Frankfurt am Main: Peter Lang, 2009).

Geudens, E., *Le compte moral de l'an X des hospices civils d'Anvers* (Antwerp: Dela Montagne, 1898).

Gilissen, J. 'Le statut des étrangers en Belgique du XIIIe au XXe siècle', *Recueils de la société Jean Bodin, vol. X* (Paris: Dessain, 1984).

Goosens, Aline, *Les inquisitions modernes dans les Pays-Bas méridionaux 1520–1633* (Brussels: Université de Bruxelles, 1997).

Gorshkow, Boris B., 'Serfs on the Move: Peasant Seasonal Migration in Pre-Reform Russia, 1800–61', *Kritika: Explorations in Russian and Eurasian History*, 1/4 (2000): 627–56.

Green, Nancy L. and François Weil (eds), *Citizenship and Those Who Leave: The Politics of Emigration and Expatriation* (Urbana/Chicago: Illinois University Press, 2007).

Greissler, Paul, *La classe politique dirigeante à Strasbourg, 1650–1750* (Strasbourg: Le Quai, 1987).

Grendi, Edoardo, 'Traffico portuale, naviglio mercantile e consolati genovesi nel Cinquecento', *Rivista storica italiana*, 3 (1968): 593–629.

Grenier, Jean-Yves, *L'économie d'Ancien Régime. Un monde de l'échange et de l'incertitude* (Paris: Albin Michel, 1996).

Grieshammer, Werner, *Studien zur Geschichte der Réfugiés in Brandenburg-Preußen bis 1713* (Berlin: Brandel, 1935).

Groppi, Angela, 'Solidarités familiales et logiques migratoires en pays de montagne à l'époque moderne', *Annales ESC*, 45 (1990): 1433–50.

Groppi, Angela, 'Il diritto del sangue. Le responsabilità familiari nei confronti delle vecchie e delle nuove generazioni (Roma secc. XVIII–XIX)', *Quaderni storici*, 92 (1996): 305–35.

Groppi, Angela, 'Ebrei, donne, soldati e neofiti: l'esercizio del mestiere tra esclusioni e privilegi (Roma XVII–XVIII secolo)', in Alberto Guenzi, Paola Massa and Angelo Moioli (eds), *Corporazioni e gruppi professionali nell'Italia moderna* (Milan: FrancoAngeli, 1999).

Groppi, Angela, 'Old People and the Flow of Resources between Generations in Papal Rome, Sixteenth to Nineteenth Centuries', in Lynn Botelho, Susannah Ottaway and Katharine Kittredge (eds), *Power and Poverty: Old Age in the Pre-Industrial Past* (Westport CT/London: Greenwood Press, 2002).

Groppi, Angela, 'Une ressource légale pour une pratique illégale. Les juifs et les femmes contre la corporation des tailleurs dans la Rome pontificale (XVIIe–XVIIIe siècles)', in Renata Ago (ed.), *The Value of the Norm: Legal Disputes and the Definition of Rights* (Rome: Biblink, 2002).

Groppi, Angela, *Il welfare prima del welfare. Assistenza alla vecchiaia e solidarietà tra generazioni a Roma in età moderna* (Rome: Viella, 2010).

Guignet, Philippe, *Le pouvoir dans la ville au XVIIIe siècle. Pratiques politiques, notabilité et éthique sociale de part et d'autre de la frontière franco-belge* (Paris: EHESS, 1990).

Guignet, Philippe, 'Cours, courées et corons. Contribution à un cadrage lexicographique, typologique et chronologique de types d'habitat collectif emblématiques de la France du Nord', *Revue du Nord*, 90/374 (2008): 29–47.

Gutton, Jean-Pierre, *La societé et les pauvres. L'exemple de la généralité de Lyon, 1534–1789* (Paris: Les Belles Lettres, 1970).

Gutton, Jean-Pierre, *L'état et la mendicité dans la première moitié du XVIIIe siècle. Auvergne, Beaujolais, Forez, Lyonnais* (Lyon: Centre D'Etudes Foreziennes, 1973).

Gutton, Jean-Pierre, *La société et les pauvres en Europe (XVIe–XVIIIe siècles)* (Paris: Presses Universitaires de France, 1974).

Gwynn, Robin D., 'James II in the Light of his Treatment of Huguenot Refugees in England, 1685–1686', *English Historical Review*, 92 (1977): 820–33.

Gwynn, Robin D., *Huguenot Heritage: The History and Contribution of the Huguenots in Britain* (Brighton: Sussex Academic Press, 2001).

Hahn, Sylvia, 'Inclusion and Exclusion of Migrants in the Multicultural Realm of the Habsburg State of Many Peoples', *Histoire sociale/Social History*, 66 (2000): 307–24.

Hahn, Sylvia, 'Migrants and the Poor Law System in Late Habsburg Empire Cities', in Mat Berglund (ed.), *Sakta vi gå genom stan – City Strolls* (Stockholm: Stockholmia förlag, 2005).

Hampson, Ethel M., 'Settlement and Removal in Cambridgeshire, 1662–1834', *Cambridge Historical Journal*, 2/3 (1928): 273–89.

Harte, Negley B. (ed.), *The New Draperies in the Low Countries and England, 1300–1800* (Oxford/New York: Oxford University Press, 1997).

Hartoy, M. de, *Histoire du passeport francais. Depuis l'antiquité jusqu'à nos jours* (Paris: Champion, 1937).

Haupt, Heinz-Gerhard (ed.), *Das Ende der Zünfte. Ein europäischer Vergleich* (Göttingen: Vandenhoeck & Ruprecht, 2002).

Heijden, Manon van der, 'New Perspectives on Public Services in Early Modern Europe', *Journal of Urban History*, 36/3 (2010): pp 269-284.

Hertner, Peter, *Stadtwirtschaft zwischen Reich und Frankreich. Wirtschaft und Gesellschaft Straßburgs 1650–1714* (Cologne/Vienna: Böhlau, 1973).

Herzog, Tamara, *Defining Nations: Immigrants and Citizens in Early Modern Spain and Spanish America* (New Haven CT: Yale University Press, 2003).

Heuer, Jennifer Ngaire, *The Family and the Nation: Gender and Citizenship in Revolutionary France, 1789–1830* (Ithaca/London: Cornell University Press, 2005).

Heusinger, Sabine von, *Die Zunft im Mittelalter. Zur Verflechtung von Politik, Wirtschaft und Gesellschaft in Straßburg* (Stuttgart: Steiner, 2009).

Heussner, Alfred, *Die französische Colonie in Cassel* (Magdeburg: Heinrichshofen, 1903).

Hindle, Steve, *On the Parish: The Micro-Politics of Poor Relief in Rural England, c. 1550–1750* (Oxford: Clarendon Press, 2004).

Hitchcock, Tim, *Down and Out in Eighteenth-Century London* (London: Continuum, 2004).

Hochstadt, Steven, 'Migration in Preindustrial Germany', *Central European History*, 16/3 (1983): 195–224.

Hochstadt, Steven, *Mobility and Modernity: Migration in Germany, 1820–1989* (Ann Arbor: University of Michigan Press, 1999).

Hocquet, Adolphe, *Tournai et le Tournaisis au XVIe siècle, au point de vue politique et social* (Brussels: Hayez, 1906).

Hohenberg, Paul M. and Lynn Hollen Lees, *La formation de l'Europe urbaine 1000–1950* (Paris: Presses Universitaires de France, 1992).

Hollifield, James F., *Immigrants, Markets, and States: The Political Economy of Postwar Europe* (Cambridge MA: Harvard University Press, 1992).

Houtte, Jan Arthur Van, 'Déclin et survivance d'Anvers (1550–1700)', *Studi in Onore di Amintori Fanfani* (6 vols, Milan: Giuffré, 1962).

Houtte, Jan Arthur Van, *Economische geschiedenis van de Lage Landen, 800–1800* (Haarlem: Fibula-Van Dishoeck, 1979).

Hovenden, R., *The Registers of the Wallon or Strangers' Church in Canterbury*, vol. 5/2 (Lymington: Huguenot Society of London, 1894).

Howell, M. and R.S. Duplessis, 'Reconsidering the Early Modern Urban Economy: The Cases of Leiden and Lille', *Past and Present*, 94 (1982): 49–84.

Hufton, Olwen, *The Poor of Eighteenth-Century France* (Oxford: Clarendon Press, 1974).

Imbert, Jean, 'De quelques bourgeoisies voisines. La bourgeoisie lorraine', in *La Bourgeoisie alsacienne. Etudes d'histoire sociale* (Strasbourg/Colmar: F.-X. Le Roux, 1954).

Imbert, Jean, 'Les rapports entre l'aubaine et la bourgeoisie en Lorraine', *Annales de l'Est*, 3 (1952): 349–64.

Innes, Joanna, 'The State and the Poor: Eighteenth-Century England in European Perspective', in John Brewer and Hellmuth Eckhart (eds), *Rethinking Leviathan: The Eighteenth-Century State in Britain and Germany* (Oxford: Oxford University Press, 1999).

Isenmann, Eberhard, 'Bürgerrecht und Bürgeraufnahme in der spätmittelalterlichen und frühneuzeitlichen Stadt', in Rainer C. Schwinges (ed.), *Neubürger im Späten Mittelalter. Migration und Austausch in der Städtelandschaft des alten Reiches (1250–1550)* (Berlin: Duncker & Humblot, 2002).

Jeggle, Christof, 'Nahrung und Markt in Ökonomien städtischer Gewerbe in der Frühen Neuzeit. Methodische Überlegungen am Beispiel des Leinengewerbes in Münster/Westfalen', in Robert Brandt and Thomas Buchner (eds), *Nahrung, Markt oder Gemeinnutz. Werner Sombart und das vorindustrielle Handwerk* (Bielefeld: Verlag für Regionalgeschichte, 2004).

Jersch-Wenzel, Stefi, *Juden und 'Franzosen' in der Wirtschaft des Raumes Berlin/ Brandenburg zur Zeit des Merkantilismus* (Berlin: Colloquium-Verlag, 1978).

Jessenne, Jean-Pierre (ed.), *L'image de l'autre dans l'Europe du Nord-Ouest à travers l'histoire* (Lille: Centre d'Histoire de la Région du Nord et de l'Europe du Nord-Ouest, 1996).

Junot, Yves, 'Mixité sociale, habitat et propriété. La paroisse Saint-Jacques de Valenciennes en 1602 d'après un registre de 100e', *Revue du Nord*, 79/320–21 (1997): 413–27.

Junot, Yves, 'L'aumône générale de Valenciennes (1531–1566). Ordre public, richesse et pauvreté jusqu'à la veille de la Révolte des Pays-Bas', *Revue du Nord*, 82/334 (2000): 53–72.

Junot, Yves, *Les bourgeois de Valenciennes. Anatomie d'une élite dans la ville (1500–1630)* (Villeneuve d'Ascq: Presses Universitaires du Septentrion, 2009).

Jütte, Robert, *Poverty and Deviance in Early Modern Europe* (Cambridge: Cambridge University Press, 1994).

Kadell, Franz-Anton, *Die Hugenotten in Hessen-Kassel* (Darmstadt/Marburg: Hessische Historische Kommission, 1980).

Kalc, Aleksej, 'Tržaško podeželje in policijski red iz leta 1777: Kratek sprehod med črko in stvarnostjo', *Annales. Annals for Istrian and Mediterranean Studies*, 18 (1999): 271–88.

Kalc, Aleksej, *Tržaško prebivalstvo v 18. stoletju: priseljevanje kot gibalo demografske rasti in družbenih sprememb* (Koper: Založba Annales, 2008).

Kaplan, Steven, 'Réflexions sur la police du monde du travail, 1700–1815', *Revue historique*, 261/1 (1979): 17–77.

Kaplan, Steven, *La fin des corporations* (Paris: Fayard, 2001).

Kaplow, Jeffrey, *Les noms des rois. Les pauvres de Paris à la veille de la Révolution* (Paris: Maspero, 1974).

Kint, An, *The Community of Commerce: Social Relations in Sixteenth-Century Antwerp* (PhD dissertation, Columbia University, New York, 1996).

Kint, An, 'Becoming Civic Community. Citizenship in Sixteenth-century Antwerp', in Marc Boone and Maarten Prak (eds), *Individual, Corporate and Judicial Status in European Cities (Late Middle Ages and Early Modern Period)* (Leuven/Apeldoorn: Garant, 1996).

Kinzelbach, Annemarie, *Gesundbleiben, Krankwerden, Armsein in der frühneuzeitlichen Gesellschaft: Gesunde und Kranke in den Reichsstädten Überlingen und Ulm, 1500–1700* (Stuttgart: Steiner, 1995).

Klep, Paul M.M., *Bevolking en arbeid in transformatie. Een onderzoek in Brabant, 1700–1900* (Nijmegen: SUN, 1981).

Klep, Paul M.M., 'Urban Decline in Brabant: The Traditionalization of Investments and Labour (1374–1806)', in Herman van der Wee (ed.), *The Rise and Decline of Urban Industries in Italy and in the Low Countries (Late Middle Ages–Early Modern Times)* (Leuven: Leuven University Press, 1988), pp. 261–86.

Klingebiel, Thomas, *Weserfranzosen. Studien zur Geschichte der Hugenottengemeinschaft in Hameln* (Göttingen: Vandenhoeck & Ruprecht, 1992).

Kloek, Joost and Karin Tilmans (eds), *Burger: Geschiedenis van het begrip van de Middeleeuwen tot eenentwintigste eeuw* (Amsterdam: Amsterdam University Press, 2002).

Kluge, Arndt, *Die Zünfte* (Stuttgart: Steiner, 2007).

Knotter, Ad and Jan Luiten van Zanden, 'Immigratie en arbeidsmarkt in Amsterdam in de 17e eeuw', *Tijdschrift voor sociale geschiedenis*, 13 (1987): 403–31.

Kohnke, Meta, 'Das Edikt von Potsdam. Zu seiner Entstehung, Verbreitung und Überlieferung', *Jahrbuch für Geschichte des Feudalismus*, 9 (1985): 241–75.

Kolchin, Peter, *Unfree Labor: American Slavery and Russian Serfdom* (Cambridge MA: Harvard University Press, 1987).

Kölle, Adolf, 'Ursprung und Entwicklung der Vermögenssteuer in Ulm', *Württembergische Vierteljahrshefte für Landesgeschichte*, 7 (1989): 1–24.

Kuijpers, Erika, *Migrantenstad. Immigratie en sociale verhoudingen in zeventiende-eeuws Amsterdam* (Hilversum: Verloren, 2005).

Kuijpers, Erika and Maarten Prak, 'Burger, ingezetene, vreemdeling. Burgerschap in Amsterdam in de 17e en 18e eeuw', Joost Kloek and Karin Tilmans (eds), *Burger: Geschiedenis van het begrip van de Middeleeuwen tot eenentwintigste eeuw* (Amsterdam: Amsterdam University Press, 2002).

Kuijpers, Erika and Maarten Prak, 'Gevestigden en buitenstaanders', in W. Frijhoff and M. Prak (eds), *Geschiedenis van Amsterdam, vol. II–1: Centrum van de Wereld, 1578–1650* (Amsterdam: SUN, 2004).

Laffont, Jean-Luc, *Policer la ville. Toulouse, capitale provinciale au siècle des Lumières* (PhD dissertation, University of Toulouse II Le Mirail, 1997).

Lameere, Jules and Henri Simont, *Recueils des ordonnances de Pays-Bas* (5 vols, Brussels: Goemare, 1910).

Lanaro, Paola, 'Economia cittadina, flussi migratori e spazio urbano in Terraferma veneta tra basso Medioevo ed età moderna', in Donatella Calabi and Paola Lanaro (eds), *La città italiana e i luoghi degli stranieri (XIV–XVIII secolo)* (Rome: Laterza, 1998), pp. 63–81.

Leenders, Marij, *Ongenode gasten. Van traditioneel asielrecht naar immigratiebeleid, 1815–1938* (Hilversum: Verloren, 1993).

Lees, Lynn Hollen, *The Solidarities of Strangers: The English Poor Laws and the People, 1700–1948* (Cambridge: Cambridge University Press, 1998).

Leeuwen, Marco H.D. van, *Bijstand in Amsterdam, ca 1800–1850. Armenzorg als beheersings- en overlevingsstrategie* (Zwolle/Amsterdam: Waanders, 1992).

Leeuwen, Marco H.D. van, 'Logic of Charity: Poor Relief in Preindustrial Europe', *Journal of Interdisciplinary History*, 24/4 (1994): 589–613.

Leeuwen, Marco H.D. van, 'Amsterdam en de armenzorg tijdens de republiek', *NEHA Jaarboek*, 59 (1996): 132–61.

Leeuwen, Marco H.D. van, *The Logic of Charity: Amsterdam, 1800–1850* (London/New York: Macmillan, 2000).

Leeuwen, Marco H.D. van, 'Migrants' Entitlements to Poor Relief in the Netherlands, 16th–20th Centuries', paper presented at the workshop 'Migrants, Entitlements and Welfare, 1500–2000: Comparative Perspectives', Brussels, 6–7 September 2010.

Leeuwen, Marco H.D. van and J.E. Oeppen, 'Reconstructing the Demographic Regime of Amsterdam 1681–1920', *Economic and Social History in the Netherlands*, 5 (1993): 61–104.

Lepetit, Bernard, 'La population urbaine', in Jacques Dupâquier (ed.), *Histoire de la population française, vol. 2. De la Renaissance à 1789* (Paris: Presses Universitaires de France, 1988): 81–93.

Lepetit, Bernard, 'Proposition et avertissement', in Jacques Bottin and Donatella Calabi (eds), *Les étrangers dans la ville. Minorités et espace urbain du bas Moyen âge à l'époque moderne* (Paris: Maison des Sciences de l'Homme, 1999), pp. 1–15.

Lesger, Clé, 'De wereld als horizon. De economie tussen 1578 en 1650', in W. Frijhoff and M. Prak (eds), *Geschiedenis van Amsterdam, vol. II–1: Centrum van de Wereld, 1578–1650* (Amsterdam: SUN, 2004), pp. 103–88.

Lesger, Clé, 'Migratiestromen en economische ontwikkeling in vroegmoderne steden. Nieuwe burgers in Antwerpen en Amsterdam, 1541–1655', *Stadsgeschiedenis*, 1 (2006): 97–121.

Levi, Giovanni, *Inheriting Power: The Story of an Exorcist* (Chicago: University of Chicago Press, 1988).

Lévy-Coblentz, Françoise, *L'art du meuble en Alsace au siècle des Lumières, vol. 2. De la paix de Ryswick à la Révolution (1698–1789)* (Saint-Dié: Le Chardon, 1985).

Lindemann, Mary, *Patriots and Paupers: Hamburg, 1712–1830* (Oxford: Oxford University Press, 1990).

Linden, Marcel van der, 'The National Integration of European Working Classes (1871–1914): Exploring the Causal Configuration', *International Review of Social History*, 33 (1988): 285–311.

Linden, Marcel van der (ed.), *Social Security Mutualism: The Comparative History of Mutual Benefit Societies* (Bern: Peter Lang, 1996).

Lindert, Peter H., *Growing Public. Social Spending and Economic Growth since the Eighteenth Century* (Cambridge: Cambridge University Press, 2004).

Linebaugh, Peter and Marcus Rediker, *The Many-Headed Hydra: The Hidden History of the Revolutionary Atlantic* (Boston MA: Beacon Press, 2000).

Lipson, Ephraim, *The Economic History of England* (vol. 3, London: Black, 1956).

Lis, Catharina, 'Sociale politiek in Antwerpen, 1779. Het controleren van de relatieve overbevolking en het reguleren van de arbeidsmarkt', *Tijdschrift voor sociale geschiedenis*, 2 (1976): 146–166.

Lis, Catharina, *Social Change and the Labouring Poor: Antwerp, 1770–1860* (New Haven CT: Yale University Press, 1986).

Lis, Catharina and Hugo Soly, *Poverty and Capitalism in Pre-Industrial Europe* (Brighton: Harvester Press, 1979).

Lis, Catharina and Hugo Soly, 'Policing the Early Modern Proletariat, 1450–1850', in David Levine (ed.), *Proletarianization and Family History* (Orlando: Academic Press, 1984).

Lis, Catharina and Hugo Soly, 'Living Apart Together: overheid en ondernemers in Brabant en Vlaanderen tijdens de tweede helft van de 18de eeuw', in Jan Craeybeckx and Etienne Scholliers, *Arbeid in Veelvoud. Een huldeboek voor Jan Craeybeckx en Etienne Scholliers* (Brussels: VUB Press, 1988).

Lis, Catharina and Hugo Soly, 'Corporatisme, onderaanneming en loonarbeid. Flexibilisering en deregulering van de arbeidsmarkt in Westeuropese steden (veertiende-achttiende eeuw)', *Tijdschrift voor sociale geschiedenis*, 20 (1994): 365–90.

Lis, Catharine and Hugo Soly, '"An Irresistible Phalanx": Journeymen Associations in Western Europe, 1300–1800', in Catharina Lis et al. (eds), *Before the Unions: Wage Earners and Collective Action in Europe, 1300–1850* (Cambridge: Cambridge University Press, 1994).

Lis, Catharina and Hugo Soly, 'Craft Guilds in Comparative Perspective: The Northern and Southern Netherlands, a Survey', in Maarten Prak et al. (eds), *Craft Guilds in the Early Modern Low Countries: Work, Power and Representation* (Aldershot: Ashgate, 2006).

Lis, Catharina and Hugo Soly, 'Export Industries, Craft Guilds and Capitalist Trajectories, 13th to 18th Centuries', in Maarten Prak et al. (eds), *Craft Guilds in the Early Modern Low Countries: Work, Power and Representation* (Aldershot: Ashgate, 2006).

Lis, Catharina and Hugo Soly, 'Subcontracting in Guild-Based Export Trades, 13th–18th Centuries', Stephan R. Epstein and Maarten Prak (eds), *Guilds, Innovation, and the European economy, 1400–1800* (Cambridge: Cambridge University Press, 2008).

Lis, Catharina, Dirk Van Damme and Hugo Soly, *Op vrije voeten. Sociale politiek in West-Europa (1450-1914)* (Leuven: Kritak, 1985).

Livet, Georges 'Une page d'histoire sociale: Les Savoyards à Strasbourg au début du XVIIIe siècle', *Cahiers d'histoire*, 4 (1959): 131–45.

Livet, Georges, 'La monarchie absolue et la bourgeoisie Alsacienne. D'après les fonds notariaux et les registres des Magistrats', in *La Bourgeoisie alsacienne. Etudes d'histoire sociale* (Strasbourg/Colmar: F.-X. Le Roux, 1954): 495–9.

Livet, Georges, 'Une enquête à ouvrir: Justice, police et délinquance dans les villes d'Alsace sous l'Ancien Régime', *Annales de l'Est*, 48 (1998): 361–81.

Longé, Gérard De, *Recueil des anciennes coutumes de Belgique. Coutumes du pays et duché de Brabant. Quartier d'Anvers* (4 vols, Brussels: Gobbaerts, 1870–1874).

Lottin, Alain, *Chavatte, ouvrier lillois. Un contemporain de Louis XIV* (Paris: Flammarion, 1979).

Lottin, Alain, *Lille, citadelle de la Contre-Réforme?* (Dunkerque: Westhoek-Editions/Editions des Beffrois, 1984).

Lottum, Jelle van, *Across the North Sea: The Impact of the Dutch Republic on International Labour Migration, c. 1550–1850* (Amsterdam: Aksant, 2007).

Lottum, Jelle van, 'Labour Migration and Economic Performance: London and the Randstad, c. 1600–1800', *Economic History Review*, 64/2 (2011): 531–70.

Lourens, Piet and Jan Lucassen, '"Zunftlandschaften" in den Niederlanden um im benachbarten Deutschland', in W. Reininghaus (ed.), *Zunftlandschaften in Deutschland und den Niederlanden im Vergleich* (Münster: Aschendorff, 2000).

Lucassen, Jan, *Migrant Labour in Europe 1600–1900: The Drift to the North Sea* (London: Croom Helm, 1987).

Lucassen, Jan, *Immigranten in Holland 1600–1800. Een kwantitatieve benadering* (Amsterdam: Centrum voor de Geschiedenis van Migranten, Working Paper 3, 2002).

Lucassen, Jan and Leo Lucassen (eds), *Migration, Migration History, History: Old Paradigms and New Perspectives* (Bern: Peter Lang, 1999).

Lucassen, Jan and Leo Lucassen, 'The Mobility Transition Revisited, 1500–1900: What the Case of Europe Can Offer to Global History', *Journal of Global History*, 4/3 (2009): 347–77.

Lucassen, Jan and Leo Lucassen, *The Mobility Transition in Europe Revisited, 1500–1900: Sources and Methods* (Amsterdam: International Institute of Social History, Research Paper 44, 2010).

Lucassen, Jan and Leo Lucassen, 'The Netherlands', in Klaus J. Bade, Pieter C. Emmer, Leo Lucassen and Jochen Oltmer (eds), *The Encyclopedia of Migration and Minorities in Europe* (New York: Cambridge University Press, forthcoming).

Lucassen, Jan, Tine de Moor and Jan Luiten van Zanden (eds), *The Return of the Guilds* (Cambridge: Cambridge University Press, 2008).

Lucassen, Leo, 'A Blind Spot – Migratory and Travelling Groups in Western European Historiography', *International Review of Social History*, 38/2 (1993): 209–35.

Lucassen, Leo, *Zigeuner. Die Geschichte eines polizeilichen Ordnungsbegriffes in Deutschland 1700–1945* (Cologne: Böhlau, 1996).

Lucassen, Leo, 'The Great War and the origins of migration control in Western Europe and the United States (1880–1920)', in A. Böcker, K. Groenendijk, T. Havinga and P. Minderhoud (eds), *Regulation of Migration: International Experiences* (Amsterdam: Spinhuis, 1998).

Lucassen, Leo, 'A Many-Headed Monster: The Evolution of the Passport System in the Netherlands and Germany in the Long Nineteenth Century', in J. Caplan and J. Torpey (eds), *Documenting Individual Identity: The Development of State Practices in the Modern World* (Princeton/Oxford: Princeton University Press, 2001).

Lucassen, Leo, 'Administrative into Social Control: The Aliens Police and Foreign Female Servants in the Netherlands, 1918–1940', *Social History*, 27/3 (2002): 327–42.

Lucassen, Leo, 'Bringing Structure Back In. Economic and Political Determinants of Immigration in Dutch Cities, 1920–1940', *Social Science History*, 26/3 (2002): 503–29.

Lucassen, Leo, *The Immigrant Threat: The Integration of Old and New Migrants in Western Europe since 1850* (Urbana/Chicago: University of Illinois Press, 2005).

Lucassen, Leo, 'Gelijkheid en onbehagen. De wortels van het integratiedebat in West-Europa', in Leo Lucassen and Wim Willems (eds), *Gelijkheid en onbehagen. Over steden, nieuwkomers en nationaal geheugenverlies* (Amsterdam: Bakker, 2006).

Lucassen, Leo, 'Between Hobbes and Locke. Gypsies and the Limits of the Modernization Paradigm', *Social History*, 44/4 (2008): 423–41.

Lucassen, Leo and Boudien de Vries, 'The Rise and Fall of a Western European Textile-Worker Migration System: Leiden, 1586–1700', in G. Gayot and P. Minard (eds), *Les ouvriers qualifiés de l'industrie (XVIe–XXe siècle). Formation, emploi, migrations* (Lille: Université Charles de Gaulle, 2001), pp. 23–42 (Revue du Nord 15, hors série).

Lucassen, Leo, David Feldman and Jochen Oltmer, 'Drawing Up the Balance Sheet', in Leo Lucassen, David Feldman and Jochen Oltmer (eds), *Paths of Integration. Migrants in Western Europe (1880–2004)* (Amsterdam: Amsterdam University Press: 2006).

Luu, Lien Bich, *Immigrants and the Industries of London, 1500–1700* (Aldershot: Ashgate, 2005).

Lynch, Katherine A., *Individuals, Families, and Communities in Europe, 1200–1800: The Urban Foundations of Western Society* (Cambridge: Cambridge University Press, 2003).

Lynch, Katherine A., 'Behavioral Regulation in the City: Families, Religious Associations, and the Role of Poor Relief', in Herman Roodenburg and Pieter Spierenburg (eds), *Social Control in Europe, Vol. 1: 1500–1800* (Columbus: Ohio State University Press, 2004).

Maeder, Adolf, *Notice historique sur la paroisse réformée de Strasbourg et recueil de pièces probantes* (Paris/Strasbourg: Berger-Levrault and Treuttel & Würtz, 1885, 2nd edn).

Manning, Patrick, 'Cross-Community Migration: A Distinctive Human Pattern', *Social Evolution and History*, 5/2 (2006): 24–54.

Marin, Brigitte, 'Compétences territoriales et transformations urbaines à Naples au XVIIIe siècle: la nouvelle *strada della marina* entre volonté monarchique et prérogatives municipales', *Pouvoirs publics (état, administration) et ville en France, Italie, et Espagne de la fin du XVIIe siècle à la fin du XVIIIe siècle, LIAME* 5 (January–June, 2000): 83–98.

Marin, Brigitte, 'Administrations policières, réformes et découpages territoriaux (XVII–XIXe siècle)', *Police et contrôle du territoire dans les villes capitales (XVIIe–XIXe siècle), MEFRIM*, 115/2 (2003): 745–50.

Marnef, Guido, *Antwerpen in de tijd van de Reformatie. Ondergronds protestantisme in een handelsmetropool 1550–1577* (Antwerp: Kritak, 1996).

Martin, L., 'The Rise of the New Draperies in Norwich, 1550–1622', in N.B. Harte (ed.), *The New Draperies in the Low Countries and England, 1300–1800* (Oxford/New York: Oxford University Press, 1997), pp. 245–74.

Maurer, Michael, 'Mit Ausländern Staat machen? Glaubensflüchtlinge im Absolutismus', *Essener Unikate*, 6/7 (1995): 74–85.

Meershoek, Guus, *Dienaren van het gezag: De Amsterdamse politie tijdens de bezetting.* (Amsterdam: Van Gennep, 1999).

Meester, Jan De, 'De gebruiks- en meerwaarde van poortersboeken voor historici. Casus: Antwerpen in de zestiende eeuw (vervolg)', *Vlaamse Stam*, 43/4 (2007): 317–31.

Meester, Jan De, 'Hulp vanuit onverwachte hoek: De inschrijvingslijsten van de Antwerpse droogscheerders-leerlingen als genealogische bron. Deel 1', *Vlaamse Stam*, 44/4 (2008): 233–61.

Meester, Jan De, 'Arbeidsmigratie vanuit westelijk Noord-Brabant naar Antwerpen in de zestiende eeuw', *Jaarboek De Ghulden Roos*, 68 (2009): 138–76.

Meier, Ulrich, 'Gemeinnutz und Vaterlandsliebe. Kontroversen über die normativen Grundlagen des Bürgerbegriffs im späten Mittelalter', in Rainer C. Schwinges (ed.), *Neubürger im Späten Mittelalter. Migration und Austausch in der Städtelandschaft des alten Reiches (1250–1550)* (Berlin: Duncker & Humblot, 2002).

Menjot, Denis and Jean-Luc Pinol (eds), *Les immigrants et la ville. Insertion, intégration, discrimination (XIIe–XXe siècles)* (Paris: l'Harmattan, 1996).

Meumann, Markus and Ralf Pröve, 'Die Faszination des Staates und die historische Praxis. Zur Beschreibung von Herrschaftsbeziehungen jenseits von teleologischen und dualistischen Begriffsbildungen', in Markus Meumann and Ralf Pröve (eds), *Herrschaft in der Frühen Neuzeit. Umrisse eines dynamisch-kommunikativen Prozesses* (Münster: Lit, 2004), pp. 11–49.

Milliot, Vincent, 'La surveillance des migrants et des lieux d'accueil à Paris du XVIe siècle aux années 1830', in Daniel Roche (ed.), *La ville promise. Mobilité et accueil à Paris (fin XVIIe–debut XIXe siècle)* (Paris: Fayard, 2000), pp. 21–76.

Milliot Vincent, *Un policier des Lumières, suivi de Mémoires de J.C.P. Lenoir, ancien lieutenant general de police de Paris écrits dans les pays étrangers dans les années 1790 et suivantes* (Seyssel, Les classiques, Champ Vallon, 2011).

Milliot, Vincent, 'Saisir l'espace urbain: la mobilité des commissaires au Châtelet et le contrôle des quartiers de police parisiens au 18e siècle', *Revue d'Histoire Moderne et Contemporaine*, 50/1 (2003): 54–80.

Milliot, Vincent (ed.), *Les mémoires policiers, 1750–1850. Écritures et pratiques policières du siècle des Lumières au Second Empire* (Rennes: Presses Universitaires de Rennes, 2006).

Moch, Leslie Page, *Moving Europeans: Migration in Western Europe since 1650* (Bloomington: Indiana University Press, 2nd edn, 2003).

Mogk, Walter, 'Voraussetzungen für die Einwanderung von Hugenotten und Waldensern nach Hessen-Kassel', in Jochen Desel and Walter Mogk (eds), *Die Hugenotten und Waldenser in Hessen-Kassel* (Kassel: Evangelischer Presseverband Kurhessen-Waldeck, 1978).

Mollwo, Carl (ed.), *Das rote Buch der Stadt Ulm* (Stuttgart: K. Kohlhammer, 1905).

Montanelli, Pietro, *Il movimento storico della popolazione di Trieste* (Trieste: Stabilimento Tipografico Giovanni Balestra, 1905).

Moon, David, 'Peasant Migration, the Abolition of Serfdom, and the Internal Passport System in the Russian Empire, c. 1800–1914', in David Eltis (ed.), *Coerced and Free Migration: Global Perspectives* (Stanford: Stanford University Press, 2007).

Morgan, Gwenda and Peter Rushton, *Eighteenth-Century Criminal Transportation: The Formation of the Criminal Atlantic* (Basingstoke: Palgrave Macmillan, 2004).

Morieux, Renaud, *Une mer pour deux royaumes. La Manche, frontière franco-anglaise (XVIIe–XVIIIe siècles)* (Rennes: Presses Universitaires de Rennes, 2008).

Munck, Bert De, *Technologies of Learning: Apprenticeship in Antwerp from the 15th Century to the End of the Ancien Régime* (Turnhout: Brepols, 2007).

Munck, Bert De, 'Construction and Reproduction: The Training and Skills of Antwerp Cabinetmakers in the Sixteenth and Seventeenth Centuries', in Bert De Munck, Steven L. Kaplan and Hugo Soly (eds), *Learning on the Shop Floor: Historical Perspectives on Apprenticeship* (New York/Oxford: Berghahn Books, 2007).

Munck, Bert De, 'Skills, Trust, and Changing Consumer Preferences: The Decline of Antwerp's Craft Guilds from the Perspective of the Product Market, c. 1500–c. 1800', *International Review of Social History*, 53 (2008): 197–233.

Munck, Bert De, 'Fiscalizing Solidarity (from Below): Poor Relief in Antwerp Guilds between Community Building and Public Service', in Manon van der Heijden, Elise van Nederveen Meerkerk, Griet Vermeesch and Martijn van der Burg (eds), *Serving the Urban Community: Public Facilities in Early Modern Towns of the Low Countries* (Amsterdam: Aksant, 2009).

Munck, Bert De, 'One Counter and Your Own Account: Redefining Illicit Labour in Early Modern Antwerp', *Urban History*, 37/1 (2010): 26–44.

Munck, Bert De, Piet Lourens and Jan Lucassen, 'The Establishment and Distribution of Craft Guilds in the Low Countries, 1000–1800', in Maarten Prak et al. (eds), *Craft Guilds in the Early Modern Low Countries: Work, Power and Representation* (Aldershot: Ashgate, 2006).

Naujoks, Eberhard, 'Ulm's Sozialpolitik im 16. Jahrhundert', *Ulm und Oberschwaben*, 33 (1953): 88–98.

Nave De, Francine, 'De oudste Antwerpse lijsten van nieuwe poorters (28 januari 1390–28 december 1414)', *Handelingen van de Koninklijke Commissie voor Geschiedenis*, 134 (1973): 67–309.

Nederveen Meerkerk, Elise van, 'Werkgelegenheid, opleiding en onderstand. De economische aantrekkingskracht van vroegmoderne steden', in Leo Lucassen and Wim Willems (eds), *Waarom mensen in de stad willen wonen, 1200–2010* (Amsterdam: Bert Bakker, 2009), pp. 103–23.

Nederveen Meerkerk, Elise van and Griet Vermeesch, 'Reforming Outdoor Relief. Changes in Urban Provisions for the Poor in the Northern and Southern Low Countries (c. 1500–1800)', in Manon van der Heijden,

Elise Nederveen Meerkerk, Griet Vermeesch and Martijn van der Burg (eds), *Serving the Urban Community: The Rise of Public Facilities in the Low Countries* (Amsterdam: Aksant, 2009).

Nieuwehuizen, Jan van den, 'Bestuursinstellingen van de stad Antwerpen (12de eeuw–1795)', in Raymond Van Uytven, Claude Bruneel and Herman Coppens (eds), *De gewestelijke en lokale instellingen in Brabant en Mechelen tot 1795* (Brussels: Algemeen Rijksarchief, 2000).

Niggemann, Ulrich, 'Huguenot Attitudes to Church Administration in Brandenburg-Prussia and Hesse-Kassel', *Proceedings of the Huguenot Society of Great Britain and Ireland*, 29 (2008): 93–104.

Niggemann, Ulrich, *Immigrationspolitik zwischen Konflikt und Konsens. Die Hugenottenansiedlung in Deutschland und England (1681–1697)* (Cologne/Weimar/Vienna: Böhlau, 2008).

Niggemann, Ulrich, '"Peuplierung" als merkantilistisches Instrument. Privilegierung von Immigranten und staatlich gelenkte Ansiedlungen', in Klaus J. Bade and Jochen Oltmer (eds), *Handbuch Staat und Migration in Deutschland seit dem 17. Jahrhundert* (Paderborn: Schöningh, forthcoming).

Nivet, Stéphane, *La police de Lyon au XVIIIe siècle. L'exemple de la police consulaire puis municipale* (Mémoire de DEA, Université Jean Moulin Lyon 3, 2003).

Noiriel, Gérard, *Le creuset français. Histoire de l'immigration, XIXe–XXe siècles* (Paris: Seuil, 1988).

Noiriel, Gérard, *La tyrannie du national. Le droit d'asile en Europe (1793–1993)* (Paris: Calmann-Lévy, 1991).

Noiriel, Gérard, 'Les pratiques policières d'identification des migrants et leurs enjeux pour l'histoire des relations de pouvoir. Contribution à une réflexion en longue durée', in M.C. Blanc-Chaléard et al. (eds), *Police et migrants, France 1667–1939* (Paris: Presses Universitaires de France, 2001).

Nooney, M.A., 'The Cant Dictionary of Bampfylde-Moore Carew: A Study of the Contents and Changes in Various Editions' (MA dissertation, University of Florida, 1969).

Nooyens, F. J., 'De borgbrieven', *Ons Heem*, 3 (1947): 141–4.

O'Reilly, William, 'The Naturalization Act of 1709 and the Settlement of Germans in Britain, Ireland and the Colonies', in Randolph Vigne and Charles Littleton (eds), *From Strangers to Citizens: The Integration of Immigrant Communities in Britain, Ireland and Colonial America, 1550–1750* (Brighton/Portland OR: Sussex Academic Press, 2001), pp. 492–502.

Odé, Arend W., *Migrant Workers in the Dutch Labour Market Today* (Amsterdam: Thesis Publishers, 1996).

Oltmer, Jochen, '"To Live as Germans among Germans": Immigration and Integration of "Ethnic Germans" in the German Empire and the Weimar Republic', in L. Lucassen, D. Feldman and J. Oltmer (eds.), *Paths of Integration: Migrants in Western Europe (1880–2004)* (Amsterdam: Amsterdam University Press, 2006), pp. 98–115.

Pais-Minne, Eva, 'Weldadigheidsinstellingen en sociale toestanden', in *Antwerpen in de achttiende eeuw. Instellingen, economie, cultuur* (Antwerp: De Sikkel, 1952), pp. 156–86.

Pallach, Ulrich-Christian, 'Fonctions de la mobilité artisanale et ouvrière. Compagnons, ouvriers et manufacturiers en France et aux Allemagnes (17e–19e siècles)', *Francia*, 11 (1983): 365–406.

Panariti, Loredana, 'Il dannato commercio. Trieste nel XVIII secolo', *Metodi e ricerche*, 2 (1998): 111–27.

Parker, G., 'Recrutement' and 'Désobéissance', in P. Janssens (ed.), *La Belgique espagnole 1585–1715, vol. 1. La politique* (Brussels, 2006), pp. 55–60, 65–6.

Patriquin, Larry, *Agrarian Capitalism and Poor Relief in England, 1500–1860: Rethinking the Origins of the Welfare State* (Basingstoke: Palgrave Macmillan, 2007).

Paugam, Serge, 'La pauvreté en Europe, entre statut transitoire et destin social', in Louis Maurin and Patrick Savidan (eds), *L'état des inégalités en France* (Paris: Belin, 2006), pp. 155–61.

Pelus-Kaplan, Marie-Louise, 'Travail, immigration et citoyenneté dans les villes hanséatiques, aux XVIe–XVIIe siècles, d'après les exemples de Lübeck, Hambourg et Danzig', in Pilar Gonzalez-Bernaldo, Manuela Martini and Marie-Louise Pelus-Kaplan (eds), *Etrangers et societies. Représentations, coexistences, interactions dans la longue durée* (Rennes: Presses Universitaires de Rennes, 2008).

Pelzer, Erich, *Der elsässische Adel im Spätfeudalismus. Tradition und Wandel einer regionalen Elite zwischen dem westfälischen Frieden und der Revolution (1648–1790)* (Munich: Oldenbourg, 1990).

Peveri, Patrice, 'L'exempt, l'archer, la mouche et le filou. Délinquance policière et contrôle des agents dans le Paris de la Régence', in Laurent Feller (ed.), *Contrôler les agents du pouvoir* (Limoges: Pulim, 2004), pp. 245–72.

Pfister, Christian, 'L'Alsace et l'Édit de Nantes', *Revue historique*, 160 (1929): 217–40.

Pfister, Christian, 'The Population of Late Medieval and Early Modern Europe', in Bob Scribner (ed.), *Germany: A New Social and Economic History, 1450–1630* (London: Arnold, 1996), pp. 55–8.

Piasenza, Paolo, 'Juges, lieutenants de police et bourgeois à Paris aux XVII et XVIIIe siècle', *Annales ESC*, 4 (1990): 1189–215.

Pinol Jean-Luc (ed.), *Histoire de l'Europe urbaine. De l'Antiquité au XVIIIe siècle* (Paris: Seuil, 2003).

Pirenne, Henri, *Early Democracies in the Low Countries: Urban Society and Political Conflict in the Middle Ages and the Renaissance* (New York: Harper & Row, 1963).

Plummer, Alfred, *The London Weavers' Company, 1600–1970* (London/Boston MA: Routledge & Kegan Paul, 1972).

Pol, Lotte van de and Erika Kuijpers, 'Poor Women's Migration to the City: The Attraction of Amsterdam Health Care and Social Assistance in Early Modern Times', *Journal of Urban History*, 32/1 (2005): 44–60.

Polaczek, Ernst, 'Das Handwerk der französischen Schreiner der Stadt Strassburg', *Elsässische Monatsschrift für Geschichte und Volkskunde*, 1 (1910): 321–30.

Poleggi, Ennio, 'La topografia degli stranieri nella Genova di antico regime', in Donatella Calabi and Paola Lanaro (eds), *La città italiana e i luoghi degli stranieri (XIV–XVIII secolo)* (Rome: Laterza, 1998), pp. 108–20.

Pool, Cathelijne, 'Open Borders: Unrestricted Migration? The Situation of the Poles with a German Passport in the Netherlands as an Example of Migration after Accession to the European Union', in Anita Böcker, Betty de Hart and Ines Michalowski (eds), *Migration and the Regulation of Social Integration* (Osnabrück: IMIS Beiträge 24, 2004), pp. 203–12.

Poole, Reginald L., *A History of the Huguenots of the Dispersion at the Recall of the Edict of Nantes* (London: Macmillan, 1880).

Prak, Maarten, 'Burghers into Citizens: Urban and National Citizenship in the Netherlands during the Revolutionary Era (c. 1800), *Theory and Society*, 26 (1997): 403–20.

Prak, Maarten, *Republikeinse veelheid, democratisch enkelvoud. Sociale verandering in het revolutietijdvak. 's-Hertogenbosch 1770–1820* (Nijmegen: SUN, 1999).

Prak, Maarten, Catharina Lis, Jan Lucassen and Hugo Soly (eds), *Craft Guilds in the Early Modern Low Countries: Work, Power and Representation* (Aldershot: Ashgate, 2006).

Prims, Floris, *Geschiedenis van Antwerpen* (22 vols, Antwerp: Standaard, 1938–1946).

Prims, Floris, *Het herfsttij van het corporatisme* (Antwerp: Standaard, 1945).

Pult Quaglia, Anna Maria, 'Citizenship in Medieval and Early Modern Italian Cities', in Stephan G. Ellis, Gudmundur Hálfdanarson and Ann Katherine Isaacs (eds), *Citizenship in Historical Perspective* (Pisa: Pisa University Press, 2006).

Racine, Pierre, 'La citoyenneté en Italie au moyen âge', *Le moyen âge*, 115/1 (2009): 87–108.

Raphaël, Freddy and Robert Weyl, *Regards nouveaux sur les juifs d'Alsace* (Strasbourg: Istra and Editions des Dernières Nouvelles d'Alsace, 1980).

Reininghaus, Wilfried, *Zünfte, Städte und Staat in der Grafschaft Mark. Einleitung und Regesten von Texten des 14. bis 19. Jahrhunderts* (Münster: Aschendorff, 1989).

Reinke, Andreas, 'Die Kehrseite der Privilegierung: Proteste und Widerstände gegen die hugenottische Niederlassung in den deutschen Territorialstaaten', *Comparativ*, 7 (1997): 39–52.

Renouard, Xavier, *L'assistance publique à Lille de 1527 à l'an VIII* (Lille: C. Robbe, 1912).

Roche, Daniel (ed.), *La ville promise. Mobilité et accueil à Paris (fin XVIIe–debut XIXe siècle)* (Paris: Fayard, 2000).

Roche, Daniel, *Humeurs vagabondes. De la circulation des hommes et de l'utilité des voyages* (Paris: Fayard, 2003).

Roes, Maria B., 'Unwanted Travellers: The Tightening of City Borders in Early Modern Germany', in Thomas Betteridge (ed.), *Borders and Travellers in Early Modern Europe* (Aldershot: Ashgate, 2007), pp. 87–112.

Roey, Jan Van, *De sociale structuur en de godsdienstige gezindheid van de Antwerpse bevolking op de vooravond van de Reconciliatie met Farnèse (17 augustus 1585)* (PhD dissertation, University of Ghent, 1963).

Roey, Jan Van, 'De bevolking' in *Antwerpen in de XVIde eeuw* (Antwerp: Mercurius, 1975).

Roitman, Jessica V., *Us and Them: Inter-Cultural Trade and the Sephardim, 1595–1640* (PhD dissertation, University of Leiden, 2009).

Romon, Christian, 'Mendiants et policiers à Paris au XVIIIe siècle', *Histoire économie et société*, 2 (1982): 259–95.

Romon, Christian, 'L'affaire des enlèvements d'enfants dans les archives du Châtelet (1749–1750)', *Revue historique*, 3 (1983): 55–95.

Rosenberg, Clifford, *Policing Paris: The Origins of Modern Immigration Control between the Wars* (Ithaca/London: Cornell University Press, 2006).

Rossetti, Gabriella, 'Le élites mercantili nell'Europa dei secoli XII–XVI. Loro cultura e radicamento', in Gabriella Rossetti (ed.), *Dentro la città. Stranieri e realtà urbane nell'Europa dei secoli XII – XVI* (Naples: Liguori, 1999).

Rothe, Kurt, *Das Finanzwesen der Reichsstadt Ulm im 18. Jahrhundert* (Stuttgart: Kommissionsverlag W. Kohlhammer, 1991).

Rousseaux, Xavier, 'L'incrimination du vagabondage en Brabant (14e–18e siècles). Langages du droit et réalités de pratique', in G. Van Dievoet, P.

Godding and D. Van Den Auweele (eds), *Langage et droit à travers l'histoire. Réalités et fictions* (Leuven/Paris: Peeters, 1989).

Sabean, David, *Power in the Blood: Popular Culture and Village Discourse in Early Modern Germany* (Cambridge: Cambridge University Press, 1984).

Sachsse, Christoph and Floran Tennstedt, *Geschichte der Armenfürsorge in Deutschland: vom Spätmittelalter bis zum Ersten Weltkrieg* (Stuttgart: W. Kohlhammer, 1980).

Sahlins, Peter, *Unnaturally French: Foreign Citizens in the Old Regime and After* (Ithaca/London: Cornell University Press, 2004).

Sassier, Philippe, *Du bon usage des pauvres. Histoire d'un thème politique (XVIe–XXe siècles)* (Paris: Fayard, 1990).

Schanz, Georg, *Zur Geschichte der Colonisation und Industrie in Franken* (Erlangen: Deichert, 1884).

Schaser, Angelika, 'Städtische Fremdenpolitik im Deutschland der Frühen Neuzeit', in Alexander Demandt (ed.), *Mit Fremden Leben. Eine Kulturgeschichte von der Antike bis zur Gegenwart* (Munich: C.H. Beck, 1995).

Schickler, Fernand Baron de, *Les églises du refuge en Angleterre* (3 vols, Paris: Fischbacher, 1892).

Scholliers, Etienne, 'Vrije en onvrije arbeiders, voornamelijk te Antwerpen in de 16de eeuw', *Bijdragen voor de geschiedenis der Nederlanden*, 11 (1956): 285–322.

Scholliers, Etienne, *De levensstandaard in de XVe en XVIe eeuw te Antwerpen. Loonarbeid en honger* (Antwerp: De Sikkel, 1960).

Scholliers, Etienne, 'Prijzen en lonen te Antwerpen en in het Antwerpse (16e–19e eeuw)', in C. Verlinden (ed.), *Dokumenten voor de geschiedenis van prijzen en lonen in Vlaanderen en Brabant, vol. 2* (Bruges: De Tempel, 1965).

Schultz, Helga, *Berlin 1650–1800. Sozialgeschichte einer Residenz* (Berlin: Akademie Verlag, 1992).

Schultz, Helga, *Das ehrbare Handwerk. Zunftleben im alten Berlin zur Zeit des Absolutismus* (Weimar: Böhlau, 1993).

Schwinges, Rainer C. (ed.), *Neubürger im Späten Mittelalter. Migration und Austausch in der Städtelandschaft des alten Reiches (1250–1550)* (Berlin: Duncker & Humblot, 2002).

Scott, Tom, *Society and Economy in Germany, 1300–1600* (Bristol: Palgrave, 2002).

Sczesny, Anke, 'Nahrung, Gemeinwohl und Eigennutz im ostschwäbischen Textilgewerbe der Frühen Neuzeit', in Robert Brandt and Thomas Buchner (eds), *Nahrung, Markt oder Gemeinnutz. Werner Sombart und das vorindustrielle Handwerk* (Bielefeld: Verlag für Regionalgeschichte, 2004), pp. 131–54.

Sharlin, Allan, 'Natural Decrease in Early Modern Cities: A Reconsideration', *Past and Present*, 79/1 (1978): 126–38.

Sharpe, James A., *Early Modern England: A Social History 1550–1760* (London: Arnold, 1987).

Shepard, A., 'Poverty, Labour and the Language of Social Description in Early Modern England', *Past and Present*, 201/1 (2008): 51–95.

Shephard, Edward J., 'Social and Geographic Mobility of the Eighteenth Century Guild Artisan: an Analysis of Guild Receptions in Dijon, 1700–1790', in Steve L. Kaplan and Cynthia Koepp (eds), *Work in France: Representations, Meaning, Organization, and Practice* (Ithaca, Cornell University Press, 1986).

Slack, Paul, *From Reformation to Improvement: Public Welfare in Early Modern England* (Oxford: Clarendon Press, 1999).

Snell, Keith D.M., *Parish and Belonging: Community, Identity and Welfare in England and Wales, 1700–1950* (Cambridge: Cambridge University Press, 2006).

Soly, Hugo, 'Economische vernieuwing en sociale weerstand. De betekenis en aspiraties der Antwerpse middenklasse in de 16de eeuw', *Tijdschrift voor geschiedenis*, 83 (1970): 520–35.

Soly, Hugo, 'Huurprijzen en reële opbrengst van arbeiderswoningen te Antwerpen in de eerste helft van de 16de eeuw', *Bijdragen tot de geschiedenis*, 53 (1970): 81–90.

Soly, Hugo, 'Grondspeculatie en kapitalisme te Antwerpen in de 16de eeuw', *Economisch en sociaal tijdschrift*, 26 (1973): 293–302.

Soly, Hugo, 'Nijverheid en kapitalisme te Antwerpen in de 16de eeuw', in *Album Charles Verlinden ter gelegenheid van zijn dertig jaar professoraat* (Ghent: RUG, 1975).

Soly, Hugo, *Urbanisme en kapitalisme in Antwerpen in de 16de eeuw. De stedebouwkundige en industriële ondernemingen van Gibert van Schoonbeke* (Brussels: Pro Civitate, 1977).

Soly, Hugo, 'Continuity and Change: Attidudes towards Poor Relief and Health Care in Early Modern Antwerp', in Ole Peter Grell and Andrew Cunningham (eds), *Health Care and Poor Relief in Protestant Europe, 1500–1700* (London: Routledge, 1997).

Soly, Hugo and Alfons K.L. Thijs, 'Nijverheid in de Zuidelijke Nederlanden', in *Algemene Geschiedenis der Nederlanden* (15 vols, Haarlem-Bussum: Fibula-Van Dishoeck, 1979).

Soly, Hugo and Alfons K.L. Thijs (eds), *Minderheden in Westeuropese steden (16de–20ste eeuw)* (Brussels: Gemeentekrediet, 1995).

Sombart, Werner, *Der moderne Kapitalismus* (6 vols, Leipzig/Berlin: Duncker & Humblot, 1928–1955).

Song, Byung Khun, 'Agrarian Policies on Pauper Settlement and Migration, Oxfordshire 1750–1834', *Continuity and Change*, 13 (1998): 363–89.

Sonkajärvi, Hanna, 'Les Juifs à Strasbourg au XVIIIème siècle: Enjeux d'inclusion et exclusion', *Annales de l'Est*, 57 (2007): 297–311.

Sonkajärvi, Hanna, *Qu'est-ce qu'un étranger? Frontières et identifications à Strasbourg (1681–1789)* (Strasbourg: Presses Universitaires de Strasbourg, 2008).

Sonkajärvi, Hanna, 'From German-speaking Catholics to French Carpenters: Strasbourg Guilds and the Role of Confessional Boundaries in the Inclusion and Exclusion of Foreigners in the Eighteenth Century', *Urban History*, 35/2 (2008): 202–15.

Sonkajärvi, Hanna, 'Un groupe privilégié de domestiques dans la ville de Strasbourg au XVIIIème siècle: Les Suisses portiers d'hôtels', in Bruno Bernard and Xavier Stevens (eds), *La domesticité au siècle des Lumières. Une approche comparative* (Brussels: Archives et bibliothèques de Belgique, 2009).

Sosson, Jean-Pierre, *Les travaux publics de la ville de Bruges XIVe–XVe siècles* (Brussels: Crédit Communal de Belgique, 1987).

Sosson, Jean-Pierre, 'Les métiers: norme et réalité. L'exemple des anciens Pays-Bas méridionaux aux XIVe et XVe siècles', in Jacqueline Hamesse and Colette Muraille-Samaran (eds), *Le travail au moyen âge. Une approche interdisciplinaire* (Actes du colloque international de Louvain-la-Neuve, 21–23 May 1987) (Louvain-la-Neuve: Institut d'Etudes Médiévales, 1990).

Spaans, Joke, *Armenzorg in Friesland, 1500–1800. Publieke zorg en particuliere liefdadigheid in zes Friese steden: Leeuwarden, Bolsward, Franeker, Sneek, Dokkum en Harlingen* (Hilversum: Verloren, 1997).

Specker, Hans Eugen, *Ulm. Stadtgeschichte* (Ulm: Süddeutsche Verlagsgesellschaft, 1977).

Spicer, Andrew, *The French-Speaking Reformed Community and their Church in Southampton, 1567–1620* (London: Huguenot Society of Great Britain and Ireland, 1997).

Stabel, Peter, *De kleine stad in Vlaanderen. Bevolkingsdynamiek en economische functies van de kleine en secundaire stedelijke centra in het Gentse kwartier (14de–16de eeuw)* (Brussels: Paleis der Academiën, 1995).

Stabel, Peter, *Dwarfs Among Giants: The Flemish Urban Network in the Late Middle Ages* (Leuven/Apeldoorn: Garant, 1997).

Stabel, Peter, 'Guilds in Late Medieval Flanders: Myths and Realities of Guild Life in an Export-Oriented Environment', *Journal of Medieval History*, 30 (2004): 187–212.

Stabel, Peter, 'Social Mobility and Apprenticeship in Late Medieval Flanders', in Bert De Munck, Steven L. Kaplan and Hugo Soly (eds), *Learning in the Shop Floor: Historical Perspectives on Apprenticeship* (New York/Oxford: Berghahn Books, 2007), pp. 158–159.

Statt, Daniel, 'The Birthright of an Englishman: The Practice of Naturalization and Denization of Immigrants under the Later Stuarts and Early Hanoverians', *Proceedings of the Huguenot Society of London*, 25 (1989): 61–74.

Statt, Daniel, 'The City of London and the Controversy over Immigration, 1660–1722', *The Historical Journal*, 33 (1990): 45–61.

Statt, Daniel, *Foreigners and Englishmen: The Controversy over Immigration and Population, 1660–1760* (Newark: University of Delaware Press, 1995).

Steinmetz, George, *Regulating the Social: The Welfare State and Local Politics in Imperial Germany* (Princeton: Princeton University Press, 1993).

Stolleis, Michael, 'Veit Ludwig von Seckendorff', in Michael Stolleis and Notker Hammerstein (eds), *Staatsdenker in der Frühen Neuzeit* (Munich: Beck, 1995), pp. 148–71.

Streitberger, Ingeborg, *Der Königliche Prätor von Straßburg, 1685–1789* (Wiesbaden: Steiner, 1961).

Stürmer, Michael, *Herbst des Alten Handwerks. Meister, Gesellen und Obrigkeit im 18. Jahrhundert* (Munich: Piper, 1986).

Styles, Philip, 'The Evolution of the Law of Settlement', *University of Birmingham Historical Journal*, 9/1 (1963): 33–63.

Swaan, Abram de, *In Care of the State: Health Care, Education, and Welfare in Europe and the USA in the Modern Era* (Oxford: Oxford University Press, 1988).

Tacoma, Laurens, 'Graveyards for Rome: Migration to the City of Rome in the First Two Centuries A.D.' (unpublished paper presented at the Seventh European Social Science History Conference, Lisbon, 26–29 February 2008).

Taylor, J.S. 'The Impact of Pauper Settlement 1691–1834', *Past and Present*, 73 (1976): 42–74.

Terlinden, Charles and Bolsée, *Jacques, Recueil des ordonnances des Pays-Bas* (7 vols, Brussels, 1957).

Thijs, Alfons K.L., *Van werkwinkel tot fabriek. De textielnijverheid te Antwerpen (einde 15de–begin 19de eeuw)* (Brussels: Gemeentekrediet, 1987).

Thijs, Alfons. K.L., 'Structural Changes in the Antwerp Industry from the Fifteenth to Eighteenth Century', in Herman van der Wee (ed.), *The Rise and*

Decline of Urban Industries in Italy and in the Low Countries (Late Middle Ages–Early Modern Times) (Leuven: Leuven University Press, 1988), pp. 207–12.

Thijs, Alfons K.L., 'Minderheden te Antwerpen (16de–20ste eeuw)', in Hugo Soly and Alfons K.L. Thijs (eds), *Minderheden in Westeuropese steden (16de–20ste eeuw)* (Brussels: Gemeentekrediet, 1995).

Thompson, E.P., 'The Moral Economy of the English Crowd in the Eighteenth Century', *Past and Present*, 50 (1971): 76–136.

Thorp, Malcolm R., 'The Anti-Huguenot Undercurrent in Late Seventeenth-Century England', *Proceedings of the Huguenot Society of London*, 22 (1970–1976): 565–80.

Thorp, Malcolm R., *The English Government and the Huguenot Settlement, 1680–1702* (PhD dissertation, University of Wisconsin, Madison, 1972).

Tilly, Charles, 'Migration in Modern European History', in William H. McNeill and Ruth S. Adams, *Human Migration: Patterns and Policies* (Bloomington: Indiana University Press, 1978).

Tilly, Charles, 'Demographic Origins of the European Proletariat', in David Levine (ed.), *Proletarianization and Family History* (Orlando: Academic Press, 1984).

Tilly, Charles, *Coercion, Capital and European states, AD 990–1992* (Cambridge: Cambridge University Press, 1990).

Tollin, Henri, *Der hugenottische Lehrstand, Wehrstand und Nährstand zu Frankfurt a.d. Oder* (Magdeburg: Heinrichshofen, 1896).

Tollin, Henri, *Geschichte der Französischen Colonie zu Magdeburg* (6 vols, Halle on Saale: Niemeyer, 1886–1892).

Torpey, John, *The Invention of the Passport: Surveillance, Citizenship and the State* (Cambridge: Cambridge University Press, 2000).

Trivellato, Francesca, *The Familiarity of Strangers: The Sephardic Diaspora, Livorno, and Cross-Cultural Trade in the Early Modern Period* (New Haven: Yale University Press, 2009).

Truant, Cynthia M., *The Rites of Labour: Brotherhoods of Compagnonnage in Old and New Regime France* (Ithaca/London: Cornell University Press, 1994).

Tucci, Ugo, 'Una descrizione di Trieste a metà del Settecento', *Quaderni giuliani di storia*, 1/2 (1980): 95–113.

Vanhaeck, Maurice, *Histoire de la sayetterie à Lille* (Lille: Lefebvre-Ducrocq, 1910).

Vanhaute, Eric, 'De armenzorg op het Antwerpse platteland, 1750–1850. Onderzoek naar een instelling tijdens de scharniereeuw', in *Machtsstructuren in de plattelandsgemeenschappen in België en aangrenzende gebieden (12de–19de eeuw)* (Brussels: Gemeentekrediet van België, 1988).

Vanroelen, Jan, 'Het stadsbestuur', in *Antwerpen in de XVIde eeuw* (Antwerp: Mercurius, 1975).

Verhalle, A., *Peilingen naar armoede en armenzorg in het Brugse Vrije van 1770 tot 1789* (MA thesis, Katholieke Universiteit Leuven, 1964).

Vogler, Bernard, 'La pénétration française en Alsace au XVIIIe siècle à travers les testaments', in *Provinces et états dans la France de l'Est. Le Rattachement de la Franche-Comté à la France, espaces régionaux et espaces nationaux* (Actes du colloque de Besançon, 3–4 October 1977) (Paris: Les Belles Lettres, 1979).

Vogler, Bernard, 'La vie économique et les hiérarchies sociales', in Georges Livet and Francis Rapp (eds), *Histoire de Strasbourg des origines à nos jours, vol. 3. Strasbourg de la guerre de Trente Ans à Napoléon, 1618–1815* (Strasbourg: Editions des Dernières Nouvelles d'Alsace, 1981).

Vries, Jan de, *European Urbanization, 1500–1800* (London: Methuen, 1984).

Wallace, Peter G., *Communities and Conflict in Early Modern Colmar, 1575–1730* (Atlantic Highlands NJ: Humanities Press, 1995).

Walle, Kees, *Buurthouden. De geschiedenis van burengebruiken en buurtorganisaties in Leiden (14de–19de eeuw)* (Leiden: Ginkgo, 2005).

Wee, Herman van der, *The Growth of the Antwerp Market and the European Economy (Fourteenth–Sixteenth Century)* (3 vols, The Hague: Nijhoff, 1963).

Wee, Herman van der, 'Structural Changes and Specialization in the Industry of the Southern Netherlands, 1100–1600', *Economic History Review*, 28 (1975): 203–21.

Wee, Herman van der, 'Industrial Dynamics and the Process of Urbanization and De-Urbanization in the Low Countries from the Late Middle Ages to the Eighteenth Century: A Synthesis', in Herman van der Wee (ed.), *The Rise and Decline of Urban Industries in Italy and in the Low Countries (Late Middle Ages–Early Modern Times)* (Leuven: Leuven University Press, 1988).

Wee, Herman van der (ed.), *The Rise and Decline of Urban Industries in Italy and in the Low Countries (Late Middle Age–Early Modern Times)* (Leuven: Leuven University Press, 1988).

Wee, Herman van der and Jan Matterné, 'De Antwerpse wereldmarkt tijdens de 16de en 17de eeuw', in Jan van der Stock (ed.), *Antwerpen. Verhaal van een metropool 16de–17de eeuw* (Ghent: Snoeck-Ducaju, 1963).

Wehler, Hans-Ulrich, *Deutsche Gesellschaftsgeschichte*, vol. 1 (Munich: Beck, 1987).

Wendelin, Harald, 'Schub und Heimatrecht', in Waltraud Heindl and Edith Saurer (eds), *Grenze und Staat. Paßwesen, Staatsbürgerschaft, Heimatrecht, und Fremdengesetzgebung in der österreichischen Monarchie (1750–1867)* (Vienna: Böhlau, 2000), pp. 173–230.

Werveke van, Hans, 'Ambachten en erfelijkheid', *Mededeelingen van de Koninklijke Vlaamse Academie voor Wetenschappen, Letteren en Schoone Kunsten van België*, 4/1 (Antwerp: Standaard, 1942).

Wiesner, Merry E., *Working Women in Renaissance Germany* (New Brunswick NJ: Rutgers University Press, 1986).

Wiesner, Merry E., 'Gender and the Worlds of Work', in Bob Scribner (ed.), *Germany: A New Social and Economic History, 1450–1630* (London: Arnold, 1996).

Wilke, Jürgen, 'Rechtstellung und Rechtsprechung der Hugenotten in Brandenburg-Preußen (1685–1809)', in Rudolf von Thadden and Michelle Magdelaine (eds), *Die Hugenotten 1685–1985* (Munich: Beck, 1985).

Wilke, Jürgen, 'Zur Sozialstruktur und demographischen Analyse der Hugenotten in Brandenburg-Preußen, insbesondere der in Berlin', in Ingrid Mittenzwei (ed.), *Hugenotten in Brandenburg-Preußen* (Berlin [GDR]: Akademie der Wissenschaften, Zentralinstitut für Geschichte, 1987), pp. 27–99.

Wilke, Jürgen, 'Die Französische Kolonie in Berlin', in Helga Schultz, *Berlin 1650–1800. Sozialgeschichte einer Residenz* (Berlin: Akademie-Verlag, 1992), pp. 353–430.

Williams, Alan, *The Police of Paris, 1718–1789* (Baton-Rouge/London: Louisiana State University Press, 1979).

Winter, Anne, 'Vagrancy as an Adaptive Strategy: The Duchy of Brabant, 1767–1776', *International Review of Social History*, 49/2 (2004): 249–78.

Winter, Anne, *Divided Interests, Divided Migrants: The Rationales of Policies Regarding Labour Mobility in Western Europe, ca. 1550–1914* (London: Global Economic History Network Working Paper No. 15, 2005).

Winter, Anne, 'Caught between Law and Practice: Migrants and Settlement Legislation in the Southern Low Countries in a Comparative Perspective, c. 1700–1900', *Rural History*, 19/2 (2008): 137–62.

Winter, Anne, *Migrants and Urban Change: Newcomers to Antwerp, 1760–1860* (London: Pickering and Chatto, 2009).

Wirth, Louis, 'Urbanism as a Way of Life', *American Journal of Sociology*, 44 (1938): 1–24.

Wissell, Rudolf, *Des alten Handwerks Recht und Gewohnheit* (6 vols, Berlin: Colloquium-Verlag, 1971–1988).

Wittmer, Charles, 'Les Origines du droit de bourgeoisie à Strasbourg', in *La Bourgeoisie alsacienne. Etudes d'histoire sociale* (Strasbourg/Colmar: Le Roux, 1954): 49–56.

Woods, Robert, 'Urban–Rural Mortality Differentials: An Unresolved Debate', *Population and Development Review*, 29/1 (2003): 29–46.

Woude, Ad van der, 'Population Developments in the Northern Netherlands (1500–1800) and the Validity of the "Urban Graveyard" Effect', *Annales de Démographie Historique* (1982): 55–75.

Wrigley, Edward A., 'A Simple Model of London's Importance in Changing English Society and Economy 1650–1750', *Past and Present*, 37 (1967): 46–70.

Yardeni, Myriam, *Le Refuge protestant* (Paris: Presses Universitaires de France, 1985).

Zanden, Jan Luiten van and Maarten Prak, 'Towards an Economic Interpretation of Citizenship: the Dutch Republic between Medieval Communes and Modern Nation States', *European Review of Economic History*, 10 (2006): 111–45.

Zeller, Gaston, 'Manants d'Alsace, derniers manants de France', *Mélanges 1945, I. Etudes alsatiques* (Paris: Les Belles Lettres, 1946): 111–20.

Zeller, Olivier, 'Géographie des troubles et découpages urbains à Lyon (XVIe–XVIIIe siècles)', *Actes du 114e Congrès National des Sociétés Savantes* (Paris: Comité des travaux historiques et scientifiques (CTHS), 1989): 43–59.

Zielenziger, Kurt, *Die alten deutschen Kameralisten. Ein Beitrag zur Geschichte der Nationalökonomie und zum Problem des Merkantilismus* (Frankfurt am Main: Sauer & Auvermann, 1966).

Zolberg, Aristide, *A Nation by Design: Immigration Policy in the Fashioning of America* (New York/Cambridge MA: Harvard University Press/Russell Sage Foundation, 2006).

Index

For Product Safety Concerns and Information please contact our
EU representative GPSR@taylorandfrancis.com | Taylor & Francis
Verlag GmbH, Kaufingerstraße 24, 80331 München, Germany.